Kingship and Ideology in the Islamic an

What were the attitudes to diplomacy and kingsh
Anne Broadbridge examines struggles over ideolog
Asia from 1260 to 1405. She explores two very differ
world of the Mamluk sultans of Egypt and Syria, and the Mongol world inhabited by the Golden Horde in Central Asia, the Ilkhanids in Iran and Anatolia, the Ilkhanids' successors and Temür. The relationships among these rival rulers were often highly charged, and frequent diplomatic missions were exchanged in an effort to promote each ruler's ideology over the ideologies of others. Using a range of sources including chancellery manuals, diplomatic letters, chronicles and travel narratives, the author examines these exchanges, the activities of individual rulers and the methods they used to proclaim their sovereignty to various audiences. This is the first book to explore what it meant to be a monarch in the pre-modern Islamic world, and how ideas about sovereignty evolved across the period. This groundbreaking work will appeal to scholars of Middle Eastern and Central Asian history, Mongol history and Islamic history, as well as historians of diplomacy and ideology.

ANNE F. BROADBRIDGE is Assistant Professor in History at the University of Massachusetts, Amherst.

Cambridge Studies in Islamic Civilization

Published titles in the series are listed at the back of the book

Kingship and Ideology in the Islamic and Mongol Worlds

ANNE F. BROADBRIDGE

University of Massachusetts, Amherst

CAMBRIDGE
UNIVERSITY PRESS

CAMBRIDGE UNIVERSITY PRESS
Cambridge, New York, Melbourne, Madrid, Cape Town, Singapore,
São Paulo, Delhi, Dubai, Tokyo, Mexico City

Cambridge University Press
The Edinburgh Building, Cambridge CB2 8RU, UK

Published in the United States of America by Cambridge University Press, New York

www.cambridge.org
Information on this title: www.cambridge.org/9780521174497

First published 2008
First paperback edition 2010

A catalogue record for this publication is available from the British Library

ISBN 978-0-521-85265-4 Hardback
ISBN 978-0-521-17449-7 Paperback

To my family

Contents

List of figures — *page* viii
List of maps — ix
List of dynastic tables — x
Acknowledgments — xi
Note on transliteration and dates — xiii
List of abbreviations — xiv

Introduction — 1
1 The ideologies and the diplomacy — 6
2 The establishment of ideologies (1260–1293/658–693) — 27
3 The age of Ilkhanid conversion (1295–1316/694–716) — 64
4 The age of patronage and Muslim supremacy (1317–1341/717–741) — 99
5 Mamluk regional sovereignty and the post-Ilkhanid order (1335–1382/736–784) — 138
6 The Temürid invasions and the destruction of Mamluk sovereignty (1382–1404/784–807) — 168
Epilogue — 198

Bibliography — 208
Index — 222

Figures

1.	Decree of the ilkhan Geikhatu	*page* 18
2.	Mongol enthronement scene	57
3.	External view of Öljeitü's tomb	68
4.	Internal view of Öljeitü's tomb	69
5.	Folio from the anonymous Baghdad Quran	97
6.	Folio from a Quran of al-Nāṣir Muḥammad	112
7.	View of Mecca and the pilgrimage	126
8.	Scene from the poems of Sulṭān-Aḥmad Jalayir	158
9.	Folio from a Quran of al-Ashraf Shaʿbān	165
10.	The school and tomb complex of Shaʿbān's mother	166
11.	Temür's tomb (the Gūr-i Mīr)	169

Maps

Dynastic tables

Acknowledgments

This project began as a dissertation in the Department of Near Eastern Languages and Civilizations at the University of Chicago. Let me first thank my advisor, John Woods, for pointing me towards the Mongols and the world they made; Cornell Fleischer, who refused to let me forget the regions and peoples beyond Cairo; and Carl Petry, whose tireless enthusiasm was always contagious.

I could not have completed this project without the generous financial support provided by a Fulbright-Hays doctoral dissertation research grant, a Fellowship from the American Research Center in Egypt, a dissertation writing grant from the Dolores Zohrab Liebmann Fund and a research leave from the Department of History at the University of Massachusetts Amherst. I am grateful to the staff of the Fulbright Commission in Cairo, the ARCE staff, the trustees of the Dolores Zohrab Liebmann Fund and my colleagues at UMass.

Not surprisingly, I am deeply indebted to several libraries. I thank the staffs at the Library of the Mashyakhat al-Azhar, the Egyptian National Library and the University of Chicago Regenstein Library, especially my friends Bruce Craig, Mark Stein and the tireless Marlis Saleh. I am grateful to the Interlibrary Loan personnel at the University of Massachusetts W. E. B. Du Bois Library, and to the Center for Middle Eastern Studies at Harvard University, which arranged for me to use the Widener Library.

Throughout this process I gained greatly from the advice of scholars far more knowledgeable than I, among them Chris Taylor, Nasser Rabbat, Peter Jackson, John Meloy, Warren Schultz and Adam Sabra. In particular I thank Dr. Hassanein Rabie, Dr. Imad Abou Ghazi, Ms. Amina Elbendary and those who conducted research with me in Cairo, including Hina Azam, Chris Toensing, Megan Reid and Persis Berlecamp. Don Little deserves particular appreciation for reading the entire work without complaint, and for sending me manuscripts with extraordinary speed. I am also grateful to Reuven Amitai and Charles Melville, without whose many insightful articles this book would be far poorer. Let me also acknowledge David O. Morgan for his timely and welcome assistance with the mysterious process of publication, for which I am very grateful. I also want to acknowledge the kindness of Amalia Levanoni and Michael Winter, who included me in their wonderful Conference on Mamluk Society in Egypt and Syria, held in Haifa and Tel Aviv in May 2000.

I am delighted to mention the support of my editors at Cambridge University Press, Marigold Acland and Isabelle Dambricourt, and I give my undying gratitude to the two anonymous readers for Cambridge, whose comments on the manuscript were helpful and encouraging. Let me also thank Walter B. Denny, not only for his expertise, good humor and invaluable assistance with every image in the book, but also for providing me with several of his own photos. I am also grateful to Dr. Bernard O'Kane and Dr. Robert Hillenbrand for sending me some wonderful architectural photographs. In addition let me express my gratitude to the following individuals and institutions for granting me permission to reproduce images: Dr. Sophie Makariou at the Louvre, Paris; the Staatsbibliothek zu Berlin and the Staatliche Museen zu Berlin; Abolala Soudavar and Massumeh Farhad, representing the Art and History Trust and the Freer Gallery in Washington DC; the British Library; Karen Mansfield at the Worcester Art Museum; the Chester Beatty Library; and the Metropolitan Museum of Art.

Finally, I could never have completed this project without the unquenchable enthusiasm of my mother, Fran Bancroft, and the insights and advice of my friend, Jean Schwartz. Let me close by thanking my husband, Dave Peters, who spent hours reading, critiquing, discussing and encouraging. By now he surely knows more about this topic than I do.

All mistakes and omissions are, of course, my own.

Note on transliteration and dates

Mongolian names and terminology conform to the model set by J. A. Boyle in his translation of Rashīd al-Dīn's *The Successors of Genghis Khan*, with the exception of the hybrid "Chingiz Khan."

Turkish uses the system used by the Encyclopaedia of Islam, 2nd edition, with some modifications: ch instead of ç, j instead of dj, q instead of k with a subscript dot, and no diacriticals suggesting long vowels (i.e., Qara Qoyunlu, not Qarā Qoyunlū), but rather only the Turkish vowels (a, ı, o, u; e, i, ö, ü).

Turkish and Mongolian names in the Mamluk Sultanate use a compromise between the written names and their probable pronunciation. This uses only the Arabic vowels (a, i, u), but without diacritical marks (i.e., Uzdamir, not Özdemir, Qalawun, not Qalāwūn), and without subscript dots (i.e., Qutuz, not Quṭuz).

Arabic names and terminology conform to the standards set in *Mamluk Studies Review*; these also have been applied to Persian, although for Persian authors I've allowed some leeway to conform to the best-known spellings of their names.

The few Armenian names follow the style of the American Library of Congress, except for Hromgla, which is transliterated as shown here.

Chinese words use the Pinyin system.

Dynasties and place names are written without diacritical marks, and conform to the most commonly recognized spelling, even if it is different from the systems mentioned above. Where possible, place names appear in English or other modern-language versions (i.e., Cairo, not al-Qāhirah, Kayseri not Qayṣarīyah).

Most dates are recorded in first Common Era and then Islamic Lunar (*hijrī*) styles, separated by a slash. Dates relating exclusively to Europeans (like papal dates) use only the Common Era style.

Abbreviations

AI	*Annales Islamologiques*
BSOAS	*Bulletin of the School of Oriental and African Studies*
CAJ	*Central Asiatic Journal*
CHIr V	*Cambridge History of Iran*. Volume V. Ed. J. A. Boyle. *The Saljuk and Mongol Periods*. Cambridge, 1968.
CHIr VI	*Cambridge History of Iran*. Volume VI. Ed. Peter Jackson. *The Timurid and Safavid Periods*. Cambridge, 1968.
CIA	Max van Berchem. *Matériaux pour un Corpus Inscriptionum Arabicarum*. Paris, 1894. Volume XIX.
Court	*The Court of the Il-Khans, 1290–1340*. Eds. Julian Raby and T. Fitzherbert. Oxford, 1996.
Domination	*L'Iran face à la domination mongole*. Ed. Denise Aigle. Tehran, 1997.
EI[2]	*Encyclopaedia of Islam*, 2nd edition. Leiden and London, 1960–.
EIr	*Encyclopaedia Iranica*. London, 1985–.
HJAS	*Harvard Journal of Asiatic Studies*
IJMES	*International Journal of Middle East Studies*
JA	*Journal Asiatique*
JAOS	*Journal of the American Oriental Society*
JESHO	*Journal of the Economic and Social History of the Orient*
JRAS	*Journal of the Royal Asiatic Society*
JSAI	*Jerusalem Studies in Arabic and Islam*
Legacy	*The Legacy of Genghis Khan: Courtly Art and Culture in Western Asia, 1256–1353*. Eds. Linda Komaroff and Stefano Carboni. New Haven, 2002.
Mongol Empire	*The Mongol Empire and its Legacy*. Eds. Reuven Amitai-Preiss and David O. Morgan. Leiden, 1999.
RCEA	Étienne Combe, Jean Sauvaget, Gaston Wiet et al. *Répertoire chronologique d'épigraphie arabe*. Cairo, 1943. Volume XII.
SI	*Studia Islamica*
Technology	*Religion, Customary Law and Nomadic Technology*. Eds. Michael Gervers and Wayne Schlepp. Toronto, 2000.
ZDMG	*Zeitschrift der Deutschen Morgenländischen Gesellschaft*

Introduction

This study is an attempt to answer a series of questions about ideologies of rule in the medieval Middle East and Central Asia. What were the dominant ideas of legitimate kingship in this period? What specific choices did individual rulers make to legitimate themselves, and why? Who were the audiences they addressed? And to what extent did rulers' attempts to buttress their claims of legitimacy affect their actions? An investigation of the ideological options available to rulers and the choices they made can reveal their assumptions about what truly mattered in a king, sultan or khan. As seen even in rulers whose power was built primarily on military strength, but who nevertheless struggled to justify themselves on loftier grounds, notions of kingship were not mere window-dressing for the reality of power, but rather inspired, shaped and constrained the decisions that rulers made.

The topic arises from a well-known historical context. In the thirteenth/seventh century a collection of warriors known as the Mongols appeared on the Central Asian horizon of the Middle East. The Mongols were sky-venerating Altaic steppe nomads with excellent archery skills, who rose to startling greatness under the charismatic leadership of Chingiz Khan. Possibly during Chingiz Khan's lifetime, and certainly after his death, members of the Chingizid family believed they were favored by the Enduring Sky (*möngke tenggeri*), which had ordered them to institute universal rule over the entire world. The Mongol campaigns of conquest were thus in part an attempt to implement the orders of the Enduring Sky.

Despite the success of these conquests, by 1260/659 the Mongols themselves were caught in a destructive civil war, and their empire had divided into four independent states in China, Central Asia, Southern Russia and the Qipchaq Steppe, and Iran. Nevertheless, the uncompromising ideology of the imperial house dominated Central Asia and the Middle East into the fourteenth/eighth century. Thereafter, nomadic and sedentary rulers strove to craft new responses to the challenges of the Mongol legacy. Among the most successful was the warlord Temür (d. 1405/807), who gathered his own hordes, articulated his own vision and set out to "revive" Chingiz Khan's empire and humble the non-Mongol world once again.

The importance of the Mongols to the history of this period is thus unmistakable. It was they who radically altered the political, military, economic and social situations in every area they reached, as their empire spread rapidly from China to Hungary and from southern Siberia to Tibet. Their nomadic lifestyle, their military superiority, their astonishing control over often miserable subjects, their extraordinary consumption and the changes they wrought to systems of world trade all left deep impressions. More subtly, the Mongols brought radical ideological changes to the rest of the world. In the medieval Middle East and Central Asia the dominant ideology of rule became that of the Mongols themselves, although only the imperial family could lay claim to power within it.

At the other end of the spectrum from the Mongols were the Mamluk sultans of Egypt and Syria, who ruled the central Islamic lands from their capital at Cairo for 267 years (1250–1517/648–923). The Mamluks were military slaves, and began their careers as young, often Turkish-speaking, captives brought to Egypt and Syria from the northern Black Sea coast or the Caucasus. Once arrived, they were converted to Islam and trained in military arts, then allowed to rise to positions in the military and in government, including that of the sultan himself. As a result, the Mamluks were entirely of nomad origin, but not themselves nomadic. The Sultanate was prosperous, with access to the silk road of Central Asia and control of the spice trade of the Indian Ocean. It was largely Muslim in population, overwhelmingly Muslim in culture and outlook, and enjoyed a clear political and ideological hegemony over the Islamic holy cities of Mecca and Medina in the Hijaz region as well.

Although the centrality of the Mongols to the history of the medieval world is clear, the importance of the Mamluks to the Mongols is less obvious. Certainly on the scale of the Great Mongol Empire the Mamluks appeared as little more than recalcitrant rebels in an out-of-the-way corner. But for two Mongol states, the Golden Horde of Southern Russia and the Qipchaq Steppe (1241–1502/638–907) and the Ilkhanids of Iran and Khurasan (1258–1335/656–736), the Mamluks occupied a unique historical position. The sultans in Cairo were the first non-Mongols to intervene in the fractured politics of the Mongol Civil War in the 1260s/660s by allying themselves with the Golden Horde against the Ilkhanids, and also held off hostile Ilkhanid forces not once, but repeatedly. Later the Mamluks played a role in the histories of the Ilkhanid successor states, then kept Temür and his Mongol look-alike hordes at bay until he crushed them on his second try.

In contrast to the Mongols, the Mamluk ideology of legitimate kingship rested on a foundation of Islamic religious ideals, with the notion of Mamluks as military Guardians of Islam, Muslims and the Islamic holy cities as its cornerstone. This ideology of kingship was in part a response to the challenge of Mongol imperial legitimacy, and an attempt to circumvent the Mamluks' ideological weaknesses in the face of the Chingizid model.[1] But after the conversion of many Chingizid khans to Islam, the Mamluks' role as Guardians of Islam slowly faded, while their position as sovereigns of the holy cities grew in importance. Muslim Mongols and their Turkic successors eventually sought to control these sites and appropriate Islamic notions of legitimate rule, and thus sparred symbolically and actually with the Mamluks.

This study investigates the major ideologies of kingship in the years 1260–1405/658–807 as they were expressed in the diplomatic contact between the Mamluks and the Mongol and Turkic groups that dominated the region: the Golden Horde and the Ilkhanids, the Ilkhanids' successors in Iran and Anatolia, and Temür. It does not focus on rulers' expressions of legitimacy to the internal audiences of their own subjects – that would be another book, or several. This study ends with the death of Temür in 1405/807, since his life and career represent a watershed in the influence of Mongol ideology. Although Temür cast himself squarely into Chingizid ideological norms, his empire-building led to the establishment of his own dynasty as a rival ideological force to that of Chingiz Khan, even though Temür's empire was far more ephemeral. In addition, Temür's reduction of the Mamluks to vassalage in 1402–03/805 was unprecedented in the history of the Sultanate, and effectively destroyed both Mamluk pretensions to sovereignty, and their image as Guardians of religion. The Mamluks later reprised many of their earlier ideological arguments, but only after rebuilding themselves laboriously from the ground up over a period of years. Thus although Temür's troublemaking did not destroy Mamluk ideology for good, the damage he wrought marked a second watershed, this time for the Mamluks, and represents a worthy point of conclusion.

Methods

Ideally this study would take place through the investigation of historical sources in several languages: Arabic, the language of the Mamluk chancellery and chronicles; Mongolian, used in Ilkhanid and Golden Horde diplomacy; and Persian, the Mongols' second diplomatic language, which was also used to write their histories. (Some later sources are composed in Turkish.) Such an ideal is impossible to realize, unfortunately, for the current state of the material is distinctly skewed. Most works are in Arabic, written in the Mamluk Sultanate, and predictably support the Mamluks and denigrate their antagonists. The Persian histories, written for the Ilkhanids, their successors or Temür, are far fewer, and compound the problem of their scarcity

[1] Scholarship on Mamluk legitimacy often assumes the internal audience of subjects or other Mamluks, not the external audiences of other rulers; this study, by contrast, will focus on outside audiences for Mamluk ideology.

either by routinely implying that the Mamluks were unimportant, or by failing to acknowledge their existence. Nor do early Persian, Turkish or Mongolian sources remain from the Golden Horde. As a result, in places this study will present an abashedly Cairo-centric view of the ideological debate. The problems of the sources also appear in the periodization, which, for lack of alternatives, relates more closely to Mamluk ideological changes than to Mongol or Turkic ones. This study also relies in part on coins, inscriptions and, to a much lesser degree, deeds for pious endowments (*waqf* documents). Although these items often expressed rulers' ideas of kingship, they tended to address the internal audiences of subjects, not the external audiences of other rulers. Therefore this study mentions those sources when they add to an overall understanding of the ideologies, or when the diplomatic evidence is sorely lacking (as in Chapter 5), but it does not pretend to be exhaustive in comparative numismatics, epigraphy or endowment studies.

The expression of rival ideologies through diplomacy developed and changed over five different phases. In the first phase (1260–93/658–93) the Mamluks created a model of kingship that rested squarely on the central concept of Mamluks as military Guardians of Islam and Muslims, which they used to combat the threat posed by the pagan Ilkhanids. The Ilkhanids in turn saw the Mamluk sultans as rebel slaves, whose insubordination against the divinely mandated Chingizid dynasty was intolerable. By contrast, in this period the Mamluk sultans and the khans of the Golden Horde developed cordial relations characterized by the notion of unity between the two sides: unity in opposition to the Ilkhanids and, frequently, unity in religion.

Next the Mamluks wrestled with the specter of Ilkhanid conversion to Islam (1295–1316/694–716). During this period, the newly Muslim ilkhans proclaimed themselves to be supreme Muslim sovereigns, while nevertheless maintaining their loyalty to Mongol imperial tradition. In response, the Mamluks developed the notion of a hierarchy of conversion, which allowed them to resist the Ilkhanids and proclaim their greater worthiness of Muslim rule, which they acquired by having professed the religion first.

The third phase (1317–35/716–36) witnessed the development of the concept of Muslim regional supremacy, which allowed the Mamluk sultan al-Nāṣir Muḥammad to proclaim his superiority as a Muslim ruler over the Ilkhanids despite their conversion and continued adherence to Islam. But the ilkhan Abū Saʿīd and his vicegerent Choban were equally eager to promote themselves as benign and pious Muslim patrons, and since this phase was marked by cordial relations between the Sultanate and the Ilkhanate, struggles over ideological supremacy moved to the ceremonial of the pilgrimage and Arabian affairs. Marriage alliances became an important arena for the expression of kingship during this period, especially through verbal sparring over the propriety of potential matches. At the same time Muḥammad and Özbek Khan of the Golden Horde inaugurated a new relationship of unity in religion, which was also bound – then badly strained – by matrimonial ties.

For the Mamluks, the fourth phase was one of regional sovereignty (1335–82/736–84) and a new emphasis on dynasty in legitimacy; by contrast, the ideological standby of Guardianship was allowed to decline. This phase began during the political disintegration of the Ilkhanate after Abū Saʿīd's death, when many of the Ilkhanid successors became Mamluk governors in return for patronage and the promise of Muḥammad's military support. At the same time, some Ilkhanid successors interacted creatively with the Muslim and Chingizid fusion left by the later Ilkhanids, while others turned to Islamic or pre-Mongol Turkic models to justify themselves. Then after Muḥammad's death in 1341/741, his generally ineffectual successors continued his relations of sovereignty with their Mongol and Turkic allies and governors, even though the strength they projected had become hollow.

In the fifth phase (1382–1405/784–807) Temür tried to "restore" his own creative version of the Mongol Empire, which caused the Mamluks to respond by reviving the anachronistic notion of the "infidel" threat formerly presented by the Ilkhanids. During this phase Mamluk ideology returned to the notion of Guardianship, which was combined with the concept of regional sovereignty by the sultan Barquq to combat the military and ideological threat that Temür posed. However, both the sultan's sovereignty and the ideal of Guardianship collapsed during the reign of Barquq's son al-Nāṣir Faraj, when Temür took advantage of Mamluk political disarray to reduce the sultan to a tribute-paying governor in 1402–03/805.

CHAPTER 1

The ideologies and the diplomacy

An ideology of kingship is the set of ideas by which a ruler defines himself as a sovereign. In the period under discussion, these ideas gave rulers models for their behavior, and helped them both assert the legality and legitimacy of their reigns, and maintain their claims to rule in the eyes of various, often overlapping audiences, frequently in opposition to the claims of others. No sovereign, no matter how well established or how much a parvenu, could resist the impulse to justify to others his actual control of lands, populations, resources and armies. Through these justifications we can see what individual rulers, their advisors and their subjects thought was important in the conception of a monarch. Nevertheless, rulers were not irrevocably bound by their ideologies – at times sovereigns sullied their images by contradicting the expectations of others for the sake of achieving specific goals. And yet even in these cases, rulers could not divorce themselves from the visions of sovereignty on which they modeled their conduct, and so always sought to rationalize their behavior, even if they did so poorly. In general, ideologies of rule were limited, conservative and slow to change. In the years 1260–1405/658–807, only a few models of sovereignty existed, which were often glaringly intolerant of one another. This intolerance appeared in the diplomatic exchanges among competing rulers, which was the most prominent arena both for expressing legitimacy, and for denigrating the claims of rivals.

Nomadic ideology

The most powerful new political entity of the thirteenth/seventh century was the Mongol Empire, from which emerged the dominant ruling ideology of the Chingizids. This model of kingship was straightforward. Like many other nomad aristocrats, Temüjin (later Chingiz Khan) began his political career by gaining followers through military prowess, diplomacy and charisma, and losing them when times were bad.[1] Eventually, however, a series of fortunate

[1] Paul Ratchnevsky, *Genghis Khan: His Life and Legacy*, ed. and tr. Thomas Nivison Haining (Oxford, 1991).

escapes, auspicious predictions and lucky breaks suggested that the Enduring Sky (*möngke tenggeri*) was favoring Chingiz Khan through a divine mandate, and had granted him a special good fortune (the imperial *su*). Although historians still debate whether Chingiz Khan himself believed in this favor, ultimately his offspring did, and claimed furthermore that the divinely granted good fortune had passed to them. The imperial fortune became linked to the four sons borne by Chingiz Khan's senior wife Börte: Jochi, Chagatai, Ögedei and Tolui, as well as to their descendants. In obedience to the will of the Enduring Sky, the members of Chingiz Khan's imperial or "golden" family attempted to impose universal Chingizid rule on the world through a remarkable series of military campaigns in the early thirteenth/seventh century.[2] In the ideological context of Chingizid expansion, any independent ruler intent on retaining his independence was a rebel against the golden family and the Enduring Sky. The merciless slaughter of such rebels was therefore necessary and good, since it both implemented the divine will and provided an object lesson for other would-be rebels. Among Altaic nomads the Chingizids' simple yet forceful concept of a divinely favored dynasty appealed to enduring traditions of ancestor reverence and belief in sacred power or fortune (the *su*), while for sedentary peoples the Chingizid claim to divine support was underscored by the speed and success of the Mongol military campaigns – surely only a dynasty supported by God could conquer so much so fast.[3]

The divine mandate's concepts of the imperial fortune and a heavenly command to institute universal rule not only continued after Chingiz Khan's death and the accession as Great Khan of his third son Ögedei (d. 1241/639), but helped inspire the Mongol conquests of the 1230s/630s and early 1240s/640s. Despite its strength, however, the divine mandate ultimately served to divide the imperial family, not unite it. Since Chingiz Khan failed to leave a clear plan for succession after Ögedei, members from widely flung branches of the family could argue for their own inclusion in the terms of the divine mandate, to the detriment of Chingiz Khan's and Börte's four sons. Even among these four houses disagreement over the application

[2] Igor de Rachewiltz, "Some Remarks on the Ideological Foundations of Chingis Khan's Empire," *Papers on Far Eastern History* 7 (1973), 21–36; J.J. Saunders, *The History of the Mongol Conquests* (London, 1971), 50, 52–53, 75; Bertold Spuler, *The Mongols in History*, tr. Geoffrey Wheeler (London, 1971), 6–8, 14–15; David O. Morgan, "The Mongols and the Eastern Mediterranean," in *Latins and Greeks in the Eastern Mediterranean after 1204*, eds. Benjamin Arbel et al. (London, 1989), 200; Marie-Lise Beffa, "*Le Concept de* tänggäri *«ciel» dans l'*Histoire secrète des Mongols," *Études Mongoles et Siberiennes* 24 (1993), 215–36; also see Anatoly M. Khazanov, "Muḥammad and Jenghiz Khan Compared: The Religious Factor in World Empire Building," *Comparative Studies in Society and History* 35 (1993), 464–66, esp. 465 on the way Mongol understandings of universal sovereignty contrasted with Turkic visions that were limited to rule over nomads.

[3] For ancestor cults and sacred power see Devin DeWeese, *Islamization and Native Religion in the Golden Horde: Baba Tükles and Conversion to Islam in Historical and Epic Tradition* (University Park, PA, 1994), 37, 46.

of the imperial *su* was rampant, and struggles over control of the empire led to great division within the family. This was most apparent in the contentious scuffles to establish the Great Khans Güyük (r. 1246–48/643–45) and Möngke (r. 1251–59/649–57).

In an attempt to validate his control of the empire and hold the imperial family together, Great Khan Möngke presented himself as a traditionalist devoted to the example of his grandfather Chingiz Khan. This he did immediately after his coronation by purging his Chagataid and Ögedeid rivals on the grounds that they had opposed the will of the Mongol ruling majority, in contravention of Mongol law and Chingiz Khan's example.[4] Möngke then reunited what remained of the imperial family by reviving the Enduring Sky's command to conquer, and called for two military campaigns – one to China under his brother Qubilai, and another to Iran under his brother Hülegü. This latter campaign had far-reaching consequences for Muslim rulers. In addition to the clear, uncompromising and universalist ideology of the divine mandate, the Mongols recognized forceful concepts of law, among them the decrees issued by Chingiz Khan himself, the *yasa* (*jasaq*).[5] Therefore Möngke also portrayed himself as a purist and supporter of his grandfather's legal ordinances in a deliberately tradition-oriented attempt to unify the family.[6] Ultimately questions of law played an important role in ideology during and long after the Mongol period.

Mongol ideas of legitimacy reached overlapping audiences comprised of the Chingizids themselves, non-Chingizid Mongols and Turks, and sedentary subjects, including the vassal rulers of subdued populations. The Mongols spread the powerful concepts of the divine mandate and the importance of the golden dynasty in several ways: through written and verbal demands for submission from non-Mongol rulers, among them the Mamluks; through the summoning of vassal rulers to Mongol courts and through the "reeducation" of vassals' hostage relatives. Some scholars furthered literate knowledge of the Mongols by writing treatises on them.[7] To describe the effect the

[4] Thomas T. Allsen, *Mongol Imperialism: The Policies of the Grand Qan Möngke in China, Russia and the Islamic Lands 1251–59* (Berkeley and Los Angeles, 1987), 34–36, 42.

[5] For the *yasa* see David Ayalon, "The Great *Yāsa* of Chingiz Khān: A Reexamination," *SI* 33 (1971), 97–140; 34 (1971), 151–80; 36 (1972), 113–58; 38 (1973), 107–56, reprinted in his *Outsiders in the Lands of Islam: Mamluks, Mongols and Eunuchs* (London, 1988); Igor de Rachewiltz, "Some Reflections on Činggis Qan's *J̌asaγ*," *East Asian History* 6 (1993), 91–104; David O. Morgan, "The 'Great Yāsā of Chingiz Khān' and Mongol Law in the Īlkhānate," *BSOAS* 49 (1986), 163–76 and "The 'Great *Yasa* of Chinggis Khan' Revisited," in *Mongols, Turks and Others: Eurasian Nomads and the Sedentary World*, eds. Reuven Amitai and Michal Biran (Leiden and Boston, 2005), 291–308; Reuven Amitai-Preiss, "Ghazan, Islam and Mongol Tradition: A View from the Mamlūk Sultanate," *BSOAS* 59:1 (1996), 3–6; Ratchnevsky, *Genghis Khan*, 187–96; Denise Aigle, "Le Grand *jasaq* de Gengis-Khan, l'empire, la culture mongole et la *sharīʿa*," *JESHO* 47:1 (2004), 31–79.

[6] Allsen, *Mongol Imperialism*, 36.

[7] For hostages see Lien-Sheng Yang, "Hostages in Chinese History," *Studies in Chinese Institutional History* (Cambridge, 1961), 48–49. For treatises on the Mongols see ʿAlāʾ al-Dīn

Mongols, their conquests and their ideology had on the non-Mongol world they dominated, Marshall Hodgson developed a unique vision of "Mongol Prestige." Mongol prestige was based on non-Mongol awe of and respect for Mongol military might, thus the prevailing political idea of the period after Chingiz Khan's conquests represented "an appeal to the greatness of Mongol imperial power."[8] At the same time, Hülegü's execution of the Abbasid caliph al-Mustaʿṣim in Baghdad in 1258/656 during the Iran campaign signaled the destruction of the idea of a universalist Islamic empire. Thus subsequent claims to universal sovereignty and to legitimacy in the Islamic lands were grounded not in Islamic tradition, but in Mongol tradition, norms and genealogy.[9] (The Mamluks were one noteworthy exception to this rule.)

The Mongol model remained dominant throughout Central Asia, the Iranian Plateau and Anatolia down to and well after the death of the last effective Ilkhanid ruler in Iran, Abū Saʿīd, in 1335/736. Thereafter nomadic, semi-nomadic and sedentary rulers attempted to express their own responses to the challenges of legitimacy and the Mongol legacy through a number of experiments in ideology. At first, non-Chingizid Mongol and Turkic warlords connected to the dominant ideology by portraying themselves as conservative protectors of Chingizid heritage. This they accomplished by marrying Chingizid princesses, ruling in the name of Chingizid puppets or swearing to uphold the *yasa*.[10] Temür's ideology began this way, although it later branched into a unique set of ideas when he claimed to be, first, protector of the Chagataid heritage, based on ancestral links between his own family and the Chingizid house, and then reviver of Chingiz Khan's entire empire.[11] Eventually post-Mongol Turkic rulers drew on older Turkic traditions to rival the Chingizid model. Muslim Turkic groups like the Ottomans and the Aq Qoyunlu took up the genealogical model of a favored dynasty, but replaced Chingiz Khan with noble Turkic ancestors.[12] Turkic rulers also employed their own concept of good fortune and divine favor,

ʿAṭāʾ Malik Juvaynī, *Taʾrīkh-i Jahān Gushā*, tr. J. A. Boyle, *The History of the World-Conqueror* (Seattle, 1997); Aḥmad al-Nuwayrī, *Nihāyat al-arab fī funūn al-adab*, ed. Saʿīd ʿĀshūr (Cairo, 1985), XXVII:197–420; Reuven Amitai, "al-Nuwayrī as a Historian of the Mongols," in *The Historiography of Islamic Egypt (c. 950–1800)*, ed. Hugh Kennedy (Leiden, 2001), 23–36; also Ibn Faḍlallah al-ʿUmarī, *Das mongolische Weltreich: al-ʿUmarī's Darstellung der mongolischen Reiche in seinem Werke Masālik al-absār fī mamālik al-amsār, mit Paraphrase und Kommentar*, ed. and tr. Klaus Lech (Wiesbaden, 1968); see also R. D. McChesney, "Zamzam Water on a White Felt Carpet: Adapting Mongol Ways in Muslim Central Asia, 1550–1650," in *Technology*, 63–66.

8 Marshall G. S. Hodgson, *The Venture of Islam* (Chicago, 1974), II:404.

9 Cornell H. Fleischer, *Bureaucrat and Intellectual in the Ottoman Empire* (Princeton, 1986), 286; John E. Woods, *The Aqquyunlu: Clan, Confederation, Empire* (Salt Lake City, 1999), 4–7.

10 Woods, *Aqquyunlu*, 8; also John E. Woods, "Timur's Genealogy," in *Intellectual Studies on Islam: Essays Written in Honor of Martin B. Dickson*, eds. Michel M. Mazzaoui and Vera B. Moreen (Salt Lake City, 1999), 100.

11 Woods, "Genealogy," 106–09.

12 Fleischer, *Bureaucrat*, 286–87; Woods, *Aqquyunlu*, 9 and Appendix A.

qut (also Persian *bakht* or *farr*), which corresponded to the Mongolian *su*.[13] Likewise, the concept of law as proclaimed by the ruler (dynastic law) appeared as the Turkic *töre* (*törü* or *ture*) and later the Ottoman *kanun*.[14] Also impervious to change was the importance of lineage and dynasty as tools of legitimacy, which had mattered ideologically for centuries, and which was only emphasized by the Mongol and later Turkic focus on ancestors, and the consequent devotion to the Golden or other imperial families.[15] But Middle Eastern rulers also experimented with dynastic adoption of non-Chingizids, where leaders with weak claims to rule linked themselves to defunct dynasties possessed of ideological power. Such rulers included the early Mamluks, who forged ceremonial ties to the Kurdish Ayyubids who had preceded them, and the Ottomans, who adopted the Turkish Muslim Seljuks of Anatolia (ca. 1071–1307/463–707).[16] Among the Mamluks, Baybars (r. 1260–77/658–76) stood out for his ephemeral attempt to connect himself to the Seljuks during his brief occupation of eastern Anatolia in 1277/675.[17]

But where were Islamic ideas of kingship in all of this? During the years of Mongol shamanistic rule, and especially after the death of the caliph al-Mustʿaṣim in 1258/656, older, primarily Islamic models of legitimacy almost disappeared from view.[18] Then they began a gradual resurgence, particularly when some Mongol sovereigns themselves converted to Islam and began to fuse the two traditions. This meant that they ruled both as divinely favored descendants of Chingiz Khan, and as Muslim sultans, advised by Islamic scholars. Mongol rulers were attracted to varied aspects of Islamic notions of kingship: Berke of the Golden Horde (r. 1257–66/654/5–63/4) explained his hostility to the Ilkhanid Hülegü as a desire to uphold Islam and avenge the Abbasid caliph, while Hülegü's Muslim descendant Ghazan (r. 1295–1304/694–703), who was inordinately proud of his imperial Mongol

13 de Rachewiltz, "Foundations," 29; also see DeWeese, *Islamization*, 46; Woods, *Aqquyunlu*, 6; Halil Inalcık, "Osmanlılar'da saltanat veraseti usulü ve Türk hâkimiyet telâkkisiyle ilgisi," *Siyasal Bilgiler Fakültesi Dergisi* 14 (1956), 69–94, translated in Inalcık, "The Ottoman Succession and its Relations to the Turkish Concept of Sovereignty," in *The Middle East and the Balkans under the Ottoman Empire: Essays on Economy and Society* (Bloomington, 1993), 37–63, see here 41–42.

14 Woods, *Aqquyunlu*, 7–9 and "Genealogy," 100–01; Fleischer, *Bureaucrat*, 274, 287; also Halil Inalcık, *The Ottoman Empire: The Classical Age, 1300–1600*, tr. Norman Itzkowitz and Colin Imber (New Rochelle, NY, 1973 repr. 1989), 65–69.

15 See DeWeese, *Islamization*, 37–41.

16 For Mamluks and Ayyubids see P. M. Holt, "The Position and Power of the Mamlūk Sultan," *BSOAS* 38 (1975), 241; for Ottomans and Seljuks see Inalcık, "Sovereignty," 44; Fleischer, *Bureaucrat*, 287–88.

17 For Baybars's appropriation of the Seljuks see Peter Thorau, *The Lion of Egypt: Sultan Baybars I and the Near East in the Thirteenth Century*, tr. P. M. Holt (London, 1992), 239. The Mamluk sultan al-Muʾayyad Shaykh made a similar claim in 1419/822. See P. M. Holt, *The Age of the Crusades: The Near East from the Eleventh Century to 1517* (London and New York, 1986), 183.

18 See Woods, *Aqquyunlu*, 4–7.

ancestry, hinted as early as 1300/699 that he himself might be the Islamic centennial renewer of religion (*mujaddid*).[19] The Muslim Ilkhanids in particular successfully fused Chingizid and Islamic ideologies, which their immediate successors then carefully copied. Muslim Mongol rulers also appropriated local artistic, literary and cultural traditions to link themselves to their subjects.[20] In the post-Mongol Turkic world, Islamic ideas continued to reappear at different times in different places, now almost invariably linked to Turko-Mongol themes. The Zoroastrian concept of the ruler as the arbiter of justice, for example, had been assimilated into Islamic political thought by the eleventh/fifth century.[21] Then in the post-Mongol Turkic world, this notion merged with the nomadic concept of the ruler as a lawgiver proclaiming a special dynastic law, and reached a pinnacle under the Ottoman Kanuni Suleiman ("the Lawgiver," r. 1520–66/926–74).[22] Despite Suleiman's success, however, the reconciliation of Islamic and nomadic laws remained an intellectual and ideological challenge to other rulers and their advisors for centuries.[23] In addition, Islamic mystic, Shiite and apocalyptic notions gave rise to the idea of a ruler whose reign was justified by a personal connection to divinity, whether mediated by holy figures or not.[24] This concept, too, survived the Mongol invasions, and resurfaced in the Ottoman Osman's marriage to the daughter of the mystic Shaykh Edebali, and in the Turkish Isma'īl Ṣafavī (r. 1501–24/907–30) when he claimed divinity.

In general, Islamic models of kingship were most attractive to those who were unable to forge connections to the Chingizid paradigm, like Muslim Turks and Mongols. The Chobanids in Azerbaijan (1335–57/736–58), who had no claim to the Chingizid heritage, toyed with the Islamic concept of the Rightly Guided One (*mahdī*) and with worthy patronage of religious architecture in Arabia.[25] Similarly Temür claimed Islamic respectability for his military campaigns through the sanction of Muslim holy men, and resorted most clearly to Islamic ideology when he fought with Chingizid princes, whose own legitimacy in Chingizid terms so clearly surpassed his own.[26] But among Muslim rulers in the Middle East, it was the Mamluk sultans who stood out for their reliance on narrowly Islamic ideas of kingship, which they used specifically to oppose Chingizid ideological domination.

19 Baybars al-Manṣūrī, *Zubdat al-fikrah fī ta'rīkh al-hijrah*, ed. D. S. Richards (Beirut, 1998), 333–34; also see Chapter 3 below.

20 On Chinese and Iranian symbols of legitimacy used for domestic audiences see Tomoko Masuya, "Ilkhanid Courtly Life," in *Legacy*, 96–102 and note 79; also Robert Hillenbrand, "The Arts of the Book in Ilkhanid Iran," in *Legacy*, 134–67, esp. 153–54.

21 A. K. S. Lambton, "Justice in the Medieval Persian Theory of Kingship," *SI* 17 (1962), reprinted in *Theory and Practice in Medieval Persia* (London, 1980), 96–97, 99.

22 Fleischer, *Bureaucrat*, 286–92, and Woods, *Aqquyunlu*, 6–9.

23 McChesney, "Zamzam Water," entire.

24 Woods, *Aqquyunlu*, 4–7.

25 See Chapters 4, 5.

26 Woods, "Genealogy," 104–06.

Mamluk ideology

Mamluk ideology was first created during the early years of the Sultanate, and, despite some necessary modifications, this model was emulated by later sultans for years. Unlike Chingizid or later Turko-Mongol notions of kingship, however, this ideology hinged consistently and exclusively on antiquated Islamic concepts, and on a vision of the Mamluk sultan as a martial Guardian of Islam and Islamic society. The Mamluk sultans used this outdated model because they suffered from two serious, linked problems: the institution of slavery and a lack of lineage.[27] The Mamluk slave institution meant that the Mamluks were singularly ill-suited to justify themselves as rulers. A sultan's professional career began in servitude (unless he was the offspring of a slave), and although within the Sultanate military slaves and their descendants formed the ruling class, outside it slaves were nobodies. Correspondingly the Mamluk sultans could claim no lineage, for their origins were unknown and assumed to be unimportant. This meant that when proclaiming their legitimacy to their own subjects the early Mamluks resorted to dynastic adoption from their predecessors, the defunct Ayyubids, which they achieved by continuing Ayyubid ceremonial practices. In addition, the Mamluk sultans consistently tried to develop their own dynasties as an alternate response to this lack of lineage, albeit with mixed results. The Mamluks also justified their rule at home by patronizing both the Islamic courts and the grievance courts (*maẓālim*), promoting themselves as warrior-kings, establishing Islamic architectural complexes, overseeing the prosecution of heresy and apostasy, and participating in processions, religious festivals or public displays of charity.[28] Most importantly, the early Mamluks promised to protect their subjects from the Mongols.

[27] Other than descendants of the sultan Qalawun (r. 1279–90/678–89), Mamluk rulers had no lineage, thus many tried (and failed) to establish dynasties. I am currently preparing an article on the Mamluk dynastic impulse.

[28] For Ayyubid ceremonial see Holt, "Position and Power," 241. For courts and the law see Joseph H. Escovitz, *The Office of Qâḍî al-Quḍât in Cairo under the Baḥrî Mamlûks* (Berlin, 1984); Jørgen S. Nielsen, *Secular Justice in an Islamic State: Maẓālim under the Baḥrī Mamlūks, 662/1264–789/1387* (Leiden, 1985). For heresy and apostasy see Eliyahu Ashtor, "L'Inquisition dans l'état mamlouk," *Rivista degli Studi Orientali* 25 (1950), 11–26; Anne F. Broadbridge, "Apostasy Trials in Eighth/Fourteenth Century Egypt: A Case Study," in *The History and Historiography of Central Asia: A Festschrift for John E. Woods*, eds. Judith Pfeiffer and Sholeh A. Quinn with Ernest Tucker (Wiesbaden, 2006), 363–82. For architecture see R. Stephen Humphreys, "The Expressive Intent of the Mamluk Architecture of Cairo: A Preliminary Essay," *SI* 35 (1972), 69–119; Nasser O. Rabbat, "The Ideological Significance of the *Dār al-Adl* in the Medieval Islamic Orient," *IJMES* 27 (1995), 3–28, and Adam Sabra, *Poverty and Charity in Medieval Islam* (Cambridge, 2000), 69–100. For the warrior-king (*Heerkönig*) see Holt, "Position and Power," 246–47. For processions and festivals see Jacques Jomier, *Le Maḥmal et la caravane égyptienne des pèlerins de la Mecque (XIIIe–XXe siècles)* (Cairo, 1953), 35–42; Boaz Shoshan, *Popular Culture in Medieval Cairo* (Cambridge, 1993), 70–76; for royal charity see Ibn ʿAbd al-Ẓāhir, *al-Rawḍ al-ẓāhir fī sīrat al-Malik al-Ẓāhir*, ed. ʿAbd al-ʿAzīz Khuwayṭir (Riyadh, 1976), 200–01, and Sabra, *Poverty and Charity*, 52–58, 138–66.

When proclaiming their right to rule to the Mongols outside their borders, by contrast, the early Mamluks faced the physical menace of Chingiz Khan's Ilkhanid descendants, the specter of Mongol prestige and the weight of the Chingizid divine mandate, while they themselves remained trapped by their own ideological weakness. To Mongol eyes, imperial lineage was the prerogative of the Chingizids, and slavery was the condition of distinctly lesser people: during Chingiz Khan's lifetime, some conquered Mongolian and Central Asian nomads had been incorporated into a system of hereditary slavery (*ötegü boghul*) in order to destroy their tribal power.[29] If slavery was therefore the fate of conquered tribes, how contemptible must the slave Mamluks have seemed as they dared call themselves independent sultans? The stigma of servitude, combined with the corresponding Mamluk lack of lineage, posed a significant and long-term ideological problem for Mamluk rulers in their interactions with the Mongols: in 1260/658 the Ilkhanid Hülegü (r. 1258–65/656–63) sent a demand for submission to the Mamluk sultan Qutuz (r. 1259–60/657–58), in which he denigrated Qutuz for his servile origins.[30] Similarly Hülegü's Armenian ally King Het'um called Baybars "a (dog) and a slave" and refused to have any dealings with him.[31] In 1300/699 Ghazan hurled accusations of ignoble origins at two different Mamluk sultans when conversing with notables in Damascus, while a century later Temür disparaged the slave origin of the Mamluk sultans Barquq and his son Faraj in letters to the Ottoman sultan Beyazid I.[32]

In addition to suffering periodic slurs from their Mongol enemies, the Mamluk sultans were entirely too familiar with the ideological problem of Chingizid legitimacy in general, for every Mongol demand for submission expressed imperial ideology in uncompromising terms. Most of the early Mamluks were Qipchaq Turks from Golden Horde territory, and so came from a pagan nomadic background similar to the Mongols' own, which allowed them to understand the nomadic ideas they encountered despite their Arabic Islamic educations. A few early Mamluks were themselves Mongols, while the Sultanate absorbed waves of immigrant Mongols in its first years: the men entered the military, while their daughters married into the elite.[33] With so many Mongols on hand and such expertise among them, therefore, the Mamluks surely knew as much about the Mongols as did those

[29] P. B. Golden, "I Will Give the People unto Thee": The Činggisid Conquests and their Aftermath in the Turkic World," *JRAS* 3rd series, 10:1 (April 2000), 24–25.
[30] See Chapter 2.
[31] Grigor of Akner, "History of the Nation of the Archers (the Mongols)," ed. and tr. Robert Blake and Richard N. Frye, *HJAS* 12:3/4 (December 1949), 355.
[32] For Ghazan see Rashīd al-Dīn, *Jāmiʿ al-tawārīkh*, ed. Muḥammad Rawshan and Muṣṭafà Musavī (Tehran, 1994), II:1293–94. For Temür see Zeki Velidi Togan, "Timurs Osteuropapolitik," *ZDMG* 108 (1958), 298, and the unpublished translation by John E. Woods.
[33] See David Ayalon, "The Wafidiya in the Mamluk Kingdom," *Islamic Culture* 25 (January–October 1951), 89–104, and reprinted in his *Studies on the Mamlūks of Egypt (1250–1517)* (London, 1977), also his "The Auxiliary Forces of the Mamluk Sultanate,"

regions that were actually under Mongol control. As a result, it is no surprise that for the Mongol audience, even more than for their own subjects, the early Mamluk sultans turned to the outdated concepts of Islamic kingship that the Mongols had destroyed, and brandished an obsolete ideology for lack of a better one with which to supplant it.

Mamluk ideology was created through cooperation among the sultan, his military men and their scholarly religious advisors. Although many sultans had distinct ideas about how to justify their reigns, which appeared in their individual expressions of ideology, the scholars played an important role in refining the religious underpinnings of Mamluk kingship. The scholars worked directly with the sultan and the ruling elite in the bureaucracy, the courts and the pious foundations that the military men established, and also wrote the endowment documents and diplomatic letters where Mamluk ideology appeared, which could either connect the Mamluks to the religiously oriented culture around them, or proclaim their protection of it to outsiders. The details of this ideology appeared in the writings of scholarly advice-givers to the sultans, and were conservatively cast in Islamic traditions of rule. They clearly reflected the concerns of an era in which Mongol military aggression was a terrifying threat, and showed that the Mamluk sultan's task was to protect his lands and subjects as a military Guardian of Islam, and also uphold Islamic law (*sharīʿah*), ideally with the advice of the scholars themselves.[34] The sultan's role as Guardian relied on several specific notions of kingly activity. Foremost was the idea of Mamluk participation in military action against non-Muslim aggressors on behalf of Islam (*jihād*).[35] Although easily the most common notion of kingship among Muslim rulers before the arrival of the Mongols, not all had focused on it to the same degree: while the Mamluks' early Ayyubid predecessors had emphasized jihad against the Crusaders, the later Ayyubids had not, and it was only the Mamluks who revived the discarded combative ideal and made it a mainstay of their ideological response to the Chingizids.[36] Closely linked to the notion of jihad was the concept of Abbasid caliphal sanction for Mamluk rule. After Hülegü's destruction of the caliphate in Baghdad in 1258/656, the Mamluk sultan

Der Islam 65 (1988), 13–37, reprinted in his *Islam and the Abode of War: Military Slaves and Islamic Adversaries* (London, 1994); Reuven Amitai-Preiss, *Mongols and Mamluks: The Mamluk–Īlkhānid War, 1260–1281* (Cambridge, 1995), 108–09.

[34] For the first seventy-five years of the Sultanate see Badr al-Dīn Muḥammad Ibn Jamāʿah, "Kitāb taḥrīr al-aḥkām fī tadbīr ahl al-islām," ed. Hans Kofler as "Handbuch des islamischen Staats- und Verwaltungsrechtes von Badr al-Dīn Ibn Gamāʿah," *Islamica* 6 (1934), 347–414; Ḥasan Ibn al-ʿAbbāsī, *Āthār al-uwal fī tartīb al-duwal*, ed. ʿAbd al-Raḥmān ʿUmayrah (Beirut, 1989/1409); Ibn al-Nafīs, *The Theologus Autodidacticus of Ibn al-Nafīs*, eds. Max Mayerhof and Joseph Schacht (Oxford, 1968), 63–71, and Remke Kruk, "History and Apocalypse: Ibn al-Nafîs' Justification of Mamluk Rule," *Der Islam* 72 (1995), 324–37.

[35] Emmanuel Sivan, *L'Islam et la croisade: idéologie et propagande dans les réactions musulmanes aux croisades* (Paris, 1968), 165–89.

[36] *Ibid.*, 93, 131, 165.

Baybars established another in Cairo in 1261/659.[37] Although not universally acknowledged outside Mamluk territory, the caliph was central to Mamluk definitions of kingship inside it, for he legitimated the reigns of the early sultans and established the ideological groundwork to expand Mamluk territory under putative Abbasid guidance. The caliph supported jihad by encouraging the Mamluk warriors for the faith (*mujāhidūn*), and legitimated their martial exertions with his prestigious name and heritage. The caliph's titles were stamped on Mamluk coins, his black banners accompanied sultanic yellow ones and the caliph himself appeared at coronations. Nevertheless, despite the caliph's symbolic importance, most Mamluk rulers severely restricted the Abbasids themselves, who often lived impotently under house arrest.[38]

The Mamluk sultans also publicly proclaimed their role as Guardians of the Islamic holy cities of Mecca, Medina and Jerusalem, and of the annual pilgrimage to Mecca, by claiming exclusive rights to pilgrimage ceremonies once dominated by the Abbasid caliphs.[39] In this way the Mamluk sultans assumed both sovereignty over the Hijaz, and ideological superiority over other Muslim rulers, which became increasingly important once the Mongols began to convert to Islam.[40] The caravan of the Guardian sultan entered the holy cities before caravans from other regions, and was led by a special camel bearing an empty silk palanquin (*maḥmal*), itself accompanied by the sultan's distinctive banners and a military band.[41] The leaders of Mecca and Medina had to bow before the palanquin as if it were the sultan.[42] When rival rulers sent palanquins, these had to enter the holy cities after the Mamluk ones. Similarly it was only the Mamluk sultan who furnished the embroidered silk curtains (*kiswah*) for the Ka'aba, which was even more important than sending the palanquin, since although several palanquins could appear during any pilgrimage season, only one set of curtains could hang at a time. The Mamluk sultan also enjoyed the exclusive prerogative of having his name and titles mentioned in the Friday sermons in Mecca, and bestowed

37 On the revived caliphate of Cairo see Stefan Heidemann, *Das Allepiner Kalifat (AD 1261): vom Ende des Kalifates in Baghdad über Aleppo zu den Restaurationen in Kairo* (Leiden, 1994); P. M. Holt, "The Structure of Government in the Mamluk Sultanate," in *The Eastern Mediterranean Lands in the Period of the Crusades*, ed. P. M. Holt (Warminster, 1977), 44–46; also his "Some Observations on the 'Abbāsid Caliphate of Cairo," *BSOAS* 47 (1984), 501–07, and "Position and Power," 243–44; for a revolutionary replacement of the caliph with the sultan see Wilferd Madelung, "A Treatise on the Imamate Dedicated to Sultan Baybars I," *Proceedings of the 14th Congress of the Union Européenne des Arabisants et Islamisants* I, ed. A. Fodor (Budapest, 1995), 91–102.

38 See Holt, "Observations," 503–07; Heidemann, *Kalifat*, 163–66, 174; Sivan, *Idéologie*, 169–70; for the caliph's uneven acceptance outside Mamluk territory see Woods, *Aqquyunlu*, 7.

39 Jomier, *Maḥmal*, 32; also see Keiko Ota, "The Meccan Sharifate and its Diplomatic Relations in the Bahri Mamluk Period," *Annals of Japan Association for Middle East Studies* 17:1 (2002), 8–15.

40 For Mamluk sovereignty see Jomier, *Maḥmal*, 3, 10, 27–34.

41 *Ibid.*, 10, and 31 for the precedence of the Mamluk palanquin. For the military band see 'Abdullah 'Ankawi, "The Pilgrimage to Mecca in Mamlūk Times," *Arabian Studies* 1 (1974), 165.

42 Jomier, *Maḥmal*, 10.

a robe, turban and hood on the preacher to wear, as well as two banners to accompany him, all in Abbasid black. The sultan provided stipends for the chief religious personnel in Mecca and Medina, and sent yearly supplies of candles and (lamp) oil for the mosques.[43] Thus the pilgrimage ceremonies gave the Mamluks a public arena to express their role as Guardians, the sovereignty it afforded them and their superiority over other Muslim rulers. It is therefore no surprise that the Mamluk sultans struggled periodically with rivals over the symbolic honors of these holy rites, among them the Rasulids of Yemen, the ilkhan Abū Saʿīd, the Temürids and various Turkic neighbors.[44]

By brandishing the concepts of military achievement in the name of religion; the promotion of Islamic law; the physical protection of Muslims, Islamic society and the holy cities; and the official sanction of the Cairene Abbasid caliphs, the Mamluks and their ideologues avoided the linked issues of slavery and unknown lineage, and responded to the ideological and military challenges of Mongol power. Being both martial and protective, this definition of kingship was well suited for a military elite. In the early years the sultan's role as Guardian contrasted easily with the infidel, caliph-murdering Ilkhanids. Thereafter, however, the creators of Mamluk ideology were forced to refine their definitions as Ilkhanid rulers converted to Islam, then were replaced by Muslim Turkic successors. Finally when Temür appeared to revive the Mongol threat, the Mamluks reverted to the ideology they had once employed against the Ilkhanids, and brandished a set of obsolete images to withstand Temür's claims.

Ideology in diplomacy

One of the most prominent places for the expression of Turko-Mongol and Mamluk ideas of kingship was diplomacy, where rulers could use both their specific message and the ceremonies and logistics of the embassy to proclaim their legitimacy.[45] A ruler's overt message appeared in two places: a formal written letter (*risālah* or *kitāb*), and an oral message (*mushāfahah*), which

[43] ʿAbdallah Ibn Baṭṭūṭah, *The Travels of Ibn Baṭṭūṭa, AD 1325–1354*, tr. with revisions and notes from the Arabic text edited by C. Defrémery and B. R. Sanguinetti by H. A. R. Gibb (Cambridge and London, 1958–2000), Hakluyt Society 2nd series, I:231–32, 247.

[44] Jomier, *Maḥmal*: for the Rasulids in 1261–82/659–81, the 1290s/690s and 1379/780 see 30–31, 43–45, 48–49; for Abū Saʿīd in 1319/718 see 45–48 and Chapter 4 below; for the Temürid Shāh Rukh in 1430–44/833–48 see 50; for the Dulqadirid Shāh Suvār and the Aq Qoyunlu Uzun Ḥasan in the 1460s–70s/870s see 50–53. These battles could be both symbolic and economic.

[45] This approach to the analysis of diplomacy was inspired by Michael McCormick, who discussed the ways Roman and Byzantine emperors communicated ideas of legitimacy to subjects with coins, inscriptions, liturgy and panegyrics, and through banquets, parades, sporting events, sacrifices, executions and speeches. See Michael McCormick, *Eternal Victory: Triumphal Rulership in Late Antiquity, Byzantium and the Early Medieval West* (Cambridge, 1986).

accompanied and expanded on the letter. Letters were produced in the chancellery, often collaboratively, and conformed to a complex stylistic protocol. In the Mamluk Sultanate the ideology expressed to outside rulers through diplomatic letters was never the product of any individual ruler, but rather arose from an amalgam of existing diplomatic protocol, the wishes of the ruler and his advisors, and the stylistic, rhetorical and ideological concerns of the officials who actually wrote the letters. Indeed, the ideas expressed in each diplomatic mission were actually the product of a great (and largely indifferentiable) collaboration of minds. Among the Mamluks, letter drafts were written and read aloud to the ruler and his chief advisors, who could make changes before the letter was sent.[46] (The protocol for Mongol and Turkic letter production may have been similar, but the evidence is lacking.)

Among all rulers, technical details like the size and quality of paper, the use of formal titles and variations in colors of ink were standardized, and conveyed the significance and worth (or lack thereof) of both the sender and the recipient. Mamluk letters to the Mongols, for example, used full-sized Baghdādī paper to indicate the importance of the recipient, since Baghdādī was the best and most expensive kind. By contrast, Mamluk letters to inferior rulers used only half- or even third-sized Baghdādī sheets.[47] Mamluk letters also bore elaborate and stylized royal signatures (*ṭughrāhs*) in gold ink until the 1370s/770s, and were further marked on every page by gold seals (*ṭamghahs*) bearing the ruler's titles.[48] Ilkhanid correspondence was written either on Baghdādī sheets, or on rolls of linen paper, and included red seals proclaiming the divine mandate in Chinese characters, or later in Arabic letters (Figure 1). Beginning at the end of the thirteenth/seventh century, Ilkhanid letters could also bear the countersignatures of Mongol commanders on the back, who acted as witnesses to the letter, and who stamped a separate black seal next to their names. Without these signatures,

[46] Ibn ʿAbd al-Ẓāhir, *Rawḍ*, 138; Shāfiʿ b. ʿAlī, *al-Faḍl al-maʾthūr min sīrat al-Malik al-Manṣūr*, ed. ʿUmar ʿAbd al-Salām Tadmurī (Beirut, 1998), 102; also P. M. Holt, "The Īlkhān Aḥmad's Embassies to Qalāwūn: Two Contemporary Accounts," *BSOAS* 49 (1986), 129.

[47] For paper sizes see Aḥmad b. ʿAlī al-Qalqashandī, *Ṣubḥ al-aʿshā fī ṣināʿat al-inshāʾ*, ed. Muḥammad Ḥusayn Shams al-Dīn (Beirut, 1987), VI:181–82, VIII:20; also see Jonathan M. Bloom, *Paper Before Print: The History and Impact of Paper in the Islamic World* (New Haven and London, 2001), 53, 62; Iraj Afshar, "Manuscript and Paper Sizes Cited in Persian and Arabic Texts," *Maqālāt va dirāsāt muhdà ilà al-duktūr Ṣalāḥ al-Dīn al-Munajjid / Essays in Honour of Ṣalāḥ al-Dīn al-Munajjid* (London, 2002), 661–62; Sheila Blair, "The Religious Art of the Ilkhanids," in *Legacy*, 130.

[48] For the *ṭughrāh* see Ibn Faḍlallah al-ʿUmarī, *al-Taʿrīf bi-al-muṣṭalaḥ al-sharīf*, ed. Samir al-Droubi (Karak, 1992/1413), 59; also Qalqashandī, *Ṣubḥ*, I:55, III:52, VII:272–73, 321, VIII:24; and XIII:170–71 for the discontinuation of the *ṭughrāh* after the 1370s/770s; also see Chapter 5 below on the Qalawunid sultan al-Ashraf Shaʿbān; for gold seals see Ibn Nāẓir al-Jaysh, *Kitāb tathqīf al-taʿrīf bi-al-muṣṭalaḥ al-sharīf*, ed. Rudolf Veselý (Cairo, 1987), 11, whence Qalqashandī, *Ṣubḥ*, VII:273–74.

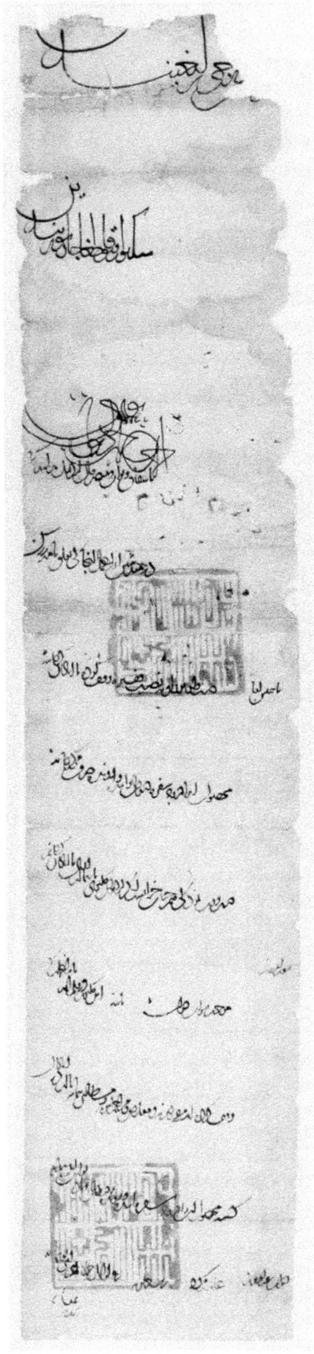

Figure 1. Like the Mongol diplomatic letters, this decree (*fīrmān*) of the ilkhan Geikhatu, written in northwestern Iran in May 1293/early Jumādà II 692, used black ink with square red seals and displayed a lavish use of white space. (Lent by the Art and History Collection; Courtesy of the Arthur M. Sackler Gallery, Smithsonian Institution, Washington, DC: LTS 1995.2.9.)

the letter could be considered invalid.[49] At both courts, letters were written with considerable amounts of blank space, which was a hallmark of royal authority, and indicated an impressive disregard for cost.[50]

The dating of letters varied depending on their origin, and indicated the differences in world views among the senders. Mamluk letters were dated according to the Islamic calendar (*hijrī*), but Mongol letters used the twelve-year Chinese-Uyghur animal cycle, to which the Islamic date was added if the khan was a Muslim, and a Christian date if Christian scribes or translators were involved. Letters from the nomadic Mongols also included the location of composition, but letters from the sedentary Mamluks did not.[51] Under the later Muslim Turkic rulers dating may have been Islamic, but it is hard to be sure since few letters remain. The language of the letters was equally varied: most had to be translated once they reached their destinations. Mongol diplomatic letters were often penned in Mongolian written in Uyghur characters (not Phags-Pa[52]), usually by civilians who had learned the script and language.[53] Mongol letters required translation into Arabic when they reached Mamluk territory, which was undertaken by prominent Mongol military figures at the Mamluk court, since civilians only rarely

49 An Ilkhanid letter to the Mamluks in 1282/681 had 13 red "tamghas" (*ṭamghah*) or (Chinese) seals. See Ibn ʿAbd al-Ẓāhir, *Tashrīf al-ayyām wa al-ʿuṣūr fī sīrat al-Malik al-Manṣūr*, ed. Murād Kāmil (Cairo, 1961), 6. For Ilkhanid seals in general and for countersignatures see Antoine Mostaert and Francis Woodman Cleaves, "Trois documents mongols des archives secrètes vaticanes," *HJAS* 15 (1952), 478–85; Francis Woodman Cleaves, "A Chancellery Practice of the Mongols in the Thirteenth and Fourteenth Centuries," *HJAS* 14 (1951), 508–25; Gottfried Herrmann and Gerhard Doerfer, "Ein persich-mongolischer Erlass des Ǧalāyeriden Šeyḫ Oveys," *CAJ* 19 (1975), 38–44; for linen paper see Antoine Mostaert and Francis Woodman Cleaves (opposing theories about cotton paper), *Les Lettres de 1289 des Ilkhans Arγun et Öljeitü à Philippe le Bel* (Cambridge, MA, 1962), 9–11.

50 Bloom, *Paper*, 62, 78.

51 Mostaert and Cleaves, *Lettres*, 18, 57; "Trois documents," 434, 452, 471; Francis Woodman Cleaves, "The Mongolian Documents in the Musée de Téhéran," *HJAS* 16 (1953), 24–25; Charles Melville, "The Chinese-Uighur Calendar of the Mongol Period," *Iran* 32 (1994), 83–98.

52 For the difference between these two ways to write Mongolian, the so-called Uyghur and Phags-Pa scripts, see "Language Situation and Scripts, Part Two: Old Turkic and Middle Turkic Languages," (D. Sinor) and "Part Three: Mongol Writing Systems," (G. Kara) in *History of Civilizations of Central Asia*, eds. C. E. Bosworth and M. S. Asimov, IV:2 (Paris, 1992–), 333, 336–37.

53 Some Mongol chancelleries also used Persian, although not to the Mamluks. For Mongolian-writing civilians see Jean Aubin, *Émirs mongols et vizirs persans dans les remous de l'acculturation* (Paris, 1995), 46–47, 83. Surviving Ilkhanid letters in Mongolian are (relatively) numerous. They include: the 1260/658 letter of the Mongol governor of Karak (L. Hambis, "La Lettre mongole du Gouverneur de Karak," *Acta Orientalia Academiae Scientiarum Hungaricae* 15 [1962], 143–46; F. W. Cleaves, "The Anonymous Scribal Note Pertaining to the *Bičig* of Ötemiş," *HJAS* 16 [1953], 478–86); a safe-conduct from Abaqa for a papal embassy in 1267/665–66 or 1279/677–78, a 1290/689 letter from Arghun to Pope Nicholas IV, and another from Ghazan to Pope Boniface VIII in 1302/701 (Mostaert and Cleaves, "Trois documents," entire); two letters to Philip IV of France: in 1289/688 from Arghun and in 1305/704 from Öljeitü (Mostaert and Cleaves, *Lettres*, entire); and the letter from Ghazan to the Mamluk sultan al-Nāṣir Muḥammad in 1301/700 (Ibn al-Dawādārī, *Kanz al-durar wa jāmiʿ al-ghurar*, ed. Hans Robert Roemer [Cairo, 1960] IX:53–56, and Author Z, *Taʾrīkh salāṭīn al-mamālīk* or *Beiträge zur Geschichte der mamlukensultane*, ed. K. V. Zetterstéen [Leiden, 1919], 93–94, although the Arabic "translation" in Ibn al-Dawādārī

learned Turkish, and never Mongolian. Mamluk letters were written primarily in Arabic, and also had to be translated at foreign courts; one exception was letters to the Golden Horde, which often used Mongolian.[54] By contrast the chancelleries of post-Mongol states were well versed in multiple languages, and could compose diplomatic correspondence in whichever was most appropriate.[55]

The colors of ink used in diplomatic letters were also significant. In both the Mamluk and Ilkhanid chancelleries, black ink was for regular text, while gold represented important people and ideas. The sender's titles always appeared in gold, as did references to God and Islamic terminology (for the Mamluks) or the Enduring Sky and the Chingizids (for the Mongols). If the recipient of a Mamluk letter was important enough, his titles were also written in gold.[56] Occasionally Ilkhanid documents called for gold ink with vermilion outlining.[57] The Ilkhanids further emphasized important figures by placing them prominently to the far right and slightly elevated on the page, but the Mamluks did not. As a result of this difference, the disgusted ilkhan Ghazan complained in 1303/702 that Mamluk styles were unseemly, their gold ink was misused and the arrangement of the page was flawed.[58]

The reception, treatment and behavior of embassies were equally loaded with portent. One important statement of a ruler's sovereignty and his opinion of his interlocutors appeared in the way envoys were permitted to travel in the host realm. Typically, envoys from hostile courts were brought into a region by secret routes and under heavy guard, and were forbidden to speak with their escorts. They were also required to leave armed members of their entourage at the border. The Mamluk sultans expressed their antagonism to the Ilkhanids and to Temür by treating their envoys as hostile, while some Ilkhanids retaliated by forcing Mamluk ambassadors to engage in ritual purification before allowing them to meet their hosts.[59] The host also

and Author Z is a forgery, not the original). For a Latin version of a lost Mongolian original see Paul Meyvaert, "An Unknown Letter of Hulagu, Il-Khan of Persia, to King Louis IX of France," *Viator* 11 (1980), 246–61.

54 ʿUmarī, *Taʿrīf*, 62–63; Qalqashandī, *Ṣubḥ*, VII:316–17. For the career of one such translator see Donald Little, "Notes on Aytamiš, a Mongol Mamlūk," in *Die islamische Welt zwischen Mittelalter und Neuzeit: Festschrift für Hans Robert Roemer zum 65. Geburtstag*, eds. Ulrich Haarmann and Peter Bachmann (Wiesbaden, 1979), 387–401; reprinted in *History and Historiography of the Mamlūks* (London, 1986).

55 See for example the multilingual Ibn ʿArabshāh (d. 1450/854), who worked for the Ottomans; also Robert G. Irwin, "What the Partridge Told the Eagle: A Neglected Arabic Source on Chinggis Khan and the Early History of the Mongols," in *Mongol Empire*, 5; also see Chapter 5 below for Jalayirid chancellery practices, and the letters in Feridun Beg, *Mecmuʾat-i munsheʾat-i selatin* ([n.p.], [1848–49]).

56 ʿUmarī, *Taʿrīf*, 59; Ibn Nāẓir al-Jaysh, *Tathqīf*, 10; Qalqashandī, *Ṣubḥ*, VII:273.

57 Cleaves, "Mongolian Documents," 7–8, 25.

58 Mostaert and Cleaves, *Lettres*, 14; for the text see Baybars al-Manṣūrī, *Zubdah*, 369; also see ʿAbd Allah Vaṣṣāf al-Ḥaẓrah, *Taʾrīkh-i Vaṣṣāf* (Tehran, 1956), 397, and ʿAbd al-Muḥammad Āyatī, *Taḥrīr-i taʾrīkh-i Vaṣṣāf* ([Tehran], 1993–94), 239–40.

59 Examples of Mamluk hostility are mentioned throughout my chapters; for Mongol purification techniques see note 73 below.

provided housing, provisions, mounts and guides to approaching embassies.[60] Among the Mamluks, Ilkhanid and Temürid ambassadors were lodged in citadels, both to guard them from the Mamluk soldiery and populace, and to keep them from seeing anything of strategic interest. By contrast, Golden Horde embassies were always considered to be friendly, and stayed in tents in the main squares of Mamluk cities, as did the envoys from Turkic nomadic governors of the Mamluk sultans. When Mamluk ambassadors went to Mongol courts, or to Temür, they were assigned tents in the ruler's camp (*ordo*), although in the later years of Ilkhanid rule Mamluk ambassadors visited both sedentary cities and tent cities.

Another of the host's kingly duties was to grant daily provisions of food, drink and spending money to his ambassador guests while they were in his realm. The amount and kinds of these provisions reflected the status of the embassy's sender. Berke Khan honored at least one Mamluk ambassador with meat, fish, cooked honey and fermented mare's milk (*qimiz, qumiz*).[61] The Mamluks tried to tailor provisions along nomadic lines, and provided sheep, horses and dairy products to eat, along with the luxury of local fruits, while Temür demonstrated his power by ensuring that ambassadors were given the best available foods, usually extensive amounts of meats and fruits in season.[62] A host also expressed his opinion of another sovereign in the initial greeting he gave the arriving embassy. In the Sultanate this took place when a Mamluk official rode out of a city to meet the ambassadors before they entered it. The rank of the official reflected the perceived importance of the embassy and the ruler it represented: embassies of great status were met by a parade led by a senior military commander, who was followed by all the commanders, armies and Mamluks, riding fine horses and dressed in their best apparel. The clothing demonstrated the ranks in the Mamluk armies, and glorified the Mamluk sultan through a display of sartorial magnificence. On such occasions, the populace also turned out both to witness the spectacle and give their own welcome.[63] Unimportant embassies were greeted with less fanfare by lesser functionaries. This welcoming delegation also became standard under the later Ilkhanids.

60 Ibn al-ʿAbbāsī, *Āthār*, 193.

61 Quṭb al-Dīn Mūsà b. Muḥammad al-Yūnīnī, *Dhayl mirʾāt al-zamān* (Hyderabad, 1954–61), I:542.

62 For examples of Mamluk provisions see Muḥammad b. al-Jazarī, *Taʾrīkh ḥawādith al-zamān wa anbāʾihi wa wafāyāt al-akābir wa al-aʿyān min abnāʾihi* or *Taʾrīkh al-Jazarī*, ed. ʿUmar ʿAbd al-Salām Tadmurī (Sidon and Beirut, 1998), II:254; Shams al-Dīn al-Shujāʿī, *Taʾrīkh al-Malik al-Nāṣir Muḥammad b. Qalāwūn al-Ṣāliḥī wa Awlādihi*, ed. Barbara Schäfer (Weisbaden, 1977), 45; for Temür see Ruy González de Clavijo, *Narrative of the Embassy of Ruy Gonzalez de Clavijo to the Court of Timour at Samarcand, AD 1403–6*, tr. Clements R. Markham, Hakluyt Society 1st series, vol. XXVI (London, 1859), 134–35.

63 Note the 1323/723 welcome for Ilkhanid envoys in Nuwayrī, *Nihāyat al-arab fī funūn al-adab*, ed. Muṣṭafà Hijāzī (Cairo, 1997), XXXIII:61–63, and in 1394/796 for the Jalayirid Sulṭān-Aḥmad in Muḥammad Ibn al-Furāt, *Taʾrīkh Ibn al-Furāt* or *Taʾrīkh al-duwal wa al-mulūk*, ed. Costantine K. Zurayk (Beirut, 1942), IX:366–68.

After the embassy had settled into its lodgings, it would meet with the ruler in a highly ceremonial reception, during which every aspect of behavior and protocol was carefully calculated to project the status of both sides. The importance of both the host and his interlocutor determined such details as what food and drink were served, where ambassadors could stand, whether or not they could sit, and the degree of obeisance they performed. At the same time the host himself used protocol to demonstrate his opinion of his interlocutor. His initial acknowledgment of the ambassadors' greeting, for example, was deeply meaningful: he could nod, stand or speak if he chose to honor the sender; if not, he could fail to meet the ambassadors' eyes, berate them or even ignore them. Likewise the ambassadors' conduct was designed to send a distinct message, and thus could be cordial, conciliatory, arrogant or even hostile, depending on their own ruler's wishes.[64]

In addition to these formalities, at receptions letters were read aloud and gifts presented (except for female slaves), but oral messages were held for later, sequestered meetings. As was true with protocol, the gifts that the ambassadors produced during these ceremonies indicated their sender's wealth, interests and intentions. At the same time, a host could seek to impress the envoys through his own show of wealth, which was communicated in part through clothing. Formal robes of honor (*khilʿah, tashrīf, kāmilīyah*) were a mainstay of political ceremonies throughout the Islamic and nomadic worlds, where rulers employed them to reinforce political bonds, express the internal hierarchies of their states, and reward special services.[65] Such robes were also an integral part of diplomatic ceremonies. A ruler would receive envoys while seated against a backdrop of officials dressed in sumptuous robes, in which gradations of material, color and ornamentation (furs, gold and gems) demonstrated hierarchies of rank. Ambassadors themselves also received one or more robes during their stay. Their quality signaled a ruler's opinion of the sender and his message, and matched the personal rank of the ambassadors. These might be military men, who surreptitiously investigated the host's capacity for war; religious scholars, who ensured lawful behavior among members of the mission; and scribes, who maintained diplomatic and chancellery protocol.[66]

64 Ibn al-ʿAbbāsī, *Āthār*, 194–95; also Doris Behrens-Abouseif, "The Citadel of Cairo: Stage for Mamluk Ceremonial," *AI* 24 (1988), 44–45.

65 See *Robes and Honor: The Medieval World of Investiture*, ed. Stewart Gordon (New York, 2001), especially Carl F. Petry, "Robing Ceremonials in Late Mamluk Egypt: Hallowed Traditions, Shifting Protocols," 353–77, and Thomas T. Allsen, "Robing in the Mongolian Empire," 305–13. For the hierarchy of robes in the early Mamluk Sultanate (as distinct from Petry's discussion of the later period) see Nuwayrī, *Nihāyah*, XXXIII:54. Also see Thomas T. Allsen, *Commodity and Exchange in the Mongol Empire: A Cultural History of Islamic Textiles* (Cambridge, 1997), entire; L. A. Mayer, *Mamluk Costume: A Survey* (Geneva, 1952), 56–64; Bethany Walker, "The Social Implications of Textile Development in Fourteenth-Century Egypt," *Mamluk Studies Review* 4 (2000), 167–217; N. A. Stillman, "Khilʿa," *EI*² V:6–7.

66 Ibn al-ʿAbbāsī, *Āthār*, 191–92.

It is impossible to describe the specific robes that Mongol rulers gave to Mamluk ambassadors, but we know that the most honored Mongol and Turkic envoys sent to the Mamluk court received full robes with sleeves, decorated with embroidered or brocaded bands, and sometimes lined with fur. Such lavish gifts might be accompanied by caps (*kalawtah*s), heavy ornamental gold belts (*ḥiyāṣah, ḥawāʾiṣ*) and, to show unusual favor, horses with full harnesses.[67] Correspondingly, lesser ambassadors were granted lesser robes, while in cases of extreme diplomatic hostility, robes might actually be withheld.[68] After the political disintegration of the Ilkhanid Empire, the Mamluks used robes to appoint some Ilkhanid successors as governors in the Mamluk administration, but these appointment robes were sent directly to their recipients, and were separate from robes bestowed on the governors' ambassadors as a diplomatic courtesy. Banners were also used to indicate one ruler's sovereignty over another: the lesser figure demonstrated his acceptance of a position as a subordinate (usually a governor) when he accepted the banner. The Mamluks routinely sent sultanic and caliphal banners to their governors among the Ilkhanid successors, then were themselves forced to accept Temür's banner after he humbled them in 1402–03/805. The only exception to the use of banners as a sign of appointment was when the Mamluks sent them to the khans of the Golden Horde. In this case they merely symbolized the position of the Mamluk sultan as a religious senior and example to follow, not an actual sovereign over the khans.

A ruler's concern with projecting royalty to other kings also appeared in the physical quality of the ambassadorial reception site. In the Golden Horde, at least one reception took place in an enormous white felt tent lined with silk. The felt represented the ruler's nomadic background, its color suggested his nobility, and the interior silk hangings, which were probably embroidered with gold (*nasīj*), reflected the khan's ability to consume expensive goods.[69] In Mamluk territory, receptions were usually held at the Cairo citadel, where the grandeur and beauty of structures like the Great Hall and Congregational Mosque built by the sultan al-Nāṣir Muḥammad, as well as the proliferation of well-guarded gates through which ambassadors passed, all emphasized the

67 See for example the Mamluk reception of Ilkhanid ambassadors to conclude the peace negotiations in 1323/723 in Nuwayrī, *Nihāyah*, XXXIII:62–63; for Mongol belts see Allsen, *Commodity and Exchange*, 16; Mark G. Kramarovsky, "The Culture of the Golden Horde and the Problem of the 'Mongol Legacy,'" in *Rulers from the Steppe: State Formation on the Eurasian Periphery*, eds. Gary Seaman and Daniel Marks (Los Angeles, 1991), 261–63.

68 The Mamluk sultan al-Nāṣir Muḥammad refused to present a robe to a Golden Horde ambassador who had angered him in 1321/721 (see Chapter 4). Similarly in 1403/806 the Mamluks temporarily withheld robes from Temür's ambassadors (see Chapter 6).

69 Ibn ʿAbd al-Ẓāhir, *Rawḍ*, 216; Yūnīnī, *Dhayl*, I:541. See also Peter Alford Andrews, *Felt Tents and Pavilions: The Nomadic Tradition and its Interaction with Princely Tentage* (London, 1999), I:389, 467–68, 470–71, 504–05, 545, 560–62; Allsen, *Commodity and Exchange*, 1–4.

sultan's magnificence, sovereignty and power.[70] Similarly Temür sent some ambassadors to view his architectural projects, which emphasized his majesty and that of his family.[71] While in host territory, envoys might also participate in festivals, games, hunting parties or family celebrations, at which rulers again displayed their kingly qualities and their affection for the envoys' sender. Conversely, envoys whose sender was on hostile terms with the host might be forced to attend military demonstrations, or even be subjected to punitive action – beatings, imprisonment or death.[72]

Whereas the ceremonies of Mamluk diplomacy were largely inherited from their Ayyubid predecessors, Mongol rulers followed distinctive elements of protocol arising from specific nomadic practices. Among these were shamanistic ceremonies designed to protect the ruler from any danger that foreign envoys posed. One such custom was the use of fire or smoke as an agent of purification, which appeared among the Ilkhanids when Mamluk ambassadors and their gifts were forced to pass between two fires in order to remove poisons or enchantments.[73] The formal audience with Mongol rulers was also regulated by strict symbolic customs, which ambassadors were warned against breaking. If the reception was held in a Mongol tent (*ger*), the ambassadors had to enter without treading on the threshold, or risk a horrible death.[74] Ambassadors were also forbidden to wear weapons in the khan's presence (although this practical custom was observed by most rulers). And since Mongol life and Mongol tents were governed by specific understandings of space, ambassadors were presented from the left, and then moved to the right once they had been received.[75] Mamluk ambassadors also had to abide by Mongol customs and taboos while in camp, at least in public. One such

70 For the ceremonial functions of the Cairo citadel under the Mamluks see Behrens-Abouseif, "Citadel," entire and 70–71 on gates; Rabbat, "*Dār al-Adl*," 1–28, and *The Citadel of Cairo: A New Interpretation of Royal Mamluk Architecture* (Leiden, 1995), entire and esp. 243–74; also Bernard O'Kane, "Monumentality in Mamluk and Mongol Art and Architecture," *Art History* 19:4 (December 1996), 510–11.

71 González de Clavijo, *Embassy*, 123–25.

72 D. Sinor, "Diplomatic Practices in Medieval Inner Asia," in *The Islamic World from Classical to Modern Times*, eds. C. E. Bosworth et al. (Princeton, 1989), 346–47.

73 Baybars's first ambassadors to Abaqa were purified in this manner. See Ibn ʿAbd al-Ẓāhir, *Rawḍ*, 399. For an eyewitness account of a similar purification ritual in 1259/657 see Reuven Amitai, "Evidence for the Early Use of the Title *Īlkhān* among the Mongols," *JRAS* 3rd series, 1:3 (1991), 355–56; similarly *The Chronicle of Novgorod, 1016–1471*, ed. and tr. Robert Michell and Neill Forbes (London, 1914, repr. Academic International, 1970), 88–89. Also see Sinor, "Diplomatic Practices," 348; Jean-Paul Roux, *La Religion des Turcs et des Mongols* (Paris, 1984), 222–24; DeWeese, *Islamization*, 258–62; Julian Baldick, *Animal and Shaman: Ancient Religions of Central Asia* (New York, 2000), 39, 88; J. A. Boyle, "Turkish and Mongol Shamanism in the Middle Ages," *Folklore* 83 (1972), 177–193, reprinted in his *The Mongol World Empire, 1206–1370* (London, 1977), 182–84.

74 This was live burial under the tent. See Baldick, *Animal and Shaman*, 99; Andrews, *Felt Tents*, I:292–94, 475.

75 Ibn ʿAbd al-Ẓāhir, *Rawḍ*, 215–16. This assumes left and right as seen by the ruler (i.e., inside the tent looking out). See Andrews, *Felt Tents*, I:561–62; also see I:305–10, I:482–91; also see Sinor, "Diplomatic Practices," 349–50.

was the Altaic taboo against the defilement of running water, which nomads maintained out of fear of angering the spirit world in general or the Enduring Sky in particular, who could respond by unleashing thunder and lightning.[76] To a people accustomed to treeless steppe, a thunderstorm could be truly terrifying: in winter 1298–99/698 Mamluk spies reported that an Ilkhanid military campaign had been postponed because of snow and lightning storms, which had been seen as a bad omen.[77] In diplomacy, therefore, the nomadic water taboo meant that ambassadors could not openly wash their clothes in camp, nor eat ice or snow.[78] Nomadic custom also dictated that all ambassadors' lives be held in high regard, as reflected in the proverb, "Fresh grass does not burn, the king's ambassador does not die."[79] As a result, when independent rulers executed Mongol ambassadors, this usually led to an ugly military reprisal.[80] The murder of ambassadors was often exacerbated by the Mongols' fine sense of social hierarchy, which designated specific methods of execution according to the rank and importance of the condemned. Since shamanistic Mongols believed that the soul was found in the blood, spilling blood on the ground became a particularly vile act because it wasted or poured out the soul.[81] The Mongols themselves acknowledged the nobility of high-ranking criminals by executing them without bloodshed, whether by strangulation with a bowstring, back-breaking or violently dragging the condemned around in a carpet.[82]

76 Aigle, "Grand *jasaq*," 64; Roux, *Religion*, 137–41; Baldick, *Animal and Shaman*, 50, 81, 89, 100, 102; see also Andrews, *Felt Tents*, I:542.

77 Nuwayrī, *Nihāyah*, XXXI:351; Jazarī, *Ta'rīkh*, I:422–23; Author Z, *Beiträge*, 47; Joseph de Somogyi, "Adh-Dhahabī's Record of the Destruction of Damascus by the Mongols in 699–700/1299–1301," in *Ignace Goldziher Memorial Volume*, ed. D. S. Loewinger (Budapest, 1948–58), 355.

78 Ibn ʿAbd al-Ẓāhir, *Rawḍ*, 215.

79 Baldick, *Animal and Shaman*, 51; Sinor, "Diplomatic Practices," 339–46.

80 See Chapter 2 for the Mamluk execution of Hülegü's envoys in 1259–60/658; see Chapter 6 for Barquq's execution of Temür's ambassadors in 1393/795, which Temürid historians compared to the Khwārazm-Shāh's execution of merchants and ambassadors from Chingiz Khan in 1218/614–15. For the Khwārazm-Shāh himself see Ratchnevsky, *Ghengis Khan*, 122–23; David O. Morgan, *The Mongols* (Oxford, 1986), 68.

81 For the theory that the soul was found in the blood, see Marco Polo, *The Description of the World*, ed. A.C. Moule and Paul Pelliot (London, 1938, repr. New York, 1976), I:199–200; Francis Woodman Cleaves, *The Secret History of the Mongols* (Cambridge, MA, 1982), 140; Ibn al-ʿIbrī/Bar Hebraeus, *The Chronography of Gregory Abū'l-Faraj, the Son of Aaron, the Hebrew Physician, Commonly Known as Bar Hebraeus*, tr. E. A. W. Budge (London, 1932), 431; also Thomas T. Allsen, "Biography of a Cultural Broker, Bolad Ch'eng-Hsiang in China and Iran," in *Court*, 16–19; George Vernadsky, *The Mongols and Russia* (New Haven, 1953), 26–27; for the bloodshedding taboo in general see Ruth I. Meserve, "The Uses of Blood in Traditional Inner Asian Societies," in *Technology*, 37–38. An alternate theory is that the spirit was found in the breathing apparatus, not the blood. So far this has been investigated for animal slaughter, but not human execution; nevertheless bloodshed was prohibited in animal slaughter as well. See Aigle, "Grand *jasaq*," 66; Roberte Hamayon, *La Chasse à l'âme: esquisse d'une théorie du chamanisme sibérien* (Nanterre, 1990), 397; Meserve, "Blood," 38.

82 Baldick, *Animal and Shaman*, 95, 104, 108; Marco Polo, *Description*, I:199–200.

Thus every diplomatic action, ceremony and ritual was imbued with significance, and afforded opportunities for rulers to proclaim and exchange ideology. It is in these encounters, as well as in the corresponding written texts, that appear the models of kingship used by the Mamluks and their Mongol and Turkic allies and rivals. The diplomatic exchanges therefore illuminate the specific elements of the Mamluk religious ideology of Guardianship, the subsequent notion of Mamluk regional sovereignty, changing versions of Mongol imperial and later Islamic legitimacy, and the eventual Turkic elaborations on Mongol themes.

CHAPTER 2

The establishment of ideologies (1260–1293/658–693)

The early Mamluk sultans spent much of their time and energy responding to the challenges posed by the Mongol Empire and the Chingizid House. Certainly the Mamluks also paid close attention to their Christian and Muslim neighbor states, especially the Crusaders, the Anatolian Seljuks and the Rasulids in Yemen. Nevertheless, consideration of the Mongols took precedence over other Mamluk concerns, and lay behind many of their policies and decisions. It was in this early phase that the Mamluk sultans met the ideological challenge of Chingizid rule and the divine mandate with a conscious invocation of martial Islamic norms, which centered on the concept of Guardianship of religion and the patronage of the Abbasid caliph. The Mamluks themselves did not loom particularly large on Mongol horizons, but nevertheless were important enough to draw the attention of two main branches of the Chingizid House: the Ilkhanids and the Golden Horde, who were simultaneously cousins and bitter rivals.

The Ilkhanid Empire was established by Hülegü during the Iran campaign of the 1250s/650s, but after the sudden death of the Great Khan Möngke in August 1259/Shaʿbān 657, Hülegü personally withdrew to Azerbaijan shortly before the end of the campaign, and his remaining forces in Syria were defeated by Mamluk-led armies at the battles of ʿAyn Jālūt (3 September 1260/25 Ramaḍān 658) and Homs (11 December 1260/5 Muḥarram 659).[1] This gave Hülegü a reason both to remember the Mamluks and to seek revenge. Meanwhile in Southern Russia and the Qipchaq Steppe the Khanate of the Golden Horde had been established in the 1240s/640s by the House of Chingiz Khan's oldest son Jochi (d. ca. 1227/624). In the 1250s/650s Berke Khan became the first Golden Horde ruler to convert to Islam and take up Islamic ideas of kingship, which he used to challenge Hülegü's dominion in Iran.[2] Berke's hostility had several causes: Hülegü's 1258/656 murder of the Abbasid caliph and destruction of Baghdad, a quarrel over the tax revenue from the Caucasus (which Berke claimed but Hülegü collected)

[1] For the battles see Amitai-Preiss, *War*, 26–48, esp. 39–45, 50–53.
[2] DeWeese, *Islamization*, 67–71, esp. note 1 on 67 for scholarly work on this topic; also 83–86.

and the fate of three Jochid princes who had participated in Hülegü's Iran campaign but died in suspicious circumstances thereafter. Even Möngke's death contributed to the hostilities, for deliberations about Möngke's successor degenerated into the Civil War (1260–64/658–662/3), during which Hülegü and Berke supported rival sides. Beginning in the autumn and winter of 1261–62/659–60, the two cousins engaged in a series of inconclusive battles in the Caucasus region.[3] In pursuing their rivalry, the ilkhans and the khans of the Golden Horde unexpectedly found themselves interacting with the Mamluk sultans, and with the Mamluk ideology of Guardianship.

The Mamluks and the Ilkhanids

The relationship between the Mamluks and the Ilkhanids was marked by mistrust, active hostility and war.[4] Although for the Ilkhanids the Mamluks never represented more than one enemy among three (the others were the Golden Horde and an alliance of Ögedeid and Chagataid Mongols to the east[5]), the Mamluk victories at ʿAyn Jālūt and Homs, their refusals to submit to Ilkhanid rule and their frequent raids into Ilkhanid territory were an irritation, an insult and an ideological thorn in Ilkhanid sides, which spurred periodic campaigns of Ilkhanid retribution. These the Mongols justified on the grounds that the Mamluks were rebels and slaves, whose resistance to the Ilkhanids, and through them to the divinely mandated rule of the golden house, simply could not be tolerated. The Mamluks responded by developing their ideology of Guardianship in direct opposition to Ilkhanid rule, which they characterized as infidel and destructive to Islamic society as a whole.

Qutuz and Hülegü

The scene was set as early as 1259–60/658, when in the course of the campaign to Syria Hülegü's scribes wrote to the Mamluk sultan al-Muẓaffar Qutuz (r. 1259–60/657–58) and demanded his immediate submission to Mongol rule on pain of annihilation.[6] This letter and the hostile Mamluk response it provoked left a long shadow in Mamluk–Ilkhanid relations, traces of which

[3] Peter Jackson, "The Dissolution of the Mongol Empire," *CAJ* 22:3–4 (1978), 208–12, 220–27, 232–35; Morgan, *The Mongols*, 117; Bertold Spuler, *Die Goldene Horde: die Mongolen in Russland 1223–1502* (Wiesbaden, 1965), 38–45; Amitai-Preiss, *War*, 78–80.

[4] For an excellent comprehensive view of the hostilities see Amitai-Preiss, *War*, entire.

[5] For the Ögedeids and Chagataids see Michal Biran, *Qaidu and the Rise of the Independent Mongol State in Central Asia* (Surrey, 1997).

[6] For versions of the text see Qalqashandī, *Ṣubḥ*, VIII:64–65; Ibn al-Dawādārī, *Kanz al-durar wa jāmiʿ al-ghurar*, ed. Ulrich Haarmann (Cairo, 1971), VIII:47–48; Ibn al-ʿIbrī/Bar Hebraeus, *Taʾrīkh mukhtaṣar al-duwal*, ed. Father Anton Ṣalaḥānī (Beirut, 1958), 278; Ibn Duqmāq, *al-Jawhar al-thamīn fī siyar al-mulūk wa al-salāṭīn*, ed. Muḥammad ʿIzz al-Dīn ʿAlī (Beirut, 1985), 60; Ibn al-Furāt, "Duwal," MS Vatican fol. 243b–244a (as cited in Amitai-Preiss, *War*, 36 and note 64; also cited in Hein, 453 [see below]); Aḥmad al-Maqrīzī, *Kitāb al-sulūk li-maʿrifat duwal al-mulūk*, ed. Muḥammad Muḥammad Amīn and Saʿīd ʿĀshūr (Cairo, 1956–73),

appeared as late as the campaigns of Temür. In it two crucial ideas arose: the question of Mamluk slavery and the execution of Mongol ambassadors. As in most Mongol demands for submission, Hülegü's letter represented him as divinely chosen, leading the armies of God on a mighty path of destruction that would overtake his opponents unless they submitted at once. In the letter Hülegü warned:

> Know . . . that we are the soldiers of God. He created us from His wrath, and gave us dominion over those on whom His anger descended . . . We do not have mercy on the one who weeps, nor do we have pity on the one who complains, for verily God has torn mercy from our hearts . . .
>
> Our hearts are like mountains and our numbers like sand. He who desires peace with us is saved, and he who desires war with us regrets it. If you accept our conditions and receive our authority, then you will have what we have. If you oppose [us] and refuse [us] and persevere in your disobedience, then blame no one but yourselves.[7]

In addition the letter made an usual and insulting remark about Qutuz's origins: "al-Muẓaffar Qutuz, who is from the race of the mamluks (*mamālīk*) who fled from our swords to this region, enjoyed its comforts and then killed its ruler."[8] This statement can be interpreted in several ways. Within Mamluk territory, a rumor identified Qutuz as the royal nephew of the last ruling Khwārazm-Shāh Muḥammad II (r. 1200–20/596–617), and claimed that Qutuz had been sold into slavery as a boy when the Mongols destroyed his uncle's empire in the 1210s/610s.[9] Although it is unclear whether Hülegü knew of Qutuz's alleged Khwārazm-Shāh connection and, more tenuously, believed it, this could have been a taunt about Muḥammad II's flight before Mongol troops in 1219–20/616–18. An alternate theory is that the Ilkhanids viewed the Mamluks as Qipchaqs (which many of them were), and thus as a subject people who had previously fled Mongol armies.[10] Or this could have

I:427–28; Rashīd al-Dīn, *Jāmiʿ*, II:1028–29; Vaṣṣāf al-Ḥaẓrah, *Tajzīyat al-amṣār wa tazjīyat al-aʿṣār*, ed. Joseph Hammer-Purgstall as *Geschichte Vaṣṣāf's: persisch herausegegeben und deutsch übersetz* (Vienna, 1856), II:85–86 (Persian) and I:81–83 (German); Horst Hein, "Hülägüs Unterwerfungsbriefe an die Machthaber Syriens und Ägyptens," *ZDMG* 150:2 (2000), 453–57; also Amitai-Preiss, *War*, 24 and note 93, 36. French translation in E. Quatremère, ed. and tr., *Histoire des Mongols de la Perse* (Amsterdam, 1968 [repr. of 1886]), 343; English translation in Bernard Lewis, ed. and tr., *Islam: From the Prophet Muḥammad to the Capture of Constantinople*, vol. I: *Politics and War* (New York, 1987), 84–85; also see William M. Brinner, "Some Ayyūbid and Mamlūk Documents from Non-Archival Sources," *Israel Oriental Society* 2 (1972), 119–21, 127–43; Eric Voegelin, "The Mongol Orders of Submission to European Powers, 1245–1255," *Byzantion* 15 (1940–41), 378–413.

7 Vaṣṣāf, *Geschichte*, II:85 (Persian) and I:82 (German); also Brinner, "Documents," 119–21, 128–31.

8 Qalqashandī, *Ṣubḥ*, VIII:64.

9 Nuwayrī, *Nihāyah*, XXIX:479–80; also Yūnīnī, *Dhayl*, I:368; Ibn al-Dawādārī, *Kanz*, VIII:40–41; also Amitai-Preiss, *War*, 35.

10 Charles J. Halperin, "The Kipchak Connection: The Ilkhans, the Mamluks and Ayn Jalut," *BSOAS* 63 (2000), 229–45; Golden, "Činggisid Conquests," 21–41, esp. 24–25; Amitai-Preiss, *War*, 36; also Sinor, "Diplomatic Practices," 344, for a Mongol letter sent to the Hungarian King Béla IV that describes the Qipchaqs as slaves, and *Chronicle of Novgorod*, 65, for another such reference.

been an insulting reference to Qutuz's actual tenure as a military slave, and a second slur on Mamluk disrespect for their Ayyubid predecessors, the last of whom the Mamluks had murdered in 1250/648.[11] Regardless of Hülegü's intent, the idea of servitude and the stigma it represented applied far too easily to the sultans in Cairo because of the Mamluk institution of military slavery. It was therefore at this moment that the troublesome question of slavery entered the diplomatic context, where it remained to challenge Mamluk rulers ideologically for decades.

Qutuz responded to Hülegü's threats and slur with the most hostile statement in the symbolic language of diplomacy: he had the Mongol envoys decapitated, after which the heads were paraded around the city of Cairo on pikes, and hung on the southern city gate (Bāb Zuwaylah).[12] In this single execution Qutuz managed to break two nomadic taboos: he violated the immunity of ambassadors, and spilled their blood and the souls it contained on the ground. He may also have hoped to force the hand of his own commanders, many of whom were apprehensive about fighting the Mongols. The execution both promoted Qutuz to his men as a warrior-king, and guaranteed that a battle would be fought. Although Qutuz's decision was ratified by his victory over the Mongol army at ʿAyn Jālūt, his hostile treatment of Hülegü's embassy, like the question of Mamluk slavery, resonated in Ilkhanid–Mamluk diplomacy for years.

Baybars, Hülegü and Abaqa

Despite Qutuz's important initial role, it was really his murderer and successor Baybars (r. 1260–77/658–76) who developed relations seriously with both the Ilkhanids and the Golden Horde. Baybars was greatly concerned with perceptions of his rule, and worked to present himself as a legitimate monarch both internally and to his Mongol interlocutors. This concern was reflected in his official biography, which portrayed him as a warrior-king and divinely favored Guardian of Muslims.[13] To enact these roles, Baybars fought the Ilkhanids, their Armenian allies and the Crusaders, promoted Islamic law over Chingizid dynastic law, and may even have spread tales of his own bravery and cunning to inspire his troops and intimidate his enemies.[14] Baybars was the first Mamluk sultan to assume sovereignty over the Hijaz by monopolizing the right to send the embroidered curtains to the Kaʿaba in

[11] For this theory see Amitai-Preiss, *War*, 36; for the last Ayyubid, al-Muʾaẓẓam Turanshah, see Holt, *Crusades*, 83.

[12] Ibn al-Dawādārī, *Kanz*, VIII:48; also Baybars al-Manṣūrī, *Zubdah*, 50, and *Kitāb al-tuḥfah al-mulūkīyah fī al-dawlah al-turkīyah*, ed. ʿAbd al-Ḥamīd Ṣāliḥ Ḥamdān (Cairo, 1987), 43; Nuwayrī, *Nihāyah*, XXIX:472.

[13] Ibn ʿAbd al-Ẓāhir, *Rawḍ*, entire.

[14] One example is in Vaṣṣāf, *Geschichte*, II:174–75 (Persian) and I:164–65 (German); Āyatī, *Taḥrīr*, 53–54; see also Amitai-Preiss, *War*, 139–56, and Baybars's letters below for law.

Mecca.[15] Furthermore it was Baybars who established the refugee Abbasid as the caliph al-Mustanṣir in 1261/659 in Cairo. In a magnificent ceremony of mutual investiture, Baybars and al-Mustanṣir publicly ended the caliphal interregnum, legitimated Baybars's reign and formalized the sultan's duty to conduct territorial expansion as al-Mustanṣir's delegate.[16] Baybars also promoted his rule through public charity, architectural patronage and reorganization of the Islamic judicial system, and worked to negate his own lack of genealogy by trying to establish a dynasty through his son, Muḥammad Berke Khan.[17]

In addition to these proclamations of kingship at home, Baybars established himself outside his own territory as a martial patron for other rulers in the region, whom he encouraged to fight the infidels in Iran. These included the three princes from the Luʾluʾid dynasty in the dangerous border region in Iraq, who defected from the Ilkhanids in 1261/659 and petitioned to become Baybars's governors. Baybars equipped them with supplies and gave them banners, which symbolized his sovereignty over them. (Ominously, however, he then sent the caliph and the Luʾluʾids to retake Iraqi territory from Hülegü, and only two Luʾluʾids survived to return.[18]) Baybars had a similar interaction with a group of Hakkārī Kurds in 1261–62/660, who traveled to Cairo for Baybars's support, then returned with it to northern Iraq.[19] Baybars equally welcomed overtures from the Seljuk ruler ʿIzz al-Dīn Kay Kawus in Mongol-dominated Anatolia, who in 1262/660 desperately promised to surrender half his territory in return for military support against his brother, Qilich Arslan IV (r. 1248–65/646–63), who was backed by the Ilkhanids. Baybars was about to send Kay Kawus an army when news arrived that he had fled to Constantinople.[20] Undeterred, Baybars wrote to petty rulers in Iraq and Iran and encouraged them to oppose the Ilkhanids.[21] In retaliation

15 Jomier, *Maḥmal*, 27.

16 Holt, "Structure," 44; Amitai-Preiss, *War*, 56–57; also Baybars's titles in inscriptions in *RCEA*, XII:55–238 (throughout) and in *CIA*, XIX:118–23, 189–90.

17 For public charity see Ibn ʿAbd al-Ẓāhir, *Rawḍ*, 200–01, 202; for architectural patronage see Rabbat, *Citadel*, 108–10 and "*Dār al-Adl*," 12–13; for the judicial system see Escovitz, *Qâḍî al-Quḍât*, 3–4, 22. Since Baybars had come to power by helping murder Qutuz, the sultan also spread a Turkish story that a regicide was God's choice as ruler, then had himself falsely recorded as the first to strike Qutuz. Ibn ʿAbd al-Ẓāhir, *Rawḍ*, 68; Baybars al-Manṣūrī, *Zubdah*, 53–54; for the corrected story see Shāfiʿ b. ʿAlī, *Ḥusn al-manāqib al-sirrīyah al-muntazaʿah min al-sīrah al-Ẓāhirīyah*, ed. ʿAbd al-ʿAzīz Khuwayṭir (Riyadh, 1989), 66–67, 318–19, 339; also Amitai-Preiss, *War*, 56 for Baybars's use of the caliph to counter the stigma of regicide.

18 For this troubling campaign and the possible reasons for sending it see Amitai-Preiss, *War*, 56–60.

19 *Ibid.*, 63.

20 *Ibid.*, 158; Claude Cahen, *The Formation of Turkey: The Seljukid Sultanate of Rūm: Eleventh to Fourteenth Century*, tr. and ed. P. M. Holt (Harlow, 2001), 188–91.

21 These were rulers in Shiraz and Luristan. Baybars also corresponded with the Georgians, the Beduin Āl Khafājah of Syria, and secretly with figures inside Ilkhanid territory. Ibn ʿAbd

for Baybars's patronage of regional rulers, Hülegü consolidated his grip on Iraq and on his vassals in that region, the Artuqids of Mardin, and sought, unsuccessfully, to form an alliance against the Mamluks with Latin Christian rulers.[22] But Hülegü was unable to focus all his attention on the Mamluks, since he was also busy with the Civil War in Mongolia and China, and with hostilities with Berke in the Caucasus.

After Hülegü's death in February 1265/Rabīʿ II 663, his oldest son Abaqa (r. 1265–82/663–80) came to the throne. Like his father, Abaqa had to divide his military attention among three different fronts: the Golden Horde, the Mamluks and the Chagataid–Ögedeid alliance. But despite these military pressures, Abaqa's relationship to the Mamluk sultan was far more active than Hülegü's had been. Abaqa began to punish severely any of his own subjects suspected of corresponding with Baybars, among them the Seljuk sultan Qilich Arslan IV, who was murdered and replaced by his young son Kay Khusraw III, with real power in the hands of the Anatolian strongman Muʿīn al-Dīn the Parvanah.[23] Like his father, Abaqa tried to enlist Christian military support against Baybars, and during the 1260s/660s and 1270s/670s wrote to arrange a campaign with European rulers, among them Pope Clement IV (1265–68), King James I of Aragon (r. 1213–76), Edward I of England (r. 1272–1307) and Louis IX of France (r. 1226–70).[24] Abaqa also married Maria, a Byzantine princess, and discussed a joint campaign with her father, Emperor Michael VIII Paleologus (r. 1259–82). Other than Edward's unproductive invasion of Syria in 1271–72, however, no Christian ruler took Abaqa up on his proposal.[25]

Finally, the ilkhan broke away from his father's simple policy of containment by exchanging hostile embassies with Baybars, in hopes of forcing the sultan to submit to Ilkhanid rule. One theory suggests that these exchanges essentially let each side wage psychological warfare against the other for the benefit of audiences at home.[26] Although this was an important part of the diplomatic interactions, the ambassadorial missions also permitted each sovereign to express his vision of kingship publicly, and justify his rule to his adversary and his adversary's court. Thus, for example, each of Abaqa's

al-Ẓāhir, *Rawḍ*, 149; Mufaḍḍal Ibn Abī al-Faḍāʾil, *Kitāb al-nahj al-sadīd wa al-durr al-farīd fīmā baʿda taʾrīkh Ibn al-ʿAmīd*, ed. and tr. E. Blochet (Paris, 1911, 1920, 1932), 126–28; also Amitai-Preiss, *War*, 144–45, 148–51.

22 Ludger Ilisch, "Geschichte der Artuqidenherrschaft von Mardin zwischen Mamluken un Mongolen 1260–1410 AD," Ph.D. dissertation (Westfälischen Wilhelms-Universität zu Münster, 1984), 41–44; Amitai-Preiss, *War*, 151–52. For Hülegü's interactions with Latin Christians see Peter Jackson, *The Mongols and the West, 1221–1410* (Harlow, 2005), 166–67.

23 Cahen, *Turkey*, 195; Amitai-Preiss, *War*, 159–60.

24 Jackson, *Mongols and the West*, 167–68, 173–75, 179–80.

25 Laurence Lockhart, "The Relations between Edward I and Edward II of England and the Mongol Īl-Khāns of Persia," *Iran* 6 (1968), 23–24; Amitai-Preiss, *War*, 98–99, 105, 125–26; Jackson, *Mongols and the West*, 168.

26 Reuven Amitai-Preiss, "An Exchange of Letters in Arabic between Abaγa Īlkhān and Sultan Baybars (AH 667/AD 1268–69)," *CAJ* 38:1 (1994), 11–33.

messages informed Baybars and all his men that Abaqa was a divinely designated ruler from the imperial Chingizid House, against whom an illegitimate rebel of tainted slave origin had risen. Abaqa sent his first embassy to Mamluk territory in 1265–66/664. The Ilkhanid ambassadors met with Baybars in Syria, bringing him unidentified "gifts" (*hadāyā*) and demanding "peace" (*ṣulḥ*). But since Abaqa's forces had begun to move against Mamluk territory at the same time, "peace" really meant obedience to Abaqa. Likewise the unnamed "gifts" must have been symbolic, with their acceptance conveying Baybars's willingness to submit. The fate of the ambassadors and their "gifts" is unknown, but their mission led to no agreement.[27]

The next exchange of envoys followed a singular chain of events. In a battle in 1265–66/664 a Mamluk force in Cilicia captured the Armenian prince Lewon, forcing Lewon's father King Het'um I (r. 1226–69) to negotiate for his son's release. Baybars made the most of this opportunity both practically and ideologically. First he retaliated for an insult of the early 1260s/660s, when Het'um had rebuffed his diplomacy and called him "a (dog) and a slave." Now Baybars was able to ask the captive prince: "Your father called me a slave and would not make peace. Am I the slave now, or you?"[28] Then Baybars demanded that Het'um send to Abaqa for a former mamluk named Sunqur al-Ashqar, Baybars's very close companion, who had been in prison in Aleppo in 1260/658 when the Mongols captured the city, and who had become part of the spoils. Het'um traveled to Abaqa's court in 1266–68/665–66 to make the petition, but Sunqur was not found until the following year, 1268–69/666–67. Then Sunqur was conveyed to Cilicia and sent to Baybars, along with the keys to several Armenian forts, in exchange for Lewon.[29]

By the time of Sunqur's dramatic ransom, Abaqa was occupied with hostilities with the Chagataids. The ilkhan therefore took advantage of this convenient opportunity to give Sunqur a message for Baybars, which led the two rulers to conduct another unfriendly diplomatic exchange, facilitated in part by the Armenian king. It began once Sunqur had returned to Mamluk territory and conveyed Abaqa's message; thereafter Baybars permitted an official Ilkhanid envoy to enter his realms and meet with him in Damascus in 1268–69/667.[30] Nevertheless the ambassador's oral message was hostile:

> When he emerged from the East, the King Abaqa took control of all the world. All entered into obedience to him, and no opposer opposed him; he who opposed him died. As for you: [even] if you rose up to the sky or sank down to the ground, you

[27] Ibn al-Furāt, "Ta'rīkh al-duwal wa al-mulūk," Dār al-Kutub, Cairo, MS 54251, fol. 110a; Maqrīzī, *Sulūk*, I:553; Amitai-Preiss, *War*, 120.
[28] Grigor of Akner, "Archers," 355, 359.
[29] For the exchange of Sunqur for Lewon see Amitai-Preiss, *War*, 116–20, with extensive source references.
[30] Amitai-Preiss, *War*, 120–21; also his "Exchange," entire.

would not free yourself from us. The best policy is that you make peace (*ṣulḥ*) with us . . . *you are a mamluk and were sold in Sivas; how [dare] you oppose the kings of the earth*? (emphasis added)[31]

Here Abaqa promoted his own divinely mandated sovereignty and struck Baybars in his weakest ideological point by combining the imperial ideology of world conquest with Mongol disdain for slavery. Clearly he had as much contempt for Mamluk bondage as had his own father, or the Armenians.

Abaqa's written letter was equally peremptory.[32] In it he acknowledged that Qutuz, not Baybars, had been responsible for executing Hülegü's envoys in 1259–60/658, which exonerated Baybars for Qutuz's behavior. This allowed Abaqa to dissociate Baybars from Qutuz and accept Baybars as a vassal, even though the belief that Baybars had advised Qutuz to kill the ambassadors, and was therefore guilty by association, remained current in Ilkhanid circles for years.[33] After discussing some Qipchaq Turks whom Baybars wanted sent to Mamluk realms, Abaqa bragged that only discord among the Mongols (with the Chagataids?) had kept him from riding towards (and destroying) Baybars. Abaqa then reached the crux of the letter, his demand for Baybars to become a vassal: "You suggested that 'We [i.e., Baybars] become subject (*naṣīr īl*) and give power [over to Abaqa]'; we deem that appropriate from you."[34] The letter emphasized the universal obedience enjoyed by Abaqa's Chingizid family, then ordered Baybars to send his brothers and sons to the Mongol court, where they would learn about Mongol law (*yāsā*, i.e., *yasa* or *jasaq*) and return to Baybars with this knowledge.[35] Reinforcing the demand for submission was the gold tablet (Per. *paizah* from Ch. *p'aizi*) that accompanied the letter, which was itself a mark of Ilkhanid rank, and therefore a sign that Baybars would be incorporated into Abaqa's administration.[36]

Baybars's response was equally unfriendly.[37] His letter opened with a dismissive tone, saying that only because of Sunqur's message had Baybars bothered to express interest in exchanging embassies to the Armenian king.[38] The letter distanced Baybars from Qutuz (the envoy murderer) by emphasizing that Baybars had sent Abaqa's embassy back unharmed, but then mocked

31 Ibn al-Dawādārī, *Kanz*, VIII:139–40; and Amitai-Preiss, "Exchange," 14–15 and note 17 for source references and discussion. Amitai translates a different version of the text in Amitai-Preiss, *War*, 121.

32 For the text see Ibn ʿAbd al-Ẓāhir, *Rawḍ*, 340–41; for a translation and commentary see Amitai-Preiss, "Exchange."

33 Rashīd al-Dīn, *Jāmiʿ*, II:1031.

34 Ibn ʿAbd al-Ẓāhir, *Rawḍ*, 340; also Amitai-Preiss, "Exchange," 18, 24, and *War*, 9, 121 for the concept of "il."

35 Ibn ʿAbd al-Ẓāhir, *Rawḍ*, 340; also Yang, "Hostages," 48–49. For *yasa* see Chapter 1 note 5.

36 Ibn ʿAbd al-Ẓāhir, *Rawḍ*, 339; for *paizah* or *p'aizi* (older *p'ai-tzu*) see Kramarovsky, "Culture," 260.

37 For the text see Ibn ʿAbd al-Ẓāhir, *Rawḍ*, 341–42; for a translation, source references and commentary see Amitai-Preiss, "Exchange," 29–31.

38 Ibn ʿAbd al-Ẓāhir, *Rawḍ*, 341.

Abaqa's attempts to reach an agreement. To demonstrate the impossibility of a relationship, and to champion the Islamic world view over the Chingizid one, the letter argued that Baybars's "*yāsā*" (implying Islamic law, *sharīʿah*) was greater than Chingizid law.[39] It did not, however, refer to Islamic law by name, or mention the Abbasid caliph, perhaps because Abaqa was so hopelessly pagan. Rather it belittled the ilkhan with a taunting reference to the battle of ʿAyn Jālūt and the death in it of Hülegü's general Kitbugha. Then Baybars invoked Abaqa's (alleged) intention of sending a relative to Cairo, and Baybars's own willingness to trade the favor. Since the Mongol imperial family accepted hostages from vassals but certainly never provided any of their own, this was a startling expression of bravado. Combined with Baybars's proclamation that Islamic law was superior to Chingizid law, this taunt projected a relationship of equals, or even suggested that Abaqa should submit to the Mamluk sultan. To emphasize this, in the oral message Baybars demanded that Abaqa surrender Anatolia, Diyarbakir and Iraq in order to save his own life and troops.[40] Such defiance both shored up Baybars's rejection of the Chingizid universal claim, and promoted Baybars as a warrior to his own men. Not surprisingly, the embassy led to nothing positive.

After this failed exchange Baybars went on the pilgrimage at the end of 1269/667.[41] Although undertaken in secret, news leaked out after the fact, and bolstered Baybars's image as both a pious Muslim ruler and a master of subterfuge. Meanwhile Abaqa's attention turned briefly to other matters, among them the Chagataid threat on his eastern border, his own official enthronement as ruler of Iran with an imperial decree (*yarligh*) sent by the Great Khan Qubilai in 1270/669 and increasingly strained relations with the Golden Horde.[42] Nevertheless, the ilkhan still increased the number and intensity of raids on Mamluk territory during this period, which forced Baybars to respond frequently, in addition to fighting Crusaders and Assassins in Syria.[43]

Nevertheless it was not until 1271–72/670 that a new diplomatic exchange took place between Baybars and Abaqa, again through intermediaries. This time the architect was the chief Mongol in Anatolia, Samaghar. In fall 1271/670 Samaghar had led a campaign into Syria, but had withdrawn without engaging Baybars. Then in a reversal of tactics six months later in May 1272/Shawwāl 670, Samaghar sent an ambassador named Majd al-Dīn Dawlat Khan to the Mamluk Sultanate, along with a translator and ambassadors

39 *Yāsā* here must be understood as Islamic law, for Baybars never established dynastic laws. See Amitai-Preiss, *War*, 122, and "Exchange," 30–31; also Aigle, "Grand *jasaq*," 36–38, 41–42, 45, 62–67. For one later example of a non-Chingizid's use of dynastic law in legitimacy see Halil Inalcık, "Suleiman the Lawgiver and Ottoman Law," *Archivum Ottomanicum* 1 (1969), 105–38.

40 Ibn al-Dawādārī, *Kanz*, VIII:140.

41 Ibn ʿAbd al-Ẓāhir, *Rawḍ*, 354–56; Nuwayrī, *Nihāyah*, XXX:166–67; Ibn al-Dawādārī, *Kanz*, VIII:142; Baybars al-Manṣūrī, *Tuḥfah*, 66; also Amitai-Preiss, *War*, 124.

42 Biran, *Qaidu*, 31; J. A. Boyle, "Political and Dynastic History of the Īl-Khāns," *CHIr* V:360; Spuler, *Goldene Horde*, 55.

43 Thorau, *Baybars*, 187–219; Amitai-Preiss, *War*, 124–25.

from the Parvanah. Through Dawlat Khan, Samaghar invited Baybars to send him envoys for Abaqa, with whom he promised to intercede for the sultan.[44] Samaghar's motive was unclear, but Baybars welcomed the gesture, and took Dawlat Khan riding with him in the polo grounds in an unusual gesture that combined cordiality with a desire to impress. Then he sent two commanders to Anatolia, where they met with Samaghar and the Parvanah and presented them with gifts.[45] The Mongol Samaghar received a single bow and an apology that this was all the ambassadors could carry, but the apology was facetious since the ambassadors also carried luxury cloth, which they gave secretly to the Muslim Parvanah.[46]

Next the Mamluk ambassadors were taken to Abaqa. The Persian historians do not even mention the envoys' presence at the Ilkhanid court, but according to Mamluk sources, the meeting was just as unfriendly as any previous one. One author claimed that the ambassadors' message combined Baybars's bravado with his reliance on an alliance he had formed with Abaqa's Golden Horde enemies: "The sultan sends greetings to you, and says that Möngke Temür's [Golden Horde] envoys have come to him repeatedly [suggesting] that the sultan [Baybars] should ride from his side, and the king Möngke Temür should ride from his side. Wherever Baybars's horse reached would be his, and wherever Möngke Temür's horse reached would be his."[47] Another historian claimed that the ambassadors told Abaqa that Baybars not only refused to submit to Abaqa's authority, but, in a kingly assumption of personal responsibility for all Muslims (and possibly as the associate of the Abbasid caliph), demanded that Abaqa give back the Muslim lands he held. Abaqa refused, but countered that each ruler should simply retain what he already had (without further attacks on the other). The treatment of gifts underscored the mutual hostility: Abaqa forced the presents and ambassadors to pass between two fires for purification before they reached him.[48] When the gifts were then revealed during the reception, they proved to be few, and exclusively items of war, which symbolically indicated hostility: a sword, a Venetian mail shirt and helmet, and a bow, quiver and nine arrows.[49] This impertinence told a Mongol audience that Baybars disrespected Abaqa's authority, the dignity of the imperial house and the will of the Enduring Sky.

44 Amitai-Preiss, *War*, 127.

45 Ibn ʿAbd al-Ẓāhir, *Rawḍ*, 399–400; Nuwayrī, *Nihāyah*, XXX:191–92; Muḥammad b. ʿAlī Ibn Shaddād, *Taʾrīkh al-Malik al-Ẓāhir*, ed. Aḥmad Ḥuṭayṭ (Wiesbaden, 1983), 34–35; Baybars al-Manṣūrī, *Tuḥfah*, 74, and *Zubdah*, 134; also Amitai-Preiss, *War*, 127–28; Thorau, *Baybars*, 220–21; Cahen, *Turkey*, 196–97.

46 Ibn Shaddād, *Taʾrīkh*, mentions a bow, 34; Ibn al-Furāt mentions nine bows and nine arrows in "Duwal," Dār al-Kutub MS 36310, fol. 205a.

47 Only snippets of the oral message remain. Ibn ʿAbd al-Ẓāhir, *Rawḍ*, 399–400, whence Nuwayrī, *Nihāyah*, XXX:191–92. Ibn ʿAbd al-Ẓāhir's claim that Abaqa stormed out of the audience should be dismissed as highly unlikely. See Amitai-Preiss, *War*, 127–28.

48 Ibn ʿAbd al-Ẓāhir, *Rawḍ*, 399.

49 *Ibid.*; Baybars al-Manṣūrī, *Zubdah*, 134; Ibn Shaddād, *Taʾrīkh*, 34; Ibn al-Furāt, "Duwal," MS 36310, fol. 205a.

The insult was surely exacerbated by the fact that it came from a Qipchaq and former slave. The only proper response from a Mongol point of view was the brutal subjugation of such a rebel, thus Abaqa insulted the ambassadors and sent them back without an agreement.[50]

Nevertheless Abaqa tried once more to make his point clear, this time by sending his own embassy to Damascus in August–September 1272/Ṣafar 671. But Baybars was determined to put Abaqa's envoys in their place, and thereby conclusively humiliate the ilkhan. This Baybars accomplished by manipulating the ceremonial movement of the *jūk* (Turkish *chök*), which involved descending to one knee and putting an elbow on the ground, and which was a sign of respect for high-ranking persons among the Mongols. When the Mongol envoys were forced to perform it three times in front of the governors of each Syrian city in turn, however, it publicly humiliated them.[51] In Damascus the ambassadors were lodged in a tower for reasons of security, and during their stay had to stand watching with their rival envoys from the Golden Horde as Baybars's finest soldiers practiced in front of them. Abaqa's message was hardly new: once more the ilkhan wanted a peace agreement with Baybars, engineered through the mediation of Sunqur al-Ashqar. But since the "peace" would be ratified when either Baybars or his heir came to the Ilkhanid court, this was clearly another demand for submission.[52] Baybars replied by echoing his defiance of the Chingizid claim: Abaqa might come to Baybars's *own* court if he wanted peace. Shortly after Baybars sent the Ilkhanid embassy back, he defeated a Mongol force at the Euphrates.[53] This victory was a turning point for the Mamluk sultan, after which Baybars's reputation increased greatly and his fear of Ilkhanid strength decreased.[54] It also marked the end of Baybars's diplomatic interactions with Abaqa, and his increased reliance on his own military abilities as a Guardian.

Thus Baybars soon increased his contact with the Parvanah and other Muslim Turkish military commanders from the Seljuk state in Anatolia. After surreptitious negotiations in 1274–76/672–75, some Anatolian commanders offered Baybars sovereignty over their territory if he would come and drive the Mongols out of it. Baybars personally led Mamluk troops to victory over a combined Anatolian–Mongol force at the battle of Elbistan on 15 April 1277/10 Dhū al-Qaʿdah 675. After the battle, more Anatolian commanders joined Baybars, but the Parvanah did not, despite his earlier promises. Nevertheless Baybars made a triumphal march to Kayseri and, in a dramatic but ephemeral example of dynastic adoption, was proclaimed Seljuk sultan there. But a lack of

50 Ibn Shaddād, *Taʾrīkh*, 35; also Amitai-Preiss, *War*, 128.

51 Amitai-Preiss, *War*, 128–29; also Ibn ʿAbd al-Ẓāhir, *Rawḍ*, 404. For *jūk* / *chök* see Nuwayrī, *Nihāyah*, XXVII:339; Sir Gerard Clauson, *An Etymological Dictionary of Pre-Thirteenth Century Turkish* (Oxford, 1972), 413–14.

52 Abaqa's second letter has not survived.

53 For the battle see Amitai-Preiss, *War*, 129–31; Thorau, *Baybars*, 220–24.

54 Baybars al-Manṣūrī, *Tuḥfah*, 76.

adequate supplies, a desire to protect the countryside and concern about Abaqa's possible reprisals led to Baybars's withdrawal to Damascus, where he suddenly sickened and died on 30 June 1277/27 Muḥarram 676. The Parvanah, whose loyalties were doubted by both sides, was executed by Abaqa in August 1277/Rabīʿ I 676.[55]

It is tempting to dismiss Baybars's coronation as heir to the Seljuks as trivial, since his unexpected demise led to the immediate loss of Anatolia. Nevertheless this temptation should be resisted. Throughout his reign Baybars worked hard to legitimate himself through a multifaceted ideology of rule, and also labored to establish his son and heir Muḥammad Berke Khan as the next in a new dynasty. Although Baybars's gains in Anatolia were both modest and ephemeral, historians should not forget that this extremely ambitious, martially skilled sultan planned to return to Anatolia and build on his initial achievements. Unfortunately for Baybars's descendants, however, this plan was thwarted by the sudden and still mysterious circumstances of the sultan's death. But certainly the concept of dynastic adoption was familiar to Baybars, who used it within Mamluk territory when he linked himself to Ayyubid ceremonial practices. By assuming the Seljuk claim for himself and his heirs, therefore, Baybars was simply adding another dynasty to his ideological repertoire, and must have intended to build on this foundation in subsequent years. But his death nullified his adoption of the Seljuks, which his immediate successors then abandoned as an ideological strategy.

Qalawun and Tegüder Aḥmad

Although Baybars was immediately succeeded by two sons in quick order, the dynasty on which he had pinned his hopes ultimately failed, and the next real sultan was al-Manṣūr Qalawun (r. 1279–90/678–89), a seasoned military commander and one of Baybars's own mamluk comrades. Like Baybars, Qalawun immediately tried to establish a dynasty through his own offspring; unlike Baybars, Qalawun enjoyed real success. Ideologically the transition from Baybars's sons to Qalawun was relatively smooth, for in legitimating his own rule Qalawun closely followed Baybars's example: he monopolized the pilgrimage ceremonies in the Arabian Peninsula, continued the patronage of worthy architecture, officially supported the Islamic legal system and dutifully took the Mamluks into the battlefield against Ilkhanids and Crusaders. Also like Baybars, Qalawun continued the rituals of the Ayyubid dynasty.[56]

[55] For this complicated campaign see Amitai-Preiss, *War*, 157–78; Cahen, *Turkey*, 196–207; Thorau, *Baybars*, 235–40.

[56] Linda S. Northrup, "The Baḥrī Mamlūk Sultanate, 1250–1390," in *The Cambridge History of Egypt*, ed. Carl F. Petry (Cambridge, 1998), I:249, 255; also Linda S. Northrup, *From Slave to Sultan: The Career of al-Manṣūr Qalāwūn and the Consolidation of Mamluk Rule in Egypt and Syria (678–689 AH/1279–1290 AD)* (Stuttgart, 1998), 85–86, 118–121; Rabbat, *Citadel*, 136–37. For Qalawun's building inscriptions see *RCEA*, 255–335 (throughout); *CIA*, 125–40.

Nevertheless, Qalawun's accession created resentment among many, including Baybars's beloved friend Sunqur al-Ashqar, who had kept his ties with the Ilkhanids, and who now took the opportunity to write inviting Abaqa to invade Syria.[57] Sunqur wanted Abaqa to defeat Qalawun in battle, and then appoint him as Ilkhanid governor over Mamluk territory. Abaqa obligingly sent a Mongol force under the leadership of his brother Möngke Temür, and Sunqur was only persuaded at the eleventh hour to rejoin the Mamluk side and fight the invaders, thereby helping Qalawun win at the battle of Homs in 1281/680.[58] Qalawun's own anxiety about the Mongol invasion, his own precarious position as new sultan and the even more precarious position of the dynasty he wanted to establish were reflected in his hasty decision to recognize his oldest son al-Ṣāliḥ ʿAlī as his heir immediately before he set out to meet the Ilkhanid armies.

After the deaths of both Abaqa and Möngke Temür later that same year, the accession of their brother Tegüder (r. 1282–84/681–83) suddenly fouled the Mamluk ideological works. Tegüder had converted to Islam and taken the Islamic name Aḥmad, and once enthroned, also took the Muslim title of "Sultan." At the same time, however, Tegüder's version of Islam seems to have retained numerous Mongol elements.[59] Thus as a Muslim Ilkhanid, Tegüder was able to combine Chingizid and Islamic ideologies to devastating effect. In particular he immediately destroyed the main argument of Mamluk legitimacy, which Qalawun had inherited from Baybars: that Ilkhanids were infidel oppressors of Muslims, against whom military action was necessarily carried out by the Mamluk sultan, Guardian of Islam and protector of Muslim society. Tegüder was well aware of the weakness of the Mamluk position, for in August–September 1282/Jumādà I 681, soon after his enthronement, he sent an embassy to demand that Qalawun become his vassal, since divisions of religion no longer separated them.[60] His ambassadors were brought under close escort to Cairo, where the handsome sultan tried to impress them by receiving them in great style, at night, in an audience lit by many candles.[61]

Tegüder had sent both oral and written messages.[62] The letter proclaimed the good news of Tegüder's conversion and his accession to the throne, from

[57] Amitai-Preiss, *War*, 182 and source references.
[58] For the battle see *ibid.*, 179–201.
[59] Reuven Amitai, "The Conversion of Tegüder Ilkhan to Islam," *JSAI* 25 (2001), 15–43; Jackson, "Aḥmad Takudar," *EIr* I:661; Jean Calmard, "Le Chiisme imamite sous les Ilkhans," in *Domination*, 264–68; Aubin, *Émirs mongols*, 32.
[60] Adel Allouche, "Tegüder's Ultimatum to Qalawun," *IJMES* 22 (1990), 437–46, revising the pioneering work of Holt, "Embassies," entire. Also Amitai-Preiss, *War*, 147, 211, and Amitai, "Conversion," 30–33; Jackson, "Takudar," 661; Boyle, "Īl-Khāns," 365; Spuler, *Mongols in History*, 44–45; D. Sinor, "Les Relations entre les Mongols et l'Europe jusqu'à la mort d'Arghoun et de Béla IV," *Cahiers d'Histoire Mondiale*, 3:1 (1956), 54.
[61] Holt, "Embassies," 129.
[62] For the texts of Tegüder's letter and Qalawun's response see Ibn ʿAbd al-Ẓāhir, *Tashrīf*, 6–16; Shāfiʿ, *Faḍl*, 94–100 and 102–13; Ibn al-Dawādārī, *Kanz*, VIII:249–60; Baybars al-Manṣūrī, *Zubdah*, 219–26; Ibn al-ʿIbrī/Bar Hebraeus, *Mukhtaṣar*, 289–92; Mufaḍḍal, *Nahj*, text and

which he intended to set right Muslim affairs. This established Tëguder immediately as a rival to Qalawun in the realm of virtuous Muslim rule, and added a new Islamic dimension to the weight of Mongol prestige and Ilkhanid hostility. Tegüder told Qalawun about a Mongol assembly (*quriltai*), in which all the participants had wanted to attack the Muslims, but he alone had dissented out of a sense of moral good. Here Tegüder may have intended to intimidate Qalawun with the threat of Mongols united against him, while emphasizing his own moral integrity. The letter then reported at length on the good deeds the new ilkhan had done in the Muslim community. Tegüder claimed as his foremost achievement the establishment of Islamic law (*nawāmīs al-sharʿ al-muḥammadī*). Tegüder also pardoned criminals, inspected Islamic pious endowments, constructed new religious buildings and regularized protection for the pilgrimage caravans.[63] Particularly in these last two areas Tegüder threatened Qalawun's legitimacy, for Qalawun was a great founder of religious buildings, and as sovereign over the holy cities was responsible not only for the pilgrims who passed through his realms, but for all pilgrimage activities in the Hijaz. The letter also informed Qalawun that Tegüder had forbidden his soldiers to harass merchants traveling between his lands and Qalawun's territory, which reflected Tegüder's interest both in proclaiming his own sovereignty, and in supporting trade.[64] Then the letter reported that Tegüder had caught one of Qalawun's spies disguised as a dervish, whom out of the goodness of his heart he had sent back to Qalawun rather than execute.[65] This allowed Tegüder to arrogate the moral high ground to himself, from which he (and his scribes) lectured Qalawun about the evil effect spies had on the Muslim community. The letter closed with Tegüder's veiled demand that Qalawun submit to his authority (*fatḥ abwāb al-ṭaʿah*) and become his vassal.

In his response, which was twice as long as Tegüder's letter, Qalawun and his chancellery were faced with the ideological ramifications of Tegüder's conversion, which denied Qalawun the easy defense of a Muslim ruler facing an infidel, and presented him with a rival in the realm of responsible Islamic rule. The letter opened by acknowledging Tegüder's conversion, and expressed Qalawun's relief over Tegüder's new-found faith. Immediately thereafter, however, the religious scholars in Qalawun's chancellery introduced the weighty concept of precedence in conversion, which enjoyed a paramount position both in Sunni–Shiite debates on legitimate Muslim leadership, and in the vast Islamic literature on qualities of moral excellence

French translation 336–61; Vaṣṣāf, *Geschichte*, texts 231–39 and German translations 215–23; Maqrīzī, *Sulūk*, I:978–84; Qalqashandī, *Ṣubḥ*, VIII:66–69 and VII:258–64. Also see Allouche, "Ultimatum," 438–40.

63 For Tegüder's rule as a Muslim see Amitai, "Conversion," 25–30, 32–34.

64 For trade see Amitai-Preiss, *War*, 208–11.

65 For spies see *ibid.*, 140–47, 155.

and precedence (*manāqib, awāʾil, sawābiq*).[66] Here the letter used this tradition to praise God that Qalawun had converted first and thus was senior in religion to Tegüder: "We thanked God for making us among the predecessors and first ones (*min al-sābiqīn al-awwalīn*) to this station and rank [or: to this religion, station and rank[67]], for making firm our feet in every situation of endeavor (*ijtihād*) and holy struggle (*jihād*) where without Him feet would quake."[68] By invoking precedence in conversion, Qalawun's chancellery established him in a position of religious seniority and gave him a solid ideological base from which to withstand Tegüder's call for vassalage.

Qalawun's letter acknowledged Tegüder's acts as a good Muslim ruler, and assured him that these were correct procedure. Coming after the assertion of Mamluk religious seniority, this reinforced Qalawun's image as a Muslim ruler who already knew what he was doing, and was therefore superior to a newcomer like Tegüder. The letter then castigated previous Ilkhanids for overrunning other rulers and their kingdoms (notably the Seljuks), and warned that this kind of oppression was not the behavior of pious kings. Such advice emphasized Qalawun's superior knowledge of kingly behavior, while setting the stage for his later treatment of the question of vassalage. On the freedom of merchants the letter asserted Qalawun's sovereignty by assuring Tegüder that Qalawun, too, had ordered his governors not to harass them, especially the governors of the al-Raḥbah and al-Bīrah border forts. This statement sent the overt message that the passage of merchants required the attention of both rulers, and covertly slapped Tegüder in the face by mentioning al-Raḥbah and al-Bīrah, which were military thorns in the Ilkhanids' sides.[69] Turning to the question of the alleged spy, the letter challenged Tegüder's moral superiority by charging first that real dervishes had been mistaken for spies and murdered in Mongol lands, and second that Tegüder himself had sent quite a few actual spies into Qalawun's territory. Thereafter Qalawun's letter came to the questions of vassalage. Carefully it avoided a direct answer, but elaborated on the importance of true friendship, and suggested that Tegüder did not understand the concept since he had used threatening language in an ostensibly cordial message.

Finally the letter addressed Tegüder's oral message: Tegüder had said he would remain in his own territory if Qalawun would reach an agreement (*ittifāq*) with him, i.e., become his vassal. In response Qalawun's letter suggested that this would only be possible if Tegüder had true friendship in mind, i.e., if Tegüder were seeking peace and not submission. Second, Tegüder had suggested that if Qalawun were not interested in expansion, he should stay in his own territories. In reply the letter lambasted Tegüder for the conduct of

[66] See Asma Afsaruddin, *Excellence and Precedence: Medieval Islamic Discourse on Legitimate Leadership* (Leiden, 2002), 36–79, esp. 52–58; also Allouche, "Ultimatum," 442 (on Mamluk control of the caliph as a point of precedence).

[67] Mufaḍḍal, *Nahj*, 348. [68] Ibn ʿAbd al-Ẓāhir, *Tashrīf*, 11. [69] Amitai-Preiss, *War*, 202–03.

his governor Qonqqurtai in Anatolia, who was shedding blood, wreaking destruction, enslaving innocents, selling free persons as slaves, and all while the Islamic tax (*kharāj*) from that land went to Tegüder. This portrayed Tegüder and his governors as oppressive, and set the stage for Qalawun to present himself as a virtuous Muslim savior-king, who might some day free the oppressed in Anatolia. Third, Tegüder had challenged that if Qalawun refused to stop raiding Tegüder's lands, he should choose a battlefield (to settle the matter). But in response Qalawun's letter ridiculed the Ilkhanid armies by pointing out that they had seen battlefields in Syria before, with disastrous results.

In this exchange Qalawun's legitimacy rested securely on the new concept of religious seniority his chancellery had introduced. Nevertheless, like Baybars, Qalawun and his scribes also referred to past Mamluk military victories over the Ilkhanids when appropriate. Qalawun also relied on the second Cairene Abbasid caliph, al-Ḥākim bi-amr Allah, who was mentioned early in the correspondence, for if all Muslims owed the caliph allegiance, then Tegüder did as well.[70] But some felt that Qalawun's ideological position was still tenuous. Thus the head chancellery official and historian Ibn ʿAbd al-Ẓāhir, whom Qalawun had inherited from Baybars, shored up Qalawun's arguments in his official biography of the sultan, where he portrayed Tegüder's conversion as fake and merely an attempt to dupe Qalawun.[71] By contrast, other Mamluk historians, especially those not writing under the sultan's patronage, were either neutral or even convinced that Tegüder's conversion was genuine.[72] Regardless, this marked the beginning of a trend for Qalawun, his descendants and their ideologues, who were reluctant to believe that any Ilkhanid conversion to Islam was genuine, although they were quick to believe it from the Golden Horde. Such a point of view allowed the Qalawunids to revert easily to the older model of Mamluks protecting Muslims from infidels or, in this case, from false converts.

Despite the ideological efforts made on his behalf, however, Qalawun himself evinced some wary interest in Tegüder's conversion, for he indicated

[70] Allouche, "Ultimatum," 442, points out that most Mamluk historians omit the caliph, thereby censuring their report of this event, but the outside sources do not. I argue that this both confirms al-Ḥākim's continued ideological role in foreign diplomacy, and suggests Qalawun's desire to suppress the caliph at home. The reference is omitted in Ibn ʿAbd al-Ẓāhir, *Tashrīf*, 10; Ibn al-Dawādārī, *Kanz*, VIII:254–55; Maqrīzī, *Sulūk*, I:980–81; Mufaḍḍal, *Nahj*, 347–49; but included in Shāfiʿ, *Faḍl*, 102–03; Vaṣṣāf, *Geschichte*, text 234–35 and translation 218; Ibn al-ʿIbrī/Bar Hebraeus, *Mukhtaṣar*, 292.

[71] Ibn ʿAbd al-Ẓāhir, *Tashrīf*, 4; also Amitai, "Conversion," 22–23. Even Rashīd al-Dīn doubted Tegüder's claim to be a genuine Muslim, although in part, perhaps, to glorify Ghazan. Peter Jackson, "The Mongols and the Faith of the Conquered," in *Mongols, Turks and Others: Eurasian Nomads and the Sedentary World*, eds. Reuven Amitai and Michal Biran (Leiden and Boston, 2005), 274.

[72] Muḥammad b. Aḥmad al-Dhahabī, "Taʾrīkh al-islām wa ṭabaqāt al-mashāhīr wa al-aʿlām," Dār al-Kutub, Cairo, MS 10682, fol. 24b; Ibn ʿAbd al-Ẓāhir, *Tashrīf*, 93; Yūnīnī, *Dhayl*, IV:211.

to the ambassador that any future embassies should include Tegüder's spiritual advisor, Shaykh 'Abd al-Raḥmān, with whom Qalawun wanted to speak.[73] Therefore Tegüder sent a second mission to Syria, led by Shaykh 'Abd al-Raḥmān, shortly before he himself set out towards Khurasan to put down a rebellion from his nephew Arghun. The embassy arrived in Damascus on 2 March 1284/12 Dhū al-Ḥijjah 682, having affronted the dignity of the Mamluk sultan as soon as it entered Mamluk territory. In Mamluk lands only the sultan rode with the royal parasol (Ar. *jitr*, from Per. *chatr*).[74] But when Shaykh 'Abd al-Raḥmān appeared at the border, he was escorted by armed men and shaded by a parasol. The significance of the parasol was clear to both sides, since the shaykh refused to relinquish it when asked, which was a challenge to Qalawun's sovereignty. Finally the Mamluk governor of Aleppo, who had gone to meet the embassy, forcibly deprived the shaykh of both his umbrella and his escort.[75] Shaykh 'Abd al-Raḥmān and the truncated remainder of his entourage were then conveyed secretly and under heavy guard to Damascus "in the medieval equivalent of a sealed train."[76] There they were lodged in the citadel and given considerable daily stipends, but were forced to cool their heels for months.[77] During this period Tegüder suffered a stunning reversal in his struggles with Arghun, and was deposed and executed in August 1284/Jumādā I 683.[78]

Qalawun waited to meet with the ambassadors until August–September 1284/Jumādā II 683, after he had verified the news of Tegüder's death. Then Qalawun received the embassy at night in impressive royal style, with himself once again set against a backdrop of lighted candles and the Royal Mamluks in their finest raiment.[79] Without telling the envoys of Tegüder's death, Qalawun heard the contents of the letter.[80] It had been written in May–June 1283/Rabī' I 682, at a time when open rebellion against Tegüder had not yet flared. In it, and as in his first letter, Tegüder tried to claim participation in a united Mongol front in order to intimidate Qalawun. This he did by outlining the way he and his cousins in other Khanates had shelved past disagreements and agreed to return to a state of unity. The letter then dropped the references to obedience and submission (*ṭā'ah*) made by the first embassy, and requested only a peaceful agreement (*ṣulḥ* and *ittifāq*).

73 See the text of Tegüder's second letter in Ibn 'Abd al-Ẓāhir, *Tashrīf*, 71; also see Ibn al-Furāt, *Duwal*, VII:249, 278; and Amitai, "Conversion," 31–32.
74 P. A. Andrews, "Miẓalla: 4. In the Persian, Indian and Turkish Lands," *EI²* VII:192–94.
75 Ibn 'Abd al-Ẓāhir, *Tashrīf*, 49; Ibn al-Dawādārī, *Kanz*, VIII:261.
76 Holt, "Embassies," 132.
77 1,000 silver coins per day for the shaykh. Ibn al-Dawādārī, *Kanz*, VIII:261.
78 Amitai, "Conversion," 34–39; Boyle, "Īl-Khāns," 365–68; also Aubin, *Émirs mongols*, 29–36.
79 Ibn al-Dawādārī, *Kanz*, VIII:265.
80 For the text see Ibn 'Abd al-Ẓāhir, *Tashrīf*, 69–71; Baybars al-Manṣūrī, *Zubdah*, 242–43; Badr al-Dīn Maḥmūd al-'Aynī, *'Iqd al-jumān fī ta'rīkh ahl al-zamān*, ed. Muḥammad Muḥammad Amīn (Cairo, 1987–92), II:297–300; also Allouche, "Ultimatum," 443; Amitai, "Conversion," 31–32.

Although this appeared to reflect Tegüder's new interest in negotiations, it was immediately followed by a severe warning to Qalawun to ignore any naysayers who might advise against an accord. This harsh statement, and the grandiose manner in which Shaykh ʿAbd al-Raḥmān had crossed into Qalawun's realm, did not suggest negotiation between equals, but rather between superior and subordinate.

Obviously Tegüder's death saved Qalawun and his ideologues from composing an appropriate response. In fact, Qalawun soon demonstrated the depth of his antagonism towards his deceased coreligionist by moving the envoys into lesser quarters in the citadel, drastically reducing their stipends, relieving them of the bulk of their possessions and leaving them to languish. Shaykh ʿAbd al-Raḥmān himself died thereafter; his cohorts remained incarcerated until most were freed by the dramatic intervention of a sympathetic poet and a Mamluk commander.[81] Thereafter Qalawun returned to diplomatic silence and ideological hostility with Tegüder's pagan successor, Abaqa's son Arghun. Arghun followed the anti-Mamluk policies of his father by trying to muster support for a grand campaign against the Mamluks from Latin Christian rulers, albeit without success.[82] Arghun's martial ambitions may also have been spurred by his belief in the suggestions by some (among them his vizier, Saʿd al-Dawlah) that he was a Lord of the Auspicious Conjunction (*ṣāḥib qirān*), or a ruler destined to achieve greatness, who was chosen once every age by God (or perhaps the Enduring Sky).[83] But the ilkhan's death on 10 March 1291/7 Rabīʿ I 690 from extreme health-saving measures nullified any threat he might have posed to the Mamluks; nevertheless the notions of the Lord of the Auspicious Conjunction and a divinely chosen monarch did reappear in the ideologies of later rulers.

Khalīl and Geikhatu

Qalawun died suddenly in his tent outside Cairo on 10 November 1290/6 Dhū al-Qaʿdah 689, just as he was setting out on a campaign against the Latin Christian city of Acre. His son and second heir al-Ashraf Khalīl (r. 1290–93/689–93) was sworn in the next day with due pomp and circumstance. Qalawun had been unenthusiastic about Khalīl as heir, and so Khalīl was anxious to prove himself as a sultan, as his father's son and as the next in a nascent dynasty of Qalawunids.[84] But Khalīl showed great promise as a

[81] Yūnīnī, *Dhayl* IV:216–17; also Faḍlallah al-Ṣuqāʿī, *Tālī kitāb wafāyāt al-aʿyān*, ed. and tr. Jacqueline Sublet (Damascus, 1974), 107–08; Ibn al-Furāt, *Duwal*, VIII:6–7; also Ibn al-ʿIbrī/Bar Hebraeus, *Mukhtaṣar*, 298–99, claiming they were not freed.

[82] Jackson, *Mongols and the West*, 169–70.

[83] Aubin, *Émirs mongols*, 43–44; Vaṣṣāf, *Taʾrīkh*, 241–42 and an unsatisfactory resume in Āyatī, *Taḥrīr*, 145–46.

[84] Qalawun's first heir, al-Ṣāliḥ ʿAlī, had died previously of illness. For Qalawun's lack of enthusiasm about Khalīl see Northrup, *Qalāwūn*, 247–49.

military commander despite his youth and relative inexperience. During his three-year reign he expelled the last Latin Christians from the Levant (1291/690), captured the Armenian fort of Hromgla (Qalʿat al-Rūm, modern Rumkale, 1292/691) and forced the Armenian king Hetʿum II (r. 1289–1307) to give him three other forts and pay tribute.[85]

Ideologically Khalīl modeled himself more closely on Baybars than on his own father. Certainly the ideological situation for Khalīl was far more straightforward than it had been for his parent, since the single Ilkhanid ruler with whom Khalīl had any interaction, Geikhatu (r. 1291–95/690–94), was not a Muslim, and in his limited dealings with Khalīl identified himself purely as a Chingizid. This allowed Khalīl to invoke the simple idea of Guardianship of Islam against infidel outsiders that Baybars had employed and Qalawun had not. Khalīl also emulated Baybars in his pugnacity and his desire to promote himself as a warrior-king: although Khalīl's interactions with Geikhatu were few, they were belligerent, and resembled Baybars's taunts to Abaqa far more than Qalawun's hostile yet cautious relations with Tegüder. Like both Baybars and Qalawun, Khalīl made use of the symbolic importance of the Abbasid caliph al-Ḥākim; unlike them, however, Khalīl permitted the caliph a public persona and role, enjoyed a personal relationship with al-Ḥākim, spent considerable sums on his upkeep and met with him regularly to hear his advice.[86] Also breaking with his predecessors, Khalīl was the first and perhaps only Mamluk sultan to describe himself as "Reviver of the Abbasid State" on his coins.[87]

The extent of Geikhatu's interest in the Mamluks is difficult to determine. His interactions with Khalīl were limited: he sent only one army against the Mamluks, which failed to engage them, and a single embassy, in which

85 Angus Donal Stewart, *The Armenian Kingdom and the Mamluks: War and Diplomacy during the Reigns of Hetʿum II (1289–1307)* (Leiden, 2001), 73–92.

86 Ibn ʿAbd al-Ẓāhir, *al-Alṭāf al-khafīyah min al-sīrah al-sharīfah al-sulṭānīyah al-Ashrafīyah*, edited as *Ur ʿAbd Allah B. ʿAbd Ez-Zahir's Biograhi Över Sultanen El-Melik El-Asraf Halil. Arabisk Täxt med Översättning, Inledning Ock Anmärkningar Utjiven*, ed. Axel Moberg (Lund, 1902), 3–15.

87 In Arabic, *muḥyī al-dawlah al-ʿabbāsīyah*. Paul Balog, *The Coinage of the Mamlūk Sultans of Egypt and Syria* (New York, 1964), 14, 120–24; Stanley Lane-Poole, *Catalogue of Oriental Coins in the British Museum* (London, 1875–90, repr. Bologna, 1967), IV:146–47; Henri Lavoix, *Catalogue des monnaies musulmanes de la Bibliothèque nationale* (Paris, 1896), III:315–22. Balog (14) mentioned the honorary epithet, Victorious One of Muḥammad's Community and Reviver of the Abbasid State (*nāṣir al-millah al-Muḥammadīyah wa muḥyī al-dawlat [sic al-dawlah] al-ʿabbāsīyah*), and argued that it was used by Khalīl, then by al-Manṣūr Kitbugha (I was unable to check Wien 6332), al-Nāṣir Muḥammad (*sic* Balog attributed Lavoix coins 797, 798 etc. incorrectly to Muḥammad instead of Khalīl) and al-Manṣūr Lajin. However, there were actually two honorary epithets, Epithet A (Victorious One of Muḥammad's Community) and Epithet B (Reviver of the Abbasid State). Some of Kitbugha's and Lajin's coins carried only Epithet A without Epithet B (Balog coins 159, 163, 165; Lavoix, *Catalogue*, III:345, coin 853). Since Balog believed the two epithets were one, he assumed that when he saw Epithet A that B was there, too, albeit worn out. But in fact Khalīl was the only sultan we can be sure to have definitely called himself "Reviver of the Abbasid State." For Khalīl's inscriptions see *CIA*, 141–47.

Geikhatu's ideology entirely followed the Chingizid model established by Hülegü and Abaqa. Whereas Khalīl's aggressive construction of a Baybars-style image depended on looking to the east, Geikhatu did not seem to be concerned with the Mamluks at all. Certainly matters in his own territories demanded great attention – his short reign was marked by financial trouble, a catastrophic introduction of paper currency, natural disasters and Geikhatu's own indulgence in vice. The level of ideological exchange between the two sides was therefore unequal: from Geikhatu it was near desultory, but from Khalīl it was distinctly aggressive. The lack of much real interaction between the two rulers suggests that the Mamluk sultan's promotion of himself as the assertive war champion of Islam was also intended for his own men, not just his enemy.

But despite Khalīl's belligerence, his initial focus was not on the Ilkhanids, but on the remnants of Latin Christian power in Syria. Almost immediately after assuming control in Cairo, Khalīl set out to complete his father's stalled campaign to Acre, which he captured in June 1291/Jumādà II 690. There Khalīl heard that Arghun had died on 10 March 1291/7 Rabīʿ I 690, and been succeeded by his brother Geikhatu.[88] Such momentous news, coming hard on the heels of Khalīl's first successful military campaign as sultan, appears to have inspired both him and others. The deaths of Qalawun and Arghun introduced a new uncertainty into the politics of the region, while Khalīl's victory at Acre so early in his reign showed him to be a promising military successor to his father. The opportunities arising from these sudden changes were not lost on Anatolian military commanders chafing under Ilkhanid domination. In September–October 1291/Shawwāl 690, therefore, two months after his return from Syria, Khalīl met with secret messengers bearing Persian letters from military commanders in Ilkhanid Anatolia, and from the Qaramanid Türkmen in the same region. Refugees from Diyarbakir may also have been among them.[89] At least as described by Mamluk historians, the authors appeared to have gauged the best appeal for a man following so conscientiously in his predecessors' footsteps, and made a clear appeal to the familiar tenets of Guardianship of Islam: they promised that they had joined in a sworn pact to offer their obedience to Khalīl and spend their lives pursuing jihad wherever he ordered it. They claimed to consider themselves soldiers of God like Khalīl's own soldiers, promised to be as obedient as Khalīl's own military and asked to participate with Khalīl's men in all things. To demonstrate their seriousness, the Anatolians asked for official banners from Khalīl to use in military campaigns on his behalf, which symbolically made them his governors. They also sweetened their requests with gifts, which Khalīl accepted. Despite this ideological rapport, however, it does not appear that the Anatolians actually participated in any Mamluk campaigns.

88 Author Z, *Beiträge*, 9.
89 Ibn ʿAbd al-Ẓāhir, *Alṭāf*, 15–16; also Ilisch, "Artuqidenherrschaft," 64.

Nevertheless, shortly after receiving the Anatolian overtures, Khalīl began to make preparations to attack the Armenian fort of Hromgla, located on the Euphrates near the Mamluk castle of al-Bīrah, as the first step in hostilities against the Ilkhanids and their allies, and as a preliminary move towards conquering Iraq.[90] To set the ideological stage, Khalīl enacted elaborate ceremonies that linked him to his own father and to Baybars, and also invoked Abbasid symbolic importance. First in September–October 1291/Shawwāl 690 Khalīl had the caliph al-Ḥākim preach in the citadel to the Mamluk military elite. Al-Ḥākim had delivered the same sermon at his own inauguration by Baybars thirty years earlier in November 1262/Muḥarram 661 (see below). Thus with thirty-year-old words the caliph evoked the horrors of Hülegü's sack of Baghdad in 1258/656, urged the Mamluk commanders to prepare for jihad and credited the sultan with restoring the caliph to an exalted position. Khalīl may have asked al-Ḥākim to repeat this anachronistic sermon in order to revive an awareness of the danger posed by the Ilkhanids, a danger that – at least to Mamluk minds – had diminished during the martial inactivity of Arghun's rule. Or Khalīl simply thought it was time to fulfill the promise of Baybars's reign, in which the invasion of Iraq had never been seriously attempted.[91]

Next Khalīl linked the Iraq campaign to Qalawun's reputation as a warrior for the faith when on 29 October 1291/4 Dhū al-Qaʿdah 690, one (Islamic) year after his father's death, he sponsored solemn evening ceremonies at Qalawun's tomb for all the leading religious and military personnel of the Sultanate. Although the sultan himself was not present, no expense was spared: the space was perfumed with incense and lit by candles "so that the night resembled the day."[92] The religious dignitaries were welcomed by the vizier, seated according to their respective legal schools and listened as four Quran reciters – one for each school – recited different sets of verses. Thereafter the entire company was treated to a sumptuous feast and stayed up all night. In the morning the sultan and the caliph processed together from the Victory Gate in the city walls to the complex, the youthful sultan in white, the elderly caliph in Abbasid black. They paid their respects at the tomb, spoke to the dignitaries, visited the patients in the adjacent hospital, then returned to the citadel in a second grand procession, distributing great largesse throughout their journey.[93]

As part of these festivities the caliph preached a set of newly written sermons to the military elite.[94] In the first sermon the caliph reminded his

[90] By contrast, Stewart suggests that the Hromgla campaign was to mop up Christians after Acre; *Armenian Kingdom*, 73–75.

[91] Heidemann, *Kalifat*, 184–88; ʿAynī, *ʿIqd*, III:87–88. [92] Ibn ʿAbd al-Ẓāhir, *Alṭāf*, 17.

[93] *Ibid.*, 17–19, quote from 17.

[94] For the texts see *ibid.*, 12–13. The precise dating of this sermon is difficult; it took place either as part of the memorial festivities, or on the following Friday (2 November 1291/8 Dhū al-Qaʿdah 690). Also see Nuwayrī, *Nihāyah*, XXXI:220–21; Ibn al-Furāt, *Duwal*, VIII:129, and Jazarī, *Taʾrīkh*, I:58.

audience that jihad was an obligation for them, with which God was giving them a chance to earn spiritual benefits. He emphasized Khalīl's close attention to the holy struggle: "When you sleep, he is awake."[95] Although the caliph did not specifically urge the conquest of Iraq, he did allude to Khalīl's secret traps for the enemy, which "extended farther than Khurasan," and assured his audience, whom he called "soldiers of God," that the opportunities of jihad were there for the taking.[96] In the second sermon he exhorted God to grant the sultan victory and make the lands of the earth submit to him. As was appropriate for the occasion, al-Ḥākim mentioned Qalawun as an exemplar of jihad, then led everyone in the prayers.

In February–March 1292/Rabīʿ I 691 as a final boost to morale, al-Ḥākim gave yet another jihad sermon in the citadel mosque.[97] Then Khalīl and the armies left on 29 March/8 Rabīʿ II, and captured Hromgla on 28 June/11 Rajab. In a public proclamation of his success as a Guardian, Khalīl promptly renamed the fort "Citadel of the Muslims."[98] Geikhatu knew of the Mamluk presence and sent out forces to stop them, but the two sides never met. It is possible that Hetʿum II also dispatched Armenians, but if so, they too failed to engage the Mamluks.[99] Regardless, Khalīl refrained from taking unnecessary risks in hostile territory, and began his homeward journey shortly after his conquest. He followed the victory at Hromgla by sending a campaign against Shiites near Beirut, and subjugating the Armenians. These bold steps suggested an aggressive policy of consolidation within Mamluk territory and expansion outside it, which resembled Baybars's tendencies far more than the relative caution of Qalawun.

Despite Geikhatu's failure to defend Hromgla successfully, Khalīl appears to have attracted his attention, for in 1292–93/692 a large group of Ilkhanid envoys passed through Aleppo on their way to meet Khalīl in an encounter that is mysteriously ill-documented in the histories.[100] Although it is difficult to make out exactly what happened, this single exchange reinforced established ideological tropes on both sides. Khalīl's interest in imitating Baybars as the Champion of Islam against infidels was clear, while Geikhatu's message – entirely based on established imperial ideology – harkened back to Abaqa's straightforward demands. The envoys' message was both a familiar Mongol demand for submission, and a reflection of Geikhatu's fondness for greater Anatolia: Geikhatu had decided to move to Aleppo, which belonged

[95] Ibn ʿAbd al-Ẓāhir, *Alṭāf*, 12. [96] *Ibid.*, 12–13.

[97] This appears to have been a third set of sermons on jihad, but no texts remain. Nuwayrī, *Nihāyah*, XXXI:225; Jazarī, *Taʾrīkh*, I:101.

[98] Ar. *qalʿat al-muslimīn*. It had been previously known in Arabic as Citadel of the Anatolians/Greeks (Ar. *qalʿat al-rūm*). Baybars al-Manṣūrī, *Tuḥfah*, 131.

[99] Stewart, *Armenian Kingdom*, 78–79; Boyle, "Īl-Khāns," 373.

[100] It appears only in the late sources of ʿAynī and Maqrīzī, and nowhere else in Persian or Arabic, which is most unusual. ʿAynī, *ʿIqd*, III:187–88; Maqrīzī, *Sulūk*, I:786.

to him, since it had been among the cities captured by his grandfather Hülegü. If Khalīl objected in any way, Geikhatu would take over all of Syria.

Khalīl's response was worthy of Baybars. He apparently smiled at the ambassadors and expressed his delight that he and the ilkhan saw eye to eye, since he had recently been talking to his own commanders about demanding Baghdad from Geikhatu. If the ilkhan refused to hand that city over, Khalīl planned to invade Iraq, capture the city, kill its fighting men and convert it back into an Islamic city. Khalīl finished with another Baybars-style flourish by instructing the ambassadors to challenge Geikhatu to see who invaded the other's land first. The envoys may also have been treated to the sight of a Mamluk military muster, designed – as usual – to intimidate them. Their departure was unrecorded, but Khalīl does not appear to have sent Mamluk messengers back with them.

While the ilkhan and the sultan were thus establishing themselves in opposition to one another, others in the region continued to send out feelers to Khalīl. In May–June 1293/Jumādà II 692, the Türkmen leader Maḥmūd b. Qaraman sent word that he had taken over an Anatolian fort in Khalīl's name.[101] Then the governor of Syria passed on a request from the Hakkārī Kurds from north of Mosul, whom Baybars had patronized years before. Unlike the Anatolians' appeal to Guardianship, the Kurdish message reflected the position of the Mamluk sultan as head of the Islamic chivalric organization of the *futūwah*. Earlier in the century the *futūwah* may have been an association of young men who combined chivalry with ties to the caliph and to Sufism, but the details in the early Mamluk period are scant.[102] At any rate, now the Kurdish leader, ʿAlāʾ al-Dīn al-Hakkārī, wanted Khalīl to bestow the *futūwah* costume on him so he could initiate his own men. This request fit nicely into Khalīl's revival of Baybars's ideology, since Baybars had once bestowed *futūwah* garments at long distance on Berke of the Golden Horde (see below). Not surprisingly, therefore, Khalīl was amenable to al-Hakkārī's request, and sent the necessary clothes, gifts, a banner and the written confirmation of *futūwah* status. In this document Khalīl's grandiose ideological visions appeared in his titles – some inherited, some new – which revealed an aggressive version of Islamic Guardianship that focused on martial conquest, expansion and universal rule. These titles included, "Sultan of the Earth ... Imam of the Age, Raiser of the Flag of Victory, Champion of the Islamic Community, Reviver of the Abbasid State, Conqueror of Lands, Forts and Garrison Cities, Defeater of Infidels, Annihilator of Franks, Armenians and Mongols ... the Highest King of Kings; Sultan of the World and Heir of Rule (*Sulṭān al-arḍ ... imām al-ʿaṣr, rāfiʿ liwāʾ al-naṣr, nāṣir al-millah al-Muḥammadīyah, muḥyī al-dawlah*

[101] Jazarī, *Taʾrīkh*, I:156.
[102] Claude Cahen, "Futuwwa," *EI*[2] II:964–65, and Fr. Taeschner, "[Futuwwa] Post-Mongol Period," *EI*[2] II:966.

al-ʿabbāsīyah, fātiḥ al-bilād wa al-qilāʿ wa al-amṣār, qāhir al-kuffār, mubīd al-firinj wa al-arman wa al-tatār … [al-]shāhinshāh al-ʿālī, sulṭān al-ʿālam, wārith al-mulk)".[103]

But in addition to these ambitious plans to extend his domains through an active version of Guardianship, like his predecessors Khalīl wanted a successor to inherit them. Khalīl's dynastic aspirations appeared in the extensive preparations he made for the circumcisions of his half-brother and unofficial heir Muḥammad, and his nephew Mūsà, in November 1293/Dhū al-Ḥijjah 692. Although Khalīl intended to celebrate their rite of passage in style, however, he really wanted to pass the Sultanate to a son of his own, and so the festivities also marked the expected delivery of Khalīl's pregnant wife, the Mongol lady Ardakin.[104] Thus outwardly for his brother and nephew, and secretly in anticipation of the royal birth, Khalīl spent tremendous sums on military equipment, robes and expensive refreshments, and ordered his soldiers to practice for a shooting competition and military review. He also took the opportunity to inaugurate the Ashrafī Hall, a magnificent structure that he had had built in the citadel, which provided a physical expression of his kingliness.[105] But although the games were a success, the circumcisions on 23 November/22 Dhū al-Ḥijjah went without trouble and the hall shone with elaborate decorations, the sultan was severely disappointed when Ardakin gave birth to a girl.[106] Shortly thereafter Khalīl named Muḥammad as his official heir.[107] Unfortunately the implementation of Khalīl's disparate ambitions came at a high price – Khalīl's military commanders were terrified of him, and assassinated the sultan only days later in December 1293/Muḥarram 693.[108] This put an end to further Mamluk offensives for some time. Geikhatu's disinterest in the Mamluks – or his preoccupation at home – became evident after Khalīl's murder, for the ilkhan failed to invade Mamluk territory, despite the unambiguous message he had sent.

The Mamluks and the Golden Horde

While relations between the Mamluks and the Ilkhanids were marked by mistrust, hostility and war, relations between the Mamluks and the khans of the Golden Horde were characterized by friendship and, frequently,

103 Ibn ʿAbd al-Ẓāhir, *Alṭāf*, 67.

104 For Khalīl's hopes for a son see Baybars al-Manṣūrī, *Tuḥfah*, 134, and *Zubdah*, 293.

105 Rabbat, *Citadel*, 150, 158–80, esp. 169–80 on the way Khalīl may have emphasized the political and military extent of his realms through decoration, including and especially mosaic.

106 For Khalīl's dashed hopes see Baybars al-Manṣūrī, *Tuḥfah*, 134, and *Zubdah*, 293; for the circumcision see Nuwayrī, *Nihāyah*, XXI:253–54; Ibn al-Dawādārī, *Kanz*, VIII:343; Author Z, *Beiträge*, 23.

107 Nuwayrī, *Nihāyah*, XXXI:268–69.

108 Ibn al-Dawādārī, *Kanz*, VIII:351; also Holt, *Crusades*, 105–06; Robert Irwin, *The Middle East in the Middle Ages: The Early Mamluk Sultanate 1250–1382* (Carbondale, 1986), 82.

solidarity in Islam against the infidels in Iran.[109] Contact was initiated by Baybars. At first the sultan's interest in the Golden Horde was economic, as shown in his 1261–62/660 agreement with the Byzantine emperor Michael VIII to ensure the passage of slave and fur merchants coming from Golden Horde ports.[110] But ideology and strategy also played a role, and so when in summer 1262/660 Baybars heard news of battles between Berke and Hülegü and rumors that Berke had converted to Islam, he found a merchant from the Alan region of the northern Caucasus to carry a letter to Berke, with which he hoped to secure a strategic alliance against Hülegü based on a unity in Islam.[111] Here Baybars employed his position as Guardian of Islam not to oppose Berke as he did the Ilkhanids, but rather to draw him into a shared enterprise of martial action on behalf of religion. Although the results of this first foray took some time to develop, ultimately for the Golden Horde the Mamluks came to represent seniors and role models in the system of thought and belief that was Islam, which helped the khans think about their sovereignty in new ways and justify their opposition to other Chingizids.

Baybars's first letter to Berke was heavily Islamic in sentiment, which was the only safe approach for a Qipchaq Turk intervening in Mongol ruling affairs. In the letter Baybars used Islam against the powerful Chingizid reverence for the golden family by urging Berke to fight Hülegü, and informed him that as a Muslim he was obligated to wage holy war against other Mongols, even if they were his relatives. In support the letter described Baybars's own efforts as a warrior for Islam (*mujāhid*), and reminded Berke that the Prophet Muḥammad had fought some of his relatives from the Quraysh tribe in order to ensure their conversion. The letter also used anti-Christian sentiment to create a dichotomy between Muslims and non-Muslims and widen the breach between Berke and his cousin:

> Reports have come one after the next, [saying] that for the sake of his wife and her Christianity [the Nestorian Dokuz Khatun], Hulāwūn has established the religion of the cross, and has advanced the observance of his wife's religion over your religion. He has settled the unbelieving Nestorian Catholicus (*jāthlīq*) in the home of the [Abbasid] caliphs, [thereby] preferring her over you.[112]

[109] For a full discussion, albeit somewhat inaccessible, see S. Zakirov, *Diplomaticheskie Otnosheniia Zolotoi Ordy s Egiptom (XIII–XIV vv.)* (Moscow, 1966).

[110] Marius Canard, "Un traité entre Byzance et l'Égypte au XIIIe siècle et les relations diplomatiques de Michel VIII Paléologue avec les sultans mamlûks Baibars et Qalâ'ûn," *Mélanges Gaudefroy-Demombynes* (Cairo, 1935–45), 211; Ibn ʿAbd al-Ẓāhir, *Rawḍ*, 88; Baybars al-Manṣūrī, *Zubdah*, 70; also Janet Martin, "The Land of Darkness and the Golden Horde: The Fur Trade under the Mongols, XIII–XIVth Centuries," *Cahiers du Monde Russe et Soviétique* 19:4 (1978), 401–21; Mayer, *Mamluk Costume*, 58–60.

[111] Only a description of the text by its author remains. Ibn ʿAbd al-Ẓāhir, *Rawḍ*, 88–89. Also see Abū Shāmah, *Tarājim rijāl al-qarnayn al-sādis wa al-sābiʿ al-maʿrūf bi-al-dhayl ʿalà al-rawḍatayn*, ed. Muḥammad Zāhid b. al-Ḥasan al-Kawtharī (Cairo, 1947), 219; also Amitai-Preiss, *War*, 80–81.

[112] Ibn ʿAbd al-Ẓāhir, *Rawḍ*, 88.

Relations developed later that year when about 200 Mongols appeared in eastern Syria, heading for Damascus. These were a remnant of the Golden Horde's contribution to Hülegü's great Iran campaign. When hostilities deepened between Hülegü and Berke, Berke ordered his troops to return home, or, if necessary, to take refuge outside Hülegü's domains, including in Mamluk territory.[113] Initially the Mongols' ominous advance across Syria caused the population to panic and the Mamluks to send out a reconnaissance force and scorch the land around Aleppo. When the Mamluks actually encountered the Mongols, however, they discovered that the "infidels" were refugees, and bore greetings to the ruler of Egypt (Baybars) from Berke himself. Once this had been established, Baybars ordered a warm welcome for them, sent robes of honor to the men and their wives, and had homes constructed for them in Cairo in a special quarter, al-Lūq. They arrived in Cairo on 9 November 1262/24 Dhū al-Ḥijjah 660, and met with the sultan two days later. Baybars presided over a great ceremonial distribution of robes, horses and money, and gave the men military positions.[114] They soon converted to Islam, which, when combined with their new ranks, allowed Baybars to incorporate them easily into Mamluk society.[115]

Immediately after the refugees' arrival, Baybars hastened to prepare envoys to send to Berke. He also scrambled to present the right image. On Thursday 16 November 1262/2 Muḥarram 661 Baybars inaugurated a refugee Abbasid as his second caliph al-Ḥākim in the solemn presence of the Mongol leaders, the Mamluk envoys Baybars had chosen, and the senior military and religious personnel in Cairo. It was a splendid ceremony, and took place at the center of Mamluk power, the Cairo citadel. It is likely that it resembled the inauguration of Baybars's first caliph, al-Mustanṣir, in 1261/659, when Baybars wore a magnificent robe of purple, black and gold, and the caliph surely wore Abbasid black.[116] Once again Baybars swore allegiance to the caliph and promised to rule in a Godly fashion and fight for God's sake. In return al-Ḥākim entrusted Baybars with the care of Muslims and Muslim lands, exhorted him to perform jihad and appointed him his partner in supporting the truth (of religion). Al-Ḥākim's lineage was verified, and a family tree composed.[117] On Friday the caliph preached to the same audience, and focused on two concepts: the leadership of the Muslim community (*imāmah*) and jihad. First al-Ḥākim evoked Hülegü's terrifying sack of Baghdad in 1258/656, then contrasted this with Baybars's revival of the

113 ʿAynī, *ʿIqd*, I:364; Amitai-Preiss, *War*, 81.

114 Ibn ʿAbd al-Ẓāhir, *Rawḍ*, 136–38; Nuwayrī, *Nihāyah*, XXX:62–64.

115 For Islamization as the deliberate adoption of a more desirable life system and the consequent process of mutual acculturation between two traditions see DeWeese, *Islamization*, 51–59.

116 Only the colors of the first ceremony are specified. Ibn ʿAbd al-Ẓāhir, *Rawḍ*, 101; also Mayer, *Mamluk Costume*, 12–16.

117 "*qasīmahu fī qiyyām al-ḥaqq*," Ibn ʿAbd al-Ẓāhir, *Rawḍ*, 142; the legend "partner of the caliph" (Ar. *qasīm amīr al-muʾmunīn*) also appeared on Mamluk coins beginning with Baybars. Balog, *Coinage*, 85–106.

imamate, his restoration of the caliph to an exalted position, his expulsion of the enemy and his provision of a willing army to the caliph. Al-Ḥākim exhorted his listeners to engage in holy struggle (*jihād*), and reminded them of their religious duty to obey those in command, meaning Baybars. After the ceremony Baybars's chancellery composed a letter to Berke detailing al-Ḥākim's lineage and describing his inauguration in Cairo. In it Baybars urged Berke to perform jihad against Hülegü, described the Mamluk armies, enumerated his allies and enemies, and reassured Berke of the warm welcome the Mongol refugees had received. A copy of the caliph's family tree accompanied the letter.[118]

Whereas Baybars had used his first caliph, al-Mustanṣir, to establish his legitimacy with his subjects and peers, al-Mustanṣir's death in Baghdad had left Baybars facing a new audience – Berke's refugee followers, and indirectly Berke – without a caliph. Baybars was ideologically weak when compared to Berke, for Berke was a ruling member of the preeminent golden dynasty, whereas Baybars was not only a Qipchaq Turk, but also a former slave. Fortunately, Berke had converted to Islam, and fortunately the Abbasid refugee Abū al-'Abbās Aḥmad was available for employment. By recognizing al-Ḥākim as his second caliph, therefore, Baybars gave himself enough credibility to approach Berke by invoking legitimating concepts that could appeal both to a new believer and to a Chingizid. These included al-Ḥākim's (newly minted) caliphal status, several hundred years' worth of lineage and formal recognition of Baybars's rule, as well as Baybars's own position as a successful warrior for Islam bearing the Abbasid seal of approval.[119]

Baybars's chief envoy was the commander Sayf al-Dīn Kusharbak, who was accompanied by a jurisconsult and two Mongol refugees as guides. They set out in November–December 1262/Muḥarram 661, and in Constantinople crossed the path of an embassy coming from Berke.[120] Berke's ambassadors arrived in Alexandria in May–June 1263/Rajab 661, and from the outset promoted a new unity of religion between the two rulers. To do this Berke had chosen two Muslim scholars as ambassadors, and gave them a response to the letter Baybars had sent with the Alan merchant in 1262/660.[121] Berke's message opened by expressing greetings and sentiments of peace, then asked for Baybars's help against their common foe, Hülegü. Portraying Hülegü as defying the law or decrees (here, "*yasaq*") of Chingiz Khan and his family (*ahl*), Berke explained that his battles with Hülegü were motivated by the desire to spread Islam and Islamic rule, return the Islamic lands to their previous good condition, and avenge the Islamic community in general (for

[118] Ibn 'Abd al-Ẓāhir, *Rawḍ*, 141–45. [119] Heidemann, *Kalifat*, 165–66.

[120] The jurisconsult fell ill and returned to Cairo with Berke's men and Byzantine envoys. Canard, "Traité," 212–13; Ibn 'Abd al-Ẓāhir, *Rawḍ*, 138, 140, whence Nuwayrī, *Nihāyah*, XXX:64–65; Baybars al-Manṣūrī, *Zubdah*, 83, claiming that Kusharbak also returned (*sic*).

[121] Ibn 'Abd al-Ẓāhir, *Rawḍ*, 215; Ibn al-Dawādārī, *Kanz*, VIII:97; Baybars al-Manṣūrī, *Zubdah*, 82; Yūnīnī, *Dhayl*, I:533. For their arrival see the previous footnote.

Hülegü's depredations). In this Berke combined loyalty to nomadic tradition, as represented by the decrees of Chingiz Khan, with his willingness to break with the imperial family and ally himself with an outsider for the sake of his new religion. If the letter referred to Berke's other reasons for disagreement with Hülegü – tax revenue, the three dead princes, the Civil War – the Mamluk sources do not mention it. Berke also asked Baybars to attack Hülegü at the Euphrates, and to help the Anatolian Seljuk ruler, Kay Kawus, who was exiled in Constantinople.[122]

The message prompted a lengthy response on seventy (half-)sheets of Baghdādī paper.[123] It was filled with Quranic verses, stories about the Prophet exhorting jihad, compliments to the recipient and heroic descriptions of the Egyptian armies and their dedication to the holy struggle.[124] Then, in an additional demonstration of piety, manliness and religious solidarity, Baybars invoked the special rituals of the *futūwah* with Berke's envoys. Baybars himself had earlier been inducted into the mysteries of the *futūwah* by his first caliph, al-Mustanṣir, and in turn initiated al-Ḥākim. Now, therefore, Baybars asked al-Ḥākim to invest Berke's envoys and his own new Mamluk ambassadors with the *futūwah* trousers to bind them to the caliph and the sultan with ties of manly solidarity. Al-Ḥākim performed the initiation, preached a new Friday sermon, and gave the ambassadors clothes for Berke, which included him in the ritual and established links of honor and chivalry among Berke, Baybars and the caliph.[125] Thereafter Baybars sent Berke's envoys to the Islamic holy cities, where Baybars had the Mongol ruler's name mentioned in the sermon after his own in a show of Islamic unity.[126]

Baybars sent out his second embassy two months later in July–August 1263/Ramaḍān 661, but this time things did not go as planned. Baybars took care to emphasize his message of religious solidarity with elaborate gifts: items of worship (prayer-carpets, a Quran), items of jihad (weapons, horses and their trappings) and more conventional gifts (clothes, slaves, candles, rare animals). Of particular interest are the female slaves, trained in cooking: were they supposed to teach Berke and his court about a proper Muslim diet?[127] The ambassadors, gifts and menagerie sailed to Constantinople, then went to meet Michael VIII, who was away on campaign, and who promised to send them to Berke soon. Unfortunately, an embassy from Hülegü was also in

[122] For a summary of Berke's letter see Ibn ʿAbd al-Ẓāhir, *Rawḍ*, 171 (using *sharīʿah*); Nuwayrī, *Nihāyah*, XXX:87 (using *yasaq*); also Yūnīnī, *Dhayl*, I:533–34, and Amitai-Preiss, *War*, 82–83; Jackson, "Dissolution," 235. For the influence of Islam on Berke's decisions see DeWeese, *Islamization*, 84–85. For Kay Kawus see Cahen, *Turkey*, 175–91.

[123] Smaller sizes of Baghdādī paper could be used when full-sized was unavailable. Qalqashandī, *Ṣubḥ*, VI:181.

[124] Ibn ʿAbd al-Ẓāhir, *Rawḍ*, 171–72. [125] Heidemann, *Kalifat*, 169–71.

[126] Ibn ʿAbd al-Ẓāhir, *Rawḍ*, 174. They traveled with Berke's returning embassy; see Yūnīnī, *Dhayl*, I:537; also Amitai-Preiss, *War*, 84 and note 32 for the polemic on this topic between A. Poliak and David Ayalon.

[127] Ibn ʿAbd al-Ẓāhir, *Rawḍ*, 172–74; Ibn al-Dawādārī, *Kanz*, VIII:97.

Byzantine territory, probably to negotiate the treaty and marriage alliance that Michael ultimately concluded with the Ilkhanids.[128] Fearing that Hülegü might hear of the Mamluk ambassadors, Michael broke his promise and sent them not to Berke, but back to Constantinople. There they and their menagerie languished for months, and most of the animals died. Eventually the ambassadors were reduced to begging Michael to let them either continue, or return to Egypt.[129] At the same time Michael held the refugee Seljuk Kay Kawus imprisoned in his territory, but Kay Kawus conspired with the Golden Horde and the Bulgarians, who mounted a joint invasion under Berke's great-nephew Noqai in 1263/662, which liberated the Seljuk.[130] In Cairo Baybars remained unaware of Michael's perfidy until one ambassador was permitted to return in June–July 1264/Ramaḍān 662. Baybars was so angry with the emperor for interfering, and for his relationship with Hülegü, that he forced Christian officials in Egypt to excommunicate Michael.[131]

Michael also delayed the Mongol ambassadors accompanying Baybars's first ambassador Kusharbak, who finally returned to Cairo in August–September 1264/Dhū al-Qaʿdah 662, over a year after setting out.[132] Fortunately their news pleased the sultan, who soon realized that Kusharbak's mission had been a success. Berke's letter, dated 11 May 1263/1 Rajab 661, emphasized the unity in religion between him and Baybars by enumerating Berke's relatives and followers who had become Muslims, along with their families, followers, servants and armies. Berke explained that he had fought Hülegü, even though Hülegü was his own flesh and blood, because Hülegü had proved to be an oppressor (*bāghin*), which made him an unbeliever.[133] Berke clarified that he had sent an eyewitness to his battles

[128] Bruce Lippard, "The Mongols and Byzantium, 1243–1341," Ph.D. dissertation (Department of Uralic and Altaic Studies, Indiana University, December 1983), 196–98; also Amitai-Preiss, *War*, 84, 91–93.

[129] Mufaḍḍal, *Nahj*, 112–13; Ibn al-Dawādārī, *Kanz*, VIII:98; also Lippard, "Mongols and Byzantium," 193.

[130] Canard hypothesized late summer for this attack; see "Traité," 215–16.

[131] For the date see Ibn ʿAbd al-Ẓāhir, *Rawḍ*, 202; for the ambassador see Ibn al-Dawādārī, *Kanz*, VIII:98. The scant detail means we must infer that the ambassador informed Baybars; Lippard, "Mongols and Byzantium," 193, esp. note 89.

[132] They were two adults, Ar-tīmū (Ara-Temür?) and Ūnāmās (?), and a youth named Arbuqa. Ibn al-Dawādārī, *Kanz*, VIII:101; Baybars al-Manṣūrī, *Zubdah*, 82 (in the letter text). For Kusharbak's stay see Ibn ʿAbd al-Ẓāhir, *Rawḍ*, 215–16; whence Nuwayrī, *Nihāyah*, XXX:105–06 and Yūnīnī, *Dhayl*, I:540–42; Ibn al-Dawādārī, *Kanz*, VIII:101, misidentifying Kusharbak as Fāris al-Dīn (from Baybars's next embassy, see below).

[133] For a partial text see Baybars al-Manṣūrī, *Zubdah*, 82–83, whence ʿAynī, *ʿIqd*, I:360–61. Baybars mistakenly claims the letter accompanied the Mongol ambassadors Jalāl al-Dīn Ibn Qāḍī Toqāt and Nūr al-Dīn ʿAlī, who arrived in May–June 1263/Rajab 661; but the letter is dated 11 May 1263/1 Rajab 661 (i.e., the same month), names the envoys as Ar-tīmū (Ara-Temür?) and Ūnāmās (or W-nāmāt), and mentions al-Ḥākim by title. Obviously it was written after Kusharbak told Berke about al-Ḥākim's investiture, and accompanied this second Golden Horde embassy. Lippard tried to reconcile this letter with Berke's first embassy to Cairo, but did not account for the reference to al-Ḥākim, and was unaware of Berke's second embassy. Lippard, "Mongols and Byzantium," 192, esp. note 83.

with Hülegü to attest to his own military accomplishments, and expressed his gratitude for Baybars's own hostilities against the ilkhan.[134] The ambassadors described Berke's clothing and his enormous white felt tent with its jewel- and silk-bedecked interior, which signaled the wealth and power the khan controlled. They also discussed Berke's lands and their distance from Egypt, and detailed Berke's affairs, customs and laws.[135]

In response Baybars tried to impress the Mongol ambassadors and display his ability to pursue jihad by inviting them to a military review, extensive games and a ceremony of investiture. At least according to Mamluk sources he achieved the desired effect, for the envoys asked him whether these were the combined military forces of Egypt and Syria, and were amazed to discover that they were only those stationed in Cairo.[136] While in Egypt the envoys also celebrated the circumcision of Baybars's son and heir Muḥammad Berke Khan, along with the sons of several military commanders (Figure 2). In a display of royal prerogative and royal wealth, Baybars paid for all the festivities himself.[137] Unlike Berke's earlier ambassadors, however, these envoys did not interact with the caliph: perhaps because Berke had agreed to relations, Baybars's legitimacy needed no further help from his Abbasid puppet. The circumcision was the only Islamic event the ambassadors attended, and it underscored Baybars's interest in his own royal house, not the caliphal house. In fact, the sultan soon dispensed with rituals involving al-Ḥākim, and restricted him to the citadel.[138]

But despite the caliph's diminished importance, Baybars did not forget to send Islamic gifts to Berke with his own new envoys as tokens of the religion that united them. Among these were three turbans that had gone to Mecca with the lesser pilgrimage (*ʿumrah*) expressly for Berke, and a bottle of sacred water from the Meccan well of Zamzam.[139] In a sign of confidence in his new relationship to Berke, Baybars also sent a letter intervening with Noqai (who was still ravaging Byzantine territory), as requested by new Byzantine ambassadors.[140] In Constantinople, therefore, Baybars's long-delayed ambassador

[134] Baybars al-Manṣūrī, *Zubdah*, 82. This man claimed to be an exiled Ayyubid from Mayyafariqin, but several Mamluk historians insisted he was an imposter, and Baybars later arrested him along with some Mamluk commanders. Nuwayrī, *Nihāyah*, XXX:123; Yūnīnī, *Dhayl*, II:323–24; Ibn al-Dawādārī, *Kanz*, VIII:115.

[135] Shāfiʿ, *Manāqib*, 175; for tents see Allsen, *Commodity and Exchange*, 13–14; Andrews, *Felt Tents*, I:389, 468, 470–71, 545, 560–62.

[136] The reply may have been disingenuous. Ibn ʿAbd al-Ẓāhir, *Rawḍ*, 213; Nuwayrī, *Nihāyah*, XXX:101.

[137] Shāfiʿ, *Manāqib*, 175.

[138] The caliph was a potential rallying point for Baybars's rivals. Later, other Abbasid refugees were intercepted by Mamluk authorities, and soon disappeared from historical view. Heidemann, *Kalifat*, 179–80.

[139] Nuwayrī, *Nihāyah*, XXX:116–17.

[140] The envoy must have waited for the gifts to return with the pilgrims in ca. October–December 1264/Muḥarram 663 but did not set out until approximately July–August 1265/Shawwāl. The month must be inferred from previous entries. Nuwayrī, *Nihāyah*, XXX:116–17; Shāfiʿ, *Manāqib*, 209; also Ibn ʿAbd al-Ẓāhir, *Rawḍ*, 202–03.

Figure 2. This depiction of a Mongol enthronement suggests the type of scene the Golden Horde ambassadors would have had in mind as they attended the circumcision festivities for Baybars's son. (Staatsbibliothek zu Berlin, Preussischer Kulturbesitz, Orientabteilung. Diez A, fol. 7, S. 22.)

Fāris al-Dīn Aqqush al-Masʿūdī promised Michael that he would swear (falsely) in writing to have lingered in Constantinople of his own free will, then met with Noqai and asked him to desist on the grounds that Michael was a friend of Baybars. Thereafter Noqai withdrew his forces, and Fāris al-Dīn and the decimated menagerie finally resumed their journey.[141] But once in Berke's lands Fāris al-Dīn's lie came to light, damaging Baybars's own reputation, and thus causing the sultan to fine and imprison his recalcitrant ambassador upon his return to Egypt in 1266–67/665.[142]

Nevertheless despite delays, distances and lies, and despite Baybars's lowly origin and tenuous ideological position, the Mamluk sultan established an alliance with Berke based on Baybars's promotion of military Islamic values. Or did he? The historical record reflects Baybars's point of view, distilled through his official biography and copied by later writers. Despite Baybars's presentation of an alliance of equals, Berke appears to have seen Baybars with the imperial Mongol world view: that is, as an obedient subject, in this case a Muslim. To support this, one historian suggested that in the letter of summer 1262/660 Baybars offered to submit to Berke.[143] Both rulers also suggested joint campaigns against the Ilkhanids, although none ever took place. Significantly the Mamluk sources quote Berke as telling Baybars that, "I will give you the [Islamic[144]] lands that Hülegü has taken over," which was the statement of sovereign to subordinate, not a ruler to an equal ally.[145] When Berke's ambassadors met with Baybars they informed the Mamluk sultan about Berke's laws, which were required knowledge for any vassal. Much later a Mamluk author pointed out that although the khans of the Golden Horde sent few gifts to Cairo, the Mamluk sultans always dispatched lavish presents.[146] Were Baybars's gifts really gifts, therefore, or did Berke see them as some form of tribute? Nevertheless Baybars never became a full vassal to Berke, for he never sent hostages to Berke's court.[147]

141 Yūnīnī, *Dhayl*, I:538–9, II:198; Mufaḍḍal, *Nahj*, 112–14; for the timing of the delayed embassy relative to the invasion see Canard, "Traité," 215–17. For the elephant and giraffe, which reached Berke, see Ibn al-Dawādārī, *Kanz*, VIII:100.

142 Baybars heard about this from Kay Kawus, who wrote to him. Yūnīnī, *Dhayl*, I:539, II:361; Nuwayrī, *Nihāyah*, XXVII:362–63 (in 1269–70/668 [*sic*]).

143 Anne F. Broadbridge, "Mamluk Legitimacy and the Mongols: The Reigns of Baybars and Qalāwūn," *Mamluk Studies Review* 5 (2001), 101; Amitai-Preiss, *War*, 83–84. Previously I suggested that Ibn Wāṣil described Baybars claiming that the Islamic armies were all obedient *to Berke* and awaiting his command, "*fī ṭāʿatihi wa sāmiʿatun li-ishāratihi*" (reading "he" as Berke), but further investigation makes it clear that "he" means Baybars, not Berke. I thus withdraw my claim that Ibn Wāṣil's text indicated an imbalance of power between the two rulers, although the claim still stands in the case of Yūnīnī, where the text reads: "*al-dukhūl fī al-īlīyah wa al-ṭāʿah.*" Yūnīnī, *Dhayl*, II:197; Ibn Wāṣil, "Taʾrīkh al-wāṣilīn min akhbār al-khulafāʾ wa al-mulūk wa al-salāṭīn," Dār al-Kutub, Cairo, MS 40477, fols. 1306–07; also see Ibn ʿAbd al-Ẓāhir, *Rawḍ*, 139; Mufaḍḍal, *Nahj*, 112.

144 Mufaḍḍal, *Nahj*, 111.

145 Yūnīnī, *Dhayl*, II:195; variations in Mufaḍḍal, *Nahj*, 111; Ibn al-Dawādārī, *Kanz*, VIII:167.

146 ʿAynī, *ʿIqd*, fol. 317v.

147 For hostages see Yang, "Hostages," 48–49.

Möngke Temür and Noqai

The Byzantine–Ilkhanid alliance appears to have impeded diplomacy between Saray and Cairo, since no embassies are recorded until after Berke's death sometime in 1266/663–64.[148] Only in October–November 1267/Ṣafar 666, after receiving the news, did Baybars write to Berke's great-nephew and heir Möngke Temür to offer condolences, congratulate him on his accession and urge him to fight Abaqa.[149] Möngke Temür wanted to maintain good relations, but for economic reasons, not ideological ones, since he was not a Muslim. Therefore he not only ignored Baybars's request for a military alliance, but came to a separate peace agreement with Abaqa in 1268–69/667.[150]

Perhaps as a result, Baybars responded with cautious warmth to a letter that arrived in Cairo in 1270–71/669 from Berke's talented general Noqai (d. 1299–1300/699).[151] Noqai was a grandson of Boal, brother of Batu and Berke, and thus a cousin to Möngke Temür. Although Noqai was a Chingizid, his position in Golden Horde territory may have been circumscribed by the fact that inheritance was passing among Batu's descendants, to which group Noqai did not belong.[152] Nevertheless Noqai maintained great standing among the Golden Horde, played an important role as a kingmaker and ultimately became an independent khan in the 1290s/690s.[153] By writing to Baybars, Noqai probably sought to gain his support against others in the Golden Horde, not against Baybars's own Ilkhanid antagonists (with whom, in fact, Noqai later conducted diplomatic relations[154]).

In addition to working for Berke as a general, Noqai had been very close to his great-uncle, had become a Muslim like him and had been present when the Mamluk ambassadors were in Berke's camp – by his own report he discussed them with Berke. Noqai therefore understood the best approach to use with Baybars, for the letter began by giving thanks for Noqai's

148 Lippard, "Mongols and Byzantium," 199.

149 Golden Horde ambassadors arrived in Cairo in autumn 1268/early 667, probably with Baybars's returning envoys, and went home with new Mamluk envoys thereafter (Ibn ʿAbd al-Ẓāhir, *Rawḍ*, 288, 334–35; Nuwayrī, *Nihāyah*, XXVII:362; Shāfiʿ, *Manāqib*, 293–94; Baybars al-Manṣūrī, *Zubdah*, 109, 117; Ibn al-Furāt, "Duwal," MS 36310, fols. 150a–b).

150 Spuler, *Goldene Horde*, 54; for Möngke Temür's economic interests see Vernadsky, *Russia*, 170–71.

151 For the texts of Noqai's letter and Baybars's response see Ibn ʿAbd al-Ẓāhir, *Rawḍ*, 371–73; Baybars al-Manṣūrī, *Zubdah*, 131–32, and *Tuḥfah*, 71.

152 For Noqai's career see Spuler, *Goldene Horde*, 64–77; Vernadsky, *Russia*, 162–65, 174–89; Rashīd al-Dīn, *The Successors of Genghis Khan*, tr. J. A. Boyle (New York, 1971), 124–30; Uli Schamiloglu, "The Golden Horde," in *The Turks, II: Middle Ages*, eds. Hasan Celac Güzel et al. (Ankara, 2002), 822–25. For his conversion and status as a Muslim see DeWeese, *Islamization*, 88–89.

153 Jackson, *Mongols and the West*, 199; also see Schamiloglu's theory of Noqai as one of four ruling commanders who formed a council of state to serve or oppose the khan in "Golden Horde," 820, 822–25.

154 Rashīd al-Dīn, *Successors*, 129–30.

conversion, which immediately established the necessary ideological common ground. Noqai informed Baybars that he had learned of his trustworthiness from Berke, and therefore intended to follow in Berke's footsteps by establishing diplomatic relations with Baybars. Noqai also intended this to be a military alliance, and promised to fight Baybars's enemies and befriend Baybars's friends.[155]

Despite Noqai's attractive religious status, Baybars seems to have feared that Noqai was presenting himself as a Muslim alternative to Möngke Temür, and did not want to jeopardize his relations with the khan. Thus the letter written in response to Noqai – although warm – was of only medium quality. The chancellery made sure to establish Noqai's position by using an address form for military commanders, "the Dear and Lofty Seat" (*sāmī al-majlis al-ʿazīz*), which was too low for an independent sovereign.[156] In the letter Baybars warned that he did not fully understand Noqai's references to following in Berke's footsteps. This allowed Baybars to protect himself from Möngke Temür should Noqai turn out to be a rebel, but did not rebuff Noqai entirely. The chancellery then sweetened Baybars's message by congratulating Noqai on his conversion, and made Baybars expound briefly on the virtues of jihad in a self-interested attempt to steer Noqai's attentions back to Baybars's own Ilkhanid foes to the south.[157] There is no record of further contact between the two men.

By contrast, Baybars maintained his alliance with Möngke Temür, and was soon rewarded for his efforts. By 1271–72/670 Möngke Temür's truce with Abaqa had fallen apart, and as a result he sent ambassadors to Baybars in that year and asked for military assistance against the Ilkhanids. Möngke Temür may also have encouraged Baybars to ally himself with the Ögedeid Qaidu Khan in the 1270s/670s.[158] In an echo of Berke's promises, the Mongol ambassadors proposed that the Muslim lands in Abaqa's hands would be returned to Baybars's control in exchange for his help.[159] This allowed a partial reestablishment of earlier policy: Baybars could at least be allied with Möngke Temür in opposition to the Ilkhanids, if not in religion. To prove his forces' military fitness, Baybars invited the envoys to watch them practice in full gear in the main square in Damascus, and forced a set of Ilkhanid ambassadors, who were also in Damascus, to watch as well. Baybars must have hoped to emphasize his alliance with Möngke Temür to them.[160] Serendipitously the Mamluk sultan then suddenly left to undertake a lightning campaign against the Ilkhanids at the Euphrates in October–November

155 Ibn ʿAbd al-Ẓāhir, *Rawḍ*, 371–72. 156 *Ibid.*, 372; also see Qalqashandī, *Ṣubḥ*, V:465.
157 Ibn ʿAbd al-Ẓāhir, *Rawḍ*, 372–73.
158 The evidence is ambiguous. See Biran, *Qaidu*, 62, esp. notes 216, 217.
159 Ibn Shaddād, *Taʾrīkh*, 35–36, whence Yūnīnī, *Dhayl*, II:472–73; see also Ibn ʿAbd al-Ẓāhir, *Rawḍ*, 399–400, whence Nuwayrī, *Nihāyah*, XXX:192; and Ibn al-Dawādārī, *Kanz*, VIII:167; Baybars al-Manṣūrī, *Zubdah*, 134.
160 Ibn ʿAbd al-Ẓāhir, *Rawḍ*, 404.

1272/Rabīʿ I 671. After returning victorious to Damascus he took Möngke Temür's ambassadors back to Cairo, and there responded to their letter with a description of his stirring victory over Abaqa's forces. Baybars sent this heartening news back in February–March 1273/Shaʿbān 671 with splendid gifts and a collection of medicines that Möngke Temür had requested.[161]

Thereafter the two monarchs exchanged messages and gifts regularly.[162] During these Baybars sought to promote his own family and dynasty, which preempted the signal role that religion had played in his interactions with Berke. In October–November 1276/Jumādà I 675 Baybars invited Möngke Temür's ambassadors to attend the week-long wedding festivities for his heir Muḥammad Berke Khan, just as he had invited Berke's envoys in 1264/662 to attend Muḥammad's circumcision. The wedding included five days of military reviews and games, a massive ceremony of investiture and a sumptuous feast, at which Baybars sat on a costly throne of ebony inlaid with ivory, gold and silver. The crowning moment in this display of Baybars's kingly house and kingly self came after the feast when the Mamluk military commanders presented the sultan with expensive gifts, which he refused in a magnificent display of royal reticence.[163] This must have been an impressive show for the Mongol ambassadors, themselves coming from a nomadic tradition in which the ruler's ability to bestow riches on his followers, or refuse them in return, were important signals of his power and success.

Qalawun and the Golden Horde

When Qalawun came to power as the next real Mamluk sultan, he was, like Baybars, a Qipchaq and a former slave, and thus ideologically weak in the face of the Golden Horde's Chingizid lineage. It is therefore no surprise that Qalawun modeled his alliance with the Golden Horde closely on Baybars's example. Early in his reign Qalawun sent a message and sixteen loads of gifts to the Golden Horde.[164] At the least Qalawun intended to maintain cordial relations; he must also have hoped to continue the trade in mamluks. At the

[161] *Ibid.*, 411; Ibn Shaddād, *Taʾrīkh*, 58; Yūnīnī, *Dhayl*, III:5.

[162] Golden Horde envoys were in Egypt in December 1275–January 1276/Rajab 674 (Ibn Shaddād, *Taʾrīkh*, 127–28; Yūnīnī, *Dhayl*, III:116; Nuwayrī, *Nihāyah*, XXX:221; Ibn al-Furāt, *Duwal*, VII:44); in September–October 1276/Rabīʿ II 675 (Ibn Shaddād, *Taʾrīkh*, 166–67; Yūnīnī, *Dhayl*, III:174; Ismāʿīl Ibn Kathīr, *al-Bidāyah wa al-nihāyah fī al-taʾrīkh*, ed. Maktab Taḥqīq al-Turāth [Beirut, 1993], XIII:317), and in September 1277/Rabīʿ II 676, just after Baybars's death on 30 June 1277/27 Muḥarram 676 (Yūnīnī, *Dhayl*, III:235; Dhahabī, "Ṭabaqāt," MS 10680, fol. 7a); also Amitai-Preiss, *War*, 90.

[163] Ibn Shaddād, *Taʾrīkh*, 166–67.

[164] For a partial text of a letter to some lesser Golden Horde functionary see Ibn al-Furāt, *Duwal*, VII:179; otherwise Ibn ʿAbd al-Ẓāhir, *Tashrīf*, 17–18. For the slave trade see Qalawun's 1280–81/679–80 negotiations with the Byzantine emperor Michael in Canard, "Traité," 197–209, 221–24.

same time, and probably with the same diplomatic mission, Qalawun wrote to encourage the Ögedeid Qaidu to fight the Ilkhanids, possibly following Baybars's precedent.[165] But Möngke Temür died before the ambassadors arrived, so they presented their gifts to his brother and successor Töde Möngke (r. 1280–85/678/79–83/84) instead, and also met with Noqai.[166]

In response Töde Möngke sent his own embassy to Cairo in 1283–84/682. Like Berke and Noqai, Töde Möngke had converted to Islam, and so unity in religion again came to the forefront in Mamluk–Golden Horde diplomacy.[167] Töde Möngke's envoys were both jurisprudents, and bore a letter in Mongolian with news of Töde Möngke's conversion, accession and intention to implement Islamic law in his lands, although it is unclear whether Töde Möngke intended to substitute this for the decrees of Chingiz Khan. Töde Möngke also adopted the title "Emperor of Islam (*pādshāh-i Islām*)" on some coins.[168] Töde Möngke asked Qalawun to give him a Muslim name, and send him sultanic and caliphal banners, as well as drums to use when riding against enemies of the faith. By making such overtly religious requests, Töde Möngke cast Qalawun into the role of a "senior in Islam," who provided the proper equipment for Töde Möngke to be a warrior for the faith. Qalawun responded by sending the envoys to the Hijaz to perform the pilgrimage at Töde Möngke's request – although it is unknown whether Töde Möngke's name was proclaimed in the sermons in Mecca – then returned them with envoys of his own.

In this way Qalawun and Töde Möngke revived the relationship of solidarity in religion that Baybars and Berke had begun, which had foundered under the non-Muslim Möngke Temür. Their diplomatic interaction also established Qalawun as the religious senior in the relationship, which was a new concept specific to him, and which echoed his hostile relationship of Islamic kingly seniority over the ilkhan Tegüder. In both cases the idea of seniority must have resonated to these members of the golden family, among whom hierarchy and status were deeply important.[169] Töde Möngke's requests for caliphal banners also gave Qalawun an opportunity to bolster his legitimacy through the caliph as Baybars had done, although al-Ḥākim himself was restricted to virtual house arrest during Qalawun's

165 Baybars al-Manṣūrī, *Zubdah*, 209. Qaidu's envoys were in Egypt in 1284–85/683 (Ibn al-Furāt, *Duwal*, VIII:1; also Nuwayrī, *Nihāyah*, XXVII:376). Qaidu apparently had sultanic banners from Baybars and Qalawun, and relations continued with him or with his heirs at least as late as 1307–08/707 (Mufaḍḍal, *Nahj*, 631–32). Möngke Temür may have encouraged the initial contact (see note 158 above), which may have also concerned economic interests like the slave trade. Biran, *Qaidu*, 62–63; Spuler, *Goldene Horde*, 54.

166 Ibn ʿAbd al-Ẓāhir, *Tashrīf*, 17–18.

167 *Ibid.*, 46; Nuwayrī, *Nihāyah*, XXXI:102–03; Baybars al-Manṣūrī, *Zubdah*, 234; Ibn al-Furāt, *Duwal*, VII:277. For Töde Möngke's Islam see DeWeese, *Islamization*, 86–88.

168 Ibrahim Artuk and Cevriye Artuk, *İstanbul Arkeoloji Müzeleri Teşirdeki İslâmî Sikkeler Kataloğu* (Istanbul, 1970–74), 814.

169 Jackson, "Dissolution," 195.

reign.[170] It therefore seems unlikely that the caliph sent his own banner to Saray. In addition to fulfilling Töde Möngke's petition, Qalawun made some unrecorded requests of the khan (perhaps for a continuation of trade relations?), all of which were granted.[171] But this was the last substantial mention of Qalawun's interactions with the Golden Horde, for Töde Möngke's rule was troubled, and did not last long.[172] After Töde Möngke's replacement with his nephew Töle Buqa in 1285/683–84 and Qalawun's death in 1290/689, Khalīl did take up the standard of diplomatic and ideological interaction, but unsuccessfully. Although he dispatched an embassy for Constantinople and Saray in 1292–93/692, Khalīl's own murder forced the ambassador to return early without completing his mission.[173] Thereafter the Golden Horde receded into the Mamluk chronicles' background until the later reigns of Qalawun's other son, the sultan al-Nāṣir Muḥammad.

170 Heidemann, *Kalifat*, 181; Spuler's theory that Töde Möngke became a vassal to the caliph here does not account for Qalawun's sultanic banner. Spuler, *Goldene Horde*, 255.

171 Ibn ʿAbd al-Ẓāhir, *Tashrīf*, 143.

172 Vernadsky, *Russia*, 176–78; Schamiloglu, "Golden Horde," 822.

173 Ibn Kathīr, *Bidāyah*, XIII:392; ʿAynī, *ʿIqd*, III:187; also Spuler, *Goldene Horde*, 71, albeit mistakenly assuming that the mission arrived.

CHAPTER 3

The age of Ilkhanid conversion (1295–1316/694–716)

After Khalīl's murder, his half-brother al-Nāṣir Muḥammad took over in December 1293/Muḥarram 693 at the age of eight, with real power in the hands of the military commander Kitbugha. Kitbugha deposed Muḥammad a year later to begin his own reign (r. 1294–96/694–96), then was himself overthrown by his vicegerent Lajin (r. 1296–99/696–98), whose murder led to Muḥammad's return (r. 1299–1309/698–708). It was during Muḥammad's second reign that the changes Qalawun had wrought to Baybars's ideology of religious Guardianship began to have an effect. In particular the notions of seniority in Islam and of a hierarchy in conversion allowed Muḥammad to combat the ideological specter of Ilkhanid conversion to Islam, which posed a serious challenge to Mamluk legitimacy.

The threat came from the Ilkhanid monarch and brand-new Muslim convert Ghazan (r. 1295–1304/694–703), who was a young, active and talented ruler.[1] After the death of the Great Khan Qubilai in China in 1294, Ghazan abandoned the fiction of subordination to China that his predecessors had maintained. Rather his energies, and those of his advisors, especially his chief minister, Rashīd al-Dīn, turned to the revitalization of his own territory and the creation of a new order. For this purpose Ghazan implemented a series of administrative and financial reforms, largely abandoned the title of "Ilkhan" for the strictly Islamic "Sultan" and "Emperor of Islam (*pādshāh-i Islām*)" and, for a brief period at the beginning of his reign, authorized his influential advisor Nauruz to destroy churches and exile Buddhists with enthusiastic bigotry.[2] Ghazan also became the first Ilkhanid ruler to break the Mongol

[1] For Ghazan's reign see Boyle, "Īl-Khāns," 379–97; B. Spuler, *Die Mongolen in Iran: Politik, Verwaltung und Kultur in der Ilchanenzeit (1220–1350)* 4th edn (Leiden, 1988), 79–90; Sir Henry H. Howorth, *History of the Mongols from the 9th to the 19th Century, III: Mongols of Persia* (London, 1876–1927), 393–533; for his conversion see Charles Melville, "*Pādshāh-i Islām*: The Conversion of Sultan Maḥmūd Ghāzān Khān," *Pembroke Papers* 1 (1990), 159–77; Amitai-Preiss, "Tradition," entire; also Calmard, "Chiisme," 269–71.

[2] For changes in Ghazan's titles see Thomas T. Allsen, "Changing Forms of Legitimation in Mongol Iran," in *Rulers from the Steppe: State Formation on the Eurasian Periphery. Proceedings of the Soviet–American Academic Symposia in Conjunction with the Museum Exhibition: "Nomads: Masters of the Eurasian Steppe,"* eds. Gary Seaman and Daniel Marks

tradition of secret burial for royalty by building an Islamic mausoleum complex for himself west of Tabriz. Inspired by tombs he had seen in Mashhad, Ghazan invested in an elaborate compound that included not only his tomb but two schools, quarters for mystics, a law center and a mosque, as well as a hospital, library, observatory, pool and fountain. Ghazan clearly sought to make a grand proclamation of his own royalty, since he ordered that the complex be more imposing than that built for the Seljuk sultan Sanjar (r. 1115–57/511–52) at Marv, which at the time was the largest known. Ghazan was later imitated in these architectural efforts by his brother and successor Öljeitü (r. 1304–16/703–16).[3]

During his reign Ghazan also initiated an aggressive series of campaigns into Mamluk territory in 1299–1300/699, 1300–01/700 and 1303/702 with the intention of forcing Mamluk submission.[4] Ghazan's new religion did not lead to solidarity with the self-consciously Muslim Mamluks, but rather gave him a religious basis for his call for Mamluk surrender, similar to that used by Tegüder. After his accession to the throne, in 1295–96/695 Ghazan sent a letter to Cairo announcing his conversion and obliquely demanding Mamluk submission to his rule. This he did by assuring the Mamluks that they had nothing to fear now as they had in the past; rather, merchants could go back and forth in peace, and the Mamluks could join all of Ghazan's other obedient subjects. In a typically Chingizid jab at Mamluk slave origins, he assured them that Egypt in particular should knuckle under to him since it was a land "where the throne has passed from kings to slaves." But to Ghazan's fury the Mamluks did not respond in any way, which was itself a refusal to submit to his authority.[5] Ghazan also experimented with using black flags, perhaps to challenge Abbasid authority in Cairo, or to link himself to Islamic eschatological ideas – he seems to have toyed with identifying himself as the Islamic centennial renewer (*mujaddid*), which itself

(Los Angeles, 1991), II:230–31; Amitai-Preiss, "Tradition," 6–7. For Nauruz's activities and downfall see Aubin, *Émirs mongols*, 61–68, although Jackson suggests that Ghazan soon abandoned this treatment of minorities; see Jackson, "Faith," 274–75. The use of titles on coins varies: the title "ilkhan" appears on two of Ghazan's copper coins without a great khan (Lane-Poole, *Catalogue*, X:101), but combinations of "Great Khan," "Sultan Maḥmūd" and "Ghazan" appear on others (Yapı Kredi Bank, *Ak Akçe: Moğol ve Ilhanlı Sikkeleri/Mongol and Ilkhanid Coins* [Istanbul, 1992], 74–79).

[3] For Ghazan's tomb see Rashīd al-Dīn, *Jāmiʿ*, II:1376. For this, and for Ghazan's and Öljeitü's buildings, see Sheila Blair, "Patterns of Patronage and Production in Ilkhanid Iran: The Case of Rashīd al-Dīn," in *Court*, 40–42, and "Religious Art," 123–29, and "The Mongol Capital of Sultaniyya: 'The Imperial,'" *Iran* 24 (1986), 139–51; O'Kane, "Monumentality," 506–09. On secret burial for Mongol royalty see DeWeese, *Islamization*, 184 and citations in notes 50, 51; 190–93.

[4] For the campaigns see Boyle, "Īl-Khāns," 387–95; Reuven Amitai, "Whither the Ilkhanid Army? Ghazan's First Campaign into Syria (1299–1300)," in *Warfare in Inner Asian History, 500–1800*, ed. N. Di Cosmo (Leiden, 2002), 221–64; D. O. Morgan, "The Mongols in Syria, 1260–1300," in *Crusade and Settlement: Papers Read at the First Conference of the Society for the Study of the Crusades and the Latin East and Presented to R. C. Smail*, ed. Peter W. Edbury (Cardiff, UK and Atlantic Highlands, NJ, 1985), 231–35.

[5] Vaṣṣāf, *Taʾrīkh*, 372 (not in Āyatī, *Taḥrīr*); de Somogyi, "Destruction," 354–55.

evoked Arghun's earlier claim to be the Lord of the Auspicious Conjunction.[6] Worse yet from the Mamluk point of view, Ghazan consistently styled himself as Guardian of Islam, which challenged the Mamluk sultan's own claims. To make matters more troubling, even ordinary Mamluk soldiers knew of Ghazan's conversion, and many believed it had been genuine, despite official Mamluk claims to the contrary. This led to a crisis of confidence in the Mamluk armies, and may have contributed to Mamluk weakness on the battlefield when Muslim Mamluks worried about the morality of fighting Muslim Mongols.[7] Within Mamluk territory the famous jurisconsult Aḥmad b. Taymīyah (d. 1328/728) went to great lengths to eradicate this dangerous notion from the minds of the army and the populace by describing the invasions as Shiite perversions, and the converted Mongols themselves as heretics and deviants.[8]

But in addition to the freshly Islamic cast of Ghazan's thinking, the new Ilkhanid sultan took enormous pride in his Chingizid heritage, and like many other nomadic converts, successfully combined the two distinct traditions into a single, amalgamated whole.[9] Ghazan's knowledge of Chingizid history was so great, for example, that he contributed enormously to the history of the Mongols written by Rashīd al-Dīn, while further signs of enduring Chingizid custom appeared in ceremonies and court protocol.[10] Ghazan's correspondence with the Mamluks also demonstrated the continued importance of Chingizid tradition, even though Ghazan's overall tone was self-consciously Islamic, while letters written for both Ghazan and Öljeitü to non-Mamluk rulers actually featured the idea that divine authority came from the Enduring Sky, and some of Ghazan's coins used both the Mongolian and Arabic names for God at the same time (Tengri and Allah).[11] Likewise shamanistic beliefs and practices remained important to Ghazan and to the newly converted Mongols who followed him: in 1298–99/698 the Ilkhanid armies aborted a winter campaign to either Anatolia or Syria when they encountered a series of storms in which lightning struck the camp. In a

6 For Arghun see Chapter 2. For the black flags see Melville, "Conversion," 164, 170–71; Jazarī, *Taʾrīkh*, I:286. For the centennial renewer, see the letters of Ghazan's first campaign below; Vaṣṣāf's description of Ghazan's advisor Nauruz in *Taʾrīkh*, 313 (not in Āyatī), and Nauruz's description of Ghazan himself in Davud Banākatī, *Taʾrīkh-i Banākatī* or *Rawḍ al-albāb fī tawārīkh al-akābir wa al-ansāb*, ed. Jaʿfar Shiʿār (Tehran, 1969), 454; also E. van Donzel, "Mudjaddid," *EI²* VII:290.

7 Thomas Raff, *Remarks on an Anti-Mongol Fatwà by Ibn Taīmiya* (Leiden, 1973), 11–12.

8 Raff, *Fatwà*, 5, 27, 38–59; Calmard, "Chiisme," 280–81; see also Dorothea Krawulsky, *Mongolen und Ilkhane, Ideologie und Geschichte: 5 Studien* (Tübingen, 1989), 137–38.

9 See DeWeese, *Islamization*, 51–59.

10 *The Compendium of Chronicles*, or *Jāmiʿ al-Tawārīkh*. Another contributor was Bolad Agha from the court of the Great Khans who lived with the Ilkhanids for twenty-odd years; see Allsen, "Cultural Broker," 7–22; Aigle, "Grand *jasaq*," 37–38. For other Chingizid customs see Tomoko Masuya, "Courtly Life," 81–84, and Blair, "Religious Art," 106–08.

11 Mostaert and Cleaves, "Trois documents," 471, and *Lettres*, 56–57; for coins see Yapı Kredi Bank, *Ak Akçe*, 75; Stephen Album, *Sylloge of Islamic Coins in the Ashmolean*, vol. IX (Oxford, 2001), xxvi, xl for coin references.

response reminiscent of ancient steppe water taboos, the Mongol forces interpreted the lightning as an evil omen and abandoned the campaign.[12] It is possible that Ghazan was elevated on a piece of felt at his coronation in solid nomadic style, but the evidence is inconclusive.[13] Ghazan also retained the trappings of shamanistic practices in his personal life. His Muslim marriage in autumn 1295/late 694 to his stepmother Bulaghan Khatun demonstrated an enduring respect for Mongol custom, in which a son was encouraged to marry any of his father's widows other than his own mother. Ghazan employed a Muslim official as celebrant at the wedding, and appeared to be unconcerned that the religion forbade such marriages.[14] Likewise Ghazan joined his Mongol commanders in a remarkably un-Islamic ceremonial dance around a ribbon-bedecked tree in autumn 1302/702 to give thanks for his rise to power against considerable odds.[15] Altaic steppe tradition also appeared in Ilkhanid architecture (Figures 3 and 4), for Öljeitü's otherwise Islamic-style tomb included a doorway that was oriented to the south in proper Mongol style, not southwest (in this case) towards Mecca (Ghazan's own tomb has not survived).[16]

In fact, even the question of Islam was unsettled for Ghazan and Öljeitü, both of whom wrestled with interpretations of faith despite their self-consciously Muslim status, and both of whom tended to favor Twelver Shiism.[17] In 1302–03/702, for example, the two became concerned when a Shiite descendant of the Prophet was murdered by Sunnis in Baghdad, allegedly because he was praying too much. A quote attributed to Ghazan demonstrated his complex allegiances:

> Muslim religious men say that he who prays more is increased in spiritual reward. How then can they kill someone for such a thing? Especially one who was a descendant of the Prophet! Even Chingiz Khan proclaimed that although Muslims and Islam are the seal of religion and rule, Muslims are the worst of people. I used to disagree with this, but now I see that Chingiz Khan was in fact correct.[18]

[12] Nuwayrī, *Nihāyah*, XXXI:351; Jazarī, *Ta'rīkh*, I:422–23; Author Z, *Beiträge*, 46; de Somogyi, "Destruction," 355.

[13] See Ron Sela, *Ritual and Authority in Central Asia: The Khan's Inauguration Ceremony* (Bloomington, IN, 2003), 25–42.

[14] Quran IV:22, "And marry not women whom your fathers married – except what is past: It was a shameful and odious – an abominable custom indeed." See also Boyle, "Īl-Khāns," 380; Masuya, "Courtly Life," 85–88; Reuven Amitai-Preiss, "Mongol Imperial Ideology and the Ilkhanid War against the Mamluks," in *Mongol Empire*, 68, and "Tradition," 2–3; Aigle, "Grand *jasaq*," 38.

[15] Boyle, "Īl-Khāns," 392; Amitai-Preiss, "Tradition," 9.

[16] Blair, "Patronage and Production," 42, also "Religious Art," 106–07; Masuya, "Courtly Life," 88–90; Amitai-Preiss, "Tradition," entire.

[17] See Calmard, "Chiisme," esp. 276–80, 282–84; Judith Pfeiffer, *Twelver Shī'ism in Mongol Iran* (Istanbul, 1999), entire; A. Bausani, "Religion Under the Mongols," *CHIr* V:538–49, esp. 541–45; also Ibn Baṭṭūṭah, *Travels*, II:302, 304.

[18] Abū al-Qāsim 'Abdallah Qāshānī, *Ta'rīkh-i pādshāh-i sa'īd Ghiyāth al-Dunyā wa al-Dīn Uljaytu Sulṭān Muḥammad*, ed. M. Hambly (Tehran, 1969), 91.

Figure 3. External view of Öljeitü's impressive tomb. (Photo courtesy of Dr. Robert Hillenbrand.)

Shock over the incident prompted the two men to investigate competing interpretations of Islam more closely, and ultimately revealed the fundamental flaws of the Sunni position. Öljeitü in particular realized that no group capable of murdering a man from the exalted lineage of the Prophet could be correct in its religious interpretations. After much discussion, the brothers realized that the very early history of the religion pointed to a usurpation of rule from its rightful place: the noble family of the Prophet Muḥammad through his daughter Fāṭimah and her sons. By consequence, all the major (Sunni) caliphal dynasties were illegitimate, among them the Abbasids, who had merely browbeaten everyone else into conforming with their views. Eventually Ghazan decided to proclaim his personal support of Shiite Islam, but was dissuaded by Rashīd al-Dīn, who recommended that Ghazan first take over Syria and Egypt and test his new religious allegiance in the sermons there before trying it in Ilkhanid territory. (Since Ghazan never established lasting control over Syria, however, the experiment never took place.)[19]

These musings about Abbasid illegitimacy must have been influenced by the Cairene Abbasid caliph al-Ḥākim, who had been routinely brandished by the Mamluks in diplomatic letters sent to the Ilkhanids since the days of Qalawun. Contempt for the Abbasids also surfaced in Ilkhanid historical

[19] Qāshānī, *Uljaytu*, 90–95; see also Krawulsky, *Studien*, 139–43.

Figure 4. Internal detail from Öljeitü's tomb. (Photo courtesy of Dr. Bernard O'Kane.)

writing: Rashīd al-Dīn consistently portrayed the dynasty as corrupt and oppressive, and lacking the divine favor (*dawlat*, also *farr-i izādah*) bestowed on the Ilkhanids themselves. Indeed, Rashīd al-Dīn's description of the death of the caliph al-Mustaʿṣim at Baghdad in 1258/656 portrayed the last bumbling scion of a dynasty whose day was over; this unfavorable image appeared in other Ilkhanid writings as well.[20] Visions both of the divine favor enjoyed

[20] Ibn Tiqtaqah denigrated the Abbasids in 1301/700–01 to the Ilkhanid governor of Mosul. Ibn Tiqtaqah, *al-Fakhrī fī al-adab al-sulṭānīyah wa al-duwal al-islāmīyah*, tr. C. E. J. Whitting (London, 1948), 14, 26, 28, 42.

by Ghazan and Öljeitü, and of Abbasid corruption, also surfaced in the Ilkhanid artistic tradition.[21] The Ilkhanid interest in Shiites can therefore be seen in part as a desire to establish a claim to Islamic authority that ran counter to the one enjoyed by the Mamluk-protected Abbasids in Cairo.

But despite Ghazan's undeniable desire to annex Mamluk territory, there was at first very little formal interaction after the Mamluk failure to respond to Ghazan's conversion announcement in 1295–96/695. Rather, contact between the two sides appeared as political rebellion when important dissidents from both sides fled to the enemy camp. The Mamluk dissidents were several commanders who had fallen foul of the sultan Lajin, among them the Mongol Mamluk governor of Syria, Sayf al-Dīn Qipchaq, and a commander from Egypt, Sayf al-Dīn Baktimur al-Silāḥdār. In December 1298–January 1299/Rabīʿ I 698 they fled across Syria to the Mongol-controlled town of Ra's al-ʿAyn. There they heard that Lajin had been assassinated on 15 January 1299/10 Rabīʿ II 698, but did not turn back for fear of a trap; instead they were sent on to Mosul, Baghdad and finally Wasit, where Ghazan welcomed them personally. These men were to play important roles in Ghazan's first invasion of Syria.

The rebel on the Ilkhanid side was Ghazan's governor in Anatolia, Sülemish, a non-Chingizid Muslim grandson of the Mongol military commander Baiju Noyan.[22] Perhaps as early as summer 1298/697 Sülemish began to consider rebellion, and sent an ambassador named Mukhliṣ al-Dīn al-Rūmī to the Mamluk sultan Lajin to establish a relationship.[23] No trace of Sülemish's letters remain, but from the surviving partial copy of the Mamluk response from (July–August 1298)/Shawwāl (697), it appears that Sülemish's approach to Lajin resembled the one used by the Anatolians who had written to Khalīl some years earlier: that is, Sülemish seems to have invoked the

[21] One image from the Great Mongol Shāhnāmah showed the mythic figure Farīdūn representing Hülegü as he wrested Iraq from the Abbasid caliph, who was portrayed as the tyrant Zahhāk. Ghazan was shown with a solar disk behind his head, representing divine favor. The intriguing and controversial theory linking these images with Mongol history comes from Abolala Soudavar, "The Saga of Abū-Saʿīd Bahādor Khān: The Abū-Saʿīdnāmé," in *Court*, 95, 130, 183; see also Hillenbrand, "Arts of the Book," 147–49 on Rashīd al-Dīn's *Compendium of Chronicles* and the absence of illustrations of the Abbasids, also 155–66, where he responds to Soudavar.

[22] Baiju Noyan was active in the region in the 1240s/640s and 1250s/650s. For Sülemish's rebellion in brief see Boyle, "Īl-Khāns," 385–87; for detail see Stewart, *Armenian Kingdom*, 128–35; also Cahen, *Turkey*, 225.

[23] It is difficult to date both Sülemish's correspondence with the Mamluks, and his rebellion. The Mamluk response to Sülemish's overture is dated Shawwāl, probably 697 (July–August 1298), since by July 1299/Shawwāl 698 Sülemish was most likely a prisoner. Stewart suggests that Sülemish wrote to Lajin, but did not go to Cairo until Muḥammad's reign; Stewart, *Armenian Kingdom*, 132–33. I suspect that Sülemish wrote twice: once to Lajin in summer 1298/697 (eliciting the response discussed here, which Stewart did not have), and once to Muḥammad in April 1299/Rajab 698. Also see Nuwayrī, *Nihāyah*, XXXI:373; Baybars al-Manṣūrī, *Zubdah*, 319; Abū al-Fidā', *The Memoirs of a Syrian Prince: Abū'l-Fidā', Sultan of Ḥamāh (672–732/1273–1331)*, tr. and ed. P. M. Holt (Wiesbaden, 1983), 30; Mufaḍḍal, *Nahj*, 460.

Mamluk ideal of religious Guardianship, since this concept was reflected in the heavily religious tone of the response.[24] The Mamluk text was a decree of appointment (*taqlīd*), and served to both bring Sülemish into the Mamluk political structure, and explain the ideological world into which he now had to fit. It focused on two lofty and intertwined points of Mamluk ideology: first, the universalist claim to rule enjoyed by the Mamluk sultan and the obedience that this claim demanded, and, second, the role of the Mamluk armies as the soldiers of God. According to the letter, God had made the Mamluk sultan inherit the earth, and then gave rule of it to him. Therefore, since obedience to God and the Prophet Muḥammad was intimately tied to obedience to those in power, the only way to cleave to God was to demonstrate obedience to His chosen ruler, the Mamluk sultan. In case Sülemish had any doubts about the divine favor claimed for Lajin, the letter also explained that all communities (*umam*) had been required to submit to him.

The concept of obedience to God and to His chosen ruler was a stoutly Islamic claim to universality that had developed much earlier in the Islamic political tradition, and provided a clear antidote to rival Chingizid claims. In the letter these arguments about obedience and universal Mamluk rule were interspersed with elaborate descriptions of the glorious Mamluk armies, which were portrayed as the soldiers chosen by God to be the party of victory. Their task was to defend Islam, support the sultan and help him maintain his control. God's direct intervention in history on the side of right was also made clear when the letter pointed out that it had been God Himself who took Sülemish away from Satan and led him to the Mamluk fold. The rest of the letter was less lofty but more practical: it accepted Sülemish's petition for recognition and aid, informed him that troops would be sent to him and formally appointed him governor of Anatolia. The decree closed by instructing Sülemish to fight the unbeliever (*kuffār*) enemies who were all around him, and, in a pointed reference to un-Islamic Mongol legal practices, to implement Islamic law in his territories, since that was the task of a good governor. The Mamluk intention here was to bring Sülemish into an established and self-consciously Islamic, anti-Mongol world view. Since Sülemish was a non-Chingizid whose own claim to legitimacy was weak, the Mamluk sultan became a natural ally and source of military support, while Mamluk notions of Islamically sanctioned kingship provided an alternative to the Chingizid model against which Sülemish himself was struggling. That said, they could also be dismissed later if necessary, for although in the Mamluk world Sülemish's position was necessarily a subordinate one, his ambitions were probably more extensive than he admitted to his brand-new patrons.

24 The author of the response, Maḥmūd al-Ḥalabī, worked in the administration in Cairo, and later ran the Damascus chancellery. See Shihāb al-Dīn Maḥmūd al-Ḥalabī, *Ḥusn al-tawassul ilà ṣināʿat al-tarassul*, ed. Akram ʿUthmān Yūsuf (Baghdad, 1980), 373–78; also Ṣuqāʿī, *Tālī*, 195; and a garbled discussion in Qalqashandī, *Ṣubḥ*, V:344, and the text, VII:370–77.

Several months after the exchange of letters, a bad winter in 1298–99/698 ensured that Anatolia was effectively cut off from Iran, allowing Sülemish to raise additional support for a rebellion. When news of Sülemish's insubordination reached Ghazan in his winter quarters near Wasit, he sent out two successive armies in February 1299/Jumādā I 698, which defeated Sülemish in battle on 27 April/24 Rajab. Sülemish was forced to flee to Mamluk territory with only a few companions.[25] Either shortly before the battle or immediately after losing it, Sülemish sent a second letter to ask for help from the Mamluk sultan, now the fifteen-year-old al-Nāṣir Muḥammad.[26] Then Sülemish himself arrived as a refugee in Mamluk territory, met with Muḥammad in Cairo, and left his brother there as a hostage.[27] In June/Ramaḍān Sülemish took troops from Aleppo to invade Anatolia and rescue his family, but this borrowed army was decimated by a Mongol and Armenian force. Sülemish himself was eventually captured, taken back to Ghazan and executed in horrible fashion in Tabriz on 27 September 1299/29 Dhū al-Ḥijjah 698.[28] Afterwards his body was burned in an indication of Ghazan's displeasure, and his ashes were scattered to the winds.[29]

In addition to the support they offered Sülemish, the Mamluks also sent independent raids into Ilkhanid territory during the summer of 1299/698. In June–July/Ramaḍān a Mamluk force ravaged the area around Mardin, which was controlled by the Ilkhanids' Muslim vassals, the Artuqids. The raiders looted everywhere, and in particular made off with a large number of riding animals. At least according to Ilkhanid sources, they also indulged in drinking and bad behavior, which seemed especially offensive in such a holy month. News of this reached Ghazan at Tabriz in the autumn. The Ilkhanid sultan was incensed and collected the necessary Islamic juridical support (*fatwàs*) to justify a military campaign against Muslims.[30] The moment was right for military action, since Ghazan was able to take advantage of his rebel

25 Karīm al-Dīn Maḥmūd al-Aqsarā'ī, *Müsâmeret ül-ahbar: Mogollar zamaninda Türkiye Selçuklari Tarihi*, ed. Osman Turan (Ankara, 1944), 245–46; Baybars al-Manṣūrī, *Tuḥfah*, 151, and *Zubdah*, 319; Yūnīnī, *Dhayl mir'āt al-zamān*, ed. and tr. Li Guo, *Early Mamluk Syrian Historiography: al-Yūnīnī's Dhayl mir'āt al-zamān* (Leiden, 1998), II:64–66 (Arabic), I:121–22 (English); Mufaḍḍal, *Nahj*, 463; also see Stewart, *Armenian Kingdom*, 130–33; Boyle, "Īl-Khāns," 385.

26 The ambassadors passed through Damascus in April 1299/Rajab 698, on their way to Cairo. Yūnīnī/Guo, *Dhayl*, II:64 (Arabic), I:121 (English); also see Ibn al-Dawādārī, *Kanz*, IX:8; Author Z, *Beiträge*, 55; 'Aynī, *'Iqd*, III:400–01; Maqrīzī, *Sulūk*, I:876–78.

27 Baybars al-Manṣūrī, *Tuḥfah*, 151, and *Zubdah*, 319; Nuwayrī, *Nihāyah*, XXXI:375; also 'Aynī, *'Iqd*, III:401; Maqrīzī, *Sulūk*, I:876–77.

28 Rashīd al-Dīn, *Jāmi'*, II:1289; also see Nuwayrī, *Nihāyah*, XXXI:375; Baybars al-Manṣūrī, *Tuḥfah*, 151, and *Zubdah*, 319; Ibn al-Dawādārī, *Kanz*, IX:10; Maqrīzī, *Sulūk*, I:878; 'Aynī, *'Iqd*, III:401.

29 Rashīd al-Dīn, *Jāmi'*, II:1289; Banākatī, *Ta'rīkh*, 460 (saying the 21st/23rd).

30 Mamluk sources say little about this raid, even though it spurred Ghazan's first invasion. The exception is Abū al-Fidā', *Memoirs*, 35. Also see Rashīd al-Dīn, *Jāmi'*, II:1289–90; [Pseudo] Ibn al-Fuwaṭī, *al-Ḥawādith al-jāmi'ah wa al-tajārib al-nāfi'ah fī al-mi'ah al-sābi'ah*, ed. Mahdī al-Najum (Beirut, 2003), 337, 338; Vaṣṣāf, *Ta'rīkh*, 372–73, and Āyatī, *Taḥrīr*, 222.

Mamluk guests and their familiarity with the terrain and forts in question; by now he also held a grudge against the Mamluks, first for refusing to acknowledge his conversion, and second for helping Sülemish.

The first campaign

In October 1299/Muḥarram 699 Ghazan set out for Mamluk Syria with a combined force of Mongols, Armenians and Georgians. As he did so, he sent one Yaʿqūb al-Sikurjī and a group of religious men to Mamluk territory to issue a final warning of his intentions and demand Muḥammad's immediate submission. But the envoys were viewed askance and imprisoned.[31] Ghazan also sought to drum up support from Henry II of Cyprus (r. 1284–1324), but the effort at coordination failed.[32] Nevertheless, Ghazan defeated the Mamluks at the battle of Wādī al-Khaznadār on 22 December 1299/27 Rabīʿ I 699 near Homs, and went on to occupy Damascus for five weeks. During his occupation he appointed governors, who were the rebel Mamluk commanders Qipchaq and Baktimur, and heavily taxed the Damascene population. Military endeavors of the occupation period included some (allegedly) unauthorized looting in the city's outskirts, raiding to the south and west as far as Jerusalem and Hebron, and a long and unsuccessful siege of the Damascus citadel, whose commander, one Arjuwash, flatly refused to surrender.[33] Ghazan set out for home in early February 1300/mid-Jumādà II 699, leaving behind his new governors, his Mongol military commanders and two armies to hold the territory. But the Mongol commanders and armies headed east shortly after Ghazan and abandoned all of greater Syria to Qipchaq and Baktimur. Both men promptly transferred their allegiance back to the Mamluk sultan, whose advisors had reestablished control of the area by spring.[34]

[31] This information comes from the text of Ghazan's letter in Nuwayrī, *Nihāyah*, XXXI:427; also in Baybars al-Manṣūrī, *Zubdah*, 352; ʿAynī, *ʿIqd*, IV:134; Maqrīzī, *Sulūk*, I:1016. One Mamluk author referred to this irregularity in the timing of the diplomatic mission years later: "At that time they [the Ilkhanids] would send messengers, and [themselves] be right behind them." Ibn al-Dawādārī, *Kanz*, IX:51. For Sikurjī, an officer – perhaps a parasol-bearer – in the khan's employ, see Baron Constantin d'Ohsson, *Histoire des Mongols, depuis Tchinguiz-Khan jusqu'à Timour Bey, ou Tamerlan* (Amsterdam and The Hague, 1835), IV:289, note 2.

[32] Peter Edbury, *The Kingdom of Cyprus and the Crusades, 1191–1374* (Cambridge, 1991), 104.

[33] See Reuven Amitai, "The Mongol Occupation of Damascus in 1300: A Study of Mamluk Loyalties," in *The Mamluks in Egyptian Politics and Society*, eds. Michael Winter and Amalia Levanoni (Leiden, 2004), 21–41.

[34] For the most complete description of Ghazan's actions at Damascus see Yūnīnī/Guo, *Dhayl*, II:99–124 (Arabic) and I:135–64 (English), and de Somogyi, "Destruction," 360–81. For the campaign see also Ibn al-Dawādārī, *Kanz*, IX:15–36; Author Z, *Beiträge*, 56–79; alternative reports in Nuwayrī, *Nihāyah*, XXXI:380–400; Baybars al-Manṣūrī, *Zubdah*, 328–45, and *Tuḥfah*, 156–59; Mufaḍḍal, *Nahj*, 471–506. In Persian see Rashīd al-Dīn, *Jāmiʿ*, II:1289–96; Banākatī, *Taʾrīkh*, 460–63; Vaṣṣāf, *Taʾrīkh*, 371–81, and Āyatī, *Taḥrīr*, 222–29; Muḥammad b. Khwāndamīr aka Mīrkhwānd, *Rawḍat al-ṣafāʾ fī sīrat al-anbiyāʾ wa al-mulūk wa al-khulafāʾ*,

This first of Ghazan's three Syrian campaigns devastated the countryside and the Syrian economy, but also produced five texts related to Ghazan's occupation of Damascus. All promulgated the ilkhan's new Muslim identity as Guardian of Islam, but simultanously echoed with a Mongol imperial ideology reminiscent of earlier Ilkhanid letters. All were issued by the Ilkhanid chancellery, possibly in Mongolian, but were recorded by Mamluk historians in Arabic. The texts illuminated both the hostilities between the two sides, and Ghazan's ideology. At the time of this campaign, Ghazan was a dynamic adult, and had ruled for several years in his own right. The ideology he deployed therefore reflected his kingly aspirations. It turned on three main ideas: the Guardianship of Islam, the fitness of kings to rule and the question of a king's divine support. Ghazan assumed the role of Guardian of Islam for himself, explained that God had favored him in that role and as king, and argued that all others were unfit to rule by comparison. With this appropriation of the ideal of Guardianship, Ghazan effectively cut the ideological legs out from under the Mamluk sultan. The Mamluks became targets of Ghazan's divinely supported righteous rage, and appeared in his letters as bad Muslims or hypocrites who routinely oppressed their subjects. Ghazan claimed that the Mamluks enjoyed no divine support whatsoever, and were inherently unfit for rule because of their lowly ethnic origins, their slavery and the stunning irregularity of their system of succession. Ghazan also used the Mamluks' appalling ignorance of kingly behavior and proper diplomatic protocol as evidence for Muḥammad's unfitness for rule. In the letters Ghazan also touched on two concepts dear to his heart: the possibility of winning the loyalty of Mamluk soldiery away from the sultan, and the rightful prominence of the descendants of Fāṭimah and ʿAlī. At other moments he appealed to Islamic notions of the king as the bringer and arbiter of justice. Despite his new fascination with his status as a Muslim ruler, however, Ghazan continued to show his enthusiasm for his own Chingizid heritage, although it was expressed in Islamic wording. Ghazan's audience for these bold proclamations was the population of Syria, whether religious officials, ordinary people or those Mamluk military personnel who had not fled to Cairo after Wādī al-Khaznadār. Ghazan's purpose was to show how much more he deserved to rule than Muḥammad, thus the ideological arguments he employed all underscored an implicit or even explicit comparison between himself and the Mamluk ruling elite.

Although Ghazan did not enter the city of Damascus during his occupation, he interacted actually and ideologically with the city's inhabitants in several ways. The first contact occurred shortly after the battle, before Ghazan had even arrived outside Damascus. Those Damascenes who had not already fled for Cairo decided that their best chance of preservation lay in

ed. Jamshīd Kayānfar (Tehran, 2001–02), V:4234–41. For modern treatments see Boyle, "Īl-Khāns," 387–89; Stewart, *Armenian Kingdom*, 136–46, especially on the role of Hetʿum II; Amitai, "Whither?"; Morgan, "Mongols in Syria."

sending a delegation to Ghazan. After much debate, a number of religious officials set out in late December 1299/early Rabīʿ II 699 to meet the approaching ruler and beg mercy for the city.[35] When he met with the dignitaries, Ghazan informed them that he had already prepared a guarantee of peace (*amān*) for Damascus.[36] Perhaps at the same meeting, Ghazan had an interesting conversation with his Damascene guests, which illuminated his belief in his own superior lineage and fitness for rule, and his corresponding contempt for Muḥammad's undeserved sovereignty. At the meeting Ghazan asked the Damascenes: "Who am I?" They responded by citing his lineage back to Chingiz Khan. Ghazan then asked: "Who is al-Nāṣir's [Muḥammad's] father?" The Damascenes responded, "Alfī," for Qalawun al-Alfī, which was one of Qalawun's nicknames. Then Ghazan asked: "Who was Alfī's father?" Qalawun's ancestry, of course, was unknown, since he had begun his military career as a mamluk. At this the notables fell silent and did not answer, once they realized that Muḥammad's claim to rule was illegitimate (*nā-istiḥqāqī*).[37] Although uncorroborated by the Arabic histories, this anecdote appeared prominently in an official Ilkhanid history. It demonstrated Ghazan's low view of Mamluk slave origin and his correspondingly high opinion of his own Chingizid, divinely favored lineage. Clearly the Ilkhanid disdain for Mamluk slavery as expressed by Hülegü and Abaqa was alive and well in Ghazan's mind.

The first written text from this campaign was the guarantee of peace (*amān*) that Ghazan promised the Damascene notables when they met with him. It was dated 30 December 1299/5 Rabīʿ II 699, and its stated audience included not only "those who have come into obedience to us," meaning the Damascenes, but also Ghazan's own armies.[38] The guarantee described Ghazan's conversion, achieved by God's bestowal of the light of faith on him, and Ghazan's subsequent realization that Mamluk rule was oppressive. It argued that the Mamluks had demonstrated their unfitness to rule by abandoning (or deviating from, *khārijūn ʿan*) the proper path of religion. This they did by failing to exhibit any sort of faith, loyalty, or attention to the requirements and covenants of religion. Their rule was not ordered and systematic, and, far worse, they oppressed their subjects by fleecing them

[35] de Somogyi, "Destruction," 365. Rashīd al-Dīn has 31 December 1299/6 Rabīʿ II, with Ghazan arriving outside Damascus on 3 January/9 Rabiʿ II. Rashīd al-Dīn, *Jāmiʿ*, II:1293.

[36] Ibn al-Dawādārī, *Kanz*, IX:20; de Somogyi "Destruction," 366; Yūnīnī/Guo, *Dhayl*, II:102 (Arabic) and I:139 (English); also Nuwayrī, *Nihāyah*, XXXI:387–88.

[37] Rashīd al-Dīn, *Jāmiʿ*, II:1293–94; Banākatī, *Taʾrīkh*, 461–62; de Somogyi, "Destruction," 358–59, note 17.

[38] For this text and event see Nuwayrī, *Nihāyah* XXXI:389–92; Ibn al-Dawādārī, *Kanz*, IX:20–23; Author Z, *Beiträge*, 60, 62–63; Yūnīnī/Guo, *Dhayl*, II:102–04 (Arabic) and I:139–42 (English, which has superseded the translation by Howorth, *Mongols of Persia*, 441–43); Dhahabī, "Ṭabaqāt," MS 10697, fols. 125b–126b; Maqrīzī, *Sulūk*, I:1011–12; ʿAynī, *ʿIqd*, IV:40 (partial text); Mufaḍḍal, text and French translation, *Nahj*, 476–80; for the event but no text see de Somogyi, "Destruction," 365–67.

unjustly. Despite the religious terminology – especially the use of "*khārijūn ʿan*," which evoked the early Kharijite rebels against the fourth caliph ʿAlī (r. 656–61/35–40), and which also appeared in Ghazan's other letters from this campaign – the concept of deviating from the path of religion also resembled the idea that rebels deviated from obedience to the imperial house.

Next the text cast Ghazan as the defender of Muslims and their rights by describing his overwhelming desire to protect religion from these oppressors. It showed Ghazan as the Just King, promising himself that he would implement justice throughout Syria if only God would grant him victory. When God did in fact lead Ghazan to defeat the Mamluk armies at Wādī al-Khaznadār, this proved not only the rightness of Ghazan's actions, but also the unmistakable divine support that Ghazan enjoyed. As evidence of Ghazan's justice, the letter pointed out that he had specifically ordered his armies not to plunder Damascus, its environs or any Muslim territory in Syria at all. This suggested an ideological rapport between Ghazan and the Damascenes, since a Muslim ruler forbidding his troops from plundering Muslim lands was much better than a ruler of one religion plundering the people of another. The purpose of Ghazan's orders was soon made clear: the Damascenes were told to go back to their business and work to rebuild their territory. To the Mamluk historians writing after the fact, however, this argument was seriously undermined by the behavior of some of Ghazan's troops – possibly Mongols, possibly Armenians – who sacked and burned the neighborhood of Sālihīyah outside Damascus in mid-January/mid-to-late Rabīʿ II, and captured some of its inhabitants. Ghazan's failure to control his soldiers as they harassed Muslims did not support the ideal of Islamic solidarity. In a possible later addition to the original guarantee, Ghazan dismissed the events at Ṣāliḥīyah as a small-scale aberration, not to be feared and unlikely to be repeated, and indicated that he had already executed the culprits to set an example for the rest of his armies.[39]

Then in a point reminiscent of earlier Mongol religious tolerance (or indifference), although at odds with the pogroms early in his own reign, Ghazan informed his soldiers and the Damascenes of his duty as a good Muslim ruler to care for Jews, Christians and Sabians as if they, too, were Muslims. This argument was supported by a quote from the fourth caliph ʿAlī, who was made to say that protected peoples paid their money as if it were Muslim money, with the result that their blood became like Muslim blood. The reference to the inviolability of minority religions may have been

[39] The reference to Ṣāliḥīyah makes dating the letter difficult. Most accounts say that Ṣāliḥīyah was looted in mid-January/mid-to-late Rabīʿ II, that is, after the composition of this letter (dated 30 December 1299/5 Rabīʿ II). I suspect this final paragraph was added later. See de Somogyi, "Destruction," 369–71, 375; Yūnīnī/Guo, *Dhayl*, II:108 (Arabic) and I:145–46 (English); Ibn al-Dawādārī, *Kanz*, IX:23–24; also Nuwayrī, *Nihāyah*, XXXI:395–96; Baybars al-Manṣūrī, *Tuḥfah* 158, and *Zubdah*, 332; Author Z, *Beiträge*, 68; Stewart, *Armenian Kingdom*, 140–45.

suggested to Ghazan by the Armenian king Het'um II, or by the Georgians who had also accompanied Ghazan on the campaign, while the reference to 'Alī indicated Ghazan's interest in Shiite personalities as antidotes to the Abbasid caliph. Beginning on 8 January 1300/14 Rabī' II 699, Damascene preachers began to give the Friday sermons in Ghazan's name to show the change in leadership in Syria.[40]

Ghazan's second, undated text was addressed to the Mamluk military commanders of Syria.[41] During the occupation it was sent to the governors of all the Syrian forts, but none ever surrendered despite the letter's threatening tone. The governors were probably strengthened by their knowledge that Mamluk forces were mustering a second time, which was communicated to the Syrian strongholds by carrier pigeon.[42] Although this second letter presented recognizably Islamic notions of kingship, in it echoes of Mongol imperial dissatisfaction were far more clearly – and threateningly – revealed, albeit still cloaked in religious terminology. It began with a discussion of those prophets sent by God to show the world the path of righteousness. Last of them was Muḥammad, whom everyone had to follow on pain of eternal hellfire. Unfortunately, the letter continued darkly, after the time of Muḥammad the community had gone astray, and Islamic law was no longer enforced. Fortunately, God also sent individuals (periodically) from among the rulers to refresh the religion. Recently, however, tyrants and rebels against God had emerged, among them not only polytheists and idol-worshippers, but – in a clear allusion to the Mamluks – so-called Muslims who did not truly believe, who failed to follow the tenets of Islam and who oppressed their own subjects by robbing them. In response, God brought about the miraculous conversion of Ghazan himself. The sequence of arguments in the letter suggested that Ghazan was the Islamic centennial renewer of religion, or *mujaddid*, although the word *mujaddid* itself did not appear.[43] To prove the point, the letter listed the good deeds that Ghazan had accomplished after his conversion, which included fighting enemies of the faith like the rulers of Egypt and Syria.

Then, in an expression of imperial Mongol ideology cloaked in religious terminology, the letter chastised the Mamluks for failing to submit to Ghazan as God's chosen sovereign, and for harboring Sülemish and providing him with an army, which by Mongol standards was clearly rebellious behavior. It condemned the Mamluks on religious grounds by presenting Sülemish as an Islamic dissident (*khārijī*) and an apostate (*murtadd*), even though these

40 de Somogyi, "Destruction," 368; Yūnīnī/Guo, *Dhayl*, II:107 (Arabic) and I:144 (English); Nuwayrī, *Nihāyah*, XXXI:394; Author Z, *Beiträge*, 66; also Ibn al-Dawādārī, *Kanz*, IX:37.

41 For this text see Baybars al-Manṣūrī, *Zubdah*, 333–37, who claims that it was written near the end of Ghazan's tenure in Damascus (i.e., February–March/Jumādà II, 333); also 'Aynī, *'Iqd*, IV:48–56.

42 A carrier pigeon brought this news to the Damascus citadel, which suggests that additional pigeons went to the other forts and citadels in Syria. Author Z, *Beiträge*, 65; Yūnīnī/Guo, *Dhayl*, II:106 (Arabic) and I:143 (English).

43 van Donzel, "Mudjaddid."

deliberately Islamic terms could also apply in Mongol ideology to someone who was a political rebel against the Chingizids. Here, too, the denunciation was based on the notion of unfitness to govern, so that Sülemish was reviled for oppressing Muslims in Anatolia, taking their money and destroying their homes. The letter then took up a new point of criticism: the Mamluk system of succession. In a reference to the fractious Mamluk politics of the 1290s/690s, it denigrated the Mamluks' tendency to establish rulers, swear loyalty to them, and then break their oaths and murder the sultans within a few months. The implication here was that Mamluk politics were disordered, and would be better replaced by Ilkhanid rule. The letter also used the Mamluks' ignorance of kingly behavior to illuminate how unfit they were to rule. Specifically it faulted their refusal to send greetings and gifts when Ghazan converted to Islam, which was a coded way of criticizing them for failing to submit politically to Ghazan's rule through the ceremonial presentation of congratulatory presents.

Ghazan then threatened the Mamluk commanders with a terrifying unity among Mongol princes, saying that he had come to an agreement (?) with his relatives, which included not only the Great Khan Temür, but also Qaidu of the Chagatai Khanate and Noqai and Toqta of the Golden Horde; because of this agreement, Ghazan himself was able to invade Mamluk territory with "unending armies" of all nations in order to deflect evil from Muslims.[44] He added that if the Mamluk governors were good people (i.e., "submissive"), they would welcome these armies. The letter ended by ordering the Mamluk governors to add Ghazan's name to sermons, turn out to greet him upon his approach and provide religious persons to escort him to the tombs of saints and other holy sites. Adding that Ghazan had sworn an oath to perform the pilgrimage soon, the letter closed with a final demand for submission to Ilkhanid rule, and a warning about the dire consequences of failing to do so.

The third and fourth Ilkhanid texts were decrees (*firmāns*), in which Ghazan appointed the two rebel Mamluk commanders, Qipchaq and Baktimur, to be his governors in southern and northern Syria.[45] The decree for Qipchaq, dated 2 February 1300/10 Jumādà I 699, presented a brief version of Ghazan's belief that God had granted him both worldly and eternal rule: "When God, may He be exalted, blessed us with faith and guided us to the most noble of the religions, we praised him and thanked him for 'adding to our rule of the earthly world our rule in the afterlife (*aḍāfa ilā mulkinā lil-dunyā mulkanā lil-ākhirah*).'"[46] The decree presented Ghazan as

[44] Baybars al-Manṣūrī, *Zubdah*, 336. This mysterious reference cannot mean the peace of 1304/703–04, which was concluded after Ghazan's death; see below for Öljeitü's reign.

[45] The decree for Qipchaq is in Baybars al-Manṣūrī, *Zubdah*, 340–41; Maqrīzī, *Sulūk*, I:1013–15; and ʿAynī, *ʿIqd*, IV:60–63; Mufaḍḍal, text and French translation in *Nahj*, 484–89. The text in Author Z, *Beiträge*, 66–68 is really a corrupt copy of the decree for Baktimur, which is found in its entirety in Baybars al-Manṣūrī, *Zubdah*, 342–43; ʿAynī, *ʿIqd*, IV:63–65.

[46] Baybars al-Manṣūrī, *Zubdah*, 340.

the arbiter of justice by claiming that when he heard of the injustice of the Mamluk rulers, he decided to make Islam triumphant and do God's work. To that end he wrote and warned the Mamluks through repeated letters and sermons, but they did not pay attention. This neatly combined Quranic references to religious warners with the Mongol tradition of warning beleaguered cities and rulers of their need to submit.

Thereafter, the decree continued, Ghazan met the Mamluks in battle, won, and reintroduced Godliness into the world. Then Ghazan, as the divinely chosen arbiter of justice, chose Qipchaq to administer that same justice in the realm. The decree reiterated that all persons were to obey Qipchaq completely, and enumerated the places under Qipchaq's jurisdiction as Damascus, Baalbak, Homs, ʿAjlūn, al-Raḥbah, ʿArīsh, Salāmīyah, and the coast and mountains. Stipulating that Qipchaq was to work in agreement with the chief Mongol official left behind, one Nāṣir al-Dīn, the decree listed the paraphernalia given to Qipchaq on this occasion: a sword, a banner, a drum and a golden tablet (*paizah*), which was surmounted with a lion's head and bore a written statement authorizing Qipchaq in his new position. He was also appointed an honor guard of 1,000 Mongols. The decree for Baktimur was similar, although Baktimur was responsible for Aleppo, Hama, Shayzar, Antioch, Baghras, those forts on the Euphrates not under Qipchaq's jurisdiction, Hromgla, Bahasna and all outlying areas.

The final surviving text of this campaign was written after the decrees and addressed to the Syrians in general.[47] Issued shortly before Ghazan left Damascus, it served as a 'State of the Khanate' address, and was the most openly Chingizid and least Islamic of Ghazan's surviving first-campaign letters. The text began with the Mongol imperial notion of the divine support for Chingizid rule when it informed the Syrians that God had bestowed royal authority on Chingiz Khan, from whom Ghazan was sixth in line: "Our grandfather Chingiz Khan was a king and the son of a king to seven degrees in Mongol lands. When God, may He be exalted, supported him, he took over the inhabited quarter of the world with his sword. Nowhere in the histories since the time of Adam to today, has it come to us that anyone ruled the territory that Chingiz Khan ruled, or was supported with such divine support. We are the sixth king [descended from] his loins."[48] Ghazan then made clear his corresponding contempt both for the unstable Mamluk system of succession and for the lowliness of Mamluk origins: "Every little while they choose a Mamluk of the lowliest race (*min ardhal al-ajnās*) from among themselves, make him rule over Islam and set him up over humanity. They thought this was what rule was about, but they do not [even] distinguish the path of deliverance from ruin."[49]

[47] For this text see *ibid.*, 337–39; ʿAynī, *ʿIqd*, IV:56–59.
[48] Baybars al-Manṣūrī, *Zubdah*, 337–38. [49] *Ibid.*, 338.

Again Ghazan criticized the Mamluks' ignorance of kingly behavior, shown through their refusal to congratulate him in 1295–96/695, and this time offered a new explanation for their failure: they were secretly afraid that their soldiers would desert to him once they knew he was a Muslim. Ghazan mocked the Mamluks as too stupid to realize that rule comes from God, as it did even to the non-Muslim Chingiz Khan. Then in another example both of Ghazan's Shiite leanings and of his antipathy to the Abbasids he wryly observed that: "If rule is obtained through piety, then the sons of Fāṭimah would be stronger and mightier [candidates] for the caliphate."[50] Ghazan censured the Mamluks again for their raid on Mardin and for helping Sülemish, and reminded them that their defeat at Wādī al-Khaznadār was a sign of God's displeasure.

Finally Ghazan referred to a discussion he had had with some of his military commanders. They had told him that the Mamluks had been murdering Muslims in Ilkhanid territory for forty years, and had killed as many people there as lived in Egypt and Syria combined. In a blatantly nomadic willingness to uproot settled peoples, the commanders suggested that Ghazan simply relocate all the inhabitants of Mamluk territory to the Ilkhanate as compensation. But with a lordly display of concern for his new flock that both showed the Syrians how much he cared for their welfare, and warned them of the dangers he was averting from them, Ghazan refused to comply. The letter concluded with a summation of the numbers and locations of Ghazan's troops, the names of governors appointed to keep the peace and an invitation to Mamluk soldiers, who were told that if they wanted to work for Ghazan, they would be granted appropriate estates as a reward. However, no one took him up on this offer, and by late May/early Ramaḍān, Syria was firmly back in Mamluk hands.

The second campaign

Ghazan invaded Mamluk territory again in the winter of 1300–01/700, but snow and rain held up the Ilkhanids near Aleppo and the Mamluks at Gaza, ultimately preventing the two sides from meeting at all.[51] This time the Cypriots sailed to meet Ghazan but did not reach him, and in February/Jumādà I Ghazan headed back to his own territory.[52] As a sign of his reverence for Islamic history, and his particular interest in ʿAlī, Ghazan took the opportunity to visit Muslim tombs near the historic site of the battle of Ṣiffīn in 657/37. Later in May–June 1301/Ramaḍān 700, while campaigning in the Kurdish mountains, Ghazan had a new text composed and sent to

[50] *Ibid.*
[51] Yūnīnī/Guo, *Dhayl*, II:205–07 (Arabic) and I:175–77 (English); de Somogyi, "Destruction," 382–86; Mufaḍḍal, *Nahj*, 536–44; Vaṣṣāf, *Ta'rīkh*, 396, and Āyatī, *Taḥrīr*, 239; Mīrkhwānd, *Rawḍah*, V:4242; also Boyle, "Īl-Khāns," 389–90; Stewart, *Armenian Kingdom*, 146–49.
[52] Edbury, *Cyprus*, 105–06.

Muḥammad.[53] This is the only surviving diplomatic letter from Ghazan to Muḥammad, and was dispatched with a small group of envoys to Syria, who were lodged in the Damascus citadel for reasons of security, then whisked to Cairo, where they arrived in July–August/Dhū al-Qaʿdah and were seen immediately.[54]

The letters preserved from Ghazan's first campaign had addressed the Syrian population, and had promoted Ghazan to the Syrians as a rightly guided alternative to Mamluk rule. By contrast, Ghazan's diplomatic letter of summer 1301/700 was directed to the Mamluk sultan himself, along with his advisors, generals, scribes and court. It was not designed to win anyone over, but rather clarified the military and political situation, explained Muḥammad's position in it and issued an official warning about the dire consequences of Muḥammad's behavior. Although when conversing with the sultan and his advisors the envoys spoke of a peace agreement between Muḥammad and Ghazan, their letter made it clear that this was a Mongol-style peace.[55] The letter was in fact no more than an imperial demand for submission: it announced to a would-be subject that the Mongol ruler enjoyed divine support, explained that obedience to the ruler and to God was mandatory, and warned of retribution should the subject fail to submit. The letter was only distinguished from similar demands composed for Ghazan's predecessors by the historical details Ghazan chose to include, and by the fact that the letter expressed imperial ideas exclusively in Islamic terminology. Unlike the letters to the Syrians, however, it did not disparage the Mamluk systems of rule and succession, nor present Ghazan as the arbiter of justice.

Ghazan's letter opened with an unequivocal statement of Muḥammad's rebelliousness against God and against God's chosen ruler, as shown when he allowed his soldiers to raid Mardin in 1299/698: "Let the exalted sultan al-Nāṣir know that in the previous year [*sic*], some of his corrupt soldiers raided our borders and wreaked havoc there, 'in opposition to God and in opposition to us (*li-ʿinād Allah wa ʿinādinā*).'"[56] It highlighted Ghazan's own fervor to defend his subjects and quash the rebel, and established that Ghazan had followed appropriate kingly procedure by sending a warning to Muḥammad immediately before the battle of Wādī al-Khaznadār. The letter then rebuked Muḥammad for his persistence in the error of independence, as well as his shoddy treatment of Ghazan's ambassadors: "You insulted them

[53] For this text see Nuwayrī, *Nihāyah*, XXXI:426–30; Baybars al-Manṣūrī, *Zubdah*, 352–53; ʿAynī, *ʿIqd*, IV:133–37; Maqrīzī, *Sulūk*, I:1016–18; French translation in D'Ohsson, *Histoire des Mongols*, IV:288–93.

[54] The envoys were the commander Nāṣir al-Dīn ʿAlī Khwājā and the judge Kamāl al-Dīn b. Yūnus of Mosul; Nuwayrī, *Nihāyah*, XXXI:426; Baybars al-Manṣūrī, *Tuḥfah*, 161, and *Zubdah*, 352; de Somogyi, "Destruction," 386 (without names).

[55] Nuwayrī, *Nihāyah*, XXXI:426; ʿAynī, *ʿIqd*, IV:132–33; also see Amitai-Preiss, "Imperial Ideology," 66–67.

[56] Nuwayrī, *Nihāyah*, XXXI:427.

and imprisoned them, and broke the tradition of kings in proper behavior."[57] Although the unfitness of Mamluk rule was not as important a theme in this letter as it had been in the Syrian ones, this still allowed Ghazan to assert his own superior knowledge of kingly behavior and diplomatic protocol.

The letter then underscored Ghazan's divine support by pointing out that God had led him to victory over the Mamluks at Wādī al-Khaznadār, and continued with a statement of Ghazan's desire that the Mamluks submit by offering an apology for their transgressions:

> [After our victory] we thought that ... perhaps they would make amends for their previous [faults], mend what they had torn apart with their treachery, and send an apology to us ... So we waited in Damascus without hurry, and held back [from departing] in the manner of those enjoying power and control. But their negligence prevented them from trying to make peace.[58]

Next the letter took up Ghazan's failed invasion of winter 1300–01/700, and blamed Mamluk cowardice for the lack of a battle. It did not mention the weather, or Ghazan's own losses of men and animals to cold and disease, but portrayed Ghazan's return to Ilkhanid territory as caused by his concern for the populace of Syria. The letter closed by enumerating the qualifications of the two ambassadors, and reminded the Mamluks that they must soon surrender to Ilkhanid rule: "After the warning, no one is excused. If you [lit. they] do not make amends for this matter, then the blood and possessions of the Muslims will [be spilled and] go unavenged because of your actions."[59]

An official Mamluk response was composed on 3 October 1301/28 Muḥarram 701 and sent back with Ghazan's own envoys.[60] Although written for Muḥammad, however, it did not present the sultan's opinions, for Muḥammad was still a powerless teenager, and in no position to assert himself to anyone. (Muḥammad's own diplomatic voice did not emerge until his third reign began in 1310/709.) Therefore it was the collective personality of the chancellery that promulgated Mamluk notions of legitimacy. Although it has been suggested that the letter was generally conciliatory, the text does not support such a conclusion.[61] Rather, the letter's tone was cautiously derogatory. By Mamluk standards, Muḥammad's confrontation with Ghazan closely resembled Qalawun's defiance of Tegüder, thus some of the arguments used to substantiate Muḥammad's position were simply recycled from points made during Qalawun's reign. Other ideas were developments of these earlier arguments, such as the charge that Ghazan's status as a

[57] *Ibid.* Imprisonment here probably refers to Mamluk restrictions on Ilkhanid envoys like night travel and house arrest. Also see Holt, "Embassies," 132.

[58] Nuwayrī, *Nihāyah*, XXXI:428. [59] *Ibid.*, 429.

[60] For this text see *ibid.*, 430–42; Baybars al-Manṣūrī, *Zubdah*, 356–61; ʿAynī, *ʿIqd*, IV:158–68; Maqrīzī, *Sulūk*, I:1018–23; Qalqashandī, *Ṣubḥ*, VII:265–72; also a partial English translation in Howorth, *Mongols of Persia*, 459–61; French translation in D'Ohsson, *Histoire des Mongols*, IV:295–309.

[61] Boyle, "Īl-Khāns," 390.

Muslim was in doubt, or were new, such as the assertion that Ghazan was wrong to claim the Godly support enjoyed by the Mamluks for decades.

Muḥammad's opening argument was an echo of his father's own appeal to the weighty concept of worthy precedence in religion, which he, too, enjoyed by virtue of being a Muslim first: "[God] ... put us among the preceders, the first ones, the leaders and the rightly guided; those who follow the way of the Prophet (*[Allāh] ... jaʿalanā min al-sābiqīn al-awwalīn al-hādīn al-muhtadīn, al-tābiʿīn li-sunnat sayyid al-mursilīn*)."[62] Following this was a pointed reference to the superiority of those Companions of the Prophet (*ṣaḥābah*) whose conversions had been earlier rather than later, and an apt Quranic citation. Apart from the difference in wording, this was the exact argument that had been composed for Qalawun in 1282/681. Muḥammad's text then aired the second argument of Qalawun's day: the idea that Ghazan's conversion was suspect. Thirty years earlier Qalawun's chancellery officials had only dared cast this aspersion on Tegüder in historical reports of Tegüder's conversion, not in letters to the ilkhan himself. But by Muḥammad's reign times had changed, and thus this letter hinged on the implication that Ghazan was not a very good Muslim, if he even was one at all.

In this vein, the letter responded to the criticism of Mamluk behavior at Mardin by suggesting that there must have been provocation, and accused Ghazan's vassal, the Artuqid lord of Mardin, al-Manṣūr Ghāzī (r. ca. 1294/95–1312/693/94–712), of unspecified slights to local Muslims. This was immediately followed by an insult to Ghazan's forebears as infidels: "Your fathers and grandfathers lived – as you know – in a state of unbelief and discord [or hypocrisy], bearing no good will towards Islam."[63] The juxtaposition of these two points implied that Ghazan, like his ancestors, might also be considered a troublemaker or hypocrite for his relationship with the corrupt Artuqid. To drive home doubt about Ghazan's purity of faith and behavior, the letter lambasted Ghazan for his close relations with members of other religions, arguing that he surrounded himself with Christians and Jews, and included Christians in his armies.

It also condemned Ghazan for his inappropriate reaction to the raid at Mardin. The letter suggested that even if Ghazan's anger was justifiable, nothing excused the way he escalated the situation by leading a full-scale invasion into Syria, especially when the invading force was of mixed religion:

> "The recompense for an injury is an injury equal thereto," (Quran 42:40) and not that you attack Islam with patched-together hordes whose members are of all different religions, traverse the pure Biqāʿ [Valley, in Syria] with the servants of the cross, and

[62] Nuwayrī, *Nihāyah*, XXXI:430. See also Qalawun's letters in Chapter 2.

[63] Discord (*shiqāq*) in Nuwayrī, *Nihāyah*, XXXI:432; hypocrisy (*nifāq*) in Baybars al-Manṣūrī, *Zubdah*, 357.

defile the sanctity of Jerusalem, which is the second sacrosanct house of God and full brother to the Prophet's mosque.[64]

Also important here was the treatment of subject populations. The Mamluk letter contrasted the depredations caused by Ghazan's invasion of Syria with the behavior of Mamluk troops in Anatolia during the reign of Baybars, where they were credited with such unwillingness to raid that they insisted on purchasing all their food with their own money. Later, to respond to Ghazan's demand for surrender "or else," the letter voiced its suspicion that no one could possibly consider himself to be a Muslim while threatening his coreligionists with bloodshed.

To rebut Ghazan's claim of divine support, the Mamluk chancellery developed its new argument: that Ghazan was misguided to claim God's approval, since God really favored the Mamluks. In support the text tried to explain away the embarrassing Mamluk defeat at Wādī al-Khaznadār by referring unspecifically to great Mamluk victories of the past, and arguing that one military defeat meant little in the grand scheme of things. (Ghazan was probably unimpressed, and indeed throughout the letter the idea of Guardianship of religion was downplayed.) Perhaps more effectively, Muḥammad's letter opined that although Ghazan was claming divine favor, in reality, God was setting Ghazan up for a terrible fall:

If you had looked closely, you would not have been proud [of your victory], but realized that it was a loss, not a gain, and that you are bringing about His words: "We grant them respite that they may grow in their iniquity" (Quran 3:178).[65]

Muḥammad's chancellery also made him brandish the Abbasid caliph al-Ḥākim as Qalawun had done thirty years earlier. The letter pointed out that obedience to the caliph was a duty for all Muslims, implied that this included Ghazan, and warned Ghazan about God's special favor to the ruler in charge of the caliph:

He who befriends [the caliph] is protected by God, and God takes him in hand, but God will humiliate the one who opposes [the caliph], or [opposes] the ruler who elevates him.[66]

Muḥammad's letter also addressed the question of diplomatic protocol. Since Ghazan had rebuked Muḥammad for his imprisonment of the warners at Wādī al-Khaznadār, Muḥammad was made to retort that they came at a poor time, arriving as they did a day or two before the battle. Muḥammad's letter criticized Ghazan's own shabby understanding of protocol by deriding the current Ilkhanid envoys:

[64] Nuwayrī, *Nihāyah*, XXXI:432. [65] *Ibid.*, 434. [66] *Ibid.*, 437.

We honored their mission, and were generous [to them] for the sake of their sender ... [we] heard their message and sent back this response, even though their inferiority and weakness were not lost on us ... One like you [lit., "him"] should not have sent such envoys to one like us, nor assigned anyone other than a person of quality and erudition to this important matter.[67]

The ambassadors were sent back in early October 1301/late Muḥarram 701, but without Mamluk counterparts.[68]

In December/Rabīʿ II Ghazan met with his returned envoys and heard of Muḥammad's behavior, manner and court. Then he set out on a long hunting trip in the southeastern Caucasus, ending up finally in Mughan, where in April 1302/Shaʿbān 701 he had a letter written to Pope Boniface VIII (1294–1303) in response to an earlier papal missive. Scholars agree that Ghazan's letter was about a planned joint military campaign, almost certainly against Muḥammad and the Mamluk Sultanate, although the target is not specified.[69] The letter was brief and to the point: it acknowledged Ghazan's receipt of the Pope's own missive, informed Boniface that Ghazan's military preparations were continuing apace, and reminded the Pope that he had promised to gather his own troops and the support of "diverse nations."[70] Most unexpected coming from a sultan whose correspondence to the Mamluks was so heavily and consciously imbued with Islamic ideology, however, were two references to the Sky: Ghazan not only explained to Boniface that he was "Praying to the Sky," but also directed the Pope to do the same.[71] It thus seems that although Ghazan was willing to use older Mongolian ideas and imagery in some of his letters, he chose to avoid them when writing to the Mamluks, to whom such references could only weaken Ghazan's own image as a Muslim.

67 *Ibid.*, 440.

68 *Ibid.*, 430; Yūnīnī/Guo, *Dhayl*, II:194 (Arabic) and I:243 (English); this is corroborated by Ghazan's April 1303/Shaʿbān 702 letter to Aybak al-Afram (Baybars al-Manṣūrī, *Zubdah*, 369, also see below), in which he complained that the Mamluks returned his ambassadors without any of their own. Three Mamluk historians claim incorrectly that two ambassadors, Ḥusām al-Dīn Uzdamir al-Mujīrī and the judge ʿImād al-Dīn Ibn al-Sukkarī, did return with Ghazan's men in 1301/701 (Ibn al-Dawādārī, *Kanz*, IX:65–66; Author Z, *Beiträge*, 98; Baybars al-Manṣūrī, *Zubdah*, 354, 356 [contradicting the message in Ghazan's letter on 369], and *Tuḥfah*, 161). But Nuwayrī says the men were sent after Ghazan's *second* embassy (i.e., in Cairo in summer 1302/702); Vaṣṣāf corroborates this by identifying the ambassadors by name when they arrived in Iraq in December 1302–January 1303/Jumādà I 702 (Aḥmad al-Nuwayrī, *Nihāyat al-arab fī funūn al-adab*, ed. Fahīm Muḥammad ʿAlawī Shaltūt (Cairo, 1998), XXXII:18; Vaṣṣāf, *Taʾrīkh*, 397, and Āyatī, *Taḥrīr*, 240). Rashīd al-Dīn also mentions Egyptian ambassadors only for 702, not for 701 (see *Jāmiʿ*, II:1301, 1309). Thus Heribert Horst, "Eine Gesandtschaft des Mamlūken al-Malik al-Nāṣir am Īlhān-Hof in Persien," *Der Orient in der Forschung: Festschrift für Otto Spies zum 5 April 1966* (Wiesbaden, 1967)," 367, 369, and Spuler, *Mongolen*, 85–87, followed the incorrect Mamluk sources and claimed mistakenly that Uzdamir and Ibn al-Sukkarī went in 1301/701.

69 Boyle, "Īl-Khāns," 390; Mostaert and Cleaves, "Trois documents," 467, 471.

70 Mostaert and Cleaves, "Trois documents," 471. 71 *Ibid.*

The forgeries

It was also during the diplomatic exchange of late summer 1301/700–01 that a set of Mamluk forgeries emerged: one from "Ghazan," and the other a response from "Muḥammad."[72] Like Muḥammad's authentic letter, the forgeries were imbued with Mamluk ideas of kingship, but they did not play an actual role in Mamluk–Ilkhanid diplomacy. Rather they were circulated in Mamluk lands and were intended for internal consumption. Although they may have been read aloud to Mamluk troops, there is no evidence that they entered Ilkhanid territory, even though Ghazan is the alleged author of one of them.[73] Rather, the texts were concocted to denigrate Ghazan and glorify Muḥammad to Mamluk subjects and soldiers, especially in the wake of the humiliating defeat at Wādī al-Khaznadār.

The contents of the forgeries were straightforward: "Ghazan's" letter was couched in terms of brotherly love and unity in Islam, becoming at most gently reproachful when discussing the military entanglements between the two sides. Ultimately it proposed a new state of cooperation and general friendship. But this cordiality was meant to be seen as fake, as became clear in "Muḥammad's" belligerent response. It insinuated that "Ghazan's" conversion, faith, letters, plans and promises were all false. The letter accused "Ghazan" of spreading lies among Mamluk troops by claiming that it would be wrong to fight other Muslims, and explained that these lies were the real reason for the Mamluk defeat at Wādī al-Khaznadār.

The forgeries appear to have been produced by Mamluk scribes, perhaps shortly after Wādī al-Khaznadār, when the chancellery was trying to restore the sultan's image as the Guardian of Islam to his subjects and soldiers. The letters seem to have been written to combat the disturbing new reluctance of Mamluk soldiers to meet the Mongols in battle, not out of fear, but out of a desire to avoid combat with newly converted Muslims. At the same time, and like the religious scholars in the Mamluk chancellery (although independently), the jurisconsult Aḥmad b. Taymīyah drew on the vast expanse of Islamic literature to eradicate this dangerous notion from the minds of the army and the populace through legal opinions.[74] If Mamluk soldiers were indeed worried about the moral and religious ramifications of battle with the Mongols, these forgeries would have circulated an unsympathetic image of Ghazan and his forces, and strengthened the collective Mamluk backbone against them. However, they were taken as true by many of the Mamluk historians themselves, who attributed them mistakenly to Ghazan's embassy of 1301/700.

[72] I am currently preparing an article on the forgeries. See also Raff, *Fatwà*, 10, 33–35. For the forgery texts see Ibn al-Dawādārī, *Kanz*, IX:53–56, 66–70; Author Z, *Beiträge*, 93–94, 98–101; Yūnīnī/Guo, *Dhayl*, II:212–14, 243–47 (Arabic) and I:181–84, 194–98 (English); texts and French translation in Mufaḍḍal, *Nahj*, 549–54, 571–81.

[73] Yūnīnī/Guo, *Dhayl*, II:212 (Arabic) and I:181 (English).

[74] Raff, *Fatwà*, entire; also see Calmard, "Chiisme," 280–81.

The third campaign

For reasons unknown, Ghazan did not attack Mamluk territory again until the winter of 1303/702. Before setting out on this third campaign, Ghazan made elaborate logistical, religious and ceremonial preparations. He met with his family, advisors, court and the Mongol nobility in Ujan in July 1302/Dhū al-Ḥijjah 701 in a major *quriltai* in which solemn Islamic ceremonies, Mongol-style festivities and serious campaign planning were included. Some activities took place in an enormous tent of golden cloth, which had been three years in preparation.[75] The occasion began with three days of Islamic religious devotion, including recitations from the Quran. This was followed first by a party, and then by the *quriltai* itself, in which the third Syrian campaign was planned.[76]

During this string of events, Ghazan took the opportunity to send another embassy to Mamluk Cairo, which arrived on 27 August 1302/2 Muḥarram 702. The ambassadors were two judges and were treated as hostile, since they were forced to journey to Cairo at night. They bore yet another demand for Muḥammad to submit to Ilkhanid overlordship, which he would demonstrate by sending tax revenue (*kharāj*) to Ghazan and including Ghazan's name on coinage and in the Friday sermons. The ambassadors were soon sent back with a response, and were followed by a Mamluk embassy, led by the Mamluk commander Ḥusām al-Dīn Uzdamir al-Mujīrī and the judge ʿImād al-Dīn b. al-Sukkarī.[77] The Ilkhanid envoys reached Ghazan first and reported on Muḥammad, his court and his behavior. By this time Ghazan had moved from Ujan into Iraq, where he was busy planning to assert himself in the Hijaz at Muḥammad's expense.[78] The ilkhan also engaged in a flurry of diplomatic activity: he met with an embassy from Toqta of the Golden Horde, and another from the Byzantine emperor Andronicus II (r. 1282–1328). Ghazan may also have written to Edward I of England at this time.[79] Next the Mamluk ambassadors Uzdamir and Ibn al-Sukkarī arrived and met with Ghazan at Hilla in December 1302–January 1303/Jumādà I 702.

From an Ilkhanid point of view, the Mamluk response was unsatisfactory. The letter was not appropriately respectful to Ghazan, since in it

[75] Andrews, *Felt Tents*, I:553–54.

[76] For the campaign see Boyle, "Īl-Khāns," 391–95; Stewart, *Armenian Kingdom*, 149–53.

[77] Mamluk sources mention the embassy but not the message. See Nuwayrī, *Nihāyah*, XXXII:18; Baybars al-Manṣūrī, *Zubdah*, 366, and *Tuḥfah*, 163; Yūnīnī/Guo, *Dhayl*, II:207 (Arabic) and I:255 (English). For the coins and sermons see Vaṣṣāf, *Taʾrīkh*, 397, and Āyatī, *Taḥrīr*, 239–40; Mīrkhwānd, *Rawḍah*, VIII:4242–44.

[78] In a clear threat to Mamluk legitimacy, Ghazan intended to send curtains for the Kaʿaba and a palanquin to Mecca, but the failure of his third campaign ruined these plans. Charles Melville, "'The Year of the Elephant': Mamluk–Mongol Rivalry in the Hejaz in the Reign of Abū Saʿīd (1317–1335)," *Studia Iranica* 21:2 (1992), 199.

[79] For the embassies from Andronicus II and Toqta see Rashīd al-Dīn, *Jāmiʿ*, II:1308–09; for the (lost) letter to Edward I, see Lockhart, "Relations," 29; also Jean Richard, "D'Älğigidäi à Gazan: la continuité d'une politique franque chez les Mongols d'Iran," in *Domination*, 65; see also Jackson, *Mongols and the West*, 170–71.

Muḥammad's name was in gold ink, while Ghazan's was in black. Worse still, the Mamluk letter stubbornly clung to the ideals of Guardianship of Islam. The Mamluk response to Ghazan's demand for tax revenue, for example, was to explain that all their tax monies went to pay for the defense of Islamic lands and the upkeep of the great commanders (who were crucial to this defense), and that there was nothing left over. As a result, if they sent any of this money to Ghazan, there would not be enough left for them to carry out their protective duty. Far more provocatively, the Mamluk letter addressed the question of coinage by suggesting that Ghazan himself mint new coins bearing his name and that of the caliph on one side, with that of Muḥammad on the other.[80] This reference to the caliph and his symbolic capital was a deliberate slight, while the suggestion that Ghazan mint coins with Muḥammad's name on them was reminiscent of the bravado favored by Baybars and Khalīl. To drive the insult home, the ambassadors then produced a locked box, and swore to Ghazan that they had no knowledge of its contents. When opened, it proved to be full of weapons, and thus an unmistakable challenge to battle.[81] Ghazan's displeasure was profound, and persuaded him to take the rare step of imprisoning the Mamluk envoys in an unused school (*madrasah*), where they languished for two full years.

A curious view of Ghazan's meeting with the Mamluk envoys emerged from Uzdamir's report, made several years later after he and the judge finally returned to Mamluk territory.[82] Uzdamir described the formal reception he and Ibn al-Sukkarī had with Ghazan, during which Ghazan interrogated Uzdamir on various topics, but virtually ignored the judge.[83] First Ghazan asked Uzdamir about the various parts of his name and his ethnic origin (*jins*), and discovered that Uzdamir was a Qipchaq Turk. Ghazan then inquired into Uzdamir's military rank, but was outraged when Uzdamir described himself as a mere soldier (*jundī*), and demanded to know why Muḥammad had sent such a lowly personage to him. Uzdamir responded that commanders and soldiers alike were *jundī*s, since they all saw themselves as soldiers of God (*jund Allah*). Uzdamir then admitted that he was actually not a plain soldier but a commander of some note, with his own military band (*tablakhānah*); furthermore, he had served not only Muḥammad, but also Khalīl, Qalawun and even Baybars.

This prompted Ghazan to ask how many battles Uzdamir had seen. He responded that he had seen them all since the time of Ghazan's grandfather

[80] Vaṣṣāf, *Ta'rīkh*, 397, and Āyatī, *Taḥrīr*, 240; Mīrkhwānd, *Rawḍah*, VIII:4243–44; Rashīd al-Dīn merely says the Egyptian message was unsatisfactory in *Jāmiʿ*, II:1309.

[81] Ibn al-ʿAbbāsī, *Āthār*, 96; Vaṣṣāf, *Ta'rīkh*, 397, and Āyatī, *Taḥrīr*, 240.

[82] The main source for this report is Ibn al-Dawādārī, whose father was a friend of Uzdamir. Ibn al-Dawādārī, *Kanz*, IX:71–76, whence Author Z, *Beiträge*, 101–04; see also Mufaḍḍal, *Nahj*, 581 (in brief); ʿAynī, *ʿIqd*, IV:168–72; for a German translation see Horst, "Gesandtschaft."

[83] Did this interview reflect a real interest in Mamluk military abilities – better represented by Uzdamir – or did Uzdamir edit the encounter to emphasize his own role? No report from Ibn al-Sukkarī has appeared.

Abaqa. Then Ghazan wanted to know why the Mamluks had fled from Ilkhanid forces (at Wādī al-Khaznadār after their defeat). Uzdamir replied at some length. First he pointed out that the Ilkhanids had fled from the Mamluks for sixty years, and that this was the first time for the Mamluks to flee. Then he claimed that the Mamluks had underestimated the Mongols because previous battles had been so easy to win. Finally Uzdamir explained that Muḥammad had left one force to guard against Beduins in Upper Egypt, and two to watch for Crusaders at Damietta and Alexandria, and thus had met Ghazan with only a quarter of his armies.[84] The interview continued, with Uzdamir at times challenged by ʿAlī b. Berke Khan, identified as a Mamluk defector. This may have been one ʿAlāʾ al-Dīn ʿAlī Shīr, who joined Ghazan with a few companions in late summer 1302/early 702.[85] But Uzdamir reduced ʿAlī to appearing incompetent by showing that he had deserted out of disgruntlement over a poor military appointment in Aleppo.

Uzdamir claimed that his only bad moment came when Ghazan chose to question him about homosexual practices among the Mamluks: "How can your commanders leave [women] and use young men?" From this question, Uzdamir said he knew that Ghazan wanted to humiliate him. He responded: "May God save the khan! Indeed, our commanders did not know a thing about this [practice]; but rather this became a new habit in our lands when Turghay [an Oirat refugee] came to us from you [in 1296/695], for he appeared among us with young Mongol boys, whom the Mamluk elite (*al-nās*) began to employ [sexually] instead of women."[86] Uzdamir claimed that Ghazan became angry at this, and spoke to his commanders in Mongolian, at which Uzdamir knew he was a dead man. Ghazan ordered the chamberlain to ask Ibn al-Sukkarī if he could confirm this, and Ibn al-Sukkarī did. Then Ghazan inquired about the differences between Mamluk women and Mongol women. Here Uzdamir prevaricated, first stating that women in the Mamluk Sultanate covered themselves up, then professing ignorance of the practices of Mongol women, saying that Ghazan presumably would know better. Thereafter Ghazan sentenced the envoys to terrible punishment, but later commuted this to imprisonment.[87] As they were roughly herded out, Uzdamir swore that he could hear Ibn al-Sukkarī's teeth chattering, which made him smile.

Although both Mamluk and Ilkhanid historians corroborate that Uzdamir and Ibn al-Sukkarī went as envoys to Ghazan, they add no further information. What then can we make of Uzdamir's story? It might be dismissed as a

[84] Although these "forces" were probably small, this gave Uzdamir an inoffensive way to explain the Mamluk defeat at Wādī al-Khaznadār. See also Amitai, "Whither?," 237.

[85] Rashīd al-Dīn, *Jāmiʿ*, II:1307–08.

[86] Ibn al-Dawādārī, *Kanz*, IX:74. For the Oirats see Holt, *Crusades*, 108.

[87] The punishment was allegedly death by being shot from a catapult, but it seems unlikely that Ghazan would have said this, since he was surely mindful of the proud Mongol tradition that forbade killing ambassadors. Perhaps this was a dramatic exaggeration by Uzdamir.

tall tale told by a man relaxing in the private company of friends. But even if allowances are made for boasting and embellishment, the story does not ring entirely untrue. Uzdamir and Ibn al-Sukkarī were the first Mamluk envoys to the Ilkhanid court since 1272/670.[88] Ghazan's questions as reported by Uzdamir indicate a basic curiosity about the main envoy and his place in Muḥammad's realm, and show Ghazan's interest in discovering Muḥammad's attitude towards him as reflected in the qualities and ranks of his ambassadors. Ghazan's pointed inquiries about the Mamluk armies after Wādī al-Khaznadār suggest a desire to put Uzdamir and Ibn al-Sukkarī in their places; that Uzdamir was aware of this desire is evident in his answers, which portray Mamluk forces in a far better light than they deserved. Uzdamir's responses underscored the Mamluk ideology of the times, especially his reference to being one of the solders of God (*jund Allah*), which illuminated the acceptance of this notion in Mamluk military society. If Ghazan really did ask about the sexual habits of the Mamluk ruling elite – and it seems unlikely that Uzdamir would have invented such questions out of whole cloth – his motive was surely to humiliate the envoys, which both Uzdamir and Ibn al-Sukkarī understood. Finally, the imprisonment of the envoys for so long was a singular occurrence, and indicated Ghazan's fury with the Mamluk sultan.

Sometime after his fruitless meeting with Uzdamir and Ibn al-Sukkarī, Ghazan began his third military invasion of Syria in January 1303/Jumādà II 702. Shortly before setting out for Syria, Ghazan sent a final embassy to the Mamluk sultan with an unidentified set of ambassadors, which was probably a demand for submission; their arrival without Uzdamir and Ibn al-Sukkarī was cause for concern at the Mamluk court. The reception and fate of these last-minute warners is unknown.[89] Then Ghazan personally led one force to besiege the Mamluk border castle of al-Raḥbah in March/Rajab, but he did not remain in Mamluk territory for long. Meanwhile, the rest of the Ilkhanid armies advanced into Syria under the commander Qutlughshah, but were roundly defeated by Mamluk forces at Marj al-Ṣuffar on 21 April 1303/3 Ramaḍān 702, and fled back east only with difficulty.[90]

Although like the others this campaign produced a flurry of propaganda texts for Syrian audiences, only one survives, along with the description of a second propaganda text, and a summary of written negotiations for the surrender of a fort. This campaign also resulted in the production of a new Mamluk forgery. The extant text was a decree (*yarligh*), addressed first to the Mamluk governor of Syria, Aybak al-Afram, and then to the Syrians in general. It was written on 3 April 1303/14 Shaʿbān 702, eighteen days before

[88] Qalawun did not send Mamluk envoys to Tegüder in 1282/681; nor did Khalīl return Mamluk counterparts with Geikhatu's envoys in 1292–93/692.

[89] Baybars al-Manṣūrī, *Tuḥfah*, 163, and *Zubdah*, 366–67; Ibn Kathīr, *Bidāyah*, XIV:25; Rashīd al-Dīn, *Jāmiʿ*, II:1311.

[90] For the campaign see Boyle, "Īl-Khāns," 394–95.

the main Ilkhanid force was defeated at Marj al-Ṣuffar.[91] Unlike the letters of the first campaign, the decree for Aybak did not present a comparison of Ghazan with Muḥammad, in which Ghazan's divine support was highlighted while Muḥammad's unkingliness was denigrated, and the Syrians were supposed to choose the better man. Rather, by 1303/702 Ghazan had moved beyond such preliminaries. As a result, the new decree was a summation of the situation, a description of what came next and a call to action. Although it still spent considerable ink enumerating Mamluk failings, both old and new, the decree focused more heavily on Ghazan's own merciful nature than had previous texts, as a way of convincing the Syrians to join his side. It dismissed the Mamluks as corrupt yet unimportant, and, significantly, challenged the Syrians to take a stand at last. Ghazan clearly felt that this was the moment of reckoning for Syria.

The decree set the stage for the Syrians' acceptance of Ghazan by opening with a combination of imperial and Islamic ideology: God had granted Ghazan both Islam and the Chingizid inheritance: "He enlightened our heart with faith, and gave us as inheritance the sultanate of our fathers and grandfathers."[92] Then, with the goal of reviling and ultimately dismissing the Mamluks as rulers, the decree revisited such well-known Mamluk failings as their lack of joy at Ghazan's conversion, and the raid on Mardin. The decree also added new offenses to the list: the Mamluks had recently attacked Armenian territory and Diyarbakir, despite their knowledge that these areas answered to Ghazan; they had also conspired against Ghazan with Kurds, Anatolians, Georgians and the Golden Horde.[93] They had even sent a Mamluk commander, Baybars (al-Jashnakīr), to harass the Meccans for mentioning Ghazan's name in the sermon. Here Ghazan took the opportunity to reproach any Muslim who went to Mecca with an irreligious purpose in mind, which served to establish the Mamluks as religious wrongdoers, and Ghazan as the one who knew the proper path. This point also foreshadowed the struggles over prominence in the Hijaz that would occupy Muḥammad when Ghazan's successors came to the throne.[94]

As in earlier letters, the decree to Aybak used diplomatic protocol to criticize Muḥammad's ignorance of kingship and dismiss him as a ruler. Among Muḥammad's faults were his imprisonment of the warners who arrived shortly before Wādī al-Khaznadār, the summer 1301/700 house arrest of the Ilkhanid ambassadors and, when Muḥammad finally freed them and returned them to Ghazan, his failure to send Mamluk envoys with them. Further infuriating Ghazan was the letter Muḥammad had sent in October 1301/Muḥarram 701:

[91] For this text see Baybars al-Manṣūrī, *Zubdah*, 368–72 and a truncated version in Maqrīzī, *Sulūk*, I:1024–27. Also see Rashīd al-Dīn, *Jāmiʿ*, II:1311.
[92] Baybars al-Manṣūrī, *Zubdah*, 368.
[93] If the Mamluks were writing to potential allies, the historical sources are silent about it.
[94] See Melville, "Elephant," entire.

If only the answer they sent back with [our envoy] had any sense or rightness in it at all! Rather, their letter demonstrated the corruptness of their beliefs, and the way they sank deeper into a continuation of their caprices ... They wrote the name of their sultan in gold with excessive titles and elevated all of this, while the names of God and the Prophet were in [black] ink, and his (our) name [i.e., Ghazan's[95]] was written several lines lower out of spite. We assumed that this was all done out of their ignorance and lack of culture, as well as their inexperience with letters and responses.[96]

According to Ilkhanid diplomatic protocol, references to God or to Ghazan should have been written with "God" to the far right of the page and elevated in a position of honor, then "Ghazan," also to the right and elevated (but less so than "God"), followed by the regular text, which was indented. Gold ink should have been used for God and the ruler.[97]

The other goal of the decree was to emphasize Ghazan's own tolerance and restraint, both to show his forbearance, and to threaten what could happen if his patience came to an end. So, for example, when castigating Muḥammad for keeping the Ilkhanid ambassadors confined in their quarters in 1301/700–01, Ghazan told the Syrians: "If not for our propensity for kindness, Syria would have become empty of houses [because of this]."[98] Likewise Ghazan explained that he had sent the embassy of 1302/702 only out of his desire to give second chances. Ghazan's mercy and sense of fair play also appeared in the discussion of warnings, since Ghazan claimed he felt morally obliged to warn oppressive rulers before exterminating them. Although backed by Quranic injunctions, this insistence on proper warnings before annihilation was a particularly Chingizid view of the Mamluks. To make it clear that the Syrians were not blameless, however, the letter cautioned them that they too had been wrong, most notably for ignoring Ghazan's conversion, and for failing to ask him to save them from Mamluk rule. The decree ended with an ultimatum. If the Syrians wanted to demonstrate their intelligence, they would divest themselves of their foolish relationship to Egypt and submit to Ghazan: "As previously they were imagining that the border was Diyarbakir and Iraq, let them imagine from now on that it is Gaza and the edges of the sand ... In the past, as they used to ask for help from them [the Egyptians, i.e., Mamluks] against us, so now they will ask us for help against them."[99] But, the letter also cautioned, if the Syrians somehow failed to understand, their fate would be terrible: "We will cut down their trees, massacre their young and old, burn their homes ..."[100]

What effect did these arguments have on the Syrians themselves? Certainly members of the Mamluk elite were unconvinced. The indignant historian Baybars al-Manṣūrī, himself a mamluk, described the decree with contempt:

95 "his" in Baybars al-Manṣūrī, *Zubdah*, 369, meaning Ghazan; "our" in Maqrīzī, *Sulūk*, I:1025.
96 Baybars al-Manṣūrī, *Zubdah*, 369.
97 Mostaert and Cleaves, *Lettres*, 14; for other uses of gold and black ink see Blair, "Religious Art," 129–32.
98 Baybars al-Manṣūrī, *Zubdah*, 369. 99 *Ibid.*, 371. 100 *Ibid.*

"He wrote a letter to the people of Syria, misguiding them and [trying to] convince them not to help the people of Egypt; [but rather he wanted] to deceive them."[101] But to the Mamluk commander al-Ghutamī, the governor at the besieged fort al-Raḥbah, either Ghazan's threat was deadly serious, or his arguments were convincing. Ghazan had only been there a couple of days when al-Ghutamī began to send messengers to him offering to submit. A continual to and fro ensured that documents were written and affixed with Ghazan's royal seal (*ṭamghah*) to establish the conditions of obedience. These documents, which were written in Arabic, resembled the decree sent to Aybak when they explained that the Egyptians' (*sic*) own injustice and refusal to listen to envoys had brought about Ghazan's campaign, and counseled al-Ghutamī and the inhabitants of al-Raḥbah to surrender at once since God was on Ghazan's side.[102] It is an open question whether al-Ghutamī was convinced or just canny, but regardless of his actual state of mind, he sent food out to Ghazan and agreed to the terms. Ghazan even took al-Ghutamī's son with him as a hostage when he headed back east.[103] Nevertheless, any agreement between Ghazan and al-Ghutamī was nullified by the Ilkhanid defeat at Marj al-Ṣuffar.

The letter sent to the governor of Aleppo also seems to have been a piece of propaganda, but one with an argument based primarily on logistics, since although it enumerated Mamluk faults, it focused on the problem of pasturage. Claiming that the combination of a drought and the increased salinity of the earth (in Iraq?) had ruined pasturage, the letter explained that the appearance of Ilkhanid forces near the Euphrates merely showed the Ilkhanids' desire to find good grazing land. As a result, the inhabitants of the region around Aleppo should not be alarmed at the sight of approaching Mongols, and above all should not run away, since they were in no danger whatsoever. If the object of this letter was indeed to reassure the populace, however, it failed completely, since as news of the invasion arrived, Aleppans fled the region in droves. If, as seems more likely, it was also intended to show ordinary people the faults of the Mamluk sultan and his advisors, the extent of its influence is unknown. Certainly officials within the Mamluk administration viewed it as no more than a blatant attempt at deception.[104] (One additional text linked to Ghazan's third invasion was an aggressive victory letter attributed to 1304–05/704, which was supposedly written on behalf of Muḥammad and sent after the battle, but which was actually another Mamluk forgery, and probably did not go to Ilkhanid territory.[105])

[101] *Ibid.*, 368.

[102] For a paraphrase in Persian see Rashīd al-Dīn, who was at the siege, although he says the letter was in Arabic. Rashīd al-Dīn, *Jāmiʿ*, II:1311.

[103] Nuwayrī, *Nihāyah*, XXXII:24–25; Baybars al-Manṣūrī, *Zubdah*, 367–68, also *Tuḥfah*, 164; Rashīd al-Dīn, *Jāmiʿ*, II:1311–12.

[104] For descriptions but not texts see Baybars al-Manṣūrī, *Zubdah*, 366–67 for drought; *Tuḥfah*, 163, for salt.

[105] For the text see Ibn al-Dawādārī, *Kanz*, IX:119–22; Author Z, *Beiträge*, 118–21; and ʿAynī, *ʿIqd*, IV:247–51.

The reign of Öljeitü (1304–16/703–16)

Ghazan's death after illness on 11 May 1304/5 Shawwāl 703 ended his aggression towards the Mamluks, and led immediately to the accession of his brother and heir Muḥammad Kharbandah, later Khudābandah, in July–August 1304/Dhū al-Ḥijjah 703. The new sultan took the regnal title of Öljeitü (Auspicious). Unlike Ghazan, who came to the throne by force and consolidated his position through a series of bloody pogroms, Öljeitü's reign began peaceably; he was also saved from large-scale Mongol strife when in 1304/703–04 he agreed to conclude a general peace with the Great Khan Temür (r. 1294–1307), the Chagataids and the Golden Horde. He seems to have wanted to continue ruling in the traditions that Ghazan had established, for he ordered the upholding of his brother's laws, and visited Ghazan's tomb frequently during the first few years of his reign.[106]

Religiously Öljeitü retained the affinity for Twelver Shiism he had displayed during Ghazan's reign, as well as the contempt for the Abbasid caliph. Öljeitü's interest in the nobility of Alid lineage in particular echoed the Chingizid belief that legitimacy came through descent from an important ancestor. Although Öljeitü did not formally proclaim support for Shiism right away, in 1309–10/709 he converted and struck coins in the names of the twelve Shiite Imams.[107] This conversion was deplored in the Mamluk Sultanate, even though Öljeitü's new version of Islam had little lasting effect on the Ilkhanid population, and was later discarded under his entirely Sunni son.[108] Although accounts of the conversion should be treated with caution, they do suggest that, as under Ghazan, Öljeitü's reign witnessed a continuation of steppe traditions: some Mongols who allegedly wanted to return to shamanism and not become Shiites, for example, were said to have been purified for their blasphemy against Islam by passing un-Islamically between two fires.[109] Likewise Öljeitü's chancellery continued to refer to the Enduring Sky as God in diplomatic letters, although perhaps not to the Mamluks.[110] Öljeitü may even have been encouraged to see himself as a world emperor on

[106] Qāshānī, *Uljaytu*, 31, 41, 44, 83.

[107] Sheila S. Blair, "The Coins of the Later Ilkhanids: A Typological Analysis," *JESHO* 25 (October 1983), 297–98; also Lane-Poole, *Catalogue*, VI:44–45, 48–51, 55, 58–59.

[108] For the conversion, see Qāshānī, *Uljaytu*, 90–108; DeWeese, *Islamization*, 259–61; Pfeiffer, *Twelver Shīʿism*, entire, also her "Conversion Versions: Sultan Öljeytü's Conversion to Shiʿism (709/1309) in Muslim Narrative Sources," *Mongolian Studies* 22 (1999), 35–67; also see Blair, "Religious Art," 118–20. For the Mamluk disgust see Ibn al-Dawādārī, *Kanz*, IX:289; Baybars al-Manṣūrī, *Tuḥfah*, 236; Ibn Kathīr, *Bidāyah*, XIV:88; also Vaṣṣāf, *Taʾrīkh*, 616, and Āyatī, *Taḥrīr*, 354; Calmard, "Chiisme," 280–84.

[109] Boyle, "Īl-Khāns," 401–02.

[110] We cannot be sure, since no letters to the Mamluks survive. For Öljeitü's Sky references to Philip IV of France see Mostaert and Cleaves, *Lettres*, 56–57.

the order of Chingiz Khan or Alexander the Great (and surpassing his brother), even though his military exploits were insignificant.[111]

In January 1305/Jumādà II 704, several months after his accession, Öljeitü found time to release Uzdamir and Ibn al-Sukkarī and send them back to Mamluk territory with a set of his own envoys. For the Mamluks this was an important occasion, and the combined party of ambassadors was welcomed everywhere: at Damascus, the governor himself rode out to greet them.[112] The ambassadors met with Muḥammad in Cairo in March–April 1305/ Ramaḍān 704. Öljeitü's envoys carried a message of peace, but warned of dire consequences should the Mamluks not be inclined to cooperate. Nevertheless for once this was not a standard Mongol peace-as-submission but a real cessation of war, albeit only because Öljeitü was unprepared to attack the Mamluks at the time – he was actually as hostile towards them as his brother had been. Nevertheless, Öljeitü's message proclaimed his intention to refrain from war and his desire for the free passage of merchants; he also asked Muḥammad to return several Mongol commanders who had been captured at Marj al-Ṣuffar.[113] Muḥammad accepted the begrudging overture, and in May–June/Dhū al-Qaʿdah sent two new Mamluk envoys to confirm the agreement. Unlike their predecessors, they returned in relatively timely fashion in March–April 1306/Ramaḍān 705.[114]

Despite this apparent accord, Öljeitü's intentions towards the Mamluks were far from conciliatory. In April–May 1305/Shawwāl 704, Öljeitü wrote to Philip IV of France (r. 1285–1314), Edward I of England and Pope Clement V (1305–14), apparently seeking support in a new military venture against Muḥammad.[115] In the letter to Philip IV, which, incidentally, contained seven different references to the Sky, Öljeitü reaffirmed his desire for good relations, announced the event of a new unity among warring Mongol nations (the peace of 1304/703–04), and concluded with an oblique reference to those not in agreement either with him or with Philip, which probably meant Muḥammad.[116] Öljeitü's request for military cooperation was to be presented

111 Soudavar, "Abū Saʿīdnāmé," 183, discussing this theme in the histories of Qāshānī and Rashīd al-Dīn, in which Öljeitü's elevated status appeared in depictions of him with a solar disk, representing divine favor. Öljeitü's status was similarly high in his seal, which read August Emperor (Ch. *huangdi*), not prince (Ch. *wang*), as had been the case for Ghazan. Mostaert and Cleaves, "Trois documents," 483–85.

112 Nuwayrī, *Nihāyah*, XXXII:86; Mufaḍḍal, *Nahj*, 610–13; also see Baybars al-Manṣūrī, *Zubdah*, 381, and *Tuḥfah*, 176; Ibn al-Dawādārī, *Kanz*, IX:127–28, 130; Author Z, *Beiträge*, 130–31; Qāshānī, *Uljaytu*, 42, 48; Vaṣṣāf, *Taʾrīkh*, 472, and Āyatī, *Taḥrīr*, 276; Boyle, "Īl-Khāns," 399.

113 Vaṣṣāf, *Taʾrīkh*, 472, and Āyatī, *Taḥrīr*, 276. Ibn al-Dawādārī's claim that Öljeitü called Muḥammad his "older brother" and said that God had struck Ghazan dead for invading Syria must be read as hyperbole in the light of Vaṣṣāf's statements. Ibn al-Dawādārī, *Kanz*, IX:127–28; also a less dramatic quote in Mufaḍḍal, *Nahj*, 611.

114 Nuwayrī, *Nihāyah*, XXXII:86–87.

115 Boyle, "Īl-Khāns," 398–99; also see Lockhart, "Relations," 29–31; Richard, "Politique franque," 66; Jackson, *Mongols and the West*, 171–72.

116 Only the letter to Philip survives. Mostaert and Cleaves, *Lettres*, 1, 56–57.

in the oral message that accompanied and amplified this letter.[117] But Öljeitü was disappointed in his grand scheme, for Philip never answered the letter; Edward II (r. 1307–27), responding after the death of his father, apologized that he would be unable to participate, and Clement V gave only vague promises of aid at an unspecified future date.[118] Militarily Öljeitü's preoccupation with campaigns to Gilan and Herat (both in 1307/706) kept him from advancing on the Mamluks as often as his brother had done; instead, he focused on his new capital city of Sultaniyah and the tomb and shrine complex he was building there, which may have been designed to compete with the Mamluk-controlled Hijaz (Figure 5).[119]

Nevertheless the combination of belief in his own right religion, the veneration of a holy lineage, the certainty that those who followed an Abbasid caliph were misguided and hostility towards the Mamluks surely contributed to Öljeitü's mindset in 1311–12/711, when strife within the Sultanate once again facilitated an Ilkhanid invasion of Syria. It began when the Mamluk governor of Aleppo, Qarasunqur, fell foul of Muḥammad and fled for Ilkhanid territory with the governor of Tripoli, Aqqush al-Afram, mirroring Qipchaq and Baktimur over a decade earlier.[120] Öljeitü welcomed the Mamluk rebels and incorporated them into his forces. Then, aided by their knowledge of Syria, Öljeitü gathered an army and besieged the fortress of al-Raḥbah, as his brother had done before him. In Cairo, Muḥammad was now in his third reign (r. 1310–41/709–41) and finally could rule as his own man. When he heard the news, he duly set out on campaign himself. No battle was ever fought, however, for before Muḥammad reached al-Raḥbah, Öljeitü retreated to his own lands with the rebel Mamluks, who lived out their lives in Ilkhanid territory.[121] When Muḥammad learned of Öljeitü's withdrawal, he sent his troops home and went on the pilgrimage from Damascus. Thereafter Muḥammad determinedly sent Assassins to kill Qarasunqur in Ilkhanid territory until 1326/726, but none was ever successful.[122] Although intermittent hostilities continued for the rest of Öljeitü's reign, this was the last full-scale Ilkhanid invasion of Syria.[123]

117 Boyle, "Īl-Khāns," 399.

118 *Ibid.*, 402. There is some evidence that Öljeitü tried to contact European rulers in the 1310s as well. See Amitai-Preiss, citing J. R. S. Phillips, "Imperial Ideology," 58.

119 Sheila Blair, "The Epigraphic Program of the Tomb of Uljaytu at Sultaniyya: Meaning in Mongol Architecture," *Islamic Art* 2 (1987), 70–73.

120 See Little's extensive and thought-provoking discussion of Qarasunqur in Donald Little, *An Introduction to Mamlūk Historiography: An Analysis of Arabic Annalistic and Biographical Sources for the Reign of al-Malik an-Nāṣir Muḥammad ibn Qalā'ūn* (Montreal, 1970), 100–36 with references to Mamluk historians.

121 For the Persian side of this campaign see Vaṣṣāf, *Ta'rīkh*, 552–5, and Āyatī, *Taḥrīr*, 305–07; Qāshānī, *Uljaytu*, 136–43; Mīrkhwānd, *Rawḍah*, VIII:4308–12.

122 Charles Melville, "'Sometimes by the Sword, Sometimes by the Dagger': The Role of the Isma'ilis in Mamlūk–Mongol Relations in the 8th/14th Century," in *Mediaeval Isma'ili History and Thought*, ed. Farhad Daftary (Cambridge, 1996), 247–63.

123 For the military exploits of Öljeitü's later reign see Reuven Amitai, "The Resolution of the Mongol–Mamluk War," in *Mongols, Turks and Others: Eurasian Nomads and the Sedentary World*, eds. Reuven Amitai and Michal Biran (Leiden, 2005), 362–64.

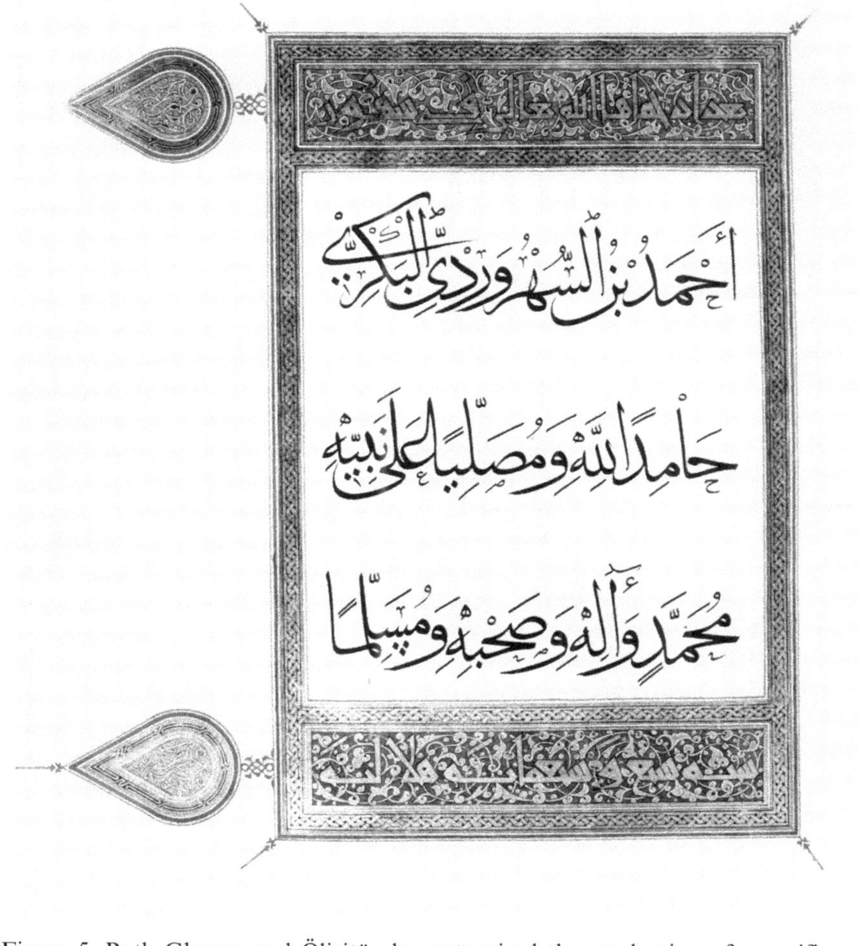

Figure 5. Both Ghazan and Öljeitü also patronized the production of magnificent Qurans like this one. (Folio from the Anonymous Baghdad Quran, Iraq [Baghdad], 1302–08/701–07. The Metropolitan Museum of Art, Rogers Fund, 1955, no. 55.44.)

Thereafter the two sides began to express themselves through covert struggles for power and prestige rather than through hostile diplomacy and war. In fact, the late 1310s/710s marked the beginning of a new ideological phase in Mamluk–Ilkhanid relations, in which the holy cities of Arabia became a central arena for the expression of ideology, especially since the Ilkhanids remained persistently Muslim. The new importance of the region was exploited by the rulers of Mecca, the Abū Numayyad Sharīfs, who were nominally loyal to the Mamluk sultan, but whose maneuverings for royal patronage more accurately reflected their own internal struggles for power.[124] For Muḥammad, this era saw a shift towards the proclamation of a new concept, that of regional Muslim supremacy, expressed through the patronage of Islam. For the Ilkhanids, this meant attempts to appropriate for themselves Muḥammad's claims to be a model Muslim ruler. Despite the urgency of this struggle, however, it remained hidden behind a new diplomatic language of Islamic unity, which became the hallmark of the upcoming decades.

124 Melville, "Elephant," 199–201, 203, 207–09; Ota, "Sharifate," 10–12.

CHAPTER 4

The age of patronage and Muslim supremacy (1317–1341/717–741)

The first third of the fourteenth/eighth century was an era dominated by three rulers. One was Muḥammad, now firmly in charge in the Mamluk Sultanate and fast emerging as idiosyncratic, paranoid and controlling. Another was the ilkhan Abū Saʿīd (r. 1317–35/717–36), although his power was gravely compromised by his own youth and by the presence of the powerful vicegerent Choban (d. 1327/728). Finally Özbek Khan of the Golden Horde (r. 1313–41/712–42) converted to Islam himself during this period and ruled as a self-consciously Muslim sovereign. Although the Mamluks and their Mongol neighbors still traded two mainstays of kingship – the relationship of the ruler to Islam, and the role of family and lineage – during these years the treatment and use of both ideas shifted significantly.

The Mamluks and the Ilkhanids

During the reign of Abū Saʿīd a new set of kingly ideologies emerged in the diplomatic arena. Just as the early, simplistic Muslim/infidel and Chingizid/rebel dichotomies had become obsolete before the turn of the century, so too the struggle over Guardianship of Islam and the elaborations on good and bad Muslim kings employed by Muḥammad, Ghazan and Öljeitü were no longer current. Rather, the 1320s/720s and 1330s/730s marked a unique phase in Mamluk–Ilkhanid relations. In 1323/723 the two sides concluded a peace treaty, which meant ideologically that the Ilkhanids dropped their view of Muḥammad as a rebel or heretic, while Muḥammad finally acknowledged the Ilkhanids as Muslims. One intriguing new theory suggests that in the 1320s/720s the Ilkhanids actually abandoned the Chingizid ideal of universal dominance they had so long proclaimed.[1] It is certainly the case that, unlike his predecessors, Abū Saʿīd did not try to take over Mamluk Syria in the name of (Muslim) Chingizid domination, while Muḥammad made no plans to capture Baghdad as Guardian of Islam against the infidels. Although the Abbasid

[1] See Amitai's thought-provoking analysis of shifts in Mongol attitudes and deliberate silence from Persian historians in "Resolution," entire, and esp. 377–78, 382–83.

caliph maintained his position in Mamluk titulature, he made no significant appearance in Mamluk proclamations of kingship, while on the Ilkhanid side there is no record of resistance to the caliph. Rather, the hostility between the Ilkhanids and the Mamluk sultan turned to friendship, and was marked by an unprecedented emphasis on unity in religion.

But despite the new era of peace, traces of the old antagonism remained, and appeared in a covert struggle for primacy over the patronage of Islam. Although Muḥammad now accepted the Islam of the Ilkhanate, he insisted on expressing his own superiority on religious grounds. This he did not by defending Islamic lands against the Ilkhanids, but by promoting himself as the supreme Muslim ruler in the region – a first among Muslim equals – which was a larger, more grandiose version of Qalawun's older position of religious seniority. To create this new expression of kingship, the sultan increased the emphasis on his relationship to the pilgrimage, so that his position as protector of pilgrims grew in visibility and importance, as did his patronage of religion within the holy cities, and his sovereignty over the Hijaz. Muḥammad ultimately became so jealous of his supremacy in the region that he went on the pilgrimage three separate times, a feat that no Mamluk ruler had ever performed before, or would again.[2] By contrast, Muḥammad's role as Guardian of Islam in general, although present, seems to have been less important.

At the same time, however, Abū Saʿīd and Choban also sought to appear as patrons of religion, and both coveted the chance to shine in the ultimate ceremonial arena of the holy cities. Although Abū Saʿīd's forays into patronage were kept largely under wraps when Choban was in control, they flourished at both the beginning and end of his reign, while Choban's own considerable ambitions of patronage in the Hijaz were expressed at Muḥammad's expense. Such ambitions only increased the covert rivalry between the two courts. Paradoxically, however, despite Muḥammad's promotion of himself as the supreme Muslim ruler and patron, the sultan was hardly the best man for the job, since he frequently let his own suspicious, paranoid personality spur him to damage the reputation he otherwise sought assiduously to maintain. In fact, on several occasions the conflict between his image as a model Muslim sovereign and his actual vicious behavior rendered the Muslim Mongols of the Ilkhanate distinctly uneasy about their own adoption of Islam.

The role of genealogy and dynasty in Mamluk–Ilkhanid exchanges of ideology also shifted during this period. If, as suggested, the Ilkhanids did drop their ideal of universal Chingizid sovereignty, they nevertheless maintained their respect for the Chingizid family. Abū Saʿīd maintained distinct

[2] Only four of forty-seven Mamluk sultans made the trip even once: Baybars, Muḥammad himself, al-Ashraf Shaʿbān (r. 1363–77/764–78) (see Chapter 5) and al-Ashraf Qaytbay (r. 1468–96/872–901). No Ilkhanid ruler ever went.

pride in his dynasty and its impressive history, while Choban kept similar sentiments alive in his single-minded dedication to Mongol tradition in general and to the Chingizid state he served.[3] The corresponding Ilkhanid contempt for Mamluk slave origin epitomized by Hülegü and Ghazan did diminish under Abū Saʿīd, perhaps because Muḥammad was not himself a slave, and the two sides were no longer at war. Nevertheless, in the context of ongoing negotiations about a royal marriage between the two courts, the repeated Ilkhanid attempts to arrange a connection between the Qalawunid and Chobanid families, not the Chingizids, indicated a lingering view of Muḥammad as inferior. Perhaps in response to his own insecure genealogical status, therefore, Muḥammad – like Khalīl and Baybars – found ways to emphasize his place in a fledgling dynasty through the use of dynastic titles, and through ceremonies highlighting his impressive predecessors.

The establishment of peace

It was not long after Abū Saʿīd's accession in 1317/717 that a peace began to seem possible. For the Ilkhanids, the resumption of hostilities with Muḥammad would have been extremely difficult in practical terms, since the first few years of Abū Saʿīd's reign saw a spate of natural disasters, invasions from the north and east, and a short-lived but ugly rebellion.[4] Choban himself had campaigned frequently in Mamluk Syria, knew the logistical problems of invasion first-hand, and – as the real power in the Ilkhanate – may have realized that maintaining rule at home was difficult enough without wasting money and men on campaigns to the west. For his own part Muḥammad had already experienced the crucible of war during Ghazan's invasions, as well as the chaos of internal rebellion. Thus he preferred to spend his third reign using his money to buy friends and allies, or pay for clandestine forms of violence, rather than troubling himself with open war.[5]

Ideologically, the reestablishment of Sunni Islam in the Ilkhanate meant that the religious problem of Öljeitü's Shiism was no longer a barrier to relations between the two sides. One complication to the situation, however,

3 For Abū Saʿīd's dynastic pride see his October–November 1330/Muḥarram 731 letter to Muḥammad Shāh b. Tughluq Shāh of Delhi, translated in Nazir Ahmed, "Diplomatic Relations between the Sultans of Delhi and the Il-Khans of Iran," *Islamic Heritage in South Asian Subcontinent* (Jaipur, 1998 [2000]), 71–75, esp. 71–72; for Choban's character, see Charles Melville, "Wolf or Shepherd? Amir Chupan's Attitude to Government," in *Court*, 79–93; for Amitai's theory see "Resolution," 373–84.

4 For natural disasters see Nuwayrī, *Nihāyah*, XXXII:290–92; ʿUmar Ibn al-Wardī, *Taʾrīkh Ibn al-Wardī*, ed. Muḥammad Mahdī al-Sayyid Ḥasan al-Khurāsānī (Najaf, 1969), II:380–81; for invasions see Spuler, *Goldene Horde*, 93–95; Boyle, "Īl-Khāns," 408; for political upheaval see Charles Melville, "Abū Saʿīd and the Revolt of the Amirs in 1319," in *Domination*, 89–120; for shifting Mongol attitudes see Amitai, "Resolution," 364, 373–74, 377–78, 382.

5 For the best study of Muḥammad see Amalia Levanoni, *A Turning Point in Mamluk History: The Third Reign of al-Nāṣir Muḥammad Ibn Qalawun (1310–41)* (Leiden, 1995).

was the activities of the Assassins, whom Muḥammad had been sending into Iran to kill the defector Qarasunqur since 1312/712. (Muḥammad had never forgiven either Qarasunqur's flight or his participation in the murder of Muḥammad's brother Khalīl.)[6] Although the Assassins never succeeded in these missions, their activities not only disrupted life at the Ilkhanid court, but undermined Muḥammad's reputation as a man of his word and a responsible Muslim ruler. The situation was also affected by matters in the Hijaz, where a struggle within the ruling Abū Numayyad branch of the Banū Qatādah Sharīfs had expanded into a regional conflict during the reign of Öljeitü, which ultimately affected both courts. Although in the end partisans of Muḥammad took the upper hand, the struggle did not play itself out until 1320/720.[7]

The religious rivalry between the Ilkhanate and the Sultanate began soon after Abū Saʿīd's enthronement, when the ilkhan decided to assert his patronage of the Islamic holy cities, and thereby issued a bold challenge to Muḥammad's position as supreme patron of Islam and sovereign of Mecca. Abū Saʿīd proclaimed his status as a patron and a ruler by outfitting a lovely palanquin to lead the Iraqi caravan for the pilgrimage of 1319/718. He also sent a beautiful set of curtains for the Kaʿaba to replace the old ones, which had been provided by Muḥammad. (His vizier, ʿAlī Shāh, added two gem-studded rings for the Kaʿaba doors.)[8] Although this was presented merely as the duty of any responsible Muslim ruler, Muḥammad's lieutenants clearly understood that a palanquin and curtains sent by someone other than the Mamluk sultan were a serious encroachment on Muḥammad's position as sovereign and supreme patron of the holy cities. They therefore prevented the Ilkhanid palanquin from entering Mecca until after Muḥammad's own, while the Ilkhanid curtains were never hung at all. When the pilgrimage was over, news of the symbolic altercation was taken home to the two sovereigns.

Immediately thereafter Muḥammad decided to go on the pilgrimage for the second time in 1319–20/719, with the object of asserting his role as protector of pilgrims and paramount patron in the Hijaz. To do this, he traveled in conspicuous style designed to show off the resources at his disposal, which included camel-borne vegetable gardens, a cook with a portable stove and enough Nile water to drink for the journey, the sojourn in the Hijaz and the return.[9] While in Mecca, Muḥammad met with all the local dignitaries and

[6] Melville, "Ismaʿilis," entire.

[7] Melville, "Elephant," 199–201, 203.

[8] Muḥammad al-Fāsī, *al-ʿIqd al-thamīn fī taʾrīkh al-balad al-amīn*, ([Cairo,] 1958), 56–57; also Maqrīzī, *Sulūk*, II:190; Ibn Baṭṭūṭah, *Travels*, I:194; Muḥammad al-Dhahabī, *Kitāb duwal al-Islām*, ed. Fāhim Muḥammad Shaltūt and Muḥammad Muṣṭafà Ibrāhīm (Qatar, 1988), 411 (but in 1319–20/719); Melville, "Elephant," 202; Jomier, *Maḥmal*, 45–48. For the duties of the pilgrimage commander from Egypt see ʿAnkawi, "Pilgrimage," 156–57.

[9] Nuwayrī, *Nihāyah*, XXXII:301–02; also Abū al-Fidāʾ (who went with Muḥammad), *Memoirs*, 76–78; Mufaḍḍal, *Nahj*, ed. and tr. S. Kortantamer as *Ägypten und Syrien zwischen 1317 und 1341 in der Chronik des Mufaḍḍal b. Abī l-Faḍāʾil* (Freiburg im Breisgau, 1973), 8 (Arabic text).

gave them expensive presents. He granted an audience to the Mongol military commanders who led the Iraqi caravan, showered them with largesse and made a point of helping to finance their trip home, even though Abū Saʿīd had already taken care of their expenses.[10] Muḥammad also performed all the pilgrimage rites, washed the Kaʿaba with his own hand and provided new curtains for it, as was his exclusive prerogative.[11] He must surely have listened to the sermons, which were given in his name by a preacher clad in the black garb of the Abbasids and accompanied by two black caliphal banners, all of which Muḥammad had provided.[12] Then, having bolstered his image as the premier patron, friend of the caliph and sovereign of the region in front of the pilgrims, the locals and Abū Saʿīd's men, Muḥammad went back to Cairo. Even the trip home reinforced his image as protector of pilgrims, since he deliberately traveled at the back of the caravan in order to pick up stragglers.[13]

This demonstration of power and patronage forced Abū Saʿīd into a role as the second Muslim ruler in the region, which he decided to accept. Although in winter 1320–21/late 720 he sent an elaborate satin palanquin studded with rubies, pearls and emeralds to Mecca, this time Muḥammad's supremacy in the Hijaz was maintained. When the caravans processed into the city, Muḥammad's banners and the Egyptian palanquin entered first without argument, followed by the Syrian palanquin, then the Ilkhanid palanquin and banners, and finally the Yemeni palanquin in a clear hierarchy of importance.[14] Abū Saʿīd did not try to send curtains this time. Heightening Muḥammad's position, the commanders accompanying the Iraqi caravan carried not only their own banners, but a yellow silk banner displaying the Mamluk sultan's insignia as well, which they may have acquired from Muḥammad himself during the pilgrimage of 1320/719.[15] This banner was visible proof that Muḥammad's position as Guardian of Pilgrims extended beyond his own territory. Even before the Iraqi caravan arrived in Mecca it proved fortunate that they had it, for the Beduin of Baḥrayn tried to double their usual protection fees, and only relented when they saw Muḥammad's flag and heard that Muḥammad had invited the Iraqi pilgrims. The Beduin then offered to guide the caravan for free, probably with a shrewd judgment

[10] Nuwayrī, *Nihāyah*, XXXII:303; also Melville, "Elephant," 203.

[11] Muḥammad al-Fāsī, *Shifāʾ al-gharām bi-akhbār al-balad al-ḥarām*, in *Die Chroniken der Stadt Mekka*, ed. Ferdinand Wüstenfeld (Leipzig, 1857–61, repr. Beirut, 1964), 277; Maqrīzī, *Sulūk*, II:197; Maḥmūd al-ʿAynī, "ʿIqd al-jumān fī taʾrīkh ahl al-zamān," Istanbul, Topkapi Library, MS Ahmed III:2912/4, fol. 323v.

[12] Ibn Baṭṭūṭah, *Travels*, I:231–32.

[13] There were so many that he had to jettison the vegetables. Nuwayrī, *Nihāyah*, XXXII:303–04.

[14] Seven caravans went from Egypt that year, and one from Iraq. Nuwayrī, *Nihāyah*, XXXII:331; Maqrīzī, *Sulūk*, II:214–15; also Fāsī, *Chroniken*, II:277–78; Dhahabī, *Duwal*, 413; ʿAynī, "ʿIqd," fol. 332r–v, on struggles over precedence between the Iraqi and Syrian caravans (the Syrians won).

[15] The dating of the Mongol acquisition of this banner is troublesome. See Melville, "Elephant," 204 and note 31, "Ismaʿilis," note 42, 261; and note 22 below.

of Muḥammad's character and wealth, which they knew from the sultan's purchase of their horses. The gamble paid off, for when Muḥammad learned they had waived their fees on his behalf, he rewarded them handsomely, since they had managed thereby to proclaim his dominion not only over the holy cities, but even over the Iraqi caravan routes to them.[16] To seal his authority and symbolize the safety of all the caravan routes he protected, Muḥammad sent his favorite wife Tughay on the pilgrimage in 1321–22/721, traveling in pomp equal to Muḥammad's own, and accompanied everywhere by yellow sultanic and black caliphal banners.[17]

Despite this apparent resolution of the tension in Arabia, the rivalry between the Ilkhanate and the Sultanate over the relationship of the ruler to Islam nevertheless emerged elsewhere, particularly in the combat of vice. When in autumn 1320/720 Abū Saʿīd became convinced that several terrifying storms of thunder, lightning and hail were a sign of divine wrath, he hastened to crack down on illegal activities in Ilkhanid territory. As soon as Muḥammad heard about this, he followed suit in his own lands.[18] Otherwise, however, the rivalry remained covert, for just as the newly cooperative Ilkhanid palanquin was reaching the Hijaz, the diplomatic realm showed an unprecedented development when the wealthy and influential slave merchant Majd al-Dīn Ismāʿīl al-Sallāmī arrived in Cairo from the Ilkhanate in February 1321/Muḥarram 721.[19] Al-Sallāmī was an excellent choice for a delicate mission, since he had access to high officials everywhere, and frequently traveled between Iran and Egypt.[20] He brought greetings to Muḥammad from Abū Saʿīd, Choban and ʿAlī Shāh, and informed the sultan of their desire to arrange a peace. Although this is the first recorded attempt at a formal agreement between the two sides, feelers seem to have been sent out

[16] They are identified unspecifically as the Beduins of Bahrayn; Muḥammad eventually used them against the rebellious Muhannā clan of the Āl Faḍl Beduin. See Nuwayrī, *Nihāyah*, XXXII:331; ʿAynī, "ʿIqd," fols. 328r–v, 332r, 338v; Maqrīzī, *Sulūk*, II:214–15, 229, 236; Levanoni, *Turning Point*, 173–84, esp. 175. For the position of the Hijaz in peace negotiations see Melville, "Elephant," 203–05.

[17] See Doris Behrens-Abouseif, "The Mahmal Tradition and the Pilgrimage of the Ladies of the Mamluk Court," *Mamluk Studies Review* 1 (1997), 92–93. Also see Khalīl al-Ṣafadī, *al-Wāfī bi-al-wafāyāt* or *Das biographische Lexicon des Ṣalāḥuddīn Halīl ibn Aibak aṣ-Ṣafadī*, ed. Hellmut Ritter et al. (Wiesbaden, 1962–), XVI:447, and *Aʿyān al-ʿaṣr wa aʿwān al-naṣr*, ed. ʿAlī Abū Zayd (Beirut and Damascus, 1998), V:599–601; Ibn al-Dawādārī, *Kanz*, IX:305; Nuwayrī, *Nihāyah*, XXX:29–30, 36; ʿAynī, "ʿIqd," fols. 338v–339v; Maqrīzī, *Sulūk*, II:232.

[18] This was in September–October 1320/Shaʿbān 720. See Melville, "Elephant," 205, including sources.

[19] See Melville, "Ismaʿilis," 253, including sources.

[20] On al-Sallāmī see Amitai, "Resolution," 366–67 and note 26; David Ayalon, *L'Esclavage du mamelouk* (Jerusalem, 1951), reprinted in *The Mamluk Military Society: Collected Studies* (London, 1979), 3; Nasser Rabbat, "The Changing Concept of *Mamlūk* in the Mamluk Sultanate in Egypt and Syria," in *Slave Elites in the Middle East and Africa: A Comparative Study*, eds. Miura Toru and John Edwards Philips (London and New York, 2000), 91 and note 27; Melville, "Ismaʿilis," 252, and 252–54 on Muḥammad's use of al-Sallāmī to shelter Assassins.

in previous years.[21] A proposal of peace from Iran was hardly new – the Ilkhanids had used this approach previously when angling for Mamluk subjugation, while even Öljeitü's peace of 1305/704 was more a result of exhaustion than a genuine interest in good relations. But this time there were no references to submission, not even veiled. Rather, the Ilkhanids confirmed that Abū Saʿīd had fully acknowledged Muḥammad's ideological supremacy in the Hijaz, for on their behalf al-Sallāmī asked Muḥammad to let Abū Saʿīd send a pilgrimage caravan to Mecca not just once but every year, along with an Ilkhanid palanquin. With this was an appeal for (another) one of Muḥammad's own banners to accompany it.[22] This request helped Muḥammad consolidate his position as supreme Muslim ruler by reviving the older ideology of seniority in religion that Qalawun had used so effectively with the Golden Horde and the Ilkhanids, and that Muḥammad had employed less convincingly against Ghazan. The message also suggested additional conditions on which the treaty would be based: Muḥammad should stop sending raids into Ilkhanid territory, dispatching Assassins to kill Qarasunqur and demanding Qarasunqur's extradition, or that of any other Mamluk defector. To this last the Ilkhanids offered in return not to demand defectors from their own territory, and also asked for free passage for merchants.[23] None of these conditions implied anything in the way of Mamluk submission.

The gifts that arrived soon after al-Sallāmī seemed by their sumptuousness to show that the Ilkhanid court was serious. Some underscored the unity in religion the two rulers shared, such as a multivolume Quran, possibly the celebrated Quran produced in 1313–14/713 for Öljeitü that later surfaced in Mamluk Cairo, as well as a steel helmet engraved with the entire holy text, which made a great impression. Other items included camels, slaves and a luxurious domed tent.[24] After deliberating with the Mamluk commanders, Muḥammad honored the Ilkhanid ruler by accepting his gifts, agreed to the treaty, sent to inform the Meccans and added some conditions about the Āl Muhannā Beduin of Syria.[25] In August/Rajab Muḥammad sent back

[21] Maqrīzī, *Sulūk*, II:164, 175 mentions such feelers, although his information is for 1316–17/716 (too early for Abū Saʿīd's reign) and 1317–18/717. See Amitai, who doubts Maqrīzī, in "Resolution," 364–66; also Melville, "Elephant," 202.

[22] This was either to add a banner to the one the Ilkhanid caravan had displayed during the pilgrimage of 1320–21/720 (i.e., just as al-Sallāmī was requesting a banner in Cairo), or to formalize the Ilkhanid right to go on the pilgrimage on a yearly basis. ʿAynī, " ʿIqd," fols. 328v, 329r; Maqrīzī, *Sulūk*, II:209–10; Melville, "Ismaʿilis," 254 esp. note 42, "Elephant," 203–05 and note 31; also note 15 above.

[23] Melville, "Ismaʿilis," 253–54 and note 42; Amitai, "Resolution," 367–68.

[24] Nuwayrī, *Nihāyah*, XXX:12 for the tent and the Quran, said by one manuscript to have been in sixty volumes; ʿAynī, " ʿIqd," fol. 329r, citing the lost portion of Yūsufī for the helmet (for Yūsufī's work see note 63 below); see also Ibn al-Wardī, *Taʾrīkh*, II:387; Abū al-Fidāʾ, *Memoirs*, 81; Mufaḍḍal, *Chronik*, 11–12. See also David James, *Qurʾāns of the Mamlūks* (New York, 1988), 111–26, also 103–10.

[25] ʿAynī, " ʿIqd," fol. 329r; Maqrīzī, *Sulūk*, II:210.

appropriate presents with al-Sallāmī, which included horses with trappings, mamluks, camels and quantities of golden cloth.[26] But despite this auspicious beginning Muḥammad did not stop sending Assassins after Qarasunqur, and thereby began to undermine his own august claim to be a trustworthy Muslim sovereign.[27]

Nevertheless, after this successful initial endeavor, Abū Saʿīd's first state embassy arrived in Cairo in mid-April 1322/late Rabīʿ I 722, led by the chief judge of Tabriz.[28] The ambassadors were met by a Mamluk commander and lodged in the citadel, where the sultan received them formally on 19 April/1 Rabīʿ II.[29] In an appeal to Muḥammad's position as supreme Muslim sovereign, the message comprised the Ilkhanid assurance that theirs was a fully Islamic state, which implied that Muḥammad should have no ideological reason to refrain from communicating with them. They also submitted a new proposal to return defectors from each side (which Muḥammad turned down), and a plea that Muḥammad stop sending Assassins to kill Qarasunqur, since doing so would be in blatant violation of the treaty. Again implying that Muḥammad was the model Muslim sovereign whose example was to be followed, the Ilkhanid proposal requested that Muḥammad choose an ambassador who could provide them with a shining example of piety. Once again, the references to subjugation and tribute that had dominated previous Ilkhanid embassies were markedly absent. To level the playing field even further, Abū Saʿīd proposed a wedding between the two royal houses.

In response to the ambassadors' stipulations, Muḥammad made a demand that underscored his insistence on ideological supremacy: he stipulated that his own name be mentioned in the sermons in Ilkhanid territory, along with (and probably after) Abū Saʿīd's name and titles. Abū Saʿīd did not receive a corresponding right either in Egypt and Syria, or in the Hijaz.[30] This emphasized Muḥammad's seniority as a Muslim ruler, as well as his sovereignty at home and in Mecca. Muḥammad also insisted that al-Sallāmī be recognized as his own slave merchant in the Ilkhanid court.[31] Then, replying to Abū Saʿīd's idea of a royal wedding, Muḥammad suggested that the ilkhan send him a

[26] Mufaḍḍal, *Chronik*, 15; also Nuwayrī, *Nihāyah*, XXXIII:12; Ibn Kathīr, *Bidāyah*, XIV:114; Melville, "Ismaʿilis," 254.

[27] Melville, "Ismaʿilis," 254; also see Mufaḍḍal, *Chronik*, 108–13; Maqrīzī, *Sulūk*, II:556–58.

[28] For this mission see Nuwayrī, *Nihāyah*, XXXIII:41; Baktāsh al-Fakhrī, *Taʾrīkh salāṭīn al-mamālīk* or *Beiträge zur Geschichte der Mamlukensultane*, ed. K. V. Zettерstéen (Leiden, 1919), 172; ʿAynī, "ʿIqd," fol. 340r; Melville, "Ismaʿilis," 254–55; Ibn al-Dawādārī, who mentions a request for Muḥammad to send boxers (*mulākimīn*), perhaps to entertain the Ilkhanid court (?) in *Kanz*, IX:308; Amitai, "Resolution," 370.

[29] Nuwayrī, *Nihāyah*, XXXIII:41.

[30] He seems to have been mentioned only occasionally in the Hijaz as a courtesy from Muḥammad. ʿAynī, "ʿIqd," fol. 332v; Ibn Baṭṭūṭah, *Travels*, I:233, 248; Melville, "Elephant," 207 and note 50; Amitai, "Resolution," 370.

[31] Melville, "Ismaʿilis," 254.

Chingizid princess to marry, which would elevate Muḥammad dynastically.[32] The request suggested that Muḥammad was just as dazzled by Chingizid genealogy as was everyone else; he may also have been emboldened to make this request because he had already managed to marry one Chingizid princess, Tulunbay of the Golden Horde, in 1320/720 (see below). To deliver the message Muḥammad sent the commander Aytamish al-Muḥammadī to the Ilkhanid court. As a Mongol Mamluk who was fluent and literate in Mongolian and well versed in Mongol lineages, history and law, Aytamish was well qualified for this weighty task. Aytamish also presented an appropriately pious image, which reinforced the idea that the Mamluk Sultanate was the home of right religion: while at the Ilkhanid court Aytamish dispensed charitable donations of food to holy persons, and refused to drink alcohol. Indeed, Aytamish so charmed everyone during his stay that Abū Saʿīd later asked Muḥammad to send no other as ambassador.[33]

After Aytamish returned home, Muḥammad received a second embassy from Abū Saʿīd in June 1323/Jumādà II 723. This time, however, matters did not run smoothly, for the senior ambassador, a Mongol commander, outraged the Mamluk ruling elite with a show of arrogance.[34] This may have reflected Ilkhanid hostility to Muḥammad's continued use of Assassins against Qarasunqur, and may also have been a covert reminder of long-held Mongol views on Ilkhanid superiority and Mamluk inferiority. By Mamluk standards, the behavior was appalling. In Homs the ambassador flabbergasted the governor by putting his hand out to be kissed, which was unheard of in Mamluk protocol for foreign envoys. By the time the embassy reached Damascus, Muḥammad's governor, Tankiz, knew what to expect. Tankiz's task as Muḥammad's highest-ranking officer in Syria was delicate, since he had to welcome the embassy appropriately enough to avoid offense, but also impress its members with Muḥammad's majesty and put the arrogant ambassador in his place. To do this, Tankiz first sent out a suitably high-ranking commander, one Sayf al-Dīn Juban, to meet the envoys outside the city. Juban had very specific orders. When he reached the ambassadors in their camp, the chief man did not even rise to greet him, but merely put out his hand for a kiss. But the well-primed Juban deliberately brushed the offending hand away, turned away himself and proceeded to ignore the man as a sign that this behavior would not do. Tankiz's next move came when the ambassadors

[32] ʿAynī, "ʿIqd," fol. 340r; also see Mufaḍḍal, *Chronik*, 11, reporting that Abū Saʿīd had wanted to marry Muḥammad's niece, the daughter of Khalīl, as early as 1320–21/721 (?). No other source corroborates this. For Muḥammad's pride in his place in an existing dynasty see Rabbat, *Citadel*, 186.

[33] ʿAynī, "ʿIqd," fols. 345r–346r; Abū al-Fidāʾ, *Memoirs*, 82; Ibn Ḥajar al-ʿAsqalānī, *al-Durar al-kāminah fī aʿyān al-miʾah al-thāminah* (Beirut, 1993), I:423–24; Little, "Aitamiš," entire; Amitai, "Resolution," 370–71.

[34] The principle report is in Nuwayrī, *Nihāyah*, XXXIII:61–63; also see Abū al-Fidāʾ, *Memoirs*, 83; Ibn al-Dawādārī, *Kanz*, IX:312–13; Fakhrī, *Beiträge*, 173; Maqrīzī, *Sulūk*, II:242, 245–46; ʿAynī, "ʿIqd," fol. 344r–v.

entered the city. Rather than having a delegation of commanders usher them in, Tankiz ordered out the entire forces of Damascus in their finest silk regalia, which blazed with gems and gold embroidery. They lined up from one of the city gates and formed a long corridor extending far out of the city, down which the ambassadors passed. The effect was simultaneously to honor and, if possible, overwhelm the guests.

Next came Tankiz's meeting with the envoys. To demonstrate Muḥammad's consequence (and his own), Tankiz did not go to meet them himself, which would have been an honor. Rather he had them brought to him, which decreased their status and increased his own (and Muḥammad's). When the ambassadors arrived they found Tankiz surrounded by chamberlains, who formed a physical barrier between him and them, symbolically lowering the ambassadors in status while elevating Tankiz.[35] To reinforce this imbalance Tankiz neither rose to meet his guests, nor even looked at them fully. He did ask about Choban and the other commanders at Abū Saʿīd's court, but made no mention of the Ilkhanid ruler himself, and soon dismissed the ambassadors.

The guests were quartered in a special tent in the square (*maydān*). Although anxious to put the chief delegate in his place, Tankiz could not afford to slight them too much, and so the tent was equipped with a parasol, which among the Mamluks normally signified the ruler. This was a great honor to the guests, and not one to be taken lightly – the Ilkhanid ambassador of 1284/682–83 had had his own umbrella confiscated at the border.[36] Once the ambassadors were settled, the senior commander demanded to meet with Tankiz again. When his request was denied, he complained that Tankiz had committed a breach of etiquette: "I came from the king, not from Choban the vicegerent, nor from the commanders. How can the sultan's governor ask me about them, [but] not ask me about the king?" Tankiz sent back a response that simultaneously reinforced the hierarchy in the Mamluk Sultanate, elevated the Mamluk sultan and diminished Choban in status: "I am a governor. I do not ask about anyone other than a governor like me, or a commander [i.e., Choban]. As for the king [Abū Saʿīd] himself: the sultan, may his reign last forever, will be the one to ask about him." The messenger went on by Tankiz's order to castigate the envoy for his arrogance, and concluded with an expression of Tankiz's religious views:

> Those lands on the far side of the Euphrates – newly in your control – are places of unbelief (*kufr*), hypocrisy (*nifāq*) and Islamic dissidents (*khāwārij*); while the lands on this side of the Euphrates – joining to Syria – are places of Islam, dwellings of the

35 The Mamluk commander Uzdamir al-Mujīrī pointed out that during his 1302–03/702 interview with Ghazan four chamberlains stood between them at first, but later they were decreased to one, indicating that Uzdamir had physically and symbolically approached the ilkhan. See Chapter 3; also Sinor, "Diplomatic Practices," 349.

36 See Chapter 2.

prophets and sites for believers, holy people, religious scholars and jurisprudents. He who comes to these lands must become polite according to the proper behavior [required by] God, may He be exalted.[37]

Tankiz's statement reflected the military elite's view that Mamluk society was one of right religion and represented the model to follow, while Mongol domains were a realm of incorrect, hypocritical or even dangerous belief. Whether because of Tankiz's convincing argument, or a desire to succeed in his mission, the envoy modified his behavior. He later complained privately to Aytamish, but was warned not to mention the matter to the sultan, who was very fond of Tankiz.[38]

In Cairo Muḥammad welcomed the dignitaries on 20 June/14 Jumādà II.[39] They announced that Abū Saʿīd and Choban had formally agreed to the treaty, and asked the sultan to swear to the terms, which he did. Thereafter they presented him with a few gifts and assured him that the rest were on their way with al-Sallāmī. In response Muḥammad accepted the gifts and showered the envoys with sweets, fruit and drinks.[40] Nevertheless the situation was not entirely cordial. At some point during the visit the ambassadors told Muḥammad that there had been another Assassin attack in Ilkhanid territory, this one shortly after Aytamish had concluded the negotiations with Choban. They asked Muḥammad why this had happened, since it completely violated the treaty. In response, Muḥammad shamelessly jeopardized his own upstanding image by lying: he disavowed any awareness of Assassins in Ilkhanid territory, swore that he had not sent any since the beginning of negotiations and then washed his hands of the matter, although he was even then secretly planning to send more.[41] Even if the ambassadors believed him at the time, subsequent attacks easily put the lie to his word.

In addition to their announcement of the treaty and their complaint about the Assassins, the Ilkhanid ambassadors of summer 1323/723 addressed the more personal topic of a marriage alliance between the two sides, albeit disappointingly for Muḥammad. Not only was Muḥammad's request for a Chingizid bride declined, but the ambassadors dealt the sultan a decided blow when they suggested on behalf of their sender that Muḥammad choose one of his own daughters to be married in Ilkhanid territory, possibly to Abū Saʿīd – which was still an honor to Muḥammad – or to a son of Choban, which was not. The Ilkhanid refusal to send a Chingizid princess to Cairo and the demand for a Qalawunid bride indicated a lingering sense of Ilkhanid superiority in general and a suggestion of Chingizid superiority in particular (a Chingizid princess being too good for Muḥammad the Qalawunid). Such implications had only been reinforced by the lead envoy's arrogance in Syria. Muḥammad read the behavior of the embassy accurately and understood the significance of the request. Therefore he postponed any decision by arguing

[37] Nuwayrī, *Nihāyah*, XXXIII:62. [38] ʿAynī, "ʿIqd," fol. 344r. [39] Fakhrī, *Beiträge*, 173.
[40] Nuwayrī, *Nihāyah*, XXXIII:62. [41] Melville, "Ismaʿilis," 255–56.

that his only marriageable daughter was five years old (which was untrue).[42] This desire for some kind of marital link resurfaced repeatedly in the 1320s/720s, suggested by both Abū Saʿīd and Choban. In these later embassies a wedding between one of Muḥammad's daughters and Choban's son Dimashq Khwājā moved firmly to the forefront of negotiations, which seriously undermined Muḥammad's dynastic position. When the bridegroom was merely Choban's son, Muḥammad's rank would drop to that of Choban, not Abū Saʿīd, which Muḥammad could see full well. As a result, Muḥammad refused each time on the grounds of his daughters' youth, which continued to be untrue – three of Muḥammad's daughters were old enough to marry into the military elite during the 1320s/720s. The only time Muḥammad did express interest in these later proposals was when he stipulated that any wedding take place in Cairo, which would have allowed him to hold the Chobanid groom as a hostage.[43]

The embassy concluded with formal presentations of robes and caparisoned horses to the ambassadors and an excursion to the polo grounds; it then departed on 28 June/22 Jumādà II, accompanied as far as Gaza by Aytamish.[44] Then, immediately thereafter, in direct contradiction to his stated acceptance of the treaty, and again careless of the threat to his image as a trustworthy ruler, Muḥammad held a secret meeting with al-Sallāmī, with whom he sent yet another Assassin for Qarasunqur.[45]

Except for the arrogance displayed by the Ilkhanid ambassador in Syria, this embassy set the tone for diplomacy in the 1320s/720s. It also set the definitions of kingship expressed by each side. Especially as explained by Tankiz, Muḥammad was the superior patron of religion. His lands were at a religious advantage because of the holy sites and scholars they contained, while the Islam practiced in them was purer than that of the Ilkhanate, and free from heresies, hypocrisy or faulty belief. In addition, and as shown through the cowing of the lead ambassador, in his own territories Muḥammad was a majestic sovereign, whom the Ilkhanids (and their ambassadors) were to take seriously, or else. As had been demonstrated previously in the negotiation over the pilgrimage ceremonial, Muḥammad was also ideologically paramount in the Hijaz as its sovereign and premier patron. For their own part, Abū Saʿīd and Choban appear to have accepted Muḥammad's basis for kingship and Abū Saʿīd's consequently secondary

[42] Nuwayrī, *Nihāyah*, XXXIII:63.
[43] Abū Saʿīd may have wanted to marry Muḥammad's daughter himself in 1323–24/724 (ʿAynī, "ʿIqd," fol. 351v); see above, note 32, for the possibility that he had earlier wanted to marry Muḥammad's niece. Then Choban wanted a bride for his son Dimashq Khwājā in July–August 1326/Ramaḍān 726; and Abū Saʿīd made the same request in May–June 1327/Rajab 727. Nuwayrī, *Nihāyah*, XXXIII:204, 231; ʿAynī, "ʿIqd," fols. 370r, 371v, 375v. The Qalawunid princesses married in 1322–23/722, 1326–27/727 and 1327–28/728. See Mufaḍḍal, *Chronik*, 17, 37; Ibn Kathīr, *Bidāyah*, XIV:117, 148; Maqrīzī, *Sulūk*, II:288, 296; ʿAynī, "ʿIqd," fol. 377r; also Irwin, *Mamluk Sultanate*, 125–26.
[44] Nuwayrī, *Nihāyah*, XXXIII:62–63. [45] Melville, "Ismaʿilis," 255–56.

role in the patronage of Islam. Nevertheless they reserved the right to challenge unkingly behavior, especially since Muḥammad continued to send Assassins. Periodically Abū Saʿīd and Choban also sought to diminish Muḥammad's position, albeit not on religious grounds, but indirectly through marriage proposals that suggested the relative inferiority of the Qalawunid lineage.

Embassies were exchanged at the rate of two per year (one for each ruler).[46] On the Ilkhanid side, both Abū Saʿīd and Choban sent ambassadors, who could travel either together, in tandem, or apart, accompanied by a staggering amount of gifts.[47] Occasionally emigrants would accompany Ilkhanid ambassadors as well.[48] The ceremonies and protocol of the receptions at both courts were similar, as were ambassadorial activities during a diplomatic stay. In the Ilkhanate Mamluk delegates engaged in long rounds of receptions with commanders, dignitaries and ladies in the ilkhan's camp. To support the new religious unity, and perhaps to prove the Mongols' Muslim credentials, Mamluk ambassadors might be invited to sermons on Fridays.[49] In Cairo Ilkhanid ambassadors attended spectacles that previously had been reserved for representatives of the Golden Horde, and that demonstrated Muḥammad's power, such as trips to the polo grounds for displays of Mamluk martial skills. Ilkhanid ambassadors also took part in religious rituals and excursions, among them visits to the holy Muslim sites of the city, or banquets on Muslim holidays (Figure 6).[50] These last allowed Muḥammad to show his patronage of religion through the provision of elaborate meals.

At other times Muḥammad sought to portray his own genealogical position through appeals to dynastic legitimacy. On one occasion in May–June 1327/Rajab 727, immediately after yet another request for a royal bride to marry Dimashq Khwājā, Muḥammad tried to impress the envoys on both

46 Ilkhanid embassies came to Cairo in November–December 1324/Dhū al-Ḥijjah 724 (Abū al-Fidāʾ, *Memoirs*, 84; Ibn al-Dawādārī, *Kanz*, IX:314; Nuwayrī, *Nihāyah*, XXXIII:72; Fakhrī, *Beiträge*, 175; Maqrīzī, *Sulūk*, II:257 although saying October–November/Dhū al-Qaʿdah); in April–May 1325/Jumādà I 725 (Fakhrī, *Beiträge*, 175); in June–July 1326/Rajab 726 (Jazarī, *Taʾrīkh*, II:110; Fakhrī, *Beiträge*, 177; Maqrīzī, *Sulūk*, II:273; ʿAynī, "ʿIqd," fol. 370r), and in May–June 1327/Rajab 727 (Jazarī, *Taʾrīkh*, II:181–82; Nuwayrī, *Nihāyah*, XXXIII:231; Maqrīzī, *Sulūk*, II:282–83). Aytamish set out for Tabriz in spring 1326/726 (Nuwayrī, *Nihāyah*, XXXIII:199; Jazarī, *Taʾrīkh*, II:108–09).

47 The Ilkhanid gifts to Muḥammad in 1324/724 included three horses of mixed breed with Egyptian-style gilded, gem-studded saddles, three belts of gold and jewels, a sword with a scabbard of gold and gems, robes with gold brocade sleeve-bands, pieces of gold brocade and eleven caparisoned Bactrian camels carrying chests that contained 700 pieces of cloth, all bearing Muḥammad's title. Abū al-Fidāʾ, *Memoirs*, 84.

48 One such was the Mongol governor of Akhlat, Tayirbugha, who was Muḥammad's maternal uncle, and who emigrated with his son Yaḥyà to Cairo in 1325–26/726, where Muḥammad gave them military positions. Nuwayrī, *Nihāyah*, XXXIII:203; Abū al-Fidāʾ, *Memoirs*, 86; Maqrīzī, *Sulūk*, II:273; ʿAynī, "ʿIqd," fol. 370r. Also see Little, "Aitamiš," 392.

49 ʿAynī, "ʿIqd," fol. 346r.

50 These included the shrines of the Prophet's grandson al-Ḥusayn and great-great-granddaughter Sayyidah Nafīsah. ʿAynī, "ʿIqd," fol. 345r. For feasts see Abū al-Fidāʾ, *Memoirs*, 84.

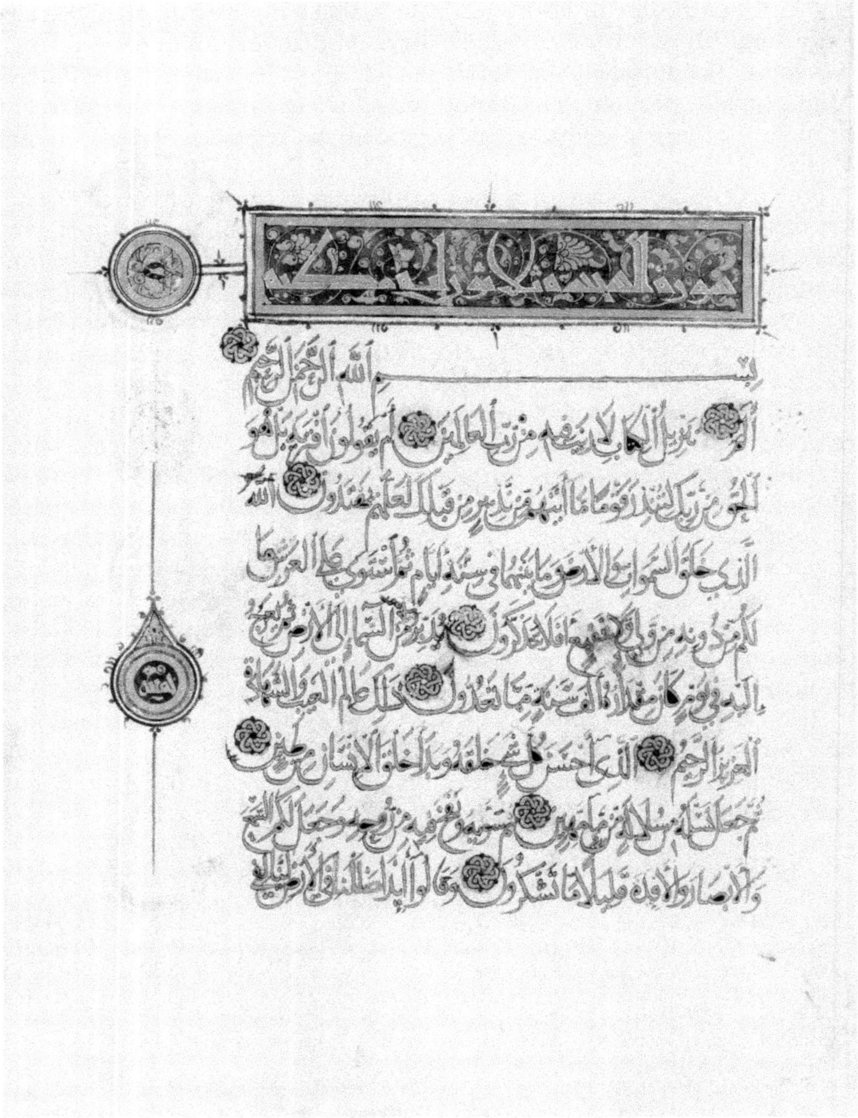

Figure 6. As a worthy Muslim sovereign, Muḥammad supported the production of this royal Quran, which was beautifully illuminated with gold, red, brown and blue ink and watercolors. (Artist: Shādhī b. Muḥammad b. Shādhī. Egypt, 1313/712–13. Freer Gallery of Art, Smithsonian, Institution, Washington, DC: Purchase, F1938.15a.)

religious and familial grounds by taking the Ilkhanid ambassadors to visit his father's tomb complex, which included a religious school and a hospital. There he sponsored a banquet for the ambassadors and the most important Islamic scholars of Cairo, which not only emphasized both Muḥammad's and Qalawun's patronage of religion, but highlighted Muḥammad's kingly heritage as Qalawun's son (and perhaps implied that Muḥammad's daughter should not marry beneath her).[51] The sultan may also have hoped to dazzle the envoys on architectural grounds, since the complex was imposing from the outside and exquisite on the inside, while the tomb chamber itself echoed the unique floor plan of the Dome of the Rock in Jerusalem.

All of these embassies were accompanied by elaborate diplomatic letters, whose protocol demonstrated the importance of the correspondence. Although no traces of Ilkhanid letters remain, some details of Mamluk practices do. As had been true for earlier Mamluk letters to the Ilkhanids, letters to Abū Saʿīd required full-sized Baghdādī paper and lavish amounts of gold and black inks. After the appropriate mention of God at the opening, letters began with a list of Muḥammad's titles, in gold, which served to illustrate his position as the Guardian of Islam and supreme Islamic patron, the consort of the Abbasid caliph of Cairo and the descendant of an earlier Mamluk ruler: "The Victorious King, Offspring of the Greatest Kings, Victorious One of the Earthly World and Religion, Partner of the Prince of the Faithful [i.e., the caliph], Sultan of Islam and Muslims, Reviver of Justice in the Worlds, Renewer (*mujaddid*) of the Splendor of Religion, Raiser of the Minarets of the Holy Fighters, Protector of the Honor of the Unitarians, Taker of Vengeance for Muslims from Heretics (*al-Malik al-Nāṣir, najl al-mulūk al-akābir, nāṣir al-dunyā wa al-dīn, qasīm amīr al-mu'minīn, sulṭān al-islām wa al-muslimīn, muḥyī al-ʿadl fī al-ʿālamīn,*[52] *mujaddid rawnaq al-dīn, muqīm manār al-mujāhidīn, ḥāmī dhimār al-muwaḥḥidīn, ākhidh tha['*]*r al-mu'minīn min al-mulḥidīn*)."[53] Particularly striking was Muḥammad's title as "Renewer of the Splendor of Religion," a concept at which Ghazan had hinted in his letters at the turn of the century, but had not employed outright.[54] Next came Abū Saʿīd's titles, also written in gold: "The Noble and Lofty Presence, the Paramount Sultan, the King-of-Kings, the Unique and Brotherly [Presence], the Khan (*al-ḥaḍarah al-sharīfah al-ʿālīyah al-sulṭānīyah al-aʿẓamīyah al-shāhinshāhīyah al-awḥadīyah al-akhawīyah al-qānīyah*)," and followed by Abū Saʿīd's personal titles and name.[55] The clearest indication of

51 Nuwayrī, *Nihāyah*, XXXIII:231.
52 This could also be read as "ʿālamayn," or "two worlds," but that would break the rhyme.
53 Baybars al-Manṣūrī, *Zubdah*, 325.
54 See Chapter 3; also Holt, "Position and Power," 247.
55 The Mamluk chancellery never used the title "the King" (*al-malik*) for Abū Saʿīd, since among the Mongols it was seen as lowly. See ʿUmarī, *Taʿrīf*, 59, whence Qalqashandī, *Ṣubḥ*, VII:273; also Ibn Nāẓir al-Jaysh, *Tathqīf*, 10, albeit replacing "Brotherly" with "Sonly" (*al-waladīyah*), and adding a few other superlatives.

new cordiality on the Mamluk side was the use of "Brotherly" for Abū Saʿīd, which signaled a warm familial relationship in which the two men were close to equals. Letters continued with pleasant expressions of friendship and news about regional politics, and closed with pious and genial exclamations.[56]

The Chobanid embassies

But Abū Saʿīd was not the only one exchanging ambassadors with Muḥammad, for Choban also sent messengers of his own. Charles Melville has characterized Choban as a devoted servant of the state, albeit an unusually powerful one, in whom Mongolian and Islamic ideas about government were at best uneasily reconciled. Consistent were Choban's devotion to the Ilkhanate itself, and to Chingizid rule within it.[57] This implied a corresponding belief in Chingizid supremacy in general, which for the Mamluks appeared most obviously in Choban's continued and insulting attempts to marry one of Muḥammad's daughters to his own son, and not to Abū Saʿīd. To compound the problem, Choban's own unease with the subtleties and flatteries of court life meant that he may not have realized the depth of his offense, since Muḥammad's refusals were consistently gracious.[58] This cost Choban dearly in his relationship to the Mamluk sultan.

To make matters worse, Choban added a sincere desire to act as a good patron of Islam to his respect for Chingizid tradition. Unlike Abū Saʿīd, who appeared to be content with his role as second regional Muslim ruler during the 1320s/720s, and who made little attempt to establish his own reputation in Mecca and Medina, Choban sought to assert his position as a charitable benefactor of religion, particularly through architectural patronage in the Hijaz. But since Muḥammad was himself the supreme patron there, Choban's efforts to establish himself thus came at Muḥammad's expense. Choban was not himself a sultan, nor aspired to be one, and never challenged Muḥammad with curtains or a palanquin – those were royal prerogatives. Nevertheless, Choban did not realize how jealously Muḥammad guarded his position as supreme Muslim patron, nor that his own repeated appeals to religion in general and to ambitious charitable projects in particular tended to offend the sultan, not warm his heart.

Early in the 1320s/720s, for example, Choban asked Muḥammad for some unused lands in Egypt to make into a pious endowment for the Haram complex in Mecca. Certainly the request bolstered Muḥammad's image as a patron of religion and reinforced his dominance within his own territory, but it also suggested that Choban had future plans in Egypt and the holy cities,

[56] ʿUmarī, *Taʿrīf*, 58–59, whence Qalqashandī, *Ṣubḥ*, VII:272–74.
[57] Melville, "Wolf or Shepherd?," 80–81, 87–91. [58] *Ibid.*, 84–86, 90.

which may have made the habitually jealous and paranoid sultan nervous.[59] Later in 1326/726 Choban honored Muḥammad by sending him three distinguished mystics, separately from Abū Sa'īd's ambassadors, but then insulted him by having them ask for a bride for Dimashq Khwājā again. The ambassadors compounded the problem by expressing Choban's hope that the jurisconsult Aḥmad b. Taymīyah would officiate at the wedding, which was impossible, since Muḥammad had recently jailed him. Although Muḥammad met with the mystics once, he refused their requests, pointed out that Ibn Taymīyah was not in favor, and then turned them over to his chief judge.[60] Later Muḥammad sent back an explanation that Ibn Taymīyah was not in the sultan's own jail (i.e., for political matters), but was in a jail for those who broke Islamic law, which Muḥammad (as its protector and upholder) could not contravene.[61]

But the Hijaz caused the most trouble between the two men, at least in Muḥammad's opinion. Choban's architectural ambitions there were considerable. In Medina he built two significant complexes: a public bath, and a school next to the Prophet's mosque. Because of their location and functions, both establishments could be appreciated frequently by the locals, and periodically by pilgrims and other visitors. This assured Choban's reputation not only in the region, but everywhere pilgrims went. Choban also built a handsome tomb for himself as part of the school, and spared no trouble or expense in doing so – he even had windows cut into the Prophet's mosque to transmit blessings into the tomb chamber.[62] But Choban was best remembered for his costly restoration of a spring outside Mecca in 1325–26/726, which he began after hearing from pilgrims that water in the city was in short supply, and therefore very expensive. When the pilgrims asked the Meccans about it, they were told that there were sufficient springs in Mecca to provide water for all, if

59 Maqrīzī, *Sulūk*, II:230 (in 1321–22/721); 'Aynī, "'Iqd," fol. 340r (in 1322–23/722); also 'Abdallah Khwāfī Ḥāfiẓ Abrū, *Dhayl-i jāmi' al-tawārīkh-i Rashīdī*, ed. Khānbābā Bāyānī (Tehran, 1971), 179; whence both 'Abd al-Razzāq Samarqandī, *Maṭla'-i Sa'dayn va majma'-yi baḥrayn*, ed. 'Abd al-Ḥusayn Navā'ī (Tehran, 1993), 110, and Mīrkhwānd, *Rawḍah*, VIII:4381.

60 This was in July–August/Ramaḍān. Nuwayrī, *Nihāyah*, XXXIII:204; also 'Aynī, "'Iqd," fol. 370r, albeit tacked on (inaccurately) to a report of Abū Sa'īd's ambassadors (in Cairo in June–July/Rajab). For mystics in Ilkhanid Islam see Charles Melville, *The Fall of Amir Chupan and the Decline of the Ilkhanate, 1327–37: A Decade of Discord in Mongol Iran*, Papers on Inner Asia No. 30 (Bloomington, IN, 1999), 21; also Denise Aigle, "Le Soufism sunnite en Fars: Sayh Amīn al-Dīn Balyānī," in *Domination*, 231–60; Reuven Amitai-Preiss, "Sufis and Shamans: Some Remarks on the Islamization of the Mongols in the Ilkhanate," *JESHO* 42:1 (1999), 27–46.

61 'Aynī, "'Iqd," fol. 371v.

62 For the bath complex see Ibn al-Wardī, *Ta'rīkh*, II:405; Ḥamdallah Mustawfī Qazvīnī, *The Geographical Part of the Nuzhat al-Qulūb*, tr. G. Le Strange (Leiden, 1919), 14 (also the school); for the school and tomb see 'Alī al-Samhūdī, *Wafā' al-wafā' bi-akhbār dār al-muṣṭafà*, ed. Muḥammad Muḥyī al-Dīn 'Abd al-Ḥamīd ([Cairo,] Egypt, 1954), II:702; 'Aynī, "'Iqd," fol. 371v; Jazarī, *Ta'rīkh*, II:270 and funeral information for Choban in note 113 below. Also see Doris Behrens-Abouseif, "Qāytbāy's *Madrasah*s and the Evolution of Haram Architecture," *Mamluk Studies Review* 3 (1999), 133–34; Melville, "Elephant," 206.

only some charity-minded person would renovate them. This report spurred Choban to send a huge sum of money with a merchant to Mecca at the end of 1325/725.[63] Choban's agent remained in the Hijaz after the holy season and, after some inquiry, found a likely project near Mount Arafat. Although in a state of great disrepair, it had great promise, since it was an extensive system built by the Abbasid queen Zubaydah (d. 831/216), and had been constructed so that water not only flowed from a spring to Mecca, but could be diverted during the pilgrimage to a set of auxiliary pools and channels at each holy site.[64] Renovating such a system would clearly cement Choban's reputation as a formidable patron of Islam. Soon work began, and in four months all the blockage had been cleared and a canal built (or rebuilt), so that water was flowing into the city "[like] a river."[65] Not only was the scope of the project vast, but Choban's timing was auspicious, since many of the wells in Mecca went dry that year.[66]

The renovation of water sources and provision of water to the needy, particularly in holy spaces, was a popular act of charity among Muslim rulers, and had a long history in the Islamic community. In the Mamluk Sultanate, especially during Muḥammad's third reign, renovating springs seems to have enjoyed a certain vogue, especially when they could be connected to Islamic spiritual sites. During his second pilgrimage in 1319–20/719 Muḥammad himself established a yearly fund to maintain the spring of Khalīṣ between Mecca and Medina; he later renovated another spring in Mecca in the course of repairing some religious buildings.[67] Within Mamluk territory, water sources associated with holy spaces were renovated under the auspices of Muḥammad's subordinates in Jerusalem and Hebron, often in conjunction with religious building projects, which led to practical and pious benefits for all.[68]

But although the Mamluks would therefore have easily understood Choban's desire to provide water in the holiest Islamic city, and although Choban's generosity inspired widespread appreciation, the Mamluk sultan's

[63] One report cites an initial outlay of 50,000 (gold) dinars, with the promise of unlimited further funds (Mūsà al-Yūsufī, *Nuzhat al-nāẓir fī sīrat al-Malik al-Nāṣir*, ed. Aḥmad Ḥuṭayṭ [Beirut, 1986], 433; whence ʿAynī, " ʿIqd," fol. 371r); others report 150,000 (silver) dirhams (Jazarī, *Taʾrīkh*, II:115), or 300,000 dirhams (Nuwayrī, *Nihāyah*, XXXIII:207; Mufaḍḍal, *Chronik*, 36; also ʿAynī, " ʿIqd," fol. 370v, citing Ibn Kathīr (this number does not appear in the edited Ibn Kathīr, *Bidāyah*, IV:142)); one total figure cited is 1,050,000 (al-Fākihī, *Kitāb al-muntaqà fī akhbār umm al-qurà*, quoting one Ibn Fahd, in *Die Chroniken der Stadt Mekka*, ed. Ferdinand Wüstenfeld [Leipzig, 1857–61, repr. Beirut, 1964], II:53).

[64] Fākihī, quoting Ibn Fahd, *Chroniken*, II:52; also see Qazvīnī, *Nuzhah*, 4.

[65] Yūsufī, *Nuzhah*, 433.

[66] Jazarī, *Taʾrīkh*, II:114–15, 125–27, 252; Yūsufī, *Nuzhah*, 433; Ibn Kathīr, *Bidāyah*, XIV:142; ʿAynī, " ʿIqd," fols. 370v–371r; Mufaḍḍal, *Chronik*, 36; Ibn al-Wardī, *Taʾrīkh*, II:399; see also Ṣafadī, *Aʿyān*, II:169.

[67] Maqrīzī, *Sulūk*, II:200–01; Ibn al-Wardī, *Taʾrīkh*, II:405.

[68] Renovations took place in Hebron in 1313–14/713 and in Jerusalem in 1326–27/727. See Maqrīzī, *Sulūk*, II:131, 289, 302; ʿAynī, " ʿIqd," fol. 377r.

response to the project was entirely negative: Muḥammad was livid when he heard that someone else had performed this great act of charity. Muḥammad hated to see royal works attributed to anyone but himself; nor, as foremost religious patron in the holy cities, could he stand the interference of a charity-minded rival. Worse still, Muḥammad had considered renovating the very same water system in Mecca, but had been dissuaded by his advisors, who thought the project untenable.[69] Choban then compounded the problem by sending news of his feat to Muḥammad in 1326/726. Muḥammad's concern with maintaining his sovereignty over the holy cities was clear in his response: the sultan roundly abused the ambassador for Choban's failure to ask for permission to renovate, and was only calmed by the man's diplomatic sop to Mamluk authority, for he assured the sultan that it was ultimately his decision whether the repairs would remain or not.[70] Given Muḥammad's extraordinary memory for slights and insults, it is no surprise that he thereafter maintained a serious grudge against Choban over this matter of the spring.

The fall of the Chobanids

In 1326–27/727 Abū Saʿīd rebelled against Choban and his sons, which led to a purge of most of the family – Choban himself was strangled in Herat at Abū Saʿīd's order in November–December 1327/Muḥarram 728.[71] For Muḥammad, who had been diplomatically involved with both men, the situation should have been clear even as the drama unfolded. Ideologically (and now practically) his relationship with Abū Saʿīd had to take priority over any relationship to a mere vicegerent, no matter how powerful. However, the matter was complicated from the outset by the question of Choban's son Temürtash, Ilkhanid governor in Anatolia, with whom Muḥammad's relations had been strained for most of the decade. Temürtash turned to Muḥammad for help, but wanted it on his own ambitious terms. Muḥammad's response to Temürtash unwittingly contributed to the ongoing tarnishing of the sultan's image as a trustworthy ruler and a model of Muslim kingship.

As early as November–December 1320/Shawwāl 720 Temürtash had begun to send Muḥammad ambassadors.[72] Despite their overlap with the Ilkhanid–Mamluk peace negotiations, however, these embassies were not an extension of general Ilkhanid goodwill, for Temürtash was actually seeking

69 Nuwayrī, *Nihāyah*, XXXIII:209; Jazarī, *Taʾrīkh*, II:127; also see Yūsufī, *Nuzhah*, 264.

70 Fākihī, quoting Ibn Fahd, *Chroniken*, II:53; Maqrīzī, *Sulūk*, II:274; ʿAynī, "ʿIqd," fol. 371r, citing the lost Yūsufī (but not in Aḥmad Ḥuṭayṭ's edition of Yūsufī, where this year is reconstructed from a different manuscript: ʿAynī MS [Istanbul?] Ahmad III:2911, vol. XVII).

71 Melville, *Decline*, 19–29, esp. 25–26 for the date, which is approximate; also see Boyle, "Īl-Khāns," 410–11.

72 Mufaḍḍal, *Chronik*, 11. A second arrived in 1321–22/721; see Abū al-Fidāʾ, *Memoirs*, 81; Ḥāfiẓ Abrū, *Dhayl*, 160, whence Samarqandī, *Maṭlaʿ*, 87, and Mīrkhwānd, *Rawḍah*, VIII:4356.

to establish himself as an independent sovereign. In Anatolia Temürtash not only ordered the sermon to be read in his own name and struck coins, forcing Abū Saʿīd to alter his own currency in response, but – far more dangerously – he promoted himself as a legitimate ruler not on any known Mongol grounds (Temürtash was not a Chingizid), but on the Islamic claim to be the Rightly Guided One (*mahdī*). It is unknown whether he used messianic black banners as Ghazan had done.[73] From Muḥammad Temürtash requested an army to invade "the two Iraqs and Khurasan" in 1321–22/721, which he did not receive; this was the first time a Mamluk sultan refrained from supporting a bid for independence in Anatolia.[74] Although in 1323–24/724 Choban dragged his son back to Iran in disgrace, Temürtash was pardoned, and soon returned to his old position and a second state of near-independence in Anatolia.[75]

Overall, relations between Muḥammad and Temürtash were tense. Temürtash feared Muḥammad's habit of hiring Assassins for dirty jobs, and therefore stationed guards in the mountain passes to ensure his own safety. This allowed him to keep merchants – including slave merchants – from entering Mamluk lands; he also forbade the slave trade, which stopped the importation of mamluks to Egypt and Syria along the land routes. In fact Temürtash reportedly hated Muḥammad so much that he would fly into a rage at the mention of the Mamluk sultan.[76] But at some point in 1327–28/727–28 when Temürtash heard that Abū Saʿīd was killing his family, he realized that his turn could be next, and, in a measure of his desperation, wrote asking Muḥammad for permission to join him in Cairo.[77] It is entirely unclear why Muḥammad acquiesced, but he did, and seems to have sent Aytamish to Anatolia to swear an oath on Muḥammad's behalf that established Temürtash's safety in Mamluk lands. This only added to the force of a similar promise to take care of Temürtash that Aytamish had made to Choban while at Abū Saʿīd's court in 1326/726.[78] Although no one saw it at the time, this oath by proxy was to cause terrible damage to Muḥammad's

[73] Ṣafadī, *Wāfī*, X:248, and *Aʿyān*, II:112; Ḥāfiẓ Abrū, *Dhayl*, 160, whence Samarqandī, *Maṭlaʿ*, 87, and Mīrkhwānd, *Rawḍah*, VIII:4356. See also Boyle, "Īl-Khāns," 409; Blair, "Coins," 303, 311; Wilferd Madelung, "Mahdī," *EI*[2] V:1230–38. For a view of Temürtash as a good man plagued by conspirators see Aqsarāʾī, *Mogollar*, 321–27.

[74] Ḥāfiẓ Abrū, *Dhayl*, 160, whence Samarqandī, *Maṭlaʿ*, 87, and Mīrkhwānd, *Rawḍah*, VIII:4356; Abū al-Fidāʾ, *Memoirs*, 81. In 1322–23/722 Muḥammad sent an army to collect tribute from the Armenians, who were expressing a new loyalty to him because Temürtash had just raided their lands in 1321–22/late 721. See Nuwayrī, *Nihāyah*, XXXIII:36–39; Ibn al-Wardī, *Taʾrīkh*, II:389; Abū al-Fidāʾ, *Memoirs*, 82.

[75] Boyle, "Īl-Khāns," 409.

[76] Yūsufī, *Nuzhah*, 439, whence ʿAynī, "ʿIqd," fol. 380r.

[77] Ḥamdallah Mustawfī Qazvīnī, *Taʾrīkh-i guzīdah*, ed. ʿAbd al-Ḥusayn Navāʾī (Tehran, 1362), 620; Ḥāfiẓ Abrū, *Dhayl*, 182, whence Samarqandī, *Maṭlaʿ*, 113–14, and Mīrkhwānd, *Rawḍah*, VIII:4383–84; Nuwayrī, *Nihāyah*, XXXIII:253; Ibn al-Dawādārī, *Kanz*, IX:346–47; ʿAynī, "ʿIqd," fol. 380r.

[78] Ṣafadī, *Aʿyān*, II:113; for Aytamish's promise to Choban to take care of Temürtash should he ever go to Egypt see ʿAynī, "ʿIqd," fol. 371v and the discussion in Little, "Aitamiš," 396–97.

image as a trustworthy and upstanding Muslim ruler. But as a result of it, Temürtash left his family behind in Anatolia and set out for Syria.[79]

Temürtash's reception in Mamluk territory showed that he was a highly honored guest; it may also have fueled his considerable ambitions for independent rule. Temürtash arrived in Damascus on 10 January 1328/25 Ṣafar. There Tankiz showed him great distinction by personally riding out to meet him, accompanied by the commanders and the assembled forces. In a greater and unprecedented display of esteem, Temürtash was lodged in the sultan's own palace before being sent on to Cairo, where he arrived on 20 January/6 Rabīʿ I.[80] Once there, however, Temürtash's expectations were not met. He had hoped that Muḥammad would ride out of the city to greet him in person as Tankiz had done in Damascus, which would have established the two men on roughly equal footing.[81] But Temürtash was met at Gaza and again outside Cairo by senior Mamluk officials in a reception appropriate for a high-ranking Mamluk commander. This signaled that Temürtash needed to fit himself into the Mamluk administration like Sülemish before him. A day after his arrival in Cairo Temürtash went to meet the sultan, who was hunting by the pyramids. There, regardless of his thoughts, Temürtash put on an appropriately grateful show, and greeted the Mamluk sultan by deferentially kissing the ground three times.[82]

From Muḥammad's point of view, the welcome of his guest was extremely warm. Muḥammad gave Temürtash an elaborate red robe and other gifts of superb quality – good enough for Muḥammad's vicegerent in Cairo, who was the highest-ranking man in the land after the sultan himself. To increase Temürtash's prestige, Muḥammad allowed him to accompany the commanders in the formal procession into the citadel, where Temürtash was lodged.[83] A few days later on 24 January/10 Rabīʿ I, Temürtash overtly declared his loyalty to Muḥammad and covertly highlighted his own kingly resources by offering Muḥammad an impressive array of luxurious gifts, including horses, mamluks and clothing. But Muḥammad countered with his own display of royal prerogative and refused almost everything. The next day Muḥammad continued to demonstrate his favor to Temürtash by permitting him to ride in the procession to a royal reception, where Temürtash sat with the commanders. By Mamluk standards, Temürtash should have been overwhelmed by such favors, but he was not. In particular, Temürtash's place at the reception was a sign of distinction from Muḥammad's point of

[79] Jazarī, *Taʾrīkh*, II:254; Nuwayrī, *Nihāyah*, XXXIII:253; Mufaḍḍal, *Chronik*, 39; Ḥāfiẓ Abrū, *Dhayl*, 182.

[80] Jazarī, *Taʾrīkh*, II:254; dates (some wrong) from Nuwayrī, *Nihāyah*, XXXIII:254–55; corrected dates in Mufaḍḍal, *Chronik*, 39–40, and Maqrīzī, *Sulūk*, II:294–95.

[81] Ṣafadī, *Aʿyān*, II:113, also *Wāfī*, X:248.

[82] Maqrīzī, *Sulūk*, II:294; ʿAynī, "ʿIqd," fol. 380v.

[83] For the clothes see Nuwayrī, *Nihāyah*, XXXIII:254; ʿAynī, "ʿIqd," fol. 380r; otherwise Ibn al-Dawādārī, *Kanz*, IX:346–47.

view, but was worrisome to Temürtash himself, since he was seated among older men of middling rank, not with the highest personnel. His distress was so apparent that Muḥammad sent to reassure his guest by explaining that he knew of Temürtash's importance, but had wanted to honor some of his father's old mamluks by placing Temürtash with them.[84]

But Temürtash's ambitions extended far beyond attaining a good place at Muḥammad's receptions. Unlike Sülemish, who had at least pretended to submit to the Mamluk sultan, Temürtash wanted total independence – including from Mamluk overlordship. Soon after his arrival, therefore, Temürtash began to show off his kingly qualities at Muḥammad's expense. Temürtash's considerable wealth in flocks and money followed him from Anatolia, and in Egypt he began to distribute enormous gifts as if he were himself sultan. Although Temürtash especially favored Muḥammad's senior commanders, no one escaped his notice: one lucky bath attendant was rumored to have been awarded hundreds of dirhams for his services.[85] Not surprisingly, this won Temürtash widespread goodwill, to Muḥammad's alarm. Worse yet, after his first demonstration of gratitude, Temürtash did not seek to charm the sultan, but rather paid far too much attention to Muḥammad's commanders and mamluks.[86] Although Muḥammad tried to disguise his own doubts and win Temürtash over with hunting parties and amusements, these outings must have fallen flat for a man with such ambitions, now reduced to dancing attendance on a sultan he despised.[87]

Certainly for a jealous man like Muḥammad there was much to fear in the tall, talented and handsome guest. This was, after all, the self-proclaimed Rightly Guided One (*mahdī*), who had dared challenge the Chingizid Abū Saʿīd. Muḥammad cannot have viewed such claims as anything but deeply disturbing, for in his role as Guardian of Islam he was responsible for the execution of apostates and heretics. If Temürtash's claims had been made in Mamluk territory, they would have guaranteed him a swift beheading under Muḥammad's auspices.[88] Temürtash's followers posed a further problem when they came to Cairo in record numbers (between 600 and 1,000) shortly after their lord.[89] Although Muḥammad found military assignments for them and for Temürtash himself, he did so grudgingly, and only at the urging of his commanders.[90] When some of the new arrivals went back to Anatolia, Muḥammad encouraged them to leave by helping pay their way.[91] The matter

[84] Maqrīzī, *Sulūk*, II:294–95; ʿAynī, "ʿIqd," fol. 380v.
[85] Ṣafadī, *Wāfī*, X:248, and *Aʿyān*, II:112–13; also Qazvīnī, *Guzīdah*, 620; Ḥāfiẓ Abrū, *Dhayl*, 182.
[86] Ṣafadī, *Wāfī*, X:248, and *Aʿyān*, II:112, 114; see also Ibn Baṭṭūṭah, *Travels*, II:339.
[87] Nuwayrī, *Nihāyah*, XXXIII:256; Yūsufī, *Nuzhah*, 439.
[88] See Broadbridge, "Apostasy Trials," 368–70, 373, 376–78.
[89] For 600 see Jazarī, *Taʾrīkh*, II:254; Nuwayrī, *Nihāyah*, XXXIII:254, and Mufaḍḍal, *Chronik*, 39; for 1,000 see Ḥāfiẓ Abrū, *Dhayl*, 182; Samarqandī, *Maṭlaʿ*, 114, and Mīrkhwānd, *Rawḍah*, VIII:4384.
[90] Ṣafadī, *Aʿyān*, II:113.
[91] Nuwayrī, *Nihāyah*, XXXIII:255.

began to seem even more serious when Muḥammad heard from the lord of the Qaramanid Türkmen, and from one of Temürtash's own sons, both in Anatolia, that the exile had designs on the Sultanate, and that astrologers had predicted Temürtash's rule in "the east" and in Egypt.[92] This made Muḥammad only more nervous.

Meanwhile the sultan was keeping track of developments in the Ilkhanate, at first through his own spy network, then by the arrival of Abū Saʿīd's envoys in Cairo in mid-December 1327/late Muḥarram 728 with official news of the trouble.[93] Next on 23 January/9 Rabīʿ I, shortly after Temürtash himself had reached Cairo, a cousin of Choban named Shāhinshāh (?) entered the city with more news of the strife, and told of Choban's intention to flee east (by this time, however, Choban was already dead).[94] In January–February/late Rabīʿ I a second set of ambassadors from Abū Saʿīd arrived in Cairo, and were surprised to find Temürtash in residence, since they had set out before word of his defection had arrived.[95] Muḥammad sent them back on 20 February/7 Rabīʿ II with his own man, a commander and seasoned ambassador named Sayf al-Dīn Uruj, who bore a message of intercession for Temürtash, and a request to settle him in Cairo with his family and followers.[96] In June/Shaʿbān Uruj returned to Syria, traveling quickly ahead of a third Ilkhanid embassy – Uruj reached Hama on the twenty-sixth/sixteenth, made it to Damascus on the twenty-seventh/seventeenth, and set out for Cairo on the same day.[97] Although his message was probably too delicate to entrust to carrier pigeons, he may have just managed to arrive in Cairo late on 30 June/20 Shaʿbān by riding his mounts at a ruinous pace. On that very evening Muḥammad arrested Temürtash, his companions and his cousin Shāhinshāh. Temürtash was jailed separately from the others.[98] Then on 20 July/11 Ramaḍān the embassy that had been following Uruj reached Cairo with the offer of a trade: Temürtash for Muḥammad's old nemesis, Qarasunqur, who was still thriving in Ilkhanid territory.[99] Muḥammad was so interested that he dispatched Aytamish on 25 July/16 Ramaḍān to make arrangements, then reconsidered and brought him back to Cairo.[100]

But Muḥammad's response to Abū Saʿīd's proposal was not to the ambassadors' liking. The sultan swore that he would not send Temürtash back alive,

[92] Yūsufī, *Nuzhah*, 439; ʿAynī, "ʿIqd," fols. 380v–381r.

[93] Nuwayrī, *Nihāyah*, XXXIII:250; Jazarī, *Taʾrīkh*, II:250; Abū al-Fidāʾ, *Memoirs*, 89; Fakhrī, *Beiträge*, 178.

[94] Nuwayrī, *Nihāyah*, XXXIII:255; Mufaḍḍal, *Chronik*, 40; also ʿAynī, "ʿIqd," fol. 380r, and Maqrīzī, *Sulūk*, II:295, both saying 2 February/19 Rabīʿ I (*sic*).

[95] Fakhrī, *Beiträge*, 178; also Jazarī, *Taʾrīkh*, II:256.

[96] Nuwayrī, *Nihāyah*, XXXIII:255–56; Maqrīzī, *Sulūk*, II:296.

[97] Abū al-Fidāʾ, *Memoirs*, 89–90; Jazarī, *Taʾrīkh*, II:265.

[98] Nuwayrī, *Nihāyah*, XXXIII:256; Jazarī, *Taʾrīkh*, II:265; Fakhrī, *Beiträge*, 178; Mufaḍḍal, *Chronik*, 40; ʿAynī, "ʿIqd," fol. 381r; Ibn al-Wardī, *Taʾrīkh*, II:406.

[99] Nuwayrī, *Nihāyah*, XXXIII:256 (albeit calling the senior envoy Ayaji [*sic*], not Abaji); ʿAynī, "ʿIqd," fol. 381r; also Ḥāfiẓ Abrū, *Dhayl*, 183; Jazarī, *Taʾrīkh*, II:266.

[100] Nuwayrī, *Nihāyah*, XXXIII:256; ʿAynī, "ʿIqd," fol. 381v.

while the ambassadors insisted that they could not possibly take him dead.[101] Aytamish himself argued passionately that killing Temürtash would cause irreparable damage to Muḥammad's image as a man of his word, since Temürtash was protected not only by his rights as a guest, but also by Muḥammad's promise of safety, which Aytamish himself had delivered. Aytamish suggested poison or some other subterfuge, but was rejected.[102] Muḥammad also discussed the matter with Abaji, the chief Mongol envoy. It is unclear what Abaji said: in one recorded scrap of the conversation he clarified that he only had orders to take Temürtash alive, while in another he cryptically suggested that a discrepancy between words and action on the part of a king meant only that the king might correct his erroneous opinion (?).[103] Regardless of what Abaji actually said, Muḥammad convinced himself that Abū Saʿīd wanted the murder to take place, and decided to carry it out, even though this would break his own promise of safety to Temürtash and ignore his ally's overt request for live extradition. On the night of 11 August/3 Shawwāl, therefore, Temürtash was smuggled out of prison in chains to be killed in the northern cemetery of Cairo. It was a grim affair. Abū Saʿīd's envoys were there, as was the unfortunate Aytamish, who hid himself from Temürtash's view when the doomed man cried out to him for help. The assembled company watched as Temürtash was strangled, then decapitated. After undergoing further indignities, the body was buried near the point of execution.[104]

What were Muḥammad's motives for this murder? He was surely hoping to force Abū Saʿīd's hand and guarantee Qarasunqur's execution by presenting Temürtash's death as a *fait accompli*. Even though this was a breach of the treaty, it was hardly the first time Muḥammad's attempts to kill Qarasunqur had threatened relations with Abū Saʿīd; in addition, Muḥammad believed he had the ilkhan's tacit approval for the murder. But Muḥammad, who was always jealous of his own position, was also showing off his power to those of his men who attended the execution, and avenging all the slights and injuries he felt Temürtash had dealt him in the past months. Nevertheless, once again Muḥammad's capacity for vicious behavior worked against him, for his betrayal of Temürtash damaged his reputation as a trustworthy Muslim sovereign, just as his earlier stubborn use of Assassins against Qarasunqur had done.

101 Ṣafadī, *Aʿyān*, II:115, and *Wāfī*, X:249. 102 ʿAynī, "ʿIqd," fol. 381v.

103 For the first, see Ṣafadī, *Aʿyān*, II:115, and *Wāfī*, X:249; for the second see ʿAynī, "ʿIqd," fol. 381v.

104 For the event and date see Nuwayrī, *Nihāyah*, XXXIII:257; Jazarī, *Taʾrīkh*, II:269; Abū al-Fidāʾ, *Memoirs*, 90; Fakhrī, *Beiträge*, 178; Ibn al-Wardī, *Taʾrīkh*, II:406 (just August–September/Shawwāl); Maqrīzī, *Sulūk*, II:299–300. A few sources give different dates: Ṣafadī, *Aʿyān*, II:115, and *Wāfī*, X:249 (in July–August/Ramaḍān); ʿAynī, "ʿIqd," fol. 381r (10 September/4 Dhū al-Qaʿdah); Ibn al-Dawādārī, *Kanz*, IX:348 claiming Temürtash died of illness (!) on 28 September/22 Dhū al-Qaʿdah.

Furthermore, the gradual Islamization of the Ilkhanate had not eradicated the Mongol preference for avoiding bloodshed when killing a high-ranking person. Choban had negotiated successfully to die by strangulation and keep his head after death, which indicated the lingering respect he commanded, but his son Dimashq Khwājā was decapitated and the head was hung up at Sultaniyah, which suggested the opposite.[105] The Mongol ambassadors must therefore have been taken aback by Temürtash's degrading decapitation, even though the blood was shed posthumously. But even if Abū Saʿīd did secretly authorize Abaji to condone murder, certainly public opinion within the Ilkhanate was outraged. Both the betrayal and the beheading were seen as violations of honor, as became clear when Aytamish and the head were sent to Azerbaijan shortly after the murder. Aytamish balked violently at the mission, but Muḥammad insisted, although the sultan did at least entrust the head to one of al-Sallāmī's servants.[106] Unfortunately for Aytamish the head arrived first, which meant that he suffered a frigid welcome throughout Ilkhanid territory, as well as embarrassing questions wherever he went. Outside several cities Aytamish and his entourage were met by crowds screaming that they were traitors and murderers – at times it was so bad that the Mongol welcoming parties had to chase the crowds away. Although the official reception was entirely correct, it, too, was stiff: "They greeted us as usual, but without the normal welcome we usually received from them."[107]

Even Abū Saʿīd was taken aback at Muḥammad's decision, and had the vizier question Aytamish privately:

> Oh Ḥājj, the sultan Abū Saʿīd asks, what was the reason for killing Temürtash and sending his head to him? He knew nothing, and then suddenly the mamluk of al-Sallāmī had come, and the head of [Temürtash] Ibn Choban was with him. He said to him: "The sultan [Muḥammad] sends greetings to you, and also sends you the head of your enemy." Abū Saʿīd was flabbergasted.[108]

Aytamish retorted that Abū Saʿīd's own envoy Abaji had implied that the murder would be welcome, but the vizier bit one finger in distress and looked at the floor, then walked out without responding.[109] Since Abū Saʿīd had personally ordered the deaths of Temürtash's father and brothers, it is unlikely that Temürtash's execution itself led to such outrage. Rather, the shock within the Ilkhanate was caused by Muḥammad's wanton betrayal of his promise of security to Temürtash. It was not helped by the terrible gaffe of

105 For Choban see Boyle, "Īl-Khāns," 411; Melville, *Decline*, 25–26. For Dimashq Khwājā see Abū al-Fidāʾ, *Memoirs*, 87; Qazvīnī, *Guzīdah*, 618; Mīrkhwānd, *Rawḍah*, VIII:4367–68; also Melville, *Decline*, 18, who highlights Abū al-Fidāʾs claim that Dimashq Khwājā's head was degradingly used as a ball by the Mongol commanders prior to being hung up.

106 ʿAynī, "ʿIqd," fol. 381v, and Little's discussion in "Aitamiš," 397. Aytamish passed through Damascus on 20 August/12 Shawwāl on his way. Jazarī, *Taʾrīkh*, II:269.

107 Yūsufī, *Nuzhah*, 441. 108 *Ibid.*, 441–42. 109 ʿAynī, "ʿIqd," fol. 384v.

the decapitation, nor the unexpected arrival of the head at court, especially since Abū Saʿīd's new wife Baghdād Khatun, a daughter of Choban, was still grieving over her dead father and brothers. But for some Temürtash's betrayal and beheading specifically represented the evils of Islamic civilization, which contrasted unfavorably with proper Mongol tradition. Aytamish was asked privately by some of the senior Mongol commanders: "Oh Ḥājj Aytamish, this thing that you did, is this a deed that Muslims do?"[110] Aytamish had to pretend to be ill to avoid meeting Baghdād Khatun, and ultimately snuck away from court without his entourage.[111] This was, perhaps, a loss of innocence on both sides; certainly Aytamish never again went to Abū Saʿīd, and Muḥammad's reputation as an example of Muslim rule was irreparably damaged.

But it developed that Muḥammad's assumptions had been correct, and Abū Saʿīd was grateful after all. Shortly after Temürtash's execution, a Mamluk spy brought news that Muḥammad's long-time nemesis Qarasunqur had died on 3 September/26 Shawwāl in Ilkhanid territory, possibly of suicide.[112] And Abū Saʿīd seemed even more cordial than ever, for he sent two more embassies to Cairo in rapid succession: one in December 1328/early Ṣafar 729, and a second in April 1329/Jumādà II 729.[113] The chief ambassador for this second mission was a toman commander named Temürbugha al-Marghinānī, and his letter contained Abū Saʿīd's request that Muḥammad send him a daughter to marry.[114] Unlike in the case of previous proposals, this time Muḥammad expressed real interest, for at last the intended bridegroom was unquestionably the ilkhan himself. Muḥammad said he would wait only three years before he sent the girl in question, although he did ask ambitiously for the territories of Diyarbakir as his daughter's bride-price. Nevertheless Temürbugha produced a sum equal to 60,000 silver coins, which Abū Saʿīd had sent to provide a feast for the Mamluk commanders in celebration of the eventual nuptials. With Muḥammad's approval the betrothal party was held on 10 May/10 Rajab, and the embassy departed with the good news shortly thereafter.

In addition to Temürtash's murder and the damage it caused to Muḥammad's position, as well as the beginning of serious marriage negotiations – and their implications of dynastic parity – between Muḥammad and

[110] Yūsufī, *Nuzhah*, 441. [111] ʿAynī, "ʿIqd," fols. 384v–385r; Little, "Aitamiš," 397.

[112] Jazarī, *Ta'rīkh*, II:272; Nuwayrī, *Nihāyah*, XXXIII:275–76; Mufaḍḍal, *Chronik*, 41; Ibn Baṭṭūṭah, *Travels*, I:109, claiming suicide by poison.

[113] For the first see Nuwayrī, *Nihāyah*, XXXIII:278–79; Fakhrī, *Beiträge*, 180; Maqrīzī, *Sulūk*, II:310; for the second, see Nuwayrī, *Nihāyah*, XXXIII:280–81; Fakhrī, *Beiträge*, 180–81; Jazarī, *Ta'rīkh*, II:324–25; Abū al-Fidā', *Memoirs*, 91. Shaykh Ḥasan the new senior commander also sent envoys, who arrived in April/Jumādà II (Nuwayrī, *Nihāyah*, XXXIII:279–80; Maqrīzī, *Sulūk*, II:310), possibly the same envoys dated to February–March/Rabīʿ II (*sic*?) by Fakhrī, *Beiträge*, 180.

[114] The negotiations for this wedding may have begun during the discussions about Temürtash; see ʿAynī, "ʿIqd", fols. 381r–v.

Abū Saʿīd, the fall of the Chobanids had a curious epilogue. In January–February 1328/Rabīʿ I 728 while Temürtash was still an honored guest in Cairo, the Mamluk sultan had several repairs made in Mecca, including the renovation of a spring, but they were not as extensive as those Choban had undertaken.[115] Nevertheless, shortly thereafter the Mamluk sultan had an unexpected opportunity to assert his ideological primacy and spite his architectural rival in the holy cities one last time. After Choban's execution, his corpse was brought back to Iran for viewing; then Abū Saʿīd ordered interment in Tabriz. But Baghdād Khatun insisted on sending her father's coffin to Medina for burial in its beautiful tomb.[116] The coffin traveled in the pilgrimage caravan of 1328/728 with all pious honors: it was carried by ten Quran-reciters, accompanied by a water-bearer and honored with the slaughter of animals in Choban's name at every stop along the way.[117] In Mecca the coffin went through the stations of the pilgrimage, "stood" with the live pilgrims on Mount Arafat, and enjoyed the pilgrims' prayers on the Feast of the Sacrifice (Figure 7). Then Choban was taken to Medina for burial. There, however, the bearers encountered an unexpected obstacle when they sought permission for interment from the Mamluk sultan. When Muḥammad learned of their request, and even though Abū Saʿīd had agreed to the burial, he felt it necessary to assert his primacy in the holy cities, not to mention his lingering resentment of the dead man, by refusing. Thus in the end Choban was never buried in the tomb on which he had lavished such care, but in the al-Baqīʿ cemetery.[118] This was the price he paid for his ideological challenge to the Mamluk sultan in the very heartland of religious patronage.

The elephant

After the early struggle with Muḥammad over the precedence of palanquins in Mecca, Abū Saʿīd had been content to remain the second Muslim ruler in the region. Or had he? Despite his overthrow of the Chobanids, he failed to increase his own authority in the Ilkhanate.[119] He did, however, manage to make inroads on Choban's patronage in the Hijaz, which came at

[115] Ibn al-Wardī, *Taʾrīkh*, II:405; also Ibn Baṭṭūṭah, *Travels*, I:206.

[116] The body of Choban's son Jelu Khan, also murdered in Herat, went as well. Ḥāfiẓ Abrū, *Dhayl*, 179, whence Samarqandī, *Maṭlaʿ*, 109–10; Mīrkhwānd, *Rawḍah*, VIII:4380.

[117] Three cows or ten sheep at each stop. Yūsufī, *Nuzhah*, 438.

[118] *Ibid.*, whence ʿAynī, "ʿIqd," fols. 379v–380r; Nuwayrī, *Nihāyah*, XXXIII:252–53; Ibn al-Wardī, *Taʾrīkh*, II:414–15; Fakhrī, *Beiträge*, 180; Mufaḍḍal, *Chronik*, 41; ʿUmarī, *Masālik*, 103; Ṣafadī, *Aʿyān*, II:169, 171; Ḥāfiẓ Abrū, *Dhayl*, 179, whence Samarqandī, *Maṭlaʿ*, 109–10; Mīrkhwānd, *Rawḍah*, VIII:4380; see also Melville, "Elephant," 207. One dramatic claim here is that burying Choban in the direction of Mecca would turn his feet towards the Prophet's mosque; although this supports Muḥammad's position as Guardian of Islamic morals, it seems to be a later interpretation. Samhūdī, *Wafāʾ*, II:702.

[119] Melville, *Decline*, 29–42, esp. 40–41.

Figure 7. A view of pilgrims in Mecca. (Anthology copied for the Temürid prince Iskandar-Sultan b. ʿUmar-Shaykh, Shiraz, 1410–11/813–14, fols. 362v–363r. London, The British Library, Add. 27261.)

Figure 7. (cont.)

Muḥammad's expense. This led to a second spate of jockeying for position between the two allies, albeit now cloaked in cordial sentiment. On the surface their relationship could not have been better, and was marked by exquisitely flattering letters, good wishes upon recoveries from medical problems and even a discussion of Abū Saʿīd's poetry, written in his own hand.[120] But at the same time Abū Saʿīd tried to promote himself in Mecca in novel fashion and at considerable expense when he sent an elephant on the pilgrimage to carry the palanquin in late summer 1330/late 730. Abū Saʿīd's intentions were entirely unclear to others at the time, but "it was clearly an ostentatious gesture designed to create an impression of the majesty and splendour of the Mongol ruler."[121] Unfortunately the favorable impression Abū Saʿīd sought did not materialize, for the elephant was viewed by many as an evil omen, and compounded the matter by dropping dead on the way to Medina.[122] Proving the pilgrims' fears, violence then broke out in Mecca. Its causes are unclear – it has been attributed to Yemeni–Meccan struggles, the misdeeds of the ruling Banū Qatādah clan or their slaves, or even a covert assassination attempt by Muḥammad himself on an Ilkhanid supporter of Choban whom he disliked.[123] What is clear is that the pilgrims were attacked, and in the fighting some Mamluk commanders were killed. Regardless of the details (or perhaps Muḥammad's own role), this was a terrible blow to Muḥammad's position as sovereign of the holy cities and protector of pilgrims. When he first heard the news, in fact, Muḥammad was so upset that he refused to eat for two days. Then he sent an army to Mecca under Aytamish to avenge the attack and reestablish his reputation and sovereignty.[124]

To complicate the situation, some of the disgraced Meccans failed to beg Muḥammad's forgiveness, and instead asked Abū Saʿīd to protect them from him. Abū Saʿīd was amenable to their request, and in winter 1330–31/early 731 dispatched a special envoy to argue the Meccans' case with the Mamluk sultan. This was one Shaykh Ibrāhīm, a conspicuously religious man and a grandson of the famous Sunqur al-Ashqar for whom Baybars had traded the Armenian prince Lewon. Shaykh Ibrāhīm's public and noteworthy piety reflected favorably upon Abū Saʿīd: when he arrived in Damascus on his

[120] In April–May 1330/Rajab 730 ambassadors arrived from Abū Saʿīd and Shaykh Ḥasan. Nuwayrī, *Nihāyah*, XXXIII:305. Also see Qalqashandī, *Ṣubḥ*, VII:275–79 for a flowery letter from Muḥammad to Abū Saʿīd, which was sent back with either the Ilkhanid embassy of December 1331/Rabīʿ I 732 (Ibn al-Dawādārī, *Kanz*, IX:361; Fakhrī, *Beiträge*, 183; Jazarī, *Taʾrīkh*, II:517), or in December 1332–January 1333/Rabīʿ II 733 (Ibn al-Dawādārī, *Kanz*, IX:372; Jazarī, *Taʾrīkh*, III:595).

[121] Melville, "Elephant," 208. [122] *Ibid.*

[123] For the Meccan–Yemeni rivalry see Ibn Baṭṭūṭah, *Travels*, II:358–59; for the Banū Qatādah clan of the Banū Ḥasan and their slaves see Nuwayrī, *Nihāyah*, XXXIII:310; Mufaḍḍal, *Chronik*, 46–47; Jazarī, *Taʾrīkh*, II:401–02; Ibn al-Dawādārī, *Kanz*, IX:353–54; Ibn Kathīr, *Bidāyah*, XIV:171; Ibn al-Wardī, *Taʾrīkh*, 420; Fāsī, *Chroniken*, 279–80; for the assassination attempt see Maqrīzī, *Sulūk*, II:323–25, 328–29; ʿAynī, "ʿIqd," fols. 389v–390r; also see Melville, "Elephant," 207–08.

[124] See Melville, "Elephant," 208–09.

way to Cairo, and unlike the usual speedy passage of Ilkhanid ambassadors, he stayed there for some time, visiting holy sites, distributing money and twice attending congregational prayers in the Umayyad mosque. Thereafter the shaykh went to Egypt to plead the Meccans' case before Muḥammad, who accepted his ally's intervention and treated the Meccans leniently.[125]

But was this a new challenge to Muḥammad's position as the premier Muslim sovereign, despite the warmth between the two men? Perhaps so. In December 1331/Rabīʿ I 732, Ilkhanid ambassadors reminded Muḥammad that he owed Abū Saʿīd a daughter. This time, however, Muḥammad stalled them, in contrast to his earlier enthusiasm.[126] Although more Ilkhanid ambassadors arrived in June–July 1332/Ramaḍān–Shawwāl, Muḥammad spared them little attention.[127] Rather his attention was turned to the holy cities, where he intended to make a timely personal demonstration of sovereignty, and for which he set out with his family on his third and final pilgrimage on 16 July/21 Shawwāl.[128] The sultan traveled with his customary display of wealth, and had sweets, pickles, fruit and even ice sent to him from Syria. As usual Muḥammad lavished gifts and cash on his own entourage, and on the ruling clans of Mecca and Medina. While performing the pilgrimage rites, Muḥammad further demonstrated his supremacy, and his alliance with Abū Saʿīd, by permitting the leader of the Iraqi caravan to stand at his right side on Mount Arafat.[129] Muḥammad capped his exertion in the pilgrimage by providing a new set of doors for the Kaʿaba in 1333/733.[130] This third and final pilgrimage, and the provision of the doors, underscored Muḥammad's position as sovereign and paramount patron in Mecca and Medina. After this Abū Saʿīd sent no more elephants, even though his relations with Muḥammad remained as cordial as ever.[131]

Indeed, the extent to which Abū Saʿīd acknowledged Muḥammad's sovereignty over the Hijaz became clear in sinister fashion during the pilgrimage of 1333/733. In that year the ilkhan secretly asked the sultan to arrange the murder of a potentially rebellious Mongol commander who was going to Mecca.[132] The intended victim, a Chingizid named Yasaʾur, had publicly criticized Abū Saʿīd's purge of the Chobanids. In response Muḥammad

125 Jazarī, *Taʾrīkh*, II:458; Fakhrī, *Beiträge*, 183.
126 ʿAynī, "ʿIqd," fol. 398r, citing the lost portion of Yūsufi; also see Jazarī, *Taʾrīkh*, II:517; Fakhrī, *Beiträge*, 183; Ibn al-Dawādārī, *Kanz*, IX:361.
127 These were probably ambassadors from Abū Saʿīd and the vizier, traveling separately and arriving on 2 June/7 Ramaḍān and 14 July/19 Shawwāl. Fakhrī, *Beiträge*, 185.
128 Mufaḍḍal, *Chronik*, 52.
129 Jazarī, *Taʾrīkh*, II:532–34 (for the fruit) and III:588 (for Mt. Arafat); Maqrīzī, *Sulūk*, II:356; also see Ibn Baṭṭūṭah, *Travels*, II:411; Ibn al-Wardī, *Taʾrīkh*, II:429; ʿAynī, "ʿIqd," fols. 397v–398r.
130 Melville, "Elephant," 209.
131 Ilkhanid envoys came in October–November 1332/Ṣafar 733 (Fakhrī, *Beiträge*, 186) and December 1332–January 1333/Rabīʿ II (Ibn al-Dawādārī, *Kanz*, IX:372; Jazarī, *Taʾrīkh*, III:595; ʿAynī, "ʿIqd," fol. 400v, saying Rabīʿ I [*sic*]).
132 Meville, "Elephant," 209 and note 60; revised in his *Decline*, 27 and note 78.

rushed a message to the leader of the Egyptian caravan, a Mamluk named Barsbugha, who hired a Beduin to stab Yasaʾur at the end of the pilgrimage. Immediately thereafter in an unsurprising double cross, Barsbugha's mamluks "accidentally" killed the murderer as he tried to escape.[133]

The reaction of the Mongol leaders from the Iraqi caravan, who rushed to confront Barsbugha, illustrated that Islam and the Chingizid heritage were equally important in their minds. They demanded to know how this could happen to a Chingizid, who had furthermore demonstrated his piety by going on the pilgrimage and standing on Mount Arafat. Barsbugha suggested that one of Yasaʾur's enemies had followed him from Ilkhanid territory, and then pointed out unconvincingly that he had only executed the murderer to prevent his escape. The discussion grew so heated that the two sides nearly came to blows. But the leader of the Iraqi caravan understood that this must have been an order from Abū Saʿīd. Even as they quarreled with Barsbugha (in Turkish), he cautioned his companions in Mongolian, saying:

By God, since the time that Yasaʾur left Abū Saʿīd and traveled with us, I knew that he would be killed, and that he would never return to Iraq. [I also knew] that his murderer would either be among us, watching him, or [Abū Saʿīd] would send to the lord of Egypt [asking him] to kill him the way he killed Temürtash.[134]

This quieted the other members of the delegation, who withdrew shortly thereafter. Nevertheless tension lingered between the Egyptian and Iraqi caravans for the rest of the 1333/733 pilgrimage season.

With the murder of a Muslim in the holiest of holy times and places, Muḥammad's capacity for vicious behavior once again overrode his desire for a pristine image. Did he believe that his involvement in the assassination could escape notice, or that he would maintain his reputation in the Hijaz and in the greater Muslim world? If so his belief was erroneous, since certainly the Mongol leader's words about Muḥammad's willingness to kill Yasaʾur "the way he killed Temürtash" revealed how distrusted Muḥammad had become in Mongol minds in particular, while the pilgrims of 1333/733 surely returned home with unflattering reports. But Muḥammad may also have viewed Abū Saʿīd's request as an opportunity to demonstrate his own power in the Hijaz, which reflected his jealous and controlling side. By arranging Yasaʾur's murder, Muḥammad was able not only to do his ally a favor, but also remind that ally (and everyone else) that the Mamluk sultan must never be taken lightly.[135] Once again, therefore, Muḥammad's paranoid

133 Yūsufī, *Nuzhah*, 170–75; whence ʿAynī, "ʿIqd," fol. 406r, and Maqrīzī, *Sulūk*, II:367–68; for an alternate story see Mufaḍḍal, *Chronik*, 5.

134 Yūsufī, *Nuzhah*, 175.

135 Even though a "Persian" (*ʿajamī*) tried to stab Muḥammad in March–April 1334/Rajab 734, while an Ilkhanid embassy was in Cairo, the incident had no recorded effect on Mamluk–Ilkhanid relations. See Ibn al-Dawādārī, *Kanz*, IX:378–79; Fakhrī, *Beiträge*, 188; Jazarī, *Taʾrīkh*, III:673; Mufaḍḍal, *Chronik*, 57.

and controlling personality pushed him to damage his own kingly reputation and call his role as protector of pilgrims into serious question. It is no wonder that some Mongols in the Ilkhanate were nervous about a religion that seemed to support such hypocrisy.

Muḥammad and Özbek of the Golden Horde

Whereas the ideas of kingship exchanged in Mamluk and Ilkhanid relations during the first third of the fourteenth/eighth century were facilitated by the peace agreement of 1323/723, and turned on subtle jockeying over the patronage of Islam and feinting over marriage alliances, the ideologies exchanged between the Mamluks and the Golden Horde were of a different sort. Certainly the relations themselves had cooled by the early 1300s/700s, when Muḥammad declined a proposal from the shamanist Toqta (r. 1290–1312/690–712) of joint military action against the Ilkhanids.[136] But on the accession of Özbek in January 1313/Ramaḍān 712, a new warmth emerged between the two sides and the diplomatic interaction was infused with energy, for Özbek's conversion to Islam permitted exchanges along the familiar lines of unity in religion. Muḥammad therefore promoted himself as a senior in religion in time-honored fashion by virtue of his relationship to the caliph, although questions of patronage in general and the holy cities in particular, especially Jerusalem, also emerged. Unlike earlier relations between sultans and khans, however, this one witnessed a striking new development in the question of lineage. For the first – and only – time a marriage took place between the two royal houses, which elevated Muḥammad dynastically in relation to the Chingizids. But when that same marriage ended in divorce, its failure was also cast in terms of lineage. Furthermore, as with Abū Saʿīd and Choban, Muḥammad could not always refrain from engaging in lies and deceit when interacting with Özbek, which undermined his reputation as an honest and upstanding ruler.

Özbek and Muḥammad entered into correspondence soon after the khan's coronation.[137] Özbek's first embassy arrived in Cairo in March–April 1314/Dhū al-Ḥijjah 713, bearing news of his accession and his conversion to Islam. Muḥammad immediately set about establishing a relationship of unity in religion: he sent back hearty congratulations and an enormous quality of gifts, mostly martial and suggestive of jihad. Muḥammad may also have sent

[136] Toqta's ambassadors went to Cairo in 1304–05/704 (Nuwayrī, *Nihāyah*, XXXII:86, Baybars al-Manṣūrī, *Zubdah*, 381; Ibn al-Dawādārī, *Kanz*, IX:128 – identifying Toqta as Anghay (?); ʿAynī, *ʿIqd*, IV:345), in 1306–07/706 (Baybars al-Manṣūrī, *Tuḥfah*, 180, and *Zubdah*, 388; Author Z, *Beiträge*, 134; ʿAynī, *ʿIqd*, IV:421–22; Maqrīzī, *Sulūk*, II:27–28), in 1310–11/710 (Baybars al-Manṣūrī, *Tuḥfah*, 220) and in 1311–12/711 (Nuwayrī, *Nihāyah*, XXXII:173–74, and probably the confusing reference to Mongol envoys on 180; Maqrīzī, *Sulūk*, II:101–02; ʿAynī, "ʿIqd," fol. 283v). Also see Spuler, *Goldene Horde*, 81–83.

[137] For Özbek's reign see Spuler, *Goldene Horde*, 85–99; Schamiloglu, "Golden Horde," 825–26; also DeWeese, *Islamization*, 90–95 (and note 46 with references to Turkish and Russian studies), 67–158 (i.e., Chapter 2) for Özbek's conversion.

sultanic and caliphal banners to Özbek, and perhaps a parasol (*jitr*) as well.[138] By contrast, the mysterious and manly rituals of *futūwah* do not seem to have been invoked.

Then when the Mamluk ambassadors with their Golden Horde counterparts came back to Cairo in December 1315/late Ramaḍān 715, Muḥammad made an unprecedented request: he charged the Mamluk envoys he dispatched in return to ask Özbek for a Chingizid bride for him.[139] In the sultan's opinion, however, the negotiations went poorly, for Özbek demanded a bride-price so high that Muḥammad lost interest: horses, armor and military equipment, as well as hundreds of thousands of gold coins, all brought to Golden Horde territory by the highest Mamluk commanders in person, accompanied by their ladies.[140] Such lofty requests were of course part of the bargaining process – indeed, Özbek intended to enjoy four years' worth of discussions, as he pointed out to Muḥammad's ambassadors in 1316–17/716: one each for negotiations, the engagement, the exchange of gifts and the wedding parties.[141] Regardless, the demands also indicated the respect that Özbek required for his relative and a lady from the Chingizid line. But Muḥammad's disinterest, whether real or feigned, led Özbek to change his terms: when the next set of Mamluk ambassadors arrived in the Golden Horde sometime in 1318–19/718, the chief envoy, Aturji, found the Chingizid princess Tulunbay Khatun waiting to be conveyed to Muḥammad for a royal wedding.[142] Although Aturji protested that he had not been authorized to negotiate further, Özbek would not be swayed, and so Aturji was forced to borrow substantial sums from merchants to pay the

[138] For the embassy see Nuwayrī, *Nihāyah*, XXVII:375 (with gifts) and XXXII:207; Fakhrī, *Beiträge*, 161; Ibn al-Dawādārī, *Kanz*, IX:279–81; Maqrīzī, *Sulūk*, II:132 (saying February–March/Dhū al-Qaʿdah) and 164 (with gifts); ʿAynī, "ʿIqd," fol. 308v. The references to the gifts are garbled: Ibn al-Dawādārī mentions banners and war material, but attributes this embassy to Toqta (*sic*); Maqrīzī mentions armor, helmets and the parasol but in 1316–17/716; Nuwayrī just says there were many gifts.

[139] This Golden Horde embassy left with Muḥammad's new ambassadors in March–April 1316/Muḥarram 716. See Nuwayrī, *Nihāyah*, XXXII:224–25 and 323; Fakhrī, *Beiträge*, 164; Maqrīzī, *Sulūk*, II:145, 163–64; ʿAynī, arguing that the proposal originated with Özbek, "ʿIqd," fols. 308v, 309r, 312r–v.

[140] The combined embassy bearing news of the stalled negotiations arrived in Cairo in early November 1317/late Shaʿbān 717, and a new joint embassy departed in April–May 1318/Ṣafar 718. Nuwayrī, *Nihāyah*, XXXII:254–55; Fakhrī, *Beiträge*, 166–67; Mufaḍḍal, *Chronik*, 3; Maqrīzī, *Sulūk*, II:174, 177, 204; ʿAynī, "ʿIqd," fol. 317v.

[141] Nuwayrī, *Nihāyah*, XXXII:324.

[142] Her lineage and exact place in the family are unclear, although none of the Mamluk historians doubt that she was a Chingizid. She is described variously as a descendant of Berke (Nuwayrī, *Nihāyah*, XXXII:324) or of Batu (ʿAynī, "ʿIqd," fol. 327v; Maqrīzī, *Sulūk*, II:204, both using impossible genealogies); as either Özbek's daughter or his sister (Ṣafadī, *Wāfī*, X:237, and *Aʿyān*, I:482; Yūsuf Ibn Taghrībirdī, *al-Manhal al-ṣāfī wa al-mustawfà baʿada al-wāfī*, eds. Muḥammad Muḥammad Amīn and Saʿīd ʿĀshūr [Cairo, 1984–], II:343); as Özbek's sister (Ibn Ḥajar, *Inbāʾ*, I:354); as a daughter (ʿUmarī, *Taʿrīf*, 62; Qalqashandī, *Ṣubḥ*, VII:316), or more generally as the daughter of kings (Ibn Kathīr, *Bidāyah*, XIV:110). Spuler, *Goldene Horde*, 259, identifies her as Özbek's daughter.

bride-price and finance the wedding festivities. Thereafter he, Tulunbay and an enormous entourage set out on the long sea journey to Egypt, which they reached in early May 1320/late Rabīʿ I 720.[143] With them was a holy man named Shaykh Nuʿmān (Khwārazmī), whom Özbek revered for his saintly qualities.[144] Although no one realized it at the time, the presence of the shaykh unwittingly strained relations considerably and damaged Muḥammad's image as a patron of Islam.

But at first the focus was entirely on Tulunbay, who was welcomed in Egypt with a dazzling display of honors.[145] Tulunbay rode from her ship to Muḥammad's residence in Alexandria in a gilded carriage, then traveled in the sultan's royal boat up the Nile, accompanied by seventeen other boats carrying her attendants and Muḥammad's escort. The party was met in Cairo by the vicegerent Sayf al-Dīn Arghun, all the important commanders, and the Royal Mamluks. Tulunbay was borne on a litter to the royal square below the citadel, where she was given not only a large hall, but also Muḥammad's own gilded satin pavilion.[146] Lavish banquets were arranged in her honor, and she and hers were plied with food and drink. On 8 May/28 Rabīʿ I Muḥammad received ambassadors from the Golden Horde, Georgia and Byzantium, then sent Arghun and another close advisor, Baktimur al-Sāqī, to meet Tulunbay, in part because both men were themselves Mongols. The next day the princess entered the citadel in a spectacular procession and was taken to the splendid Great Hall that Muḥammad had built.[147] On 16 May/6 Rabīʿ II a marriage contract was arranged for a dowry of 30,000 gold pieces. Muḥammad and Tulunbay consummated the marriage, then Muḥammad lavished gifts on the Golden Horde envoys and sent them home in September–October/Shaʿbān.[148]

This wedding was a coup on Muḥammad's part. No other Mamluk sultan had ever managed to marry into the dynasty of Chingiz Khan, nor would again. From this moment on Muḥammad displayed increased confidence in his relations with Mongol rulers, particularly in the realm of royal marriages, as shown in his later refusals of all attempts to link him to the Chobanid family. Unfortunately, the marriage itself was a failure. Ever alert to slights and insults, Muḥammad came to believe that Tulunbay was an impostor, and that Özbek had foisted a non-Chingizid onto him. Muḥammad's reasons for this belief are

143 Nuwayrī, *Nihāyah*, XXXII:323–25, whence Maqrīzī, *Sulūk*, II:203–04 and ʿAynī, "ʿIqd," fols. 327v–328r; also Ibn al-Dawādārī, *Kanz*, IX:302–03, who claims that of 2,400 people in the entourage, 400 died at sea; Abū al-Fidāʾ, *Memoirs*, 79, approximating 3,000.

144 ʿAynī, "ʿIqd," fol. 340r–v.

145 See Nuwayrī, *Nihāyah*, XXXII:323–25, whence Maqrīzī, *Sulūk*, II:203–04, and ʿAynī, "ʿIqd," fols. 327v–328r; also Ibn al-Dawādārī, *Kanz*, IX:302–04; Abū al-Fidāʾ, *Memoirs*, 79; Mufaḍḍal, *Chronik*, 10; Fakhrī, *Beiträge*, 170.

146 Ibn al-Dawādārī, *Kanz*, IX:302, says she stayed in the Ẓāhirī square built by Baybars, but this seems unlikely.

147 *Ibid.*, IX:302–03; for the hall see Rabbat, "*Dār al-Adl*," 14–18.

148 One judge stayed for the pilgrimage and went home in 1321–22/721. Nuwayrī, *Nihāyah*, XXXII:326.

unknown, as is the exact time his suspicions began, but he reportedly became disenchanted almost immediately.[149] And yet he was making a serious mistake. Unlike the Byzantine emperors, the khans of the Golden Horde do not appear to have passed off a set of well-mannered, ordinary girls as royalty.[150] Rather, the marriage of actual Chingizid princesses to worthy rulers was not uncommon, and had even served to bind vassal princes to the khans – the most recent such alliance had taken place only a few years earlier when Özbek had married the princess Konchak to Yuri Danilovich of Moscow.[151] It is unclear whether Özbek saw Muḥammad as a vassal like Yuri (or as Berke had viewed Baybars so many years earlier), although the enormous dowry he demanded suggested that he did. But regardless, it is highly unlikely that poor Tulunbay was anything other than what she claimed to be.

Özbek's decision to send Tulunbay was also an attempt to secure strategic goals, for in a separate embassy in 1320–21/720 he pressed Muḥammad to join him in military action against the Ilkhanids in the Caucasus. Since at this point covert motions seem to have been underway to engineer the treaty with the Ilkhanids, Muḥammad refused to comply, and may even have warned the Ilkhanids surreptitiously in an effort to win their trust.[152] As a result, when in November–December 1321/Dhū al-Qaʿdah 721 another Golden Horde embassy arrived in Cairo, the ambassadors were found to be inferior to previous ones, which suggested that Özbek did not respect Muḥammad. Muḥammad was himself displeased to see the ambassadors, perhaps because of his doubts about Tulunbay, and his unwillingness to jeopardize his forming alliance with Abū Saʿīd. Thus at first he refused to grant them the customary robes of honor, which was a terrible insult to Özbek. Later Muḥammad thought better of his behavior (or was advised to do so), for he relented, gave them robes and sent them back with an ambassador named Tuqsuba.[153]

But Özbek treated Tuqsuba correspondingly shabbily. First the khan failed to welcome his guest according to established protocol, then met with him only once during Tuqsuba's entire stay. Worse yet, when during that single

149 Maqrīzī, *Sulūk*, II:205; also Ṣafadī, *Aʿyan*, I:482; Yūsufī, *Nuzhah*, 235.

150 See John S. Langdon, "Byzantium's Initial Encounter with the Chinggisids: An Introduction to the Byzantino-Mongolica," *Viator* 29 (1998), 138–39; also Lippard, "Mongols and Byzantium," 210, 217–19.

151 Prior to the marriage of Konchak (christened Agatha) and Yuri in 1317, Prince Gleb Vasil'kovich of Belozero had married a Golden Horde princess in 1257, and Grand Duke Fedor Rostislavovich of Smolesnk had married a princess christened Anna in 1285. See Vernadsky, *Russia*, 169, 199–200; Charles J. Halperin, *Russia and the Golden Horde: The Mongol Impact on Medieval Russian History* (Bloomington, 1985), 18, 111; Spuler, *Goldene Horde*, 259–60. King Laszlo IV of Hungary (r. 1272–90), whose mother was a Qipchaq, also had some relationship with nomadic women, but historians disagree over whether he married two Chingizid princesses from the house of Noqai (Vernadsky, *Russia*, 180; Spuler, *Goldene Horde*, 67–68), or merely had Kipchak (i.e., non-Chingizid) concubines (Nora Berend, *At the Gate of Christendom: Jews, Muslims and "Pagans" in Medieval Hungary, c. 1000–c. 1300* [Cambridge, 2001], 175).

152 ʿAynī, "ʿIqd," fols. 328r, 333r–v, 345r, 351v.

153 Nuwayrī, *Nihāyah*, XXXIII:28.

meeting Tuqsuba announced that Muḥammad's health was good, Özbek responded that his own was fine, too, but failed to express gladness about Muḥammad's health or inquire further, which was stunningly rude. Özbek's fury had two causes: Muḥammad's refusal to join him in opposition to the Ilkhanids, and the mediocre treatment of Özbek's Shaykh Nuʿmān, who had been rebuked in Egypt by one of Muḥammad's diplomatic officials, who was both unaware of Shaykh Nuʿmān's importance to Özbek, and frustrated with the logistics of housing Tulunbay's entourage. To compound the problem, the khan had provided the shaykh with funds to construct a pious endowment in Jerusalem, but when Shaykh Nuʿmān went there, he does not seem to have been permitted to build anything. News of this had recently found its way back to Özbek, who was livid, and took it out on a merchant the Mamluks tended to favor.[154] Although Muḥammad's first offense rankled Özbek the Chingizid, who thought he had secured military assistance through an imperial wedding, the second rankled Özbek the Muslim, since this poor treatment of a man Özbek revered as holy suggested that Muḥammad was not as impressive a guardian and patron of Muslims as he ought to be. When Tuqsuba returned with Mongol ambassadors in April–May 1322/Rabīʿ II 722 and reported Özbek's treatment of him, Muḥammad snubbed Özbek in turn by refusing to hear the Mongol ambassadors' oral message and sending them away after showing them the bare minimum in diplomatic courtesies.[155]

Although embassies were exchanged irregularly thereafter, relations continued at first to be strained by Özbek's recriminations about the military campaign. Nevertheless, by 1324–25/725 Özbek seemed to have relented, and even acknowledged Muḥammad's position as a senior in Islam by asking the sultan to send him books on jurisprudence and Prophetic traditions.[156] None of the letters that accompanied these embassies remains, but their style demonstrated the importance of the relationship, since the Mamluks used the same luxurious inks and paper as they did in correspondence to Abū Saʿīd, albeit here in Mongolian.[157] Eventually, and probably with Özbek's facilitation, Muḥammad also conducted a distant diplomatic relationship with the Muslim Chagataid Tarmashirin Khan of Central Asia (r. ca. 1331–34/731–35), although the details are largely unknown.[158]

154 ʿAynī, "ʿIqd," fol. 340r–v; also see Spuler, *Goldene Horde*, 94; DeWeese, *Islamization*, 128–29.

155 ʿAynī, "ʿIqd," fol. 340v; Maqrīzī, *Sulūk*, II:236.

156 A joint embassy arrived bearing recriminations in 1323–24/724 (ʿAynī "ʿIqd," fol. 351v; also Nuwayrī, *Nihāyah*, XXXIII:69, and Fakhrī, *Beträge*, 174, neither of whom report problems); then came Özbek's request for religious books in 1324–25/725 (Maqrīzī, *Sulūk*, II:264).

157 ʿUmarī, *Taʿrīf*, 62–63, whence Qalqashandī, *Ṣubḥ*, VII:316–17. Mamluk chancellery titles for Özbek included, "The Full Brother . . . the Glorified Khan . . . Sultan of Islam and Muslims . . . Support of the House of Chingiz Khan (*al-akh al-shaqīq . . . al-qān al-muʿaẓẓam . . . sulṭān al-islām wa-al-muslimīn . . . rukn bayt Jenkiz Khan*)." Ibn Nāẓir al-Jaysh, *Tathqīf*, 12.

158 ʿUmarī, *Taʿrīf*, 63, whence Qalqashandī, *Ṣubḥ*, VII:328; Michal Biran, "The Chaghadaids and Islam: The Conversion of Tarmashirin Khan (1331–34)," *JAOS* 122:4 (October–December 2002), 742–52, esp. 747; also Biran, *Qaidu*, 63.

But eventually the situation began to worsen. In 1325–56/726 Muḥammad favored his Chingizid wife by sending her on the pilgrimage, but by summer 1327–28/728 the relationship had become insupportable for reasons unknown, and so he divorced Tulunbay and married her to one of his Mongol commanders.[159] In that same year a joint Mamluk–Golden Horde mission reached Cairo in May–June/Rajab. The Mongols spent three months camped below the citadel, met with the sultan on several occasions, then departed in late August 1328/mid-Shawwāl 728, along with Mamluk representatives.[160] This was also the period of Temürtash's residence in Cairo, arrest and execution, news of which was known in mid-August/early Shawwāl, several days before the ambassadors' departure.[161] Quite possibly they were aware of Muḥammad's broken promise to Temürtash, since they were lodged in the open with unrestricted access to gossip. Thus they may have carried not only news of Tulunbay's divorce back to Özbek, but also knowledge of Muḥammad's capacity for dishonesty. But despite the ongoing exchange of ambassadors, it was not until 1334–35/735 that Muḥammad openly found himself in trouble with his northern Mongol ally, although we do not know the reasons for the delay.[162] In that year Özbek sent an ambassador with an angry letter that censured Muḥammad for his divorce. Özbek's high opinion of his own dynasty and his contempt for Mamluk origin were clear when he castigated Muḥammad for mistreating a Chingizid, "*Someone like you* [emphasis added] should not injure the daughters of the Qaans."[163] Özbek argued that Muḥammad should have sent Tulunbay back to her family after the divorce, and not passed her off to some nobody (i.e., her second husband), since this was beneath the dignity of a Chingizid.[164] In response Muḥammad admirably demonstrated his talent for deceit. Since Muḥammad had anticipated this moment years earlier when he divorced Tulunbay, he had already authorized a judge to claim that Tulunbay had died of a mysterious illness. The judge then recorded this information and convinced some witnesses to sign this fake legal document, which Muḥammad simply produced to convince the ambassadors that Özbek's information was untrue. When the ambassadors left, they took with them a letter detailing Tulunbay's "death," in addition to the standard gifts. After their departure, Muḥammad dealt with his ex-wife, still very much alive and

[159] For the pilgrimage see Nuwayrī, *Nihāyah*, XXXIII:217; Ibn al-Dawādārī, *Kanz*, IX:320; for the divorce and remarriage in summer 1328/728 see Maqrīzī, *Sulūk*, II:298; for Tulunbay's three husbands after Muḥammad see Ṣafadī, *Wāfī*, VIII:237, and *Aʿyān*, I:482; Shujāʿī, *Taʾrīkh*, 120.

[160] Nuwayrī, *Nihāyah*, XXXIII:259–60; Fakhrī, *Beiträge*, 179–80; Maqrīzī, *Sulūk*, II:296; ʿAynī, "ʿIqd," fol. 378v.

[161] Ibn Kathīr, *Bidāyah*, XIV:155.

[162] Muḥammad's ambassador returned to Cairo in mid-November 1330/late Muḥarram 730 (Fakhrī, *Beiträge*, 181), and was followed by a Golden Horde envoy (Jazarī, *Taʾrīkh*, II:382). There were no indications of trouble.

[163] Yūsufī, *Nuzhah*, 162. [164] *Ibid.*, 235.

now a widow from her second husband, by arranging yet another marriage for her.[165]

Özbek appeared to have been mollified, since although another diplomatic exchange took place in 1336–37/737, it centered on Muḥammad's purchase of slaves, and his request that Özbek send the relatives of a Mamluk commander to Cairo.[166] Özbek complied, but then appears to have wanted a favor in return. Thus when on 28 December 1338/14 Jumādà II 739 the Mamluk ambassadors of 1336–37/737 returned to Cairo with their Golden Horde counterparts, the latter bore an ominous message: Özbek asked Muḥammad to send him a daughter to marry, in order to confirm their friendship and brotherly relations. Being no fool, Muḥammad understood that Özbek planned to exact retribution for his own treatment of Tulunbay: "The sultan understood that their intent was to do to him as he had done to them."[167] Consequently he apologized with the same argument he had employed to the Ilkhanids: he did not have a daughter old enough for marriage, but promised to send one later. This time it was a particularly egregious lie, since Muḥammad actually celebrated the weddings of two daughters to members of the military elite while the ambassadors were still in Cairo (although they were surely not invited to the festivities).[168] But despite Muḥammad's refusal to send a bride to Özbek, relations continued in a state of apparent civility: the next time Özbek's ambassadors were in town in August–September 1340/ Rabīʿ I 741, one died unexpectedly, oddly enough, just a few days after Tulunbay herself had passed away quietly. In a public display of respect for the khan, Muḥammad ordered all the senior commanders to attend the funeral. Stranger still, the ambassador was buried in the tomb of one of Tulunbay's husbands.[169] Nevertheless, Özbek never received real satisfaction in the matter of the unfortunate princess. Indeed, although his relationship to Muḥammad turned on unity in Islam and a marital connection of lineage, like the Ilkhanids Özbek learned the hard way that Muḥammad's image as an upright sovereign and devout Muslim could be compromised by his shifty behavior. Muḥammad's refusal to join Özbek in action against the Ilkhanids, the slights his subordinates dealt Shaykh Nuʿmān and the divorce of Tulunbay all proved that Muḥammad was hardly the shining example of Muslim kingliness he claimed to be.

[165] *Ibid.*, 235–36, whence ʿAynī, "ʿIqd," fol. 411v.
[166] The Mongol embassy passed through Damascus towards Cairo in December 1336–January 1337/Jumādà I 737 (Jazarī, *Taʾrīkh*, III:930), and Muḥammad sent envoys of his own in June–July 1337/Dhū al-Ḥijjah (Fakhrī, *Beiträge*, 194; Yūsufī, *Nuzhah*, 379).
[167] Shujāʿī, *Taʾrīkh*, 45. [168] *Ibid.*; Fakhrī, *Beiträge*, 200–01.
[169] Tulunbay died on 8 September/15 Rabīʿ I, followed by the ambassador on the 19th/26th. In February–March 1341/Ramaḍān 741 the Mongol embassy set out, followed by Mamluk envoys in April–May/Dhū al-Qaʿdah. Fakhrī, *Beiträge*, 215–16, 221; Shujāʿī, *Taʾrīkh*, 120.

CHAPTER 5

Mamluk regional sovereignty and the post-Ilkhanid order (1335–1382/736–784)

Immediately after Abū Sa'īd's death without male heir on 30 November 1335/ 13 Rabī' II 736, his empire devolved into factional struggle over the establishment of a new sovereign.[1] Many of the contenders were former members of the Ilkhanid administration, who seem to have been looking for a king. At first this meant making a conservative appeal to the golden dynasty by raising Ilkhanid candidates for rule, although other branches of the Chingizid tree were represented as well, as were key Chingizid women like Abū Sa'īd's sister, Sātī Beg.[2] But the search for a sovereign expanded to include the Mamluk sultan, whose deceitful practices and general hypocrisy were now overlooked as Ilkhanid successors sought to win Muḥammad's recognition and military support. This led to a further elaboration of the Mamluk ideology of kingship, which centered on two new concepts: the notion of Muḥammad as a senior sovereign and patron of other kings, and the notion of a supreme Guardian of Islam.

In this new version of his ideology Muḥammad transformed his persona as the religious senior and premier patron of the Hijaz into a simpler idea of seniority in rule. This meant that Muḥammad was no longer a first among Muslim equals, but a senior sovereign surrounded by a constellation of junior rulers. As such, Muḥammad's new role became that of a patron to lesser kings, and often even a sovereign over them. At the same time, and in response to the warfare in Ilkhanid territory, Muḥammad revived the older responsibility of military Guardianship of Islam that had lain dormant for some years. But whereas earlier versions of the Guardian ideal had been proclaimed in opposition to infidels, now there were no infidels in sight, and Muḥammad was interacting entirely with rulers whose commitment to Islam he accepted. The enemy therefore now became heretics and apostates,

[1] For this period of complex military and political struggle see Melville's admirable *Decline*, esp. 43–59; also Boyle, "Īl-Khāns," 413–15; Ilisch, "Artuqidenherrschaft," 98–104.

[2] There was also fleeting interest in the unborn child of Abū Sa'īd's pregnant Chobanid widow, Dilshād Khatun, but the infant turned out to be a girl. See Charles Melville and Abbas Zaryab, "Chobanids," *EIr* V:499–500.

and Muḥammad himself became a supreme Guardian, who shared this weighty responsibility with other rulers as part of his patronage of them.

Factional struggle after the death of Abū Saʿīd

As the seat of Ilkhanid power, Iraq and Azerbaijan took Muḥammad's immediate attention after Abū Saʿīd's death, especially since the contenders there were several. First was Prince Arpa, a formidable descendant of Chingiz Khan's Toluid grandson Ariq Böke, and the new husband of the Ilkhanid Sātī Beg. Second was Mūsà Khan, who was allegedly a grandson of the Ilkhan Baidu (r. 1295/694), and who was backed by the Oirat ʿAlī Pādshāh, himself governor of Baghdad and one of Abū Saʿīd's uncles. Third was a descendant of Hülegü's son Möngke Temür, a child named Muḥammad b. Yolqutluq, who was a puppet for Abū Saʿīd's former chief commander, Shaykh Ḥasan Jalayir, and his sometime Mongol ally Ḥājjī-Taghay. Members of the Chobanid family also entered the fray, although they never allied themselves with Muḥammad.

The Mamluk sultan interacted directly with several of these contenders. In doing so, his chancellery used paper size and a variety of titles to underscore Muḥammad's new position of seniority. Full-sized Baghdādī paper had been a sign of the importance of the khans during Ilkhanid rule, but after Abū Saʿīd's death, no Chingizid in Ilkhanid territory received it (although the Golden Horde still did).[3] Rather, contenders and their puppets might receive half-sized paper (for "the greatest kings below the khans"), third-sized paper (for "the second tier of kings") or even "ordinary" paper (for "the smallest kings, governors and others").[4] Chancellery forms of address displayed a hierarchy of titles, which reflected the status of each addressee and ranged from "His Dignity" (*maqām*, for royalty), "The Seat" (*maqarr*, for the highest military men and administrators) and "His Honor" (*janāb*, for the next level of military men) to a second "The Seat" (*majlis*, for ordinary military men).[5]

Muḥammad first corresponded with ʿAlī Pādshāh, who defeated Arpa in battle on 29 April 1336/17 Ramaḍān 736.[6] During Abū Saʿīd's lifetime Muḥammad and ʿAlī Pādshāh had conducted an epistolary friendship in which Islamic norms were certainly present – ʿAlī Pādshāh apparently told Muḥammad about his wish to go on the pilgrimage, and was also known for his desire to uphold Islam in society.[7] Now, however, he wanted military assistance even after defeating Arpa, and wrote in Mūsà's name asking for a Mamluk army in May–June 1336/Shawwāl 736. Clearly ʿAlī Pādshāh knew that the price of support was acknowledging Muḥammad's seniority and

[3] Ibn Nāẓir al-Jaysh does cite, secondhand, a suggestion that the Chingizid puppet Taghay Temür (r. 1338–39/739) received diplomatic honors equal to those for Abū Saʿīd, but if so he was the only one. See Ibn Nāẓir al-Jaysh, *Tathqīf*, 11; Qalqashandī, *Ṣubḥ*, VII:279.
[4] Qalqashandī, *Ṣubḥ*, VIII:20. [5] *Ibid.*, V:463–65. [6] See Melville, *Decline*, 48.
[7] Yūsufī, *Nuzhah*, 301–02; for ʿAlī Pādshāh's complex personality see Melville, *Decline*, 63–66.

asking for his patronage, for he promised to swear allegiance to Muḥammad and rule Baghdad as his governor.[8] Muḥammad was receptive, and invoked the religious basis for their earlier friendship by taking the ambassadors to visit tombs of Muslim holy figures, and of Muḥammad's father Qalawun.[9] Despite this warm welcome, however, Muḥammad's letter to ʿAlī Pādshāh's candidate Mūsà was a subtle lesson in Mūsà's inferiority and a reinforcement of the Mamluk sultan's new authority.[10] On the surface Muḥammad honored Mūsà as a Chingizid: Mūsà's titles were nearly identical to Abū Saʿīd's own, and included "Sultan," which declared Mūsà's membership in the Golden House (non-Chingizids received the lower-ranking "Noyan"). Muḥammad also praised Mūsà's supporters (including ʿAlī Pādshāh) for rendering service to one great in "the Qaan's lineage."[11] Nevertheless the letter appears to have used only half-sized Baghdādī paper, not full, which lowered Mūsà's status from that of Abū Saʿīd, while its message focused on the linked notions of unity in religion and unity in Guardianship of that religion, which promoted Muḥammad's seniority both as a Muslim ruler and as a supreme Guardian.[12]

The letter opened with Quranic citations that expressed Muḥammad's gratitude for God's support for the victors of Islam. It then linked religion and kingship on the one hand, and rebellion and infidelity on the other, by congratulating Mūsà on his victory over his enemy (Arpa), who was described not as an infidel, but as a rebel against religion and rule (*al-khārijī ʿalà al-dīn wa al-mulk*). The letter promoted Muḥammad's new position as the supreme Guardian by assuring Mūsà that the sultan had been leading out his own victorious Islamic armies to help Mūsà in his struggles, but had stopped when the good news of Mūsà's victory reached him. Muḥammad then emphasized his seniority when he took up the Qalawunid mantle of a great king guiding a lesser one in kingly and religious affairs: he advised Mūsà on how to reward his supporters, and promised further suggestions in the oral message on how to behave.[13] The letter also invoked fictitious familial bonds to define the relationship of patronage between the two men. Mūsà's letter had described him as being "like a son" to Muḥammad; here Muḥammad claimed that Mūsà was dearer to him than any of his real sons, and went on to address Mūsà as a (younger) brother as well. Shortly after this exchange, however, ʿAlī Pādshāh was killed in a battle with Shaykh Ḥasan and

[8] Embassies from Mūsà and his advisors arrived in Cairo in early June 1336/late Shawwāl 736 (Jazarī, *Taʾrīkh*, III:872–73; Fakhrī, *Beiträge*, 192; Yūsufī, *Nuzhah*, 302; Mufaḍḍal, *Chronik*, 62; Maqrīzī, *Sulūk*, II:397; also Melville, *Decline*, 47) and in February–March 1337/Rajab 737 (Yūsufī, confusing ʿAlī Pādshāh with his brother, Muḥammad Bek, *Nuzhah*, 364–65; Maqrīzī, *Sulūk*, II:410 [saying October–November 1336/Rabīʿ I], 417–18).

[9] Maqrīzī, *Sulūk*, II:397. [10] For the text see Qalqashandī, *Ṣubḥ*, VII:280–82. [11] *Ibid.*, 281.

[12] Qalqashandī did not know the paper size but hypothesized half-Baghdādī since "no one after Abū Saʿīd was written to with [his] style." See *ibid.*, 279, 282, drawing on Ibn Nāẓir al-Jaysh, *Tathqīf*, 10, 12. Mūsà's titles were nearly identical to Abū Saʿīd's titles, but also included "The World-Renowned (*al-ʿālamīyah*)." Qalqashandī, *Ṣubḥ*, VII:280; also see Chapter 4 above.

[13] Qalqashandī, *Ṣubḥ*, VII:282.

Ḥājjī-Taghay on 24 July 1336/14 Dhū al-Ḥijjah 736.[14] ʿAlī Pādshāh's brother Muḥammad Beg took over immediately, but although the Mamluk sultan sent the promised army to Cilicia in March–April 1337/Shaʿbān 737, overtly to collect Armenian tribute and covertly to stand ready for Mūsà and Muḥammad Beg, they never reached it.[15]

But Mūsà's advisors were not the only ones interested in Muḥammad's patronage, for Shaykh Ḥasan also sought Mamluk support for his own Chingizid puppet, Muḥammad b. Yolqutluq.[16] Shaykh Ḥasan therefore criticized Muḥammad's favor towards Mūsà and the Oirats, and in doing so demonstrated the way both Chingizid lineage and submission to Muḥammad's sovereignty were guiding him: "we are closer to you [than Muḥammad Beg], for *we are more obedient to you than he is* [emphasis added]. Let us be united, for we are closer to you than anyone else ... How is this Mūsà from the lineage of the Qaan? The one who is from the lineage of the Qaan, and about whom the greatest Mongols agree, is Muḥammad b. Yolqutluq."[17] It is unknown whether Muḥammad ever addressed Muḥammad b. Yolqutluq as "Sultan" and "Khan," or praised his membership in the Chingizid house, as he did Mūsà. But certainly Shaykh Ḥasan, as a non-Chingizid commander, received only third-sized paper and the lower appellations of "His Noble Lofty Honor (*al-janāb al-karīm al-ʿālī*)" and "Noyan." As supreme Guardian and now patron of other Guardians, Muḥammad was able to address Shaykh Ḥasan with a range of martial Islamic titles: "Support of Islam and Muslims ... Victorious One of Islamic Holy Fighters, Commander of the Armies of the Unitarians ... Support of the Islamic Community ... (*ʿawn al-islām wa al-muslimīn ... nāṣir al-ghuzāh wa al-mujāhidīn,*

14 Melville, *Decline*, 51–53.

15 For Muḥammad's secret intentions see Yūsufī, *Nuzhah*, 367; Maqrīzī, *Sulūk*, II:417–18; for the Armenian campaign see Shujāʿī, *Taʾrīkh*, 4; Fakhrī, *Beiträge*, 193; Ibn al-Wardī, *Taʾrīkh*, II:448; Jazarī, *Taʾrīkh*, III:936.

16 Multiple embassies from Shaykh Ḥasan or Ḥājjī-Taghay reached Cairo. The first was from Shaykh Ḥasan in August–September 1336/Muḥarram 737 (Maqrīzī, *Sulūk*, II:407), then another in October–November 1336/Rabīʿ I 737 (Fakhrī, *Beiträge*, 193; Jazarī, *Taʾrīkh*, III:929; Maqrīzī, *Sulūk*, II:410); a response went back immediately (Jazarī, *Taʾrīkh*, III:930; Mufaḍḍal, *Chronik*, 65). Thereafter an embassy from Shaykh Ḥasan arrived in Cairo in February–March 1338/Shaʿbān 738 (Fakhrī, *Beiträge*, 197, claiming a joint embassy from Shaykh Ḥasan and Ḥājjī-Taghay; Maqrīzī, *Sulūk*, II:446, mentioning Shaykh Ḥasan only), and one from Ḥājjī-Taghay in May–June 1338/Dhū al-Qaʿdah 738 (Fakhri, *Beiträge*, 198). Thereafter a rift developed between the two. Therefore an independent embassy came from each man in April–May 1339/Shawwāl 739 (Fakhri, *Beiträge*, 202 for Ḥājjī-Taghay; ʿAynī, *ʿIqd*, as cited in ʿAbbas al-ʿAzzāwī, *Taʾrīkh al-ʿIrāq bayna Iḥtilālayn: Ḥukūmat al-Jalāyirīyah* (Baghdad, 1935–49), II:30–31 for Shaykh Ḥasan). Additional embassies from Shaykh Ḥasan arrived in December 1339–January 1340/Jumādà II 740 (Fakhrī, *Beiträge*, 206; Shujāʿī, *Taʾrīkh*, 68; Mufaḍḍal, *Chronik*, 80, claiming Shaykh Ḥasan wanted Muḥammad to reconcile him to Ḥājjī-Taghay; similarly Maqrīzī, *Sulūk*, II:489) and in April–May 1340/Dhū al-Qaʿdah (Fakhrī, *Beiträge*, 209).

17 Yūsufī, *Nuzhah*, 365; Shaykh Ḥasan also cryptically claimed a family relationship to Muḥammad's Mongol mother, Ashlun, but the details are not clear. See Melville, *Decline*, 57–58 note 173.

zaʿīm juyūsh al-muwaḥḥidīn . . . ʿimād al-millah, ʿawn al-ummah . . .)." As patron of the caliph, Muḥammad gave Shaykh Ḥasan a special, caliphal title: "Arm of the Commander of the Believers (*ʿaḍud amīr al-muʾminīn).*" At the same time, however, Muḥammad's chancellery used other titles to acknowledge that Shaykh Ḥasan's ideology also relied on the preservation of Ilkhanid tradition: "Servant of the [Chingizid] State, Guardian of the Eastern Kingdom, Commander of the Tomans, Commander of the Ulus [state, people], Supporter of Kings and Sultans (*kāfī al-dawlah al-qānīyah, kāfil al-mamlakah al-sharqīyah, āmir al-tawāmīn, amīr al-ulūs, ẓahīr al-mulūk wa al-salāṭīn*)."[18]

Despite his correspondence with Shaykh Ḥasan, Muḥammad continued to favor Mūsà and the Oirats, but they were defeated, and Mūsà killed, by summer 1337/late 737.[19] Only then did Muḥammad turn his full attention to Shaykh Ḥasan and his ally Ḥājjī-Taghay, and maintained a relationship with each man even after their puppet died in battle in summer 1338/738 and a rift developed between them.[20] Although Muḥammad's relationship with Shaykh Ḥasan was established on a presumption of Muḥammad's patronage, the record does not reveal whether this state of affairs continued.[21] But certainly by 339/739 Shaykh Ḥasan was again (or still) bowing to Muḥammad's sovereignty out of military necessity when he asked Muḥammad to send him an army under competent leadership – perhaps one of Muḥammad's sons. In return Shaykh Ḥasan swore he was at the sultan's service, and promised to have Muḥammad's name read in sermons in his lands. But although Muḥammad had covertly directed the army to Cilicia for Mūsà and the Oirats, he refused to provide one for Shaykh Ḥasan under any leadership. Nevertheless Muḥammad did dispatch an official to broker a reconciliation between Shaykh Ḥasan and Ḥājjī-Taghay in 1339–40/740.[22] He also tried to assert a position of patronage over Ḥājjī-Taghay, and asked him to send a son to Cairo to marry one of the Qalawunid princesses in 1338–39/739. Although Ḥājjī-Taghay claimed to be flattered, Muḥammad's suggestion that the bridegroom travel to Egypt resembled his earlier interactions with the Chobanids, especially his attempts to make them bow to his

18 Qalqashandī, *Ṣubḥ*, VII:286, and see VII:314–15, where Qalqashandī explains that Muḥammad also wrote to Shaykh Ḥasan's wives, but used "ordinary" (i.e., fourth-tier) paper for them.

19 Melville, *Decline*, 51–55. For news, refugees and occasional messengers sent to Mamluk territory see Mufaḍḍal, *Chronik*, 66; Shujāʿī, *Taʾrīkh*, 5–7, 17–18; Jazarī, *Taʾrīkh*, III:1013–14; Fakhrī, *Beiträge*, 195–97, 206–08; Yūsufī, *Nuzhah*, 448; Maqrīzī, *Sulūk*, II:437–38; also Melville, *Decline*, 70 note 205, citing also Muqrī, "Nathr al-jumān," Chester Beatty Library MS 4113, fol. 29r–v; also see note 16 above.

20 S. Album, "Studies in Ilkhanid History and Numismatics II: A Late Ilkhanid Hoard (741/1340) as Evidence for the History of Diyar Bakr," *Studia Iranica* 14:1 (1985), 73; also Melville, *Decade*, 59, 69.

21 We have no record of the messages exchanged in 1336–37/737 or 1338/738. See note 16 above for specific references.

22 Mufaḍḍal, *Chronik*, 80; Maqrīzī, *Sulūk*, II:489, 491; also Album, "Studies II," 73.

own dynastic importance. Ultimately Ḥājjī-Taghay declined the offer on the grounds that he needed an army more than a daughter-in-law.[23]

At the same time that Muḥammad was playing the role of patron to claimants in the Ilkhanid heartlands who both appealed to his own seniority and continued to uphold Chingizid norms, he also interacted with regional figures who were merely seeking to carve out positions for themselves without Chingizid candidates. In these cases the petitioners not only recognized Muḥammad's seniority as a ruler, but bowed to his sovereignty outright. One such was the Anatolian commander Eretna, an Uyghur who had worked for years in Ilkhanid service.[24] Although at first loyal to Shaykh Ḥasan, Eretna soon threw off his allegiance. When Shaykh Ḥasan mustered an army to go to Anatolia and rebuke him, Eretna looked to Cairo for protection, and in 1337–38/738 asked to become Muḥammad's governor.[25] Since Eretna had neither status nor a Chingizid puppet, it was a simple matter for Muḥammad to incorporate him directly into the Mamluk administration, especially since there was a precedent for the relationship: Sülemish had earlier been appointed governor of Anatolia.

Although the single remaining text sent from Muḥammad to Eretna is corrupt, some recognizable concepts of Guardianship and patronage do emerge from the conflicted verbiage.[26] The letter opened with an appeal to Guardianship when it stated that God had protected the lands of Islam with Muḥammad's sword. It then made a grand statement of Muḥammad's sovereignty and right to universal rule by explaining that God had united Muḥammad's territories, and that Muḥammad hoped his realm would reach all civilized lands and last until the end of time. In its body the letter highlighted Muḥammad's position as the paramount patron of religion: it described the sultan as the performer of God's good works on earth, and claimed that God had used Muḥammad to recover religion (*istaradda*, from an unspecified poor state). It pointed out that Muḥammad had responded to all those who called upon him to support Islam: he had welcomed immigrants (Ilkhanid refugees?), distinguished them and brought them close to "the sword of our state, which saved [them]."[27] Immediately thereafter it claimed cryptically that "We praised God for testing us," which may have been a veiled allusion to the refugee Temürtash, meant to act as a warning (?).[28] Next the letter related Anatolia to Muḥammad's role as supreme Guardian by describing the region both in glowing terms, and as a land of polytheism (*shirk*), where Muḥammad's sword had done (unspecified) great deeds. It closed by appointing Eretna governor there, since he had taken charge of the region for Muḥammad's sake. Eretna's status appeared in the third-sized

[23] Shujāʿī, *Taʾrīkh*, 36–39.
[24] Claude Cahen, "Eretna," *EI*[2] II:705–06; Golden, "Činggisid Conquests," 27.
[25] Shujāʿī, *Taʾrīkh*, 25–27; Maqrīzī, *Sulūk*, II:445–46; Ṣafadī, *Aʿyān*, I:448.
[26] For the text see Shujāʿī, *Taʾrīkh*, 26–27. [27] *Ibid.*, 26. [28] *Ibid.*

paper and form of address used: "His Lofty Honor (*al-janāb al-ʿālī*)," which was lower than the address for Shaykh Ḥasan (His Noble Lofty Honor, *al-janāb al-karīm al-ʿālī*). Also like Shaykh Ḥasan and as a non-Chingizid, Eretna was identified as "Noyan," while in keeping with his incorporation into the Mamluk model of Guardianship he received a caliphal title: "Sword of the Commander of the Believers (*sayf amīr al-muʾminīn*)."[29] But like Sülemish and Temürtash, Eretna was interested in Muḥammad only to achieve his own ends, and saw the Mamluk sultan as merely one possible patron. Eretna therefore failed to include Muḥammad's titles on coins and in sermons as promised, then later renewed his loyalty to Shaykh Ḥasan, and by 1339–40/740 was issuing coins in the name of Shaykh Ḥasan's Chingizid puppet.[30] But Muḥammad himself was quite serious about maintaining his sovereign position. When his spies discovered Eretna's transgressions, therefore, Muḥammad sent a Mamluk army to raid Eretna's borders, and also asked the Dulqadirid Türkmen, who had successfully petitioned to become Mamluk governors in Elbistan in 1338–39/739, to harass Eretna as well.[31] As a result Eretna bowed to Muḥammad's sovereignty by apologizing in winter 1340/740 with gifts, and promised to (re-)instate Muḥammad's name in sermons and on coins.[32]

In terms of ideology, therefore, Muḥammad had become a patron, a senior sovereign and the supreme Guardian for several Ilkhanid successors by 1340–41/741. Nevertheless, although Muḥammad demanded much from his petitioners, he returned little to them: in particular he provided only one army, to Mūsà and the Oirats in 1337/737, which never reached them. Despite this poor record, however, Ilkhanid successors continued to bow to Muḥammad's ideology to achieve their goals, as shown in January–February 1341/Shaʿbān 741, when Shaykh Ḥasan and Ḥājjī-Taghay, now reconciled and rulers of Baghdad and Diyarbakir respectively, asked once again for an army with which to conquer in Muḥammad's name, in return for the usual promises about coins, sermons and ruling as Muḥammad's governors. But Muḥammad, wary after Eretna's behavior, responded with a challenge: "If you want this, then first strike coinage, have me mentioned in the sermons, and swear formally that we are united. Then send me someone I can trust, to whom I will give the army."[33] The answer to this challenge came in May–June/Dhū al-Ḥijjah, when Shaykh Ḥasan's nephew Ibrāhīm Shāh

[29] Qalqashandī, *Ṣubḥ*, VII:299–300; also Ibn Nāẓir al-Jaysh, *Tathqīf*, 43–44.

[30] Album, "Studies II," 65–66. Eretna's ambitions had appeared even during Abū Saʿīd's reign. See Melville, *Decline*, 37–39.

[31] Shujāʿī, *Taʾrīkh*, 40–41; Maqrīzī, *Sulūk*, II:459. The sultan granted a similar request from the Kurds of Niṣībīn in 1339–40/740. See Maqrīzī, *Sulūk*, II:471.

[32] The ambassadors arrived in Cairo in December 1339–January 1340/Rajab 740. Shujāʿī, *Taʾrīkh*, 68; Fakhrī, *Beiträge*, 206–07; also Maqrīzī, *Sulūk*, II:490. For coins in Muḥammad's name see Album, "Studies in Ilkhanid History and Numismatics I: A Late Ilkhanid Hoard (743/1341)," *Studia Iranica* 13:1 (1984), 94, 96 and notes 130, 137.

[33] Shujāʿī, *Taʾrīkh*, 98.

arrived in Cairo, followed by one of Ḥājjī-Taghay's sons, Pīr Ḥusayn.[34] At the audience Ibrāhīm Shāh presented the sultan with coins minted in his name in Baghdad, and a document in which Shaykh Ḥasan, Ḥājjī-Taghay and the Artiqud ruler of Mardin swore loyalty to the Mamluk sultan. Pīr Ḥusayn and Ibrāhīm Shāh were to remain in Cairo as hostages.[35] This proof of fidelity was at last enough, and Muḥammad ordered the muster of an army. The papers were actually being drawn up when suddenly Muḥammad received new reports of trouble brewing in the east, which made him delay the campaign and dispatch his own man to learn more.[36] But shortly thereafter the sultan began to suffer from pain, weakness and fainting, and died in the citadel on 7 June 1341/21 Dhū al-Ḥijjah 741. One month later the powerless new sultan al-Manṣūr Abū Bakr (r. 1341/741) sent the frustrated ambassadors home with promises of assistance, but no army.[37] Thus ended Muḥammad's tenure as the regional patron and supreme Guardian. Thereafter the political reality of Qalawunid rule began to crumble silently behind the edifice of kingly supremacy that Muḥammad had built.

Later Qalawunids and Ilkhanid successors

For several decades after Muḥammad's death, politics in the Mamluk Sultanate were fractious: twelve Qalawunids reigned but few ruled, while a majority were deposed and murdered, and power rested with senior commanders.[38] But the commanders played no role in ideology, and thus proclamations of kingship to external rulers continued to be made in the names of the Qalawunids. Meanwhile the struggles among the Ilkhanid successors continued, although now the contenders had to interact with Muḥammad's descendants, not Muḥammad. Unfortunately the picture is hard to extricate from the extremely poor historical record: Arabic sources in this period are few, terse and repetitive; the Persian sources mostly ignore the Mamluks, and outside works, coins and inscriptions are scant at best. The following points must therefore be considered tentative.

By the time the later Qalawunids came to the throne, the era of conflict with Chingizid Iran and Anatolia was long past, and the concept of Guardianship had become an inherited ideological laurel: impressive and regularly displayed, but no longer foremost in anyone's mind. Nor did the sultan's

34 Ibrāhīm Shāh should not be confused with Ḥājjī-Taghay's nephew of that name. Fakhrī, *Beiträge*, 221; Mufaḍḍal, *Chronik*, 100–01; Shujā'ī, *Ta'rīkh*, 99; Maqrīzī, *Sulūk*, II:519–20; also Album, "Studies II," 46–47, 74–75.

35 No such coins have been found. See 'Azzāwī, *Ta'rīkh al-'Irāq*, II:31; Album, "Studies I," 96 and note 137.

36 Shujā'ī, *Ta'rīkh*, 99–101; Fakhrī, *Beiträge*, 221–22; Mufaḍḍal, *Chronik*, 102–04; Maqrīzī, *Sulūk*, II:520–21.

37 Shujā'ī, *Ta'rīkh*, 133.

38 For the ugly political details of this period see Holt, *Crusades*, 121–29; Irwin, *Mamluk Sultanate*, 125–51.

position as sovereign of the Hijaz and protector of pilgrims vanish, but it similarly dwindled in prominence for lack of strong rivals. Instead, later Qalawunid understandings of kingship turned to the elusive gold standard of legitimacy: dynasty. Never before had such a long series of Mamluk sultans enjoyed membership in an august house and freedom from the stigma of recent servitude, but now assertions of the Qalawunid dynasty surfaced on coins, in inscriptions and most clearly in diplomatic letters, regardless of the actual power the Qalawunids themselves held. This new awareness of dynasty affected Mamluk relationships to the Ilkhanid successors, for the Qalawunid sultans inherited the position of seniority and often sovereignty over them that Muḥammad had built up at the end of his reign. But just as Muḥammad had paradoxically claimed to be an upstanding Muslim ruler even when his behavior was hypocritical and false, so too the later Qalawunids maintained their position of supremacy to outside rulers even when they themselves were powerless.

Meanwhile the post-Ilkhanid contenders continued to rely on Muslim Ilkhanid tradition to legitimate themselves, which meant using Chingizid puppets until the 1350s/750s, and maintaining Ilkhanid ceremonies and diplomatic traditions.[39] Titles reflected this conservative appeal: some early successors simply kept their Ilkhanid administrative titles, while their descendants styled themselves protectors or upholders of the Chingizid legacy. But because the model the successors copied was that of the Muslim Ilkhanids, not Chingizids per se, they also invoked the familiar Islamic ideals of kingship like sponsoring charitable architectural projects, although rarely in the Hijaz.[40] Similarly many proclaimed their support for law, which could be either Islamic law, Turkic versions of Mongol dynastic law, or both.[41] The Ilkhanid successors also made tentative attempts to move beyond Chingizid or Ilkhanid tradition through experiments in legitimacy. Some rulers therefore used Islamic ideas of kingship not to invoke the Muslim Ilkhanids, but to provide an alternative to Chingizid legitimacy, just as the Mamluks had once done. Others simply abandoned Muslim Ilkhanid or Chingizid models for Islamic norms, usually modeled on the Seljuk example, while a few successors moved outside both the Chingizid and Islamic models by engaging in dynastic adoption from old Persian families or appealing to Persian cultural traditions. In addition, all continued to acknowledge the kingly seniority of the Qalawunid sultans, and many even accepted Qalawunid sovereignty by

[39] It seems unlikely, however, that they ritually elevated the ruler on felt, which was a Chingizid coronation prerogative. See Sela, *Inauguration*, 25–42.

[40] Patronage of the Hijaz played a smaller role in ideology in this period, except for occasional struggles between the Mamluks and the Rasulids of Yemen, including one in 1342–43/743 (Shujāʿī, *Taʾrīkh*, 232; Abu Bakr Ibn Qāḍī Shuhbah, *Taʾrīkh Ibn Qāḍī Shuhbah*, ed. ʿAdnān Darwīsh [Damascus, 1977–], I:299); also Ota, "Sharifate," 12–14.

[41] See Woods, *Aqquyunlu*, 7–9; Inalcık, *Ottoman Empire*, 66–68.

offering to become clients to the Mamluks, or governors in the Mamluk administration.

The Qalawunid dynasty

The clearest promotion of dynasty appeared in three diplomatic letters written for two different Qalawunid sultans. The first was sent in 1340/750 to the Byzantine emperor John VI Cantacuzenus (r. 1341–54) for al-Nāṣir Ḥasan (r. 1347–51/748–52; 1354–61/755–62). It referred twice to the cordial relations enjoyed by Ḥasan's ancestors and the emperors, and also described Ḥasan as a member of an august house, neither of which concepts was common to earlier Mamluk diplomatic practice.[42] The second letter was dated August–September 1374/Rabīʿ I 776, and was sent from the sultan al-Ashraf Shaʿbān (r. 1363–77/764–78) to Mehmed Bulaq of the Golden Horde.[43] In the letter Shaʿbān sought to resume the relations enjoyed by both sides' forebears, which had lapsed. Although the purpose of the letter was hardly new, the ideology of kingship that accompanied it was. Earlier the sultans Qalawun and Muḥammad had thanked God for making them Muslims before others. Now, by contrast, Shaʿbān proclaimed the overarching sovereignty of the Qalawunid house, first by thanking God for creating him a king to whom other kings were subject and before whom great leaders bowed down, then by praising God for making him inherit the rule of his forebears and ensuring that rule would pass down in one family.[44] Although Shaʿbān's letter went on to reprise existing ideas of Mamluk legitimacy by invoking God-given victories over infidel enemies, the service of the two holy shrines and the figure of the Abbasid caliph, these were not the primary focus of the text. Shaʿbān's admiration for the general concept of dynasty as a worthy institution appeared in the third letter, a 1367–68/769 missive to the Artuqid al-Ṣāliḥ Maḥmūd that praised Maḥmūd for following his predecessors' example, congratulated him on his inheritance of rule from them and lauded the Artuqid dynasty itself: "he and his noble house remain elevated to us."[45] The importance the later Qalawunids attached to their own membership in a dynasty of rulers also appeared on their coins, which frequently included the sultan's lineage back to Qalawun, even on copper coins with

[42] Marius Canard, "Une lettre du Sultan Malik Nâṣir Ḥasan à Jean VI Cantacuzène (750/1349)," *Annales de l'Institut d'Études Orientales* 3 (Paris, 1939), 47–48.

[43] For the text see Ibn Nāẓir al-Jaysh, *Tathqīf*, 13–15; Qalqashandī, *Ṣubḥ*, VII:318–21. The chancellery thought the khan's name was Muḥammad, which must have been Mehmet Bulaq, a puppet who "ruled" beginning in 1370/771–72, mostly in the Crimea. Coins were minted in his name until 1375–76/777. See Spuler, *Goldene Horde*, 121, 453; Lane-Poole, *Catalogue*, VI:165–68.

[44] Shaʿbān was fourth in a line of Qalawunids: his father was al-Amjad Ḥusayn (who never ruled), son of Muḥammad, son of Qalawun.

[45] Qalqashandī, *Ṣubḥ*, VII:291.

abbreviated legends. This was at odds with the practices of contemporary dynasties (and earlier Mamluk sultans), which might include some lineage, but rarely three or four generations' worth.[46] The chancellery may also have contributed to ideological continuity, since its head under al-Nāṣir Muḥammad, ʿAlā' al-Dīn ʿAlī b. Faḍlallah, kept his position until 1368/769–70.[47]

The lightweights: Qalawunid clients and governors

Ideologically the smaller rulers in the Ilkhanid heartland or Anatolia, many of them Türkmen, did not appear to engage with Chingizid or Muslim Ilkhanid legitimacy. Certainly Türkmen had no claims to these models of kingship, nor did they appear to want them. Rather, in a possible revival of Seljuk tradition, some Türkmen used Seljuk chancellery practices and Seljuk titles, including at times even the supreme Islamic title, "Sultan," but the Mamluk chancellery never deigned to acknowledge it.[48] Even the Uyghur Eretna used titles that suggested he favored Islamic concepts and Seljuk protocol as an alternative to the Chingizid and Ilkhanid models. Although some rulers eventually elaborated on Oghuz Turkic traditions to rival the Chingizid favored dynasty, divine fortune and special law, the scant evidence from this period keeps us from knowing precisely how and when these developments began.[49] Certainly they made no appearance in Türkmen interactions with the Mamluks. Rather, many of these lesser Ilkhanid successors developed relations of submission to the Qalawunid sultans, who acted as their patrons, and as the supreme regional sovereigns, based on the position of superiority they had inherited from Muḥammad.

The relationships between the Qalawunids and their governors and clients involved a straightforward exchange: as sovereign and patron, the sultan

46 For the Mamluks see Balog, *Coinage*, 164–246; Lane-Poole, *Catalogue*, IV:160–91, IX:351–63; Lavoix, *Catalogue*, III:347–95; Artuk and Artuk, *Sikkeler*, 261–64. To contrast them with other contemporary dynasties see Lane-Poole, *Catalogue*, VI:206–26 and X:128–31 (Jalayirids), VIII:21–23 (Qaramanids) and VIII:41–49 (early Ottomans), IX:301–02 (Artuqids); Artuk and Artuk, *Sikkeler*, 404–07 (Artuqids), 441–42 (Qaramanids), 806–14 (Chingizid puppets after Abū Saʿīd), 823–26 (Eretnayids), 828–30 (Jalayirids), 833 (Qara Qoyunlu); similarly Album, "Studies I," entire, "Studies II," entire, and *Ashmolean*, xxxix–xli for coin references; H. L. Rabino, "Coins of the Jalā'ir, Ḳara Ḳoyūnlū, Mus͟haʿs͟haʿ, and Āḳ Ḳoyūnlū Dynasties," *Numismatic Chronicle* 6th series, 10 (1950), 94–139. For the inscriptions of the later Qalawunids see *CIA*, 197–98, 247–49, 152–73, 278–88.

47 Irwin, *Mamluk Sultanate*, 131–32.

48 Heath W. Lowry, *The Nature of the Ottoman State* (New York, 2003), 38–39, 41–42, 74; ʿUmarī, *Taʿrīf*, 51–55; Ibn Nāẓir al-Jaysh, *Tathqīf*, 56; Qalqashandī, *Ṣubḥ*, VII:297–305, esp. VII:304–05, VIII:11–25; see below for the Qaramanid adoption of "Sultan." Also see Rustam Shukurov, "Turkoman and Byzantine Self-Identity: Some Reflections on the Logic of the Title-Making in Twelfth- and Thirteenth-Century Anatolia," in *Eastern Approaches to Byzantium*, ed. Antony Eastmond (Aldershot, 2001), 262.

49 See Chapter 1.

promised (but only occasionally delivered) military support to his clients and governors, and gave them the luxurious regalia of office. Sometimes the sultan sent banners, or dies to cast coins. Since governorates in particular were accompanied by financial rights to property (*iqṭāʿ*), sultans also told governors which lands they could claim, and in some cases provided additional lower-ranking positions and their associated property rights, which governors distributed to their own men. For correspondence, clients and governors could expect third-sized paper and a range of middling to lesser titles, depending on the regulations of the chancellery.[50] In return governors and clients expressed loyalty to the Qalawunid sultan by including his titles on coins and in sermons, or by sending financial contributions to Cairo: in 1354–55/755 a Ramadanid paid 1,000 horses for the governorate of Elbistan, command of the Anatolian Türkmen, the usufruct from an estate and the right to distribute military posts to his men.[51] It is nevertheless unclear whether such donations were gifts, bribes or taxes. Governors were also supposed to join Mamluk military campaigns (although this often failed in practice), while the Türkmen in particular liked to visit the sultan at court. This allowed them to see the great cities of Damascus and Cairo, meet members of the Mamluk administration and experience the wealth of the Sultanate through gracious receptions. Perhaps as a result of these visits, some Türkmen sent their relatives to join the military in Cairo. This allowed them both to establish contacts in Egypt for times of need, and to provide the sultans with hostages.[52]

One particular aspect of the relationship between the Qalawunid sultans and their clients and governors was the use of the Abbasid caliph as a legitimating figurehead: caliphal banners accompanied the sultanic ones that governors received, and governors might also be granted a caliphal title. And yet it is unclear what benefit the sultans actually derived from the caliphs in these relationships. The evocation of Abbasid symbolism may have represented a simple continuation of older ideological concepts like that of Guardianship or the patronage of the holy cities, none of which was discarded during the Qalawunid period even though they lacked in force when compared to the concept of dynasty. But the Qalawunid sultans seem to have

[50] ʿUmarī, *Taʿrīf*, 41–55; Ibn Nāẓir al-Jaysh, *Tathqīf*, 50–56; Qalqashandī, *Ṣubḥ*, VII:297–305, VIII:11–25.

[51] Maqrīzī, *Sulūk*, II:921. The Dulqadirids also sent gifts in 1345–46/746 and 1346–47/747, and tribute (*taqdimah*) in 1355–56/756 (Maqrīzī, *Sulūk*, II:691, 722, III:21).

[52] Examples include various Dulqadirids, who visited in 1355–56/756 and 1365–66/767; another arrived to stay in 1386–87/788 (Maqrīzī, *Sulūk*, III:21, 120, 542; Ibn Qāḍī Shuhbah, *Taʾrīkh*, III:180). Similarly a Doğerid named Aḥmad emigrated in 1374–75/776 (Maqrīzī, *Sulūk*, III:236–37; Ibn Qāḍī Shuhbah, *Taʾrīkh*, II:449), while the chief Doğerid, Sālim, visited the Mamluk governor at Aleppo and went on to Cairo in 1383–84/785 (Ibn Qāḍī Shuhbah, *Taʾrīkh*, III:105). Other Türkmen living in Cairo include the Qaramanids Mūsā, ʿAlī Khan and Temür Khan (Maqrīzī, *Sulūk*, III:340, 491).

omitted the Abbasids from coins in this period, which suggests they found the caliphs unimportant. Thus when the Qalawunids interacted with client rulers and governors, they appear to have done so primarily as sultans of a royal house, not as partners of the caliph, as Baybars, Qalawun and especially Khalīl had once done. It is even more difficult to determine what the clients and governors themselves thought of their own symbolic connections to the caliph, especially since, like the sultans themselves, they did not appear to refer to the caliph on coins.[53]

And yet the Abbasids did not entirely disappear from politics. Twice in the 1380s/780s the caliph al-Mutawakkil ʿalà Allah (d. 1405–06/808) was considered as a candidate to replace the sultan in Cairo: first in 1376–77/778 after the murder of the Qalawunid al-Ashraf Shaʿbān, and again in summer 1383/785, when officers in the Mamluk armies were foiled as they plotted to overthrow the sultan Barquq for al-Mutawakkil, which they intended to do with Türkmen and Kurdish military support.[54] The rebels' willingness to promote the Abbasids suggests that they saw the caliph as a legitimate political alternative to the sultan, although whether they viewed al-Mutawakkil as a genuine or merely symbolic leader is unknown.[55] It is similarly unclear whether the Türkmen and Kurds involved in 1383/785 in particular were nomads living within Mamluk territory, or came from the autonomous confederations of Anatolia and Iraq. Nevertheless this political endorsement of the caliph inside Mamluk territory may have resonated with rulers outside as well: certainly interest in the caliph and his symbolic importance surfaced after the Qalawunid period when the Jalayirid Sulṭān-Aḥmad (r. 1382–1410/784–813) promoted himself on coins as the "Helper of the Commander of the Faithful," and the Ottoman Beyazid (r. 1389–1402/791–804) actively sought to acquire official Abbasid patronage for his rule from the Mamluk sultan.[56]

[53] For a complete lack of caliph references on coins see Lane-Poole, *Catalogue*, VI:206–26 and X:128–31 (Jalayirids), VIII:21–23 (Qaramanids) and 41–49 (early Ottomans); Artuk and Artuk, *Sikkeler*, 404–07 (Artuqids), 441–42 (Qaramanids), 823–26 (Eretnayids), 828–30 (Jalayirids), 833 (Qara Qoyunlu); similarly Album, *Ashmolean*, xxv–xxxi for formulas, xxxix–xli for coin references. The Jalayirid Sulṭān-Aḥmad (r. 1382–1410/784–813) is an exception to this rule; see below and note 56.

[54] They were Qurṭ b. ʿUmar "The Turkman" and Ibrāhīm b. Qutlughtimur. See Lutz Wiederhold, "Legal-Religious Elite, Temporal Authority and the Caliphate in Mamluk Society: Conclusions Drawn from the Examination of a 'Zahiri Revolt' in Damascus in 1386," *IJMES* 31 (1999), 213–14 and source references; also see Maqrīzī, *Sulūk*, III:493–95; Jalāl al-Dīn ʿAbd al-Raḥmān al-Suyūṭī, *Taʾrīkh al-khulafāʾ*, ed. Muḥammad Muḥyī al-Dīn ʿAbd al-Ḥamīd (Saida and Beirut, 1997), 556–57, and al-Suyūṭī, *History of the Caliphs*, tr. Henry Sullivan Jarrett (Amsterdam, 1970), 531–32.

[55] This topic deserves much more study, which could build on Wiederhold's promising "Zahiri Revolt."

[56] This was one of Sulṭān-Aḥmad's coin legends (*mughīth amīr al-muʾminīn*). See Rabino, "Coins," 106. Beyazid asked for an Abbasid caliphal decree from Cairo in the 1390s/790s; see chapter 6 note 40.

The Ilkhanid heartland

Qalawunid governors and clients in the Ilkhanid heartland included the Artuqids of Mardin, the lords of Sinjar, and the Qara Qoyunlu and Doğerid Türkmen.[57] Of these, the Artuqids had the longest relationship with the Mamluks: as loyal clients to the Ilkhanids, the Artuqids had at first been targets of Mamluk military aggression during the thirteenth/seventh century, despite being staunchly Muslim; nevertheless some believed that the Artuqids secretly enjoyed private contacts with the sultans in Cairo.[58] Certainly after the Mamluk–Ilkhanid peace of 1323/723 good relations prevailed between Cairo and Mardin as well, but only after Abū Saʿīd's death did the Artuqid al-Ṣāliḥ Ṣāliḥ (r. 1312–64/712–66) take on a new role by providing the Mamluk sultan with regular news of the Ilkhanid successors – it was Ṣāliḥ's last-minute warning that stopped Muḥammad from sending the army to Shaykh Ḥasan and Ḥājjī-Taghay in 1341/741.

Ṣāliḥ himself was independent of the Ilkhanid successors by 1346–47/747.[59] In an assertion of Seljuk-style Islamic norms of kinship, Ṣāliḥ had styled himself "Sultan" as early as 1330–31/731, although the Mamluks only ever accorded him the lower-ranking "King" (*malik*).[60] Chancellery evidence suggests that Ṣāliḥ maintained a good relationship to the Mamluks despite the political turmoil in Cairo, and he may also have continued to provide them with news.[61] Then in 1349–50/751 the relationship grew closer when a strongman in Sinjar began to threaten both the Artuqid city of Mardin and the Mamluk fort of al-Raḥbah. In response Ṣāliḥ wrote to Cairo for help, even though he was undergoing marriage negotiations with Choban's son Malik Ashraf at the time, and could have applied to him as well. The Mamluks sent an army from Syria to join Ṣāliḥ in a siege of Sinjar. Despite the cooperation between the two forces, the Mamluks were in charge, and the Qalawunid sultan Ḥasan (first r. 1347–51/748–52) – not the Artuqid Ṣāliḥ – was sovereign over the whole affair, for when the strongman asked for a pardon, it was the Mamluk officers who granted one on the sultan's behalf. The terms of the agreement also demonstrated Qalawunid supremacy: the lord of Sinjar became a client of Cairo, not Mardin, and was required to perform sermons and mint coins in Ḥasan's name, send hostages to Egypt to ratify the

[57] See articles in *EI*²: "Artuḳids" (Claude Cahen, I:662–67); "Ḳarā-Ḳoyunlu" (Faruk Sümer, IV:584–88); "Döger" (Faruk Sümer, II:613–14).

[58] Jazarī, *Taʾrīkh*, I:238, 427–28, 436; Ibn al-Dawādārī, *Kanz*, IX:10; Ilisch, "Artuqidenherrschaft," 68–69, 78–82.

[59] Ilisch, "Artuqidenherrschaft," 108.

[60] Max van Berchem, *Amida: matériaux pour l'épigraphie et l'histoire musulmanes du Diyar-Bekr* (Paris, 1910), 112; ʿUmarī, *Taʿrīf*, 41; Ibn Nāẓir al-Jaysh, *Tathqīf*, 20; Qalqashandī, *Ṣubḥ*, VII:289; also Artuk and Artuk, *Sikkeler*, 407.

[61] ʿUmarī, *Taʿrīf*, 41–42; Qalqashandī, *Ṣubḥ*, VII:288–89.

agreement and thereafter pay a yearly tribute.[62] Ṣāliḥ appears to have approved of this arrangement, and when one hostage escaped en route to Egypt, Ṣāliḥ not only captured and beheaded him, but demonstrated his own loyalty by sending the head to Aleppo.[63] When Ṣāliḥ subsequently took over Sinjar entirely in 1353–54/754, the Mamluks did not protest, which suggests that they approved his maneuver. Ṣāliḥ then lost the city to the Qara Qoyunlu in 1356/757, and neither he nor the Mamluks regained control until 1361–62/763, when the Mamluks sent ambassadors to Sinjar and to Mosul with the appropriate robes, documents, banners and gifts to establish the Qara Qoyunlu as Mamluk governors. In a statement of the sultan's role as supporter of Islamic law, the ambassadors were accompanied by judges, who had been designated to remain in each city after the ambassadors left.[64]

Then when the Jalayirids began to expand (see below), Ṣāliḥ himself bowed more deeply to the notion of Qalawunid supremacy and formally asked to become a Mamluk governor in 1358–59/760, although he stamped the sultan's titles only intermittently on his coins, perhaps in response to Jalayirid pressure.[65] The Artuqids appear to have enjoyed favored status among the small rulers patronized by the Mamluks: when Ṣāliḥ died in 1364/766, prayers were said over him in the Umayyad mosque in Damascus, and the robe appointing his son al-Manṣūr Aḥmad (r. 1364–67/766–69) as heir was promptly sent out from Cairo.[66] In 1365–66/767, when Aḥmad faced another round of Jalayirid pressure, the Artuqid preference for Qalawunid patronage was apparent, since Aḥmad's secret message to Cairo caused the Mamluks to dispatch a reconnaissance force, although nothing developed from this.[67] A further demonstration of Qalawunid patronage appeared when Aḥmad died of illness in 1367/769, and Aḥmad's son al-Ṣāliḥ Maḥmūd sent word of his accession to al-Ashraf Shaʿbān in 1367–68/769.[68] The response letter made the sultan's role as a ruling authority clear when it assured Maḥmūd that Shaʿbān approved his succession: "Our noble orders . . . stipulate that he take his [father's] place, and protect with his care [his father's] rights and the best interest of those lands. And so we order that this happen according to custom, out of the goodness of our noble house, which began it and returned it."[69] To underscore Shaʿbān's authority, the letter explained that if Maḥmūd did not

[62] Maqrīzī, *Sulūk*, II:830; al-Ḥasan Ibn Ḥabīb, *Tadhkirat al-nabīh fī ayyām al-Manṣūr wa banīhi*, eds. Muḥammad Muḥammad Amīn and Saʿīd ʿĀshūr (Cairo, 1976), III:144; Ibn Qāḍī Shuhbah, *Taʾrīkh*, II:9; Ṣafadī, *Aʿyān*, II:257; also see Ilisch, "Artuqidenherrschaft," 113.

[63] Ilisch, "Artuqidenherrschaft," 113.

[64] Ibn Qāḍī Shuhbah, *Taʾrīkh*, II:201; Ibn Kathīr, *Bidāyah*, XIV:335; Qalqashandī, *Ṣubḥ*, VII:297; also ʿAzzāwī, *Taʾrīkh al-ʿIrāq*, II:73; see also Sümer, "Ḳarā-Ḳoyunlu," 584–86.

[65] Coins were stamped for the Mamluk sultan in 1358–59/760 and 1362–63/764. Ilisch, "Artuqidenherrschaft," 117.

[66] Maqrīzī, *Sulūk*, III:95 (but in 1363–64/765); Ibn Ḥajar, *Durar*, II:203; Ilisch, "Artuqidenherrschaft," 119, albeit citing Ibn Kathīr (*sic*), not Ibn Ḥajar.

[67] Maqrīzī, *Sulūk*, III:122; also see Ilisch, "Artuqidenherrschaft," 121.

[68] For the text of Shaʿbān's response see Qalqashandī, *Ṣubḥ*, VII:290–91. [69] *Ibid.*, 291.

choose to rule, it would be the Qalawunid sultan who would choose his successor: "If not, then [we] will bring out someone to remedy that shortcoming and settle that situation."[70] The letter also reminded Maḥmūd that he needed to continue the obedient and friendly relations maintained by his father and grandfather, and asked him to write often. But Qalawunid sovereignty over Mardin ended a few months later when Maḥmūd was overthrown by his uncle, al-Muẓaffar Dāwūd (r. 1368–76/769–78), who abandoned his predecessors' subservience for a position of neutral independence. Thereafter, however, Dāwūd's son and successor al-Ẓāhir ʿĪsà (r. 1376–94/778–96, 1396–1407/798–809) reestablished the older relationship to the Mamluks soon after taking power.[71] The Qalawunids also continued their intermittent sovereignty over Sinjar: although the Mamluk-appointed governor and a Mamluk army from Syria were pushed out in 1371–72/773 by the unsubmissive Artuqid Dāwūd, another Mamluk army recaptured Sinjar in spring 1375/late 776, and held it for over a year until finally leaving it for good to the Qara Qoyunlu in 1376/777.[72] The Qalawunids also developed a relationship of intermittent sovereignty over the Doğerid Türkmen in the 1370s/770s, but few details are known.[73]

Anatolia

Qalawunid governors and clients in Anatolia included Eretna and the Türkmen confederations of the Dulqadirids, Qaramanids and Ramadanids.[74] Here relationships ranged from alliances between the sultan and a client, like the Qaramanids, to the direct incorporation of an Anatolian into the Mamluk administration, like Eretna, the Ramadanids and the Dulqadirids. A full history of these relationships is beyond the scope of this book, but a few points should be made here. As mentioned, the Türkmen do not appear to have engaged ideologically with the concepts of Chingizid legitimacy. The Qaramanids, whose relationship with the Mamluks was excellent, longstanding yet poorly recorded in the histories, are one example: even during the early days of Ilkhanid rule the Qaramanids showed greater allegiance to the Seljuks than to the Mongols, and enjoyed repeated positive interactions with the Mamluk sultans as well, which by Ilkhanid terms was treasonous.[75] The Qaramanids maintained their rapprochement with Cairo by developing a relationship of intermittent subservience to the sultans

[70] *Ibid.* [71] Ilisch, "Artuqidenherrschaft," 126–27, 131–32.

[72] *Ibid.*, 128–29; Ibn Qāḍī Shuhbah, *Taʾrīkh*, II:483–84; Aḥmad Ibn Ḥajar al-ʿAsqalānī, *Inbāʾ al-ghumr bi-abnāʾ al-ʿumr*, ed. Ḥasan Ḥabashī (Cairo, 1969), I:105.

[73] See Maqrīzī, *Sulūk*, III:236–37, 341, 489; Ibn Qāḍī Shuhbah, *Taʾrīkh*, II:449, III:105, 385–86.

[74] See articles in *EI²*: "Eretna" (Cahen, II:705–07); "Dhu ʾl-Ḳadr" (J. H. Mordtmann and V. L. Ménage, II:239–40); "Ḳarāmān-Oghulları" (Faruk Sümer, IV:619–25); "Ramaḍān-Oghulları" (Franz Babinger, VIII:418–19); also Salim Koca, "Anatolian Turkish Beyliks," *The Turks, II: Middle Ages*, eds. Hasan Celac Güzel et al. (Ankara, 2002), 508–14, 546–48.

[75] For a claim that the Qaramanids were "of the race of the Seljuks" see Qazvīnī, *Nuzhat*, 99.

al-Ashraf Khalīl and al-Nāṣir Muḥammad, despite living under active Ilkhanid control, and maintained this subservient relationship even after the death of Abū Saʿīd.[76] Despite the length and warmth of the relations, however, the Qalawunids never saw the Qaramanids as equals, and never addressed them with a title higher than "Commander (*amīr*)."[77] Thus when the Qaramanid Alāʾ al-Dīn (d. 1397–98/800) adopted the title "Sultan" in the 1350s/750s, the Mamluks refused to honor it; and thereafter the relationship soured, in part because Alāʾ al-Dīn's considerable ambitions did not include any more subservience.[78]

But despite the Qalawunids' proclamations of unchallenged sovereignty, the sultans had more practical and ideological trouble with their Anatolian subordinates than with anyone else, which demonstrated how hollow Qalawunid sovereignty really was. One problem was Anatolian support for Mamluk rebels. Although factional struggle over the Sultanate usually centered in Cairo, some rebellions arose in Syria. But whereas earlier Syrian rebels had looked east to the Ilkhanid court for assistance, in the post-Ilkhanid world, Syrian insurgents turned north towards Anatolia – four of five major Syrian rebellions from 1341–89/742–91 relied on Anatolian military support. The Anatolians seemed to have backed rebels not to dispense with the Qalawunid sultan, but to change to a new one and see their own status improve. Not surprisingly, rebellions were led exclusively by Mamluk governors who had served in Aleppo, and who were able to court the Anatolian military powers while in office.[79]

Nor did Anatolians always take Qalawunid sovereignty as seriously as the Qalawunids themselves did, which also showed how hollow the ideology was. Eretna had originally seen his submission to al-Nāṣir Muḥammad's rule as a mere convenience, although later he sheltered a rebel commander who helped bring Muḥammad's son al-Nāṣir Aḥmad (r. 1342/742–43) to the throne.[80] But Aḥmad failed to last, and thereafter the extent of Eretna's loyalty is unclear: he took the Islamic title of "Sultan" for himself and minted coins only in his own name, but upon occasion sought patronage from Shaykh Ḥasan

[76] The Qaramanids minted coins in the name of al-Ashraf Khalīl in 1291–92/691 (Jazarī, *Taʾrīkh*, I:156); and al-Nāṣir Muḥammad in 1318–19/718 (Mufaḍḍal, *Chronik*, 6; Maqrīzī, *Sulūk*, II:185–86), in 1324–25/725 (Maqrīzī, *Sulūk*, II:259) and in 1340–41/741 (Shujāʿī, *Taʾrīkh*, 115; Ibn Qāḍī Shuhbah, *Taʾrīkh*, I:129). Evidence for Qaramanid–Mamluk relations after 1340–41/741 is sparse, although by the 1380s/780s the Qaramanids had definitely turned against the Mamluks. See Sümer, "Ḳarāmān-Oghullarι," 622–23.

[77] ʿUmarī, *Taʿrīf*, 51, 55; Qalqashandī, *Ṣubḥ*, V:346.

[78] See Sümer, "Ḳarāmān-Oghullarι," 622–23; also Lane-Poole, *Catalogue*, VIII:21.

[79] These were the rebellions of Tashtimur "Green Chick-Pea," in 1341–42/742, Baybugha Arus in 1352–54/753–54, Tashtimur, Ishiq Timur and Timurbay in 1377–78/779, and Yalbugha and Mintash in 1388–89/790–91; there were also lesser uprisings. The fifth major rebel, Yalbugha al-Yaḥyāwī in 1347–48/748, made too many enemies as governor of Aleppo, and looked to the Chobanids for support. See note 103 below; also Irwin, *Mamluk Sultanate*, 127–29, 139–40.

[80] Shujāʿī, *Taʾrīkh*, 173–94; Maqrīzī, *Sulūk*, II:581–82; Ibn Qāḍī Shuhbah, *Taʾrīkh*, I:268–69; also Irwin, *Mamluk Sultanate*, 127–28.

the Jalayirid as well, and yet asked to be renewed as a Mamluk governor "as usual" in 1350–51/751.[81] But Eretna was punished for his inconstant loyalty, for the Mamluks never sent him any actual military assistance as he struggled with his enemies, and even authorized the Chobanid Malik Ashraf to attack him (see below).

A similar case was that of the Dulqadirid Qaraja (d. 1353–54/754), Mamluk governor of Elbistan. Like Eretna, Qaraja had initially approached Muḥammad in 1338–39/739 (through the governor of Syria, Tankiz), but Qaraja's ambitions, too, were greater than they seemed. Qaraja supported two different Mamluk rebellions, skirmished periodically with the governors of Aleppo and by the late 1340s/740s was rumored to be calling himself the "Victorious King (*al-malik al-qāhir*)," which was far too elevated a title for a Mamluk official. He was also said to have demanded that the Armenians pay him the annual tribute they normally sent to Cairo, which was clear insubordination.[82] But Qaraja paid a higher price for his unruliness than did Eretna, for Qaraja was eventually captured, sent to Egypt and executed by the Mamluk state in 1353–54/754, while Eretna seems to have died naturally.[83] Thereafter Eretna's successors maintained a distant relationship with the Qalawunids; by contrast, the later Dulqadirids, although less ambitious than Qaraja, alternated among submission to Qalawunid rule, struggles with local Mamluk officials and armed support of rebels against Cairo. In fact, the Dulqadirids asked for forgiveness so often that one Mamluk chancellery manual included a model letter of pardon composed specifically for them.[84] Whenever relations soured with the Anatolians, the Mamluks sent armies to bring the region under control, which was unfortunate both for the Mamluk state and for Qalawunid sovereignty. Despite their orderly and expensive showing, these armies failed in almost every campaign they undertook, either because they simply could not find their adversaries among the Anatolian mountains, or because they found them but were humiliatingly routed: of seventeen Mamluk campaigns in Anatolia between 1343–44/744 and 1384–85/786, only two were successful.[85] This demonstrated to all watching that the Qalawunid role of patron and regional sovereign was actually fraught

[81] Cahen, "Eretna"; for the Mamluks (and the quote) see Maqrīzī, *Sulūk*, II:816; for independent coins see Album, "Studies I," 94 and *Ashmolean*, xxviii for formulas, and xxxix for coin references; Artuk and Artuk, *Sikkeler*, 824. For Shaykh Ḥasan's patronage in 1344–45/745 and 1348–49/749 see Samarqandī, *Maṭla'*, 233, 261.

[82] The rebellions were in 1341–42/742 and 1352–54/753–54; see note 79 above. For skirmishes see Shujā'ī, *Ta'rīkh*, 263–64; Maqrīzī, *Sulūk*, II:657; Ibn Qāḍī Shuhbah, *Ta'rīkh*, I:461, 561. For Qaraja's visions of grandeur see Ibn al-Wardī, *Ta'rīkh*, II:501.

[83] Mordtmann and Ménage, "Dhu 'l-Ḳadr," 240; Cahen, "Eretna," 706.

[84] Qalqashandī, *Ṣubḥ*, VII:230–32.

[85] Mamluk campaigns into Anatolia, usually against the Dulqadirids, took place in 1343–44/744, 1345–46/746, 1352–54/753–54, 1354–55/755, 1361–62/763, 1365–66/767, 1376–77/778, 1377–78/779 (two campaigns), 1379–80/781 (planned but not carried out), 1381–82/783 (two campaigns), 1382–83/784, 1383–84/785 (three campaigns) and 1386–87/788. The Mamluks were successful only in 1354–55/755, and in the second campaign of 1381–82/783.

with trouble, while Qalawunid inherited sovereignty and actual Mamluk strength, although proclaimed from Cairo, were not all they seemed to be.

The heavyweights: the Chobanids and the Jalayirids

The two most prominent groups in the Ilkhanid heartland were the competing dynasties of the Jalayirids and the Chobanids, who were linked by marriage, yet ferocious rivals.[86] They had enjoyed similar relationships to the Ilkhanids: both families were descended from Mongol tribes (the Jalayirids and the Süldüz), claimed an ancestor who had been in Chingiz Khan's immediate service (Ilka and Sorgan Shira) and could boast of high-level service to the Ilkhanid branch of the dynasty, whether through Shaykh Ḥasan (for the Jalayirids), or through Choban and Temürtash (for the Chobanids). To define their understandings of kingship, both groups relied on Muslim Ilkhanid tradition, but only the Chobanids deliberately used Islamic norms to compete with the Ilkhanid model. Both the Jalayirids and Chobanids seemed to acknowledge Qalawunid seniority and their own relative inferiority, as expressed in chancellery and ceremonial diplomatic protocol. They were also aware of the Qalawunids' sovereignty over clients and governors, but did not accept it over themselves: neither the Jalayirids nor the Chobanids ever sent tribute or hostages to Cairo, as did other rulers, and the Mamluk administration played no role in succession.

The Jalayirids maintained the strongest ties to Chingizid tradition in general and to the memory of the Muslim Ilkhanid house in particular, just as the early Mamluks had done with the Ayyubid dynasty. This was especially true for Shaykh Ḥasan, who used Chingizid puppets intermittently until 1346–47/747, after which he let the position lapse. Shaykh Ḥasan enjoyed a maternal link to the Chingizid family, for his mother Öljetei had been a daughter of the Ilkhan Arghun. One of Shaykh Ḥasan's contemporaries therefore chose to recognize his ties to the golden dynasty by identifying him as Shaykh Ḥasan "Uljatāʾī" ("the one from Öljetei"), not Jalayirid or Ilkanid, names from his father's family.[87] Nevertheless a maternal connection to the Chingizids was no substitute for a paternal link, and as a result Shaykh Ḥasan at first limited himself to the highest title he had achieved under Abū Saʿīd, "Commander of the State."[88] In the 1350s/750s, however, he seems to have adopted the

86 Dilshād Khatun, the Chobanid widow of Abū Saʿīd, married the Jalayirid Shaykh Ḥasan and later bore Shaykh Uvais, the first Jalayirid heir.

87 Zayn al-Dīn b. Ḥamdallah Qazvīnī, *Dhayl-i taʾrīkh-i guzīdah*, ed. Iraj Afshar (Tehran, 1993–94), 27 and thereafter; esp. 67.

88 His title under Ilkhanid rule was Ulus Beg (*ulus* = "state," "people" in Mongolian; *beg* = "commander" in Turkish) also *amīr-i ulus* (*amīr* = "commander" in Arabic), for which see H. R. Roemer, "The Jalayirids, Muzaffarids and Sarbadārs," *CHIr* VI:5; also see John Masson-Smith, "Djalāyir, Djalāyirids," *EI*² II:401.

sovereign title of "Sultan."[89] Throughout his reign Shaykh Ḥasan maintained a warm relationship of mutual affection with the Qalawunids, but the details are scant.[90]

The Jalayirids also maintained their ties to the Ilkhanids by following Ilkhanid models in chancellery and administrative protocol: they issued some documents in both Persian and Mongolian, mimicked Ilkhanid paper preferences and copied their predecessors in page arrangements and ink colors: in diplomacy the Ilkhanids had used square seals with red ink stating the divine mandate in Chinese characters through the reign of Öljeitü, then had added Arabic seals with the same message under Abū Saʿīd; the Jalayirids thereafter used square seals with Islamic phrases in Arabic as well.[91] Some Jalayirid coins were also bilingual, as Ilkhanid coins had been.[92] As had been the case for the early Mamluks and the Ayyubids, it was the first Jalayirids who seemed to imitate earlier protocol most closely: although Shaykh Ḥasan's chancellery practices are unrecorded, his son Shaykh Uvays's scribes mimicked Ilkhanid models, and styles began to change only under Sulṭān-Ḥusayn (r. 1374–82/776–84), whose chancellery introduced a round seal and may have reapportioned white space.[93] Also like their Muslim Ilkhanid predecessors, the Jalayirids were energetic patrons of architecture and art, especially the arts of the book, and may have promoted their legitimacy through artistic media, although the evidence is inconclusive (Figure 8).[94]

Like the Jalayirids, the Chobanid Ḥasan b. Temürtash (d. 1343/744) invoked Ilkhanid tradition through puppets.[95] Unlike the Jalayirids,

[89] Scholars debate whether Shaykh Ḥasan considered himself an independent sovereign. See Roemer, "Jalayirids," 5, and Boyle, "Īl-Khāns," 415; Spuler, *Mongolen*, 112, 253 note 27; Masson-Smith, "Djalāyirids," 401. Numismatic evidence suggests that Shaykh Ḥasan did recognize his own sovereignty. See Rabino, "Coins," 105 and plate VII coin 4; Artuk and Artuk, *Sikkeler*, 828; Album, *Ashmolean*, coins 336 and 368.

[90] For the warmth see Ibn Qāḍī Shuhbah, *Taʾrīkh*, II:105; Ṣafadī, *Aʿyān*, II:191; also Qalqashandī, *Ṣubḥ*, VII:282–83 for a similar warmth under Shaykh Uvays. For evidence of diplomatic relations see note 122 below.

[91] Herrmann and Doerfer, "Šeyḫ Oveys," 59, also 38–44; see also Mostaert and Cleaves, "Trois documents," 484–85.

[92] Lane-Poole, *Catalogue*, X:129.

[93] For similarity to Ilkhanid styles see Herrmann and Doerfer, "Šeyḫ Oveys," 3, 34–35, 58–59; Gottfried Herrmann and Gerhard Doerfer, "Ein persich-mongolischer Erlaß aus dem Jahr 725/1325," *ZDMG* 125:2 (1975), 317–46. For stylistic innovations see Gottfried Herrmann and Gerhard Doerfer, "Ein Erlass des Ǧalāyiriden Solṭān Ḥoseyn aus dem Jahr 780/1378," *Erkenntnisse und Meinungen* 1 (1973), 149–54. Also see Henri Massé, "Ordonnance rendue par le prince ilkanien Aḥmad Jalair en faveur du Cheikh Sadr od-Dîn (1305–1392)," *JA* 230 (1938), 465–68; A. D. Papazian, "Deux nouveaux iarlyks d'Ikhans," *Banber Matenadarani* 6 (1962), 379–401.

[94] Unfortunately few Jalayirid miniatures and almost no buildings have survived. See Norah M. Titley, *Persian Miniature Painting and its Influence on the Art of Turkey and India* (Austin, TX, 1983), 26–34; Gonzàlez de Clavijo on Shaykh Uvais's palace, *Embassy*, 89; ʿAzzāwī, *Taʾrīkh al-ʿIrāq*, II:79–80, 84–94, 99–101, 105.

[95] See Melville and Zaryab, "Chobanids," 499–501. This figure is known as Ḥasan b. Temürtash in some Mamluk sources, although he is often called Shaykh Ḥasan in Persian sources. I have omitted the shaykh here to avoid confusion with Shaykh Ḥasan the Jalayirid.

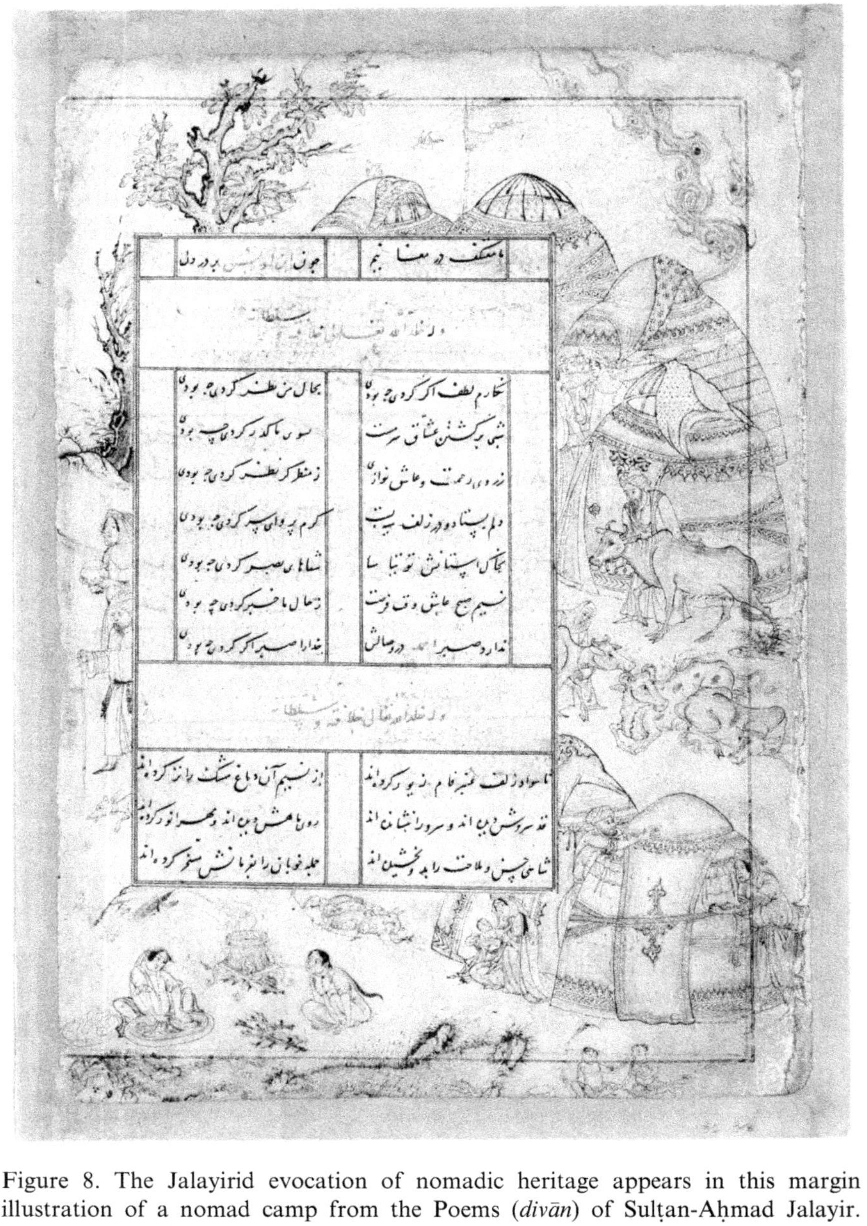

Figure 8. The Jalayirid evocation of nomadic heritage appears in this margin illustration of a nomad camp from the Poems (*divān*) of Sulṭan-Aḥmad Jalayir. (Freer Gallery of Art, Smithsonian Institution, Washington DC: Purchase, F1932.34.)

however, the Chobanids soon branched into more creative responses to the Chingizid legacy, as in 744/1343, when Ḥasan's brother and successor Malik Ashraf (r. 1343–57/744–58) set up a puppet known as both Anūshirvān Khan, and Anūshirvān the Just (*Anūshirvān-i ʿĀdil*) after the Sassanian king Khusraw I (r. 531–79). The puppet's identity is unclear: he was Malik Ashraf's wardrobe keeper (*qabjājī*), described as a member of the Turkli tribe, or an "Obscure Chankizkhanid scion, (*ke'ün*)."[96] Regardless of his actual lineage, his titles suggested that Malik Ashraf was using him conservatively to invoke the Chingizids (with "Khan") and innovatively to adopt the distant Sassanian dynasty (with "Anūshirvān the Just"). Malik Ashraf also installed a Sassanian-style chain with bells at his residence, which petitioners were supposed to ring in order to demand justice.[97] Although the Ilkhanids themselves had used Iranian cultural traditions to promote their legitimacy to their own subjects, the Chobanids' faux-Sassanian dynastic experiments were unprecedented and of unknown effect.[98]

The Chobanids also made creative connections not just to the Chingizid family and the Sassanians, but to their own would-be dynasty through the figures of Choban and Temürtash. This technique allowed them to incorporate strictly Islamic ideas into their legitimacy, create an alternative to the Chingizid model and come into closer contact with the Qalawunids. The most dramatic promotion of the Chobanid dynasty, and most threatening to the Qalawunids, came in 1337–38/738 when Ḥasan used a slave with a physical resemblance to the dead Temürtash to claim that Temürtash was still alive. This false Temürtash gained followers, and was sighted with a yellow, Mamluk-style sultanic banner – acquired without Mamluk authorization – which bore the Muslim statement of faith and the phrase "Temürtash is the freedman of God (*dimurdāsh ʿatīq Allah*)."[99] It is unknown, however, whether the doppelgänger also employed Temürtash's claim to be the "Rightly Guided One (*mahdī*)." Later Ḥasan wrote to the Qalawunid sultan al-Ṣāliḥ Ismāʿīl (r. 1342–45/743–46) and asked him to send the body of the real Temürtash home for burial, but Ismāʿīl rebuffed him by claiming ignorance of Temürtash's final resting place, and turned the messenger away disappointed.[100] After Ḥasan's death, Malik Ashraf may have been deliberately advised to circumvent the problem of Chingizid legitimacy through Islamic

96 For the Turkli tribe see Abū Bakr Ahrī, *Taʾrīkh-i Shaikh Uwais (History of Shaikh Uways): An Important Source for the History of Ādharbaijān in the Fourteenth Century*, tr. J. B. van Loon (The Hague, 1954), 71 and text, 171; for "Obscure Chankizkhanid scion," see Woods, *Aqquyunlu*, 8 (citing Zayn al-Dīn Qazvīnī, *Dhayl*, 35, whence Ḥāfiẓ Abrū, *Dhayl*, 224 and Samarqandī, *Maṭlaʿ*, 221); Mīrkhwānd, *Rawḍah*, V:4431. Also see Boyle, "Īl-Khāns," 415.

97 Qazvīnī, *Dhayl*, 55–56 whence Ḥāfiẓ Abrū, *Dhayl*, 231–32, and Samarqandī, *Maṭlaʿ*, 275; Mīrkhwānd, *Rawḍat*, V:4440.

98 For Ilkhanid use of Iranian cultural traditions see Chapter 3.

99 The sultan al-Nāṣir Muḥammad was both angry at and afraid of this news. Shujāʿī, *Taʾrīkh*, 38; also Ahrī, *Shaikh Uwais*, 65; see also Ṣafadī, *Aʿyān*, II:26–27, 115.

100 This was in August–September 1343/Rabīʿ II 744. Maqrīzī, *Sulūk*, II:648.

norms: "No sons remain in the house of Changiz Khan. You should assume the honorific 'Ashraf' (most noble) in the manner of past [Islamic] kings [Ar. *mulūk*, singular *malik*] and seize control of the kingdom and the community with the blows of your resplendent sword."[101] But whether Malik Ashraf took this advice is unclear, since he continued to maintain his puppet Anūshirvān, and did not mint independent coinage.[102]

At first the Mamluks remained wary of the Chobanids, especially after a rebellious governor of Damascus was caught trying to flee to Chobanid territory in 1347–48/748.[103] But then in 1350–53/751–53 Malik Ashraf sent three diplomatic missions to the Qalawunid sultans al-Nāṣir Ḥasan and al-Ṣāliḥ Ṣāliḥ (r. 1351–54/752–55), with messages of goodwill and friendship.[104] At the time Malik Ashraf was cementing relations with neighbors through marriage and engaging in military endeavors.[105] His embassies therefore can be seen both as an olive branch, and as an acknowledgement of Qalawunid sovereignty over other rulers in the region, particularly Eretna, whom Malik Ashraf wanted to subdue. Despite the Chobanids' stated peaceful intentions, the Mamluks viewed the embassies with distrust: when the first arrived in July–August 1350/Jumādà I 751, they wrote and informed Shaykh Ḥasan, who warned them that the envoys must be secret agents sent to spy on the Mamluk armies. The Mamluks therefore isolated the second embassy of May–June 1351/Jumādà I 752 in its quarters in Cairo, even though its message was a request for peace (*ṣulḥ*). The Mamluks also maintained the sultan's inherited position of seniority by addressing Malik Ashraf as they would Eretna with the low titles of "His Lofty Honor (*al-janāb al-'ālī*)" and "Noyan," written on only third-sized Baghdādī paper.[106] Finally in the third mission in December 1352–January 1353/Dhū al-Qa'dah 753 Malik Ashraf revealed the military rationale behind his embassies by explaining that he intended to attack Eretna, and asking the Qalawunid Ṣāliḥ, as Eretna's sovereign, to stay out of the affair. Despite Eretna's status as a sometime Mamluk governor – a status that he had petitioned to renew as recently as 1350–51/751 – and their earlier mistrust of Malik Ashraf, Ṣāliḥ's advisors granted this request, for reasons that are entirely unclear. Nevertheless, Malik Ashraf never sent a campaign to Anatolia.[107]

[101] Translation modified from Woods, *Aqquyunlu*, 7–8, but also see Mu'īn al-Dīn Naṭanzī, *Muntakhab al-tawārikh-i mu'īnī*, ed. Parvīn Istakhrī (Tehran, 2004), 127, where "sons" (*oghul*), as here, replaces "charisma" (*ughur*), as in Woods and in the earlier edition (Mu'īn al-Dīn Naṭanzī, *Muntakhab al-tawārikh-i mu'īnī*, ed. Jean Aubin [Tehran, 1957], 158).

[102] For Anūshirvān's coins see Lane-Poole, *Catalogue*, VI:115–17 and X:119–20; Album, *Ashmolean*, xxxix; Artuk and Artuk, *Sikkeler*, 813–14.

[103] This was Yalbugha al-Yaḥyāwī. See Ibn Kathīr, *Bidāyah*, XIV:252–53, 256–58; Ibn al-Wardī, *Ta'rīkh*, II:494–95; Maqrīzī, *Sulūk*, II:733.

[104] For all three embassies see Maqrīzī, *Sulūk*, II:820, 840, 883.

[105] Qazvīnī, *Dhayl*, 49–56.

[106] Ibn Nāẓir al-Jaysh, *Tathqīf*, 42; Qalqashandī, *Ṣubḥ*, VII:284, 299–300, 301.

[107] Maqrīzī, *Sulūk*, II:816, 883.

But despite the Jalayirid and Chobanid attempts both to connect themselves to Muslim Ilkhanid tradition and to move beyond it, and despite their intermittent interactions with the Qalawunid sultans, Chingizid legitimacy was still a force in its own right. This became clear when Özbek's son, Janibek Khan of the Golden Horde (r. 1342–57/742–58), invaded Azerbaijan in 1357/758.[108] Like Özbek, Janibek was a Muslim Chingizid whose ambitions were not confined to Golden Horde territory; unlike his father, Janibek assumed the supreme Chingizid title, "Great Khan (*khāqān*)," at the beginning of his reign, although it is unclear whether he kept it.[109] During his invasion of Azerbaijan Janibek wrote to regional rulers as a Chingizid and demanded their submission. Many acquiesced, among them the Jalayirid Shaykh Uvays.[110] Janibek also wrote to Malik Ashraf, to whom he clearly expressed his intention of reviving Chingizid dominance: "I am coming to take possession of the *ulus* (state, people) of Hülegü. You are the son of Choban whose name was in the decree (*yarligh*) of the four *ulus*es. Today three realms are under my command, and I also wish to appoint you commander (*emīr*) of the *ulus*; get up and come to meet [me]."[111] But Malik Ashraf refused to bow to the Chingizid claim, and dismissed Janibek as sovereign only in Golden Horde territory, who had no right to Ilkhanid lands, where Malik Ashraf was in charge for the Ilkhanid family (meaning the puppet Anūshirvān?).[112] When Janibek's messenger criticized this resistance, Malik Ashraf imprisoned him, which was tantamount to treason. Nevertheless Malik Ashraf understood how untenable his position was, both ideologically and militarily, for even to his own followers he admitted that, "This is the son of King Özbek. He is of the family of Chingiz Khan and has an overwhelming army of three hundred thousand men. I cannot hold out against him."[113] Soon thereafter Malik Ashraf's forces were defeated, and he was captured and executed at Janibek's orders, which marked the effective end of Chobanid rule.

In addition to his proclamation of Chingizid superiority, Janibek also drew on Islamic ideas of kingship, which he expressed to the Mamluks as his forebears had done. The stated impetus for Janibek's campaign had been Malik Ashraf's oppression, which refugees from Azerbaijan – among them Muslim scholars – had brought to Janibek's attention. As a Muslim ruler, Janibek had felt obliged to act.[114] After killing Malik Ashraf, therefore, Janibek sent the second embassy of his reign to Cairo (the first had announced his accession), to inform the Mamluk sultan (al-Nāṣir Ḥasan)

108 For Janibek's reign see Spuler, *Goldene Horde*, 99–109, and 101–02 for the invasion; Schamiloglu, "Golden Horde," 826–27.
109 Lane-Poole, *Catalogue*, VI:132–33, coins 383, 387.
110 Naṭanzī/Istakhrī, *Muntakhab*, 69, also see Ilisch, "Artuqidenherrschaft," 115–16.
111 Ahrī, *Shaikh Uwais*, 76–77, with slight editing.
112 "He is king of the *ulus* of Berke, he has nothing to do with the *ulus* of Abaqa, for King Ghazan exists here [meaning the Ilkhanids?] and the emirship belongs to me." *Ibid.*, 77, with slight editing.
113 *Ibid.*, with slight editing. 114 Qazvīnī, *Dhayl*, 57–58.

that he had conquered Azerbaijan from the tyrant.[115] There is no indication that Janibek expected the sultan to bow to Chingizid rule, and the Mamluks received the embassy with great honors and accepted Janibek's gifts of falcons, sables and slaves, which they are unlikely to have done if he had demanded their obedience.[116] Although the Mamluk response has been lost, it probably drew on the older model of religious seniority over the Golden Horde to express good wishes, congratulations and perhaps solidarity against tyrants and the enemies of religion. Stylistically it resembled earlier letters to the Golden Horde and to Abū Saʿīd with large paper, colored inks and the appropriate Muslim and Chingizid titles of "Sultan" and "Khan."[117] But thereafter Janibek withdrew to the steppe and died of illness in 1357/758; his heir Birdibek, whom Janibek had left governing Azerbaijan, returned to the north and abandoned his father's conquests.

The rise of the Jalayirids

After the withdrawal of the Golden Horde and in the absence of a Chobanid threat, the Jalayirids began to rise to power under Shaykh Uvays (r. 1356–74/757–76). Ideologically Shaykh Uvays took the Ilkhanid fusion of Chingizid and Islamic ideology that his father had employed, but increased his own prestige within these combined traditions. His acceptance of Janibek's authority had been less submission to Chingizid dominance than a nod to military circumstance, for he fought with Birdibek's deputy Akhījūq over Tabriz in summer 1358/759, which was technically treason.[118] By October–November 1358/Dhū al-Qaʿdah 759 Shaykh Uvays was even using "Bahadur Khan," which had been Abū Saʿīd's own title, and which suggested that the position of khan was no longer a privilege of the Chingizids alone.[119] Nevertheless, Shaykh Uvays also maintained a clear respect for the Golden House, for some of his titles emphasized his preservation of the Chingizid legacy, among them "Resurrector of the Traditions of the Chingizid State (Per. *muḥyī-yi marāsim-i dawlat-i jankizkhānī*)" and "[One] Ornamented by the Mark of the Chingizid State (Ar. *muzayyan shuʿār*

115 Ibn Qāḍī Shuhbah, *Taʾrīkh*, II:116; Maqrīzī, *Sulūk*, III:34. For the earlier embassy see Shujāʿī, *Taʾrīkh*, 247; also Spuler, *Goldene Horde*, 100.

116 Egypt does not appear in a list of regions whose rulers submitted to Janibek. Naṭanzī/Istakhrī, *Muntakhab*, 69.

117 Janibek's letter was on paper that was three fingerwidths short of full Baghdādī, to which the chancellery responded in kind. Qalqashandī, *Ṣubḥ*, VII:318. Letters were also sent to lesser Golden Horde figures. These included one in August 1351/Jumādà II 752 to the commander Qutlubugha Inaq, one to a certain Qaja ʿAlī Beg in 1363–64/765, and a third to the commander Mamay in early November 1371/late Rabīʿ II 773 (Ibn Nāẓir al-Jaysh, *Tathqīf*, 39–40, 42).

118 For this event see Roemer, "Jalayirids," 6; Masson-Smith, "Djalāyirids"; ʿAzzāwī, *Taʾrīkh al-ʿIrāq*, II:97–99.

119 Herrmann and Doerfer, "Šeyḫ Oveys," 29–30, 70–71, 78.

al-dawlah al-jankizkhānīyah)."[120] Other titles reflected his reliance on Islamic elements of kingship: "Unfurler of the Banners of the Sacred Law of the Prophet, Kindler of the Flame of the Muḥammadan Faith (Per. *bar afrāzandah-yi rāyāt-i shar'-i nabavī, bar furūzandah-yi sham'-i dīn-i Muṣṭafavī*)," as well as "Reviver of the Customs of Muḥammad's Community (Ar. *muḥyī marāsim al-millah al-Muṣṭafawīyah*)."[121] In addition Shaykh Uvays called himself "Sultan," as had the Ilkhanids since Ghazan, and as his own father had at first refused to do.[122]

Shaykh Uvays also inherited his father's cordial relationship to the Qalawunids, although now Mamluk chancellery protocol reflected Shaykh Uvays's new status, for he was promoted from "Noyan" to "Sultan" in diplomatic letters, and received greater honors, a higher rank and loftier titles than those accorded to his father: half-sized Baghdādī paper instead of third-sized, and one of two kingly forms of address, "His Lofty [or Noble] Dignity (*al-maqām al-'ālī* [or *al-sharīf*])," rather than the non-royal "His Noble, Lofty Honor (*al-janāb al-karīm al-'ālī.*)."[123] Despite these changes, at first Shaykh Uvays's relationship with the Mamluks simply reinforced the cordial inequality between the two sides: early in his reign Shaykh Uvays wrote to Cairo and received in response a Mamluk letter that contained a few perfunctory references to Guardianship, but otherwise consisted of expressions of goodwill, fulsome appreciation for Shaykh Uvays's clientage (*walā', muwālāh*) to them, and exhortations to write often.[124] At some point, however, the militarily energetic Shaykh Uvays began to look like a danger to Mamluk governors and a rival to Qalawunid supremacy: when the Artuqid ruler al-Ṣāliḥ of Mardin became loyal to the Qalawunid sultan Ḥasan in 1358–59/760, it was to protect himself against Shaykh Uvays.[125] The situation became openly hostile when Shaykh Uvays's own governor in Baghdad, Khwājā Marjān, rebelled against his lord and sent a diplomatic mission to Cairo in January–February 1366/early Jumādà I 767 to enlist Mamluk support. This pitted the Qalawunid sultan against the Jalayirid sultan and khan for the first time. In his letter Marjān explained that he considered himself to be the new

[120] For the first see Muḥammad Nakhjavānī, *Dastūr al-kātib fī ta'yīn al-marātib*, ed. A. A. Alizade (Moscow, 1964–76), I:1:14, also quoted in Woods, *Aqquyunlu*, 7; for the second see 'Azzāwī, *Ta'rīkh al-'Irāq*, III:88, citing an architectural document (in a pious endowment, *waqf*).

[121] For the first two see Nakhjavānī, *Dastūr al-kātib*, 1:1:14, also quoted in Woods, *Aqquyunlu*, 7; for the third see 'Azzāwī, *Ta'rīkh al-'Irāq*, III:88.

[122] Herrmann and Doerfer, "Šeyḫ Oveys," 29–30; Lane-Poole, *Catalogue*, VI:207–11, X:128–29; Artuk and Artuk, *Sikkeler*, 829; Album, *Ashmolean*, coins 371, 534; 'Azzāwī, *Ta'rīkh al-'Irāq*, III:92.

[123] Ibn Nāẓir al-Jaysh, *Tathqīf*, 16; Qalqashandī, *Ṣubḥ*, VII:282–83, and 286 for a variant, also 287.

[124] The text is undated and the Mamluk sultan's name absent, but the address form (Ar. *al-maqām al-'ālī*) indicates the beginning of Shaykh Uvays's reign. Qalqashandī, *Ṣubḥ*, VII:283–84.

[125] Ilisch, "Artuqidenherrschaft," 116.

Qalawunid governor in Baghdad, swore to fight Shaykh Uvays, promised to include Qalawunid titles in sermons and on coins, and assured his audience that he had sworn the Baghdad populace to allegiance to the sultan, who was now al-Ashraf Shaʿbān (r. 1363–77/764–78). Although Marjān was surely seeking Qalawunid patronage primarily to further his own ends (he intended to flee to Cairo if he failed), the Mamluk administration was enthusiastic, treated the envoys well and sent back a robe, an appointment decree, sultanic and caliphal banners, and additional robes for Marjān's men.[126]

But these developments did not please Shaykh Uvays, whose own envoys appeared in Cairo in February/late Jumādà I asking the sultan to forbid Marjān from taking refuge in Mamluk territory. In an assertion of Shaʿbān's lofty status, royal displeasure and general strength, however, the ambassador was informed that the sultan would not only allow Marjān into Mamluk territory, but would send him an army against Shaykh Uvays if need be. The sultan (or his advisors) then deliberately insulted the ambassador, and sent the embassy home disappointed (*khāʾib*).[127] But this declaration of Qalawunid power did little in practical terms for Marjān himself, whom Shaykh Uvays soon suppressed.[128] Shaʿbān and his advisors were angry at the loss of their new governor and the corresponding affront to Qalawunid royal dignity, for they later refused to turn over fugitives to Shaykh Uvays or ban them from Mamluk territory as he requested.[129] Thereafter Shaykh Uvays forced the Artuqid al-Manṣūr Aḥmad of Mardin to mint coins in his name. Aḥmad did so, but he also sent an embassy notifying Shaʿbān of Shaykh Uvays's actions. The Mamluks sent out a reconnaissance force to learn more, but nothing seems to have come of it, which underscored the hollowness of Qalawunid sovereignty.[130]

Shaykh Uvays also threatened an older mainstay of Mamluk legitimacy, the sultan's sovereignty in the Hijaz, by sending enough money and candles to Mecca to have the sermon pronounced in his name for several years during the 1370s/770s.[131] There is no evidence that Shaykh Uvays received permission for this from the sultan Shaʿbān. Furthermore, providing candles for the Kaʿaba had been an exclusive prerogative for al-Nāṣir Muḥammad, and had surely been inherited by his successors. As a sultan Shaʿbān was not only ambitious and capable enough eventually to take power for himself from his advisors, but was extremely proud of his status as a Qalawunid, promoted the antiquated notion of Guardianship and acted as a formidable patron of

126 Maqrīzī, *Sulūk*, III:112; Ibn Qāḍī Shuhbah, *Taʾrīkh*, II:275; Ibn Ḥajar, *Durar*, IV:345.
127 Maqrīzī, *Sulūk*, III:114.
128 *Ibid.*, 121; Ibn Qāḍī Shuhbah, *Taʾrīkh*, II:275–76; Qazvīnī, *Dhayl*, 77, 83, 91; Ibn Ḥajar, *Durar*, IV:345; also ʿAzzāwī, *Taʾrīkh al-ʿIrāq*, II:128.
129 Maqrīzī, *Sulūk*, III:121–22. 130 Ilisch, "Artuqidenherrshaft," 121.
131 Ibn Ḥajar, *Inbāʾ*, I:82; Fāsī, *Chroniken*, II:286; Ghiyāth al-Dīn al-Kātib al-Baghdādī, *al-Taʾrīkh al-Ghiyāthī: al-faṣl al-khāmis min sanat 656–891/1258–1486*, ed. Ṭāriq Nāfiʿ al-Ḥamdānī (Baghdad, 1975), 88.

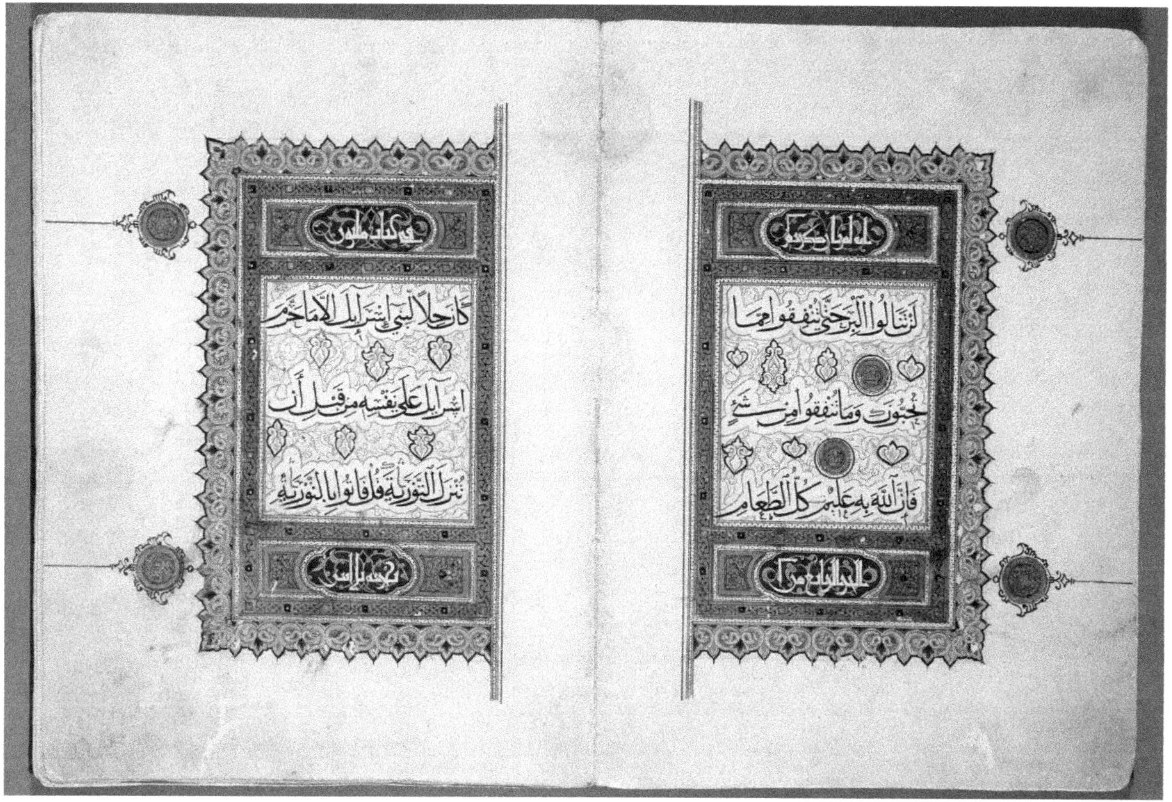

Figure 9. This elegant and expensive Quran, resplendent in blue, red, gold, black, white and turquoise inks, is thought to have been produced under the patronage of al-Ashraf Shaʿbān. (Folio from a Quran of Sultan Shaʿbān, CBL Is. 1464, fols. 2v–3r. 1370–75/771–77. © The Trustees of the Chester Beatty Library, Dublin.)

Figure 10. The best surviving example of Shaʿbān's architectural patronage is the combined school and mausoleum he built for his mother, Khwand Baraka or Umm al-Sulṭan Shaʿbān, in 1368–69/770. Side view of the complex. (Photo courtesy of Dr. Bernard O'Kane.)

Islam: Shaʿbān trumpeted his dynasty in his letters and on coins, sponsored an ambitious religious building program, and with his mother presided over the illumination of several exceedingly lovely Qurans (Figures 9 and 10).[132] Shaʿbān was also the last sultan to use a stylized royal signature (*ṭughrāh*) on

[132] The Guardian titles appeared prominently in Shaʿbān's legal documents and inscriptions. See James, *Qur'āns*, 181–82, also 178–214 for the illuminated Qurans and for the buildings; for dynasty see my discussion above; also Shaʿbān's coins in Balog, *Coinage*, 208–29; Lane-Poole, *Catalogue*, IV:178–85, IX:358–62; Lavoix, *Catalogue*, III:369–82 and note 46 above. For Shaʿbān's inscriptions see *CIA*, 278–88.

state letters.[133] Although Shaykh Uvays died in 1374/776, it is tempting to wonder whether Shaʿbān chose to undertake the pilgrimage in 1377/778 out of a desire to assert his role as a Qalawunid, a Muslim sovereign and even a Guardian in this public, traditionally Mamluk-dominated arena, and thus respond to the Jalayirid challenge as al-Nāṣir Muḥammad had once responded to the Ilkhanids. But Shaʿbān's overthrow during his pilgrimage and his murder by rebel Mamluk commanders rendered the question moot, and by the time the later Jalayirids Sulṭān-Ḥusayn (r .1374–82/776–84) and Sulṭān-Aḥmad (r. 1382–1410/784–813) sent embassies to Cairo in 1381–82/783 and 1383–84/785, the matter seems to have been settled, for the ambassadors met with no hostility.[134]

This was then a period of ideological change for both the Mamluks and the Ilkhanid successors. For the Mamluks, expressions of kingship seem to have shifted to the idea of dynasty, enshrined in the Qalawunid family, and the concept of Qalawunid sovereignty over the Ilkhanid successors, which the sultans had inherited from Muḥammad. Meanwhile the Ilkhanid successors themselves cast their visions of rule in the context of the Chingizid legacy in general and the Muslim Ilkhanid model in particular, but also responded to Qalawunid claims of seniority and sovereignty. Ilkhanid successors experimented both with straightforward challenges to Mongol traditions, like adopting the Sassanians or creating alternative dynasties, and with adaptations of Mongol norms, like appropriating the title "Khan." Some Ilkhanid successors began to challenge Mamluk ideology, whether the idea of regional supremacy, or even the older models of patronage of the Hijaz. Although this was a period of ideological experimentation, not fierce competition, all of these expressions of kingship became far more urgent once Temür appeared on the scene.

133 Qalqashandī, *Ṣubḥ*, XIII:170–71; this practice appears later to have been revived under al-Nāṣir Faraj, see VII:321.

134 Maqrīzī, *Sulūk*, III:444–45, 487; Ibn Qāḍī Shuhbah, *Taʾrīkh*, III:59–60.

CHAPTER 6

The Temürid invasions and the destruction of Mamluk sovereignty (1382–1404/784–807)

The three major invasions of the Middle East by the Mongol warlord Temür in 1386–88/788–90, 1392–96/794–98 and 1399–1404/801–07 took place during the reigns of the Mamluk sultans al-Ẓāhir Barquq (r. 1382–89/784–91, 1390–99/792–801) and his son al-Nāṣir Faraj (first r. 1399–1405/801–08), who had replaced the defunct Qalawunid family. Despite the continuity of this new dynasty in Egypt, the warlord's ideological effects on the two sultans could not have been more different. Temür's activities helped Barquq simultaneously revive the old notion of Mamluk Guardianship of Islam and hone a new version of Qalawunid-style regional sovereignty based on his identity as a Circassian. During the reign of Faraj, by contrast, Temür destroyed Mamluk claims to rule completely and thus ended an ideological era for the sultans in Cairo.

Temür himself was one of the most ideologically creative rulers in the post-Mongol age (Figure 11). As a non-Chingizid, Temür fell hopelessly outside the lineage of the golden family, which he admired to the point of obsession. Like the Chobanids, Jalayirids and other contemporary parvenus, therefore, Temür at first connected himself to the Chingizid heritage in conservative, recognizable ways. In particular Temür wedded Chingizid princesses and took the title of "Imperial Son-in-Law (*küregen*)," claimed to uphold Chingiz Khan's dynastic law (*yasa* / *jasaq*, or *töre*) and used Chingizid puppets as figurehead khans while styling himself modestly as commander (*amīr*).[1] But unlike other parvenus, Temür also creatively manipulated Chingizid imperial history in order to make a place for himself within it.[2] Temür's overarching claim was a conservative assertion of his duty to restore

[1] For Temür's Chingizid wives and puppets, and for the *tore* (also *törü* and *ture*) see Woods, "Genealogy," 100–03; for Temür's legitimacy in general see Beatrice Forbes Manz, "Tamerlane and the Symbolism of Sovereignty," *Iranian Studies* 21:1–2 (1988), 105–22; for coins see Linda Komaroff, "The Epigraphy of Timurid Coinage: Some Preliminary Remarks," *Museum Notes* 31 (1986), 207–32, esp. 211–12. For Temür's possible elevation of his puppets on a felt blanket at their coronation see Sela, *Inauguration*, 32–40.

[2] Beatrice Forbes Manz, "Mongol History Rewritten and Relived," *Revue des Mondes Musulmans et de la Méditerranée* 89–90 (2000), 129–49.

Figure 11. Temür's assertions of kingliness were particularly evident in his architectural patronage, as shown here in his monumental tomb complex, the Gūr-i Mīr. (Photo courtesy of Dr. Walter B. Denny.)

the decaying Chingizid world order.[3] Under this rubric, however, his specific arguments were unique. Temür began by presenting himself as a protector and reviver of the Chagataid heritage, but during his invasions of Iran he purported to champion the Ögedeid cause as well, and also alternated between denying the authority of the Toluid House and appropriating Toluid claims for his own purposes. This multifaceted approach appeared in Temür's interactions with actual Chingizids: Temür availed himself not only of Chagataid wives and Ögedeid puppets, but patronized Jochids and Toluids as well.[4] Later Temür's descendants used Mongol imperial history to connect their ancestors indirectly to Chingiz Khan, and thereby inherited the right to a special double kingship with the Chingizids.[5] Temür himself developed an alternative to the Chingizid divine mandate by claiming to be a divinely favored world-conqueror, the

[3] Manz, "Sovereignty," 111–12.

[4] Woods, "Genealogy," 100–09; Manz, "Sovereignty," 111, 112–14, 119, 121–22. Temür's clients included the Jochid Toqtamish, a Toluid in China, and an "Ilkhanid" in Mazandaran. See Manz, "Mongol History," 139, 141, and "Temür and the Problem of a Conqueror's Legacy," *JRAS* 3rd series 1 (April 1998), 23–25.

[5] Although these links were fully codified only after Temür's death, during his lifetime he himself named several offspring after Mongol ancestral figures. Woods, "Genealogy," 85–114, esp. 87, 91–96, 99–100, 109; see also Beatrice Forbes Manz, "Family and Ruler in Timurid Historiography," *Studies on Central Asian History in Honor of Yuri Bregel*, ed. Devin DeWeese (Bloomington, IN, 2001), 64–68.

"Lord of the Auspicious Conjunction (*ṣāḥib qirān*)," with whom God communicated through an angel with fiery wings.[6]

Like other post-Mongol Muslim rulers, Temür also used Islam to justify both his rule and his military campaigns, which he did by asserting a desire to restore and safeguard religious order as well as Chingizid order.[7] Despite his stated intentions, however, Temür actually used Islamic norms to counteract the challenges posed by genuine Chingizids, as had the Mamluks, the Chobanids and other ideologically weak rulers before him. Temür's greatest Chingizid rival was the Jochid Toqtamish, who used Temür's patronage to take over first the White Horde in Central Asia in 1379/780–81 and then the Golden Horde, after which he turned against his patron. Partly in response to Toqtamish, therefore, Temür made sure to seek the blessings of Muslim holy men for his actions, and appealed to elements of Guardianship of Islam like protecting pilgrims, ousting tyrants and conducting religiously sanctioned warfare (*ghazā'*).[8] Although useful against Chingizids, the Islamic components of Temür's ideology brought him into conflict with a variety of rulers, among them the Mamluk sultans, whom Temür regarded with disgust. Temür's veneration of Chingizid lineage was paired with a corresponding contempt for the institution of slavery. This led him to believe that the Mamluks were unworthy of rule because of their lowly origins, which had reemerged as an ideological problem once the Qalawunid dynasty was replaced by slaves.[9] But unlike the Ilkhanids before him, Temür expressed this contempt indirectly, either behind the Mamluks' backs to other rulers, or through the cunning use of humiliation in diplomacy.

Unfortunately for the warlord, his main opponent in Mamluk territory, Barquq, was the first capable, intelligent and energetic ruler after the long series of beleaguered Qalawunids, and used Temür's violent inroads into the region to focus his own definitions of kingship. Barquq and his ideologues did this by reviving the quintessentially Mamluk role of Guardian of Islam and presenting the warlord as an infidel enemy like the early Ilkhanids, despite Temür's own appeal to Islamic claims to justify his actions.[10] In addition, Barquq looked to the more recent model of Qalawunid regional sovereignty and infused it with new energy by living up to the role of sovereign that the Qalawunids had only been able to playact.[11] Temür's incursions therefore

[6] Manz, "Sovereignty," 117, 118, and "Family and Ruler," 63–64; Jean Aubin, "Comment Tamerlan prenait les villes," *SI* 19 (1963), 88. See also Chapter 2 for Arghun's use of this title.

[7] Manz, "Sovereignty," 111–12, and "Conqueror's Legacy," 23, 25–26.

[8] Manz, "Conqueror's Legacy," 25–26, and "Sovereignty," 111–12.

[9] Temür's contempt for slavery was disastrous for his own dynasty, since he omitted most of his offspring from considerations of overall succession because they had had slave mothers. See Woods, "Genealogy," 112–13.

[10] For Temür's willingness to let his troops mistreat Muslims at times see Aubin, "Les Villes," 85–86.

[11] It is likely that Barquq intended to replace the Qalawunids – whom he had helped overthrow – with his own family. I am currently preparing an article on Barquq's dynastic ambitions.

had the unintentional effect of affirming Mamluk sovereignty and the old Mamluk role as Guardian by causing other rulers in the region either to renew their commitment to Barquq, or to rush to prove their loyalty to him in hopes of winning his protection against Temür. Nevertheless, even though Barquq was the first militarily successful Guardian in decades, Barquq let his actions speak for his Guardian qualities, and himself made few overt references to the concept. His ideological use of the Abbasids was also very limited (especially because one Abbasid gave him significant political trouble), and so the caliph appeared only rarely in diplomatic letters or on coins.[12] Instead, and like Temür, Barquq emerged as an original thinker: he used Mamluk history to rebuff Temür, promote himself as a Circassian and assert his status as a kingly patron and host. Barquq also proclaimed his kingship conservatively through his relationship to Mecca and Medina. After Barquq's death in 1399/801, however, the situation changed drastically when Temür attacked again, captured Damascus, forced Faraj to become his vassal and destroyed all existing models of Mamluk kingship.

Initial forays and Temür's first campaign: 1384–88/786–90

Although Temür's three major invasions of Iran were in large part an attempt to extend dominion over its relatively wealthy territories, ideologically they led him to his most creative interactions with Chingizid history. Initially, however, Temür seems to have justified his actions with conservative Islamic norms. In 1384–86/786–87 Temür made a preliminary foray as far as Azerbaijan, where he left a governor over Sultaniyah and Tabriz; he then began his first long campaign in 1386/788.[13] During this time Temür acted in the name of his Chingizid puppet, Suyurghatmish Khan, but identified him primarily as the "Emperor of Islam" (a title that Ghazan had used), not as a Chingizid.[14] Temür also appropriated the Islamic notion of Guardianship, and thus began his campaign by attacking the Lurs in southwestern Iran because they had been harassing pilgrimage caravans; he may have used this same argument later against the Qara Qoyunlu.[15] In addition Temür exchanged letters with Barquq in January 1386/Dhū al-Ḥijjah 787, but their content and ideology are unknown.[16] Regardless of Temür's proclamations,

[12] No caliphal references appear on Barquq's coins in Balog, *Coinage*, 249–75; Lane-Poole, *Catalogue*, VI:192–98, IX:364; or Lavoix, *Catalogue*, III:397–410, although some could appear on coins in collections I have not seen. Barquq imprisoned the caliph al-Mutawakkil 'alà Allah in 1383/785 for conspiring to overthrow him. See Wiederhold, "Zahiri Revolt," 203–35; also Chapter 5 above. Al-Mutawakkil later joined the 1389–90/791–92 rebellion against Barquq. For Barquq's inscriptions see *CIA*, 297–306.

[13] Beatrice Forbes Manz, *The Rise and Rule of Tamerlane* (Cambridge, 1989), 70–71; H. R. Roemer, "Tīmūr in Iran," *CHIr*, VI:51, 57–59.

[14] Woods, "Genealogy," 105; Manz, "Sovereignty," 112.

[15] Roemer, "Tīmūr in Iran," 58; for the Qara Qoyunlu see Mīrkhwānd, *Rawḍah*, VI:1:4715.

[16] Maqrīzī, *Sulūk*, III:537; Ibn Qāḍī Shuhbah, *Ta'rīkh*, III:139.

his incursions infused the sultan's inherited role as regional sovereign with new life as rulers who had formerly been governors for the Qalawunids in Iran, Azerbaijan and Iraq now began to renew their right to Mamluk protection.[17]

The first to ask Barquq for help was Qara Muḥammad of the Qara Qoyunlu, whose concerns began in 1384–85/786 during Temür's initial invasion of Azerbaijan. This foray announced Temür's interest in Ilkhanid territory to all watching, and drew an immediate response from Temür's protégé-turned-rival, Toqtamish, who modeled himself on earlier Jochids like Özbek and Janibek by sending ambassadors to Barquq in early spring 1385/787 and asking to reestablish relations as in olden days.[18] A year later in winter 1385–86/787, Toqtamish further proclaimed the ancient Golden Horde claim to Azerbaijan and his opposition to Temür when he descended south through the Caucasus and raided Tabriz, which was now Temür's possession.[19] During this second brief invasion, Qara Muḥammad rushed to forge a connection with Barquq like those between his predecessors and the Qalawunids, and sent his paternal uncle Miṣr Khwājā in November–December 1385/Shawwāl 787 to Cairo, where he met with Barquq and offered his allegiance, so that the "two minds [could] be as one."[20] On Qara Muḥammad's behalf Miṣr Khwājā asked the sultan to support them in times of need, promised they would fight Barquq's enemies if the opportunity arose and was rewarded with Barquq's acceptance of the petition.[21]

During Temür's longer campaign (1386–88/788–90), smaller Muslim rulers joined Qara Muḥammad in relying on the Mamluk sultan to defend themselves. First was the Artuqid al-Ẓāhir ʿĪsà of Mardin, who carefully continued the Artuqid tradition of sending news to the Mamluks when he alerted them in March–April 1386/Ṣafar 788 that Temür had conquered Tabriz and forced the Jalayirid Sulṭān-Aḥmad to flee to Baghdad.[22] A few months later in May–June/Jumādà I Sulṭān-Aḥmad himself sent Barquq a gift, followed by an embassy in late autumn 1386/788. Sulṭān-Aḥmad's ambassadors added to the news from Mardin by telling of Temür's military abilities and strength, detailing the destruction he had wreaked in the region and his attempts to subjugate local rulers, and outlining the warlord's plans for winter and spring.[23] Later Barquq received ambassadors from the Ottoman sultan

[17] I have not yet determined how often vassals and governors sent tribute or taxes to the Mamluk sultan.

[18] Maqrīzī, *Sulūk*, III:531; Ibn Qāḍī Shuhbah, *Taʾrīkh*, III:155; Ibn Ḥajar, *Inbāʾ*, I:301. See also Manz, "Conqueror's Legacy," 24, and "Mongol History," 139–40; Spuler, *Goldene Horde*, 129.

[19] Manz, *Rule*, 71; Roemer, "Tīmūr in Iran," 51, 58; Spuler, *Goldene Horde*, 129.

[20] Ibn Qāḍī Shuhbah, *Taʾrīkh*, III:164.

[21] Ibn Ḥajar, *Inbāʾ*, I:301; Ibn Qāḍī Shuhbah, *Taʾrīkh*, III:164; Ibn Duqmāq, *Jawhar*, 264; Ilisch, "Artuqidenherrschaft," 132–33.

[22] Ibn Duqmāq, *Jawhar*, 264; Maqrīzī, *Sulūk*, III:542; Ibn Qāḍī Shuhbah, *Taʾrīkh*, III:181.

[23] Maqrīzī, *Sulūk*, III:545, 552 (saying the embassy came [to Cairo] in November–December 1386/Dhū al-Qaʿdah 788); Ibn Qāḍī Shuhbah, *Taʾrīkh*, III:189 (saying it came [to Damascus] in October–November/Shawwāl); Ibn Ḥajar, *Inbāʾ*, I:312.

Murad I (r. 1361–89/761–91), who may have been responding to Temür's incursion.[24]

In addition to this stream of embassies, Barquq sent out his own men to gather information, who brought alarming news throughout the summer of 1387/789 that Temür was struggling with Qara Muḥammad.[25] Soon after receiving the first report, therefore, Barquq responded to the ideological demands made by his position as a regional sovereign, and sent an army from Cairo to Aleppo in July–August/Rajab. Before the Mamluks could continue on to join the Qara Qoyunlu or engage Temür, however, news arrived that Qara Muḥammad had defeated Temür's forces on his own, and the warlord himself had returned first to Tabriz, and then to Samarqand.[26] Despite the Mamluk failure to reach him in time, Qara Muḥammad clearly appreciated the sultan's support and wanted to continue the relationship, for a little over a year later in November–December 1388/Dhū al-Ḥijjah 790, he sent word that he had recaptured Tabriz, had had the sermons pronounced there in Barquq's name and had minted coins with Barquq's titles on them, some of which he sent as evidence of his loyalty. This allowed him to ask Barquq to appoint him Mamluk governor of Tabriz, which Barquq obligingly did.[27]

Barquq's position as regional sovereign was also useful to the sultan himself, for his governors and allies needed him to remain in power, and some were willing to fight to ensure this. Thus when a Mamluk rebellion arose in early 1389/791, Qara Muḥammad and ʿĪsà of Mardin sent a joint embassy to Barquq and asked permission to enter Mamluk territory and fight the rebels. But Barquq was unwilling to reveal the very real threat this opposition posed to his sovereignty, and so thanked his petitioners for their concern but refused their offer, explaining that they were too valuable to waste on such an unimportant matter.[28] Shortly thereafter Barquq was indeed briefly deposed, and Qara Muḥammad killed in an internal struggle, but within a year Barquq had returned to power, while Qara Muḥammad's son Qara Yūsuf took over his father's rule, and eventually renewed an acknowledgment of Barquq's sovereignty as well. Meanwhile ʿĪsà demonstrated his continued loyalty by capturing some of the Mamluk rebels and sending them to Barquq.[29] This state of cooperation only continued when Temür returned to the region.

[24] Murad's embassy arrived in January–February 1388/Muḥarram 790. Ibn al-Furāt, *Duwal*, IX:24; Maqrīzī, *Sulūk*, III:574.

[25] Ibn al-Furāt, *Duwal*, IX:7, 9, 10, 12; Maqrīzī, *Sulūk*, III:563–64; Ibn Qāḍī Shuhbah, *Taʾrīkh*, III:216–17; Ibn Duqmāq, *Jawhar*, 266–67; Mīrkhwānd, *Rawḍah*, VI:1:4715–16.

[26] Ibn al-Furāt, *Duwal*, IX:14, 24; Maqrīzī, *Sulūk*, III:564, 574.

[27] Ibn Ḥajar, *Inbāʾ*, I:349–50; Ibn al-Furāt, *Duwal*, IX:37; Maqrīzī, *Sulūk*, III:585; Ibn Duqmāq, *Jawhar*, 269; also see Ilisch, "Artuqidenherrschaft," 133.

[28] This was in February–April 1389/Rabīʿ I or II 791. Ibn al-Furāt, *Duwal*, IX:62; Maqrīzī, *Sulūk*, III:598; Ibn Qāḍī Shuhbah, *Taʾrīkh*, III:269; also see Ilisch, "Artuqidenherrschaft," 133–34.

[29] Ibn al-Furāt, *Duwal*, IX:177, 269; Ibn Ḥajar, I:378; Ibn Qāḍī Shuhbah, *Taʾrīkh*, III:273, 313; Ibn Duqmāq, *Jawhar*, 282–83. Also see Ilisch, "Artuqidenherrschaft," 135; Sümer, "Ḳarā-Ḳoyunlu," 586.

Temür's second campaign: 1392–96/794–98

Although during his second campaign Temür continued to deploy Islamic notions of kingship when useful, it was here that his most creative interactions with the Chingizid heritage emerged. This campaign also witnessed an increase in Temür's struggles not only with Barquq's established governors and allies, but with other rulers, lacking previous connections to Barquq, who now rushed to seek Barquq out as both regional sovereign and as a newly revived Guardian of Islam.[30] Temür also interacted with Barquq himself in several hostile exchanges, which served to clarify both men's ideological positions, and their unswerving opposition to one another. The letters and messages Temür sent directly to Barquq made it clear that he wanted to intimidate the sultan and force his submission, while indirectly the warlord expressed his contempt for Barquq's slave origins behind Barquq's back to other rulers. In return Barquq used Temür's poor treatment of Muslims to characterize Temür as a hypocrite and a liar, and to prove that Temür was an infidel, despite his claims to the contrary.

Among the new petitioners hastening to acquire the military support of the Guardian sultan was Qāḍī Burhān al-Dīn, ruler of Sivas, who had succeeded the house of Eretna. Although it is unclear who initiated the relationship between Cairo and Sivas, by the time Temür wrote and demanded Qāḍī Burhān al-Dīn's submission in 1393–94/796, the latter was able to refuse and send Temür's written order to Barquq along with a letter of his own.[31] When writing to Barquq, Qāḍī Burhān al-Dīn appealed to a revived unity in Guardianship of Islam by expressing indignation at Temür's hypocritical and un-Islamic behavior, and criticized Temür as a criminal, sinful oppressor, "bare of the adornments of Islam."[32] The judge contrasted Temür's flawed understanding of kingship (to conquer, torture and ruin) with proper kingship (to support and further Islamic society), then told Barquq that he fervently opposed Temür, had gathered an army and was prepared to fight at any moment in defense of Islam. The judge then expressed his hope for Barquq's military support as a Guardian and patron by promising that if Barquq sent the Syrian armies to Malatya, he would lead his own forces to Erzerum and fight Temür there. As with his other petitioners, Barquq responded positively to this advance, which caused Temür later to criticize Qāḍī Burhān al-Dīn's "rebellion" (against himself) and support for the sultan.[33]

[30] For Temür's struggles with rulers in Azerbaijan see Manz, *Rule*, 103–04.

[31] For either the actual text of the judge's letter or a close paraphrase see ʿAzīz Astarābādī, *Bazm wa razm*, ed. Köprülü Zadeh Mehmet Fuat (Istanbul, 1928), 457–58.

[32] *Ibid.*, 457.

[33] Astarābādī claimed that Barquq contacted Qāḍī Burhān al-Dīn; the Mamluk historians claimed the opposite, and also stated that the judge became loyal to Barquq; Temür also believed this last. Nevertheless the judge also corresponded with Beyazid. *Ibid.*, 456–60; Ibn Ḥajar, *Inbāʾ*, I:473; Aḥmad Ibn ʿArabshāh, *ʿAjāʾib al-maqdūr fī nawāʾib Tīmūr*, ed. Aḥmad

Barquq's interactions with the Ottomans similarly increased during Temür's second invasion. A full discussion of early Ottoman ideas of kingship is beyond the scope of this book, but a few points should be made here.[34] In February–March 1392/Rabīʿ II 794 Barquq himself sent envoys to Beyazid I (r. 1389–1402/791–804), who took up the relationship his father had begun.[35] Some Mamluk historians claim that the Ottoman ruler accepted the ideology of Barquq's sovereignty and professed public loyalty to Barquq in 1392–93/794–95 in the presence of the sultan's ambassadors when he put on the robe and sword that Barquq had sent and declared: "I am the mamluk of our lord the sultan; whatever he orders me to do, I will do."[36] Given Beyazid's own considerable ambitions, however, this may have been either an exaggeration by the Mamluk historians, or at most a profession of temporary, insincere loyalty because of Temür. Certainly despite his own position of sovereignty, Barquq was wary of Beyazid, and once said: "I am not afraid of al-Lank [Temür], for everyone supports me against him, but I *am* afraid of Ibn 'Uthmān [Beyazid]."[37] Nevertheless the two rulers exchanged ambassadors, gifts and letters, and planned joint campaigns as Temür came nearer.[38] Although the extent to which Beyazid acknowledged Barquq's sovereignty is unclear, it is at least apparent that Barquq's role in the relationship was as a patron, a Guardian of Islam and the sovereign over Mecca and Medina: he sent Beyazid a doctor and medicine for an injured hand, had Cairo decorated in thanksgiving for Beyazid's victory over Crusader forces at Nicopolis in 1396/798 and allowed Ottoman pilgrims to pass through Syria in record numbers.[39] Barquq also benefited from his position as protector of the Abbasid caliph when Beyazid made a neat combination of Islamic ideology and dynastic adoption and asked Barquq to send a caliphal decree to Anatolia establishing him as the heir to the Seljuks.[40]

Fā'iz al-Ḥumṣī (Beirut, 1987), 152–55, also translated as *Tamerlane or Timur the Great Amir*, tr. J. H. Sanders (Lahore, 1936, repr. 1976), 88–91; also Ibn al-Furāt, *Duwal*, IX:386; Maqrīzī, *Sulūk*, III:817. For the text of Temür's 1394/796–97 letter (to Beyazid), in which he complained about Qāḍī Burhān al-Dīn, see Togan, "Osteuropapolitik," 294–98; there is also an unpublished translation by John E. Woods.

34 See Lowry, *Ottoman State*, 55–94, esp. 73–79.

35 Ibn al-Furāt, *Duwal*, IX:313; Maqrīzī, *Sulūk*, III:763; Ibn Qāḍī Shuhbah, *Taʾrīkh*, III:424.

36 Ibn al-Furāt, *Duwal*, IX:339, whence Ibn Qāḍī Shuhbah, *Taʾrīkh*, III:471.

37 Ibn Ḥajar, *Inbāʾ*, I:492.

38 The Ottomans under Orhan rated only small paper and the fourth-tier title of "The Lofty Seat (*al-majlis al-ʿālī*)." It is unclear whether their diplomatic honors increased with the size of their territory. See Ibn Nāẓir al-Jaysh, *Tathqīf*, 44–45; Qalqashandī, *Ṣubḥ*, VIII:15.

39 For the medical assistance see Ibn al-Furāt, *Duwal*, IX:347, whence Ibn Qāḍī Shuhbah, *Taʾrīkh*, III:476; Maqrīzī, *Sulūk*, III:790. For the embassies of 1395–96/798 see Ibn Qāḍī Shuhbah, *Taʾrīkh*, III:583; for those of 1396–97/799, including the announcement about Nicopolis, see Ibn al-Furāt, *Duwal*, IX:456–57, 464–66; Ibn Qāḍī Shuhbah, *Taʾrīkh*, III:607–08, 615; Maqrīzī, *Sulūk*, III:873, 879; Ibn Ḥajar, *Inbāʾ*, I:525; for pilgrims see Ibn Qāḍī Shuhbah, *Taʾrīkh*, III:584–85, 605.

40 Inalcık, *Ottoman Empire*, 56; also see his "Ottoman Succession," 45, and Fleischer, *Bureaucrat*, 288. The Mamluk sources do not refer specifically to this petition, but it may have taken place

In addition to these newly formed relationships, Barquq's existing governors and allies increasingly relied on the sultan as Temür advanced farther into the region. Whereas previously they had merely relayed news to Cairo, therefore, now they forwarded the paraphernalia that Temür had sent them, so that Barquq could be fully informed of Temür's activities and better help protect them. In summer 1393/795 Temür sent robes of honor, coinage dies and written demands for submission from Tabriz to both ʿĪsà of Mardin and Sulṭān-Aḥmad Jalayir. ʿĪsà refused Temür's demand by explaining that his actions were governed by the ruler of Egypt, and promptly dispatched to Cairo everything Temür had sent. Barquq wrote back instructing ʿĪsà to continue to perform the sermon in his own name (i.e., to continue in his allegiance) while he looked into the matter.[41] Contemporary historians disagree over whether Sulṭān-Aḥmad acquiesced to Temür's demands (thereby abandoning Barquq) or not, but certainly Temür himself was not interested in exacting submission so much as hoping to seize Sulṭān-Aḥmad on the grounds of protecting Muslims from oppression (Temür had heard secret complaints about Sulṭān-Aḥmad from disgruntled residents of Baghdad).[42] Temür thus made a surprise attack on Baghdad in August–September/Shawwāl, which Sulṭān-Aḥmad escaped, but many of his family members did not. Sulṭān-Aḥmad then turned (or turned back) to Barquq's protection and fled to the Mamluk fort of al-Raḥbah with the help of the Beduin Āl Faḍl leader Nuʿayr. There Sulṭān-Aḥmad wrote to Barquq and asked for permission to enter his lands. Barquq did not begrudge Sulṭān-Aḥmad's brief submission to Temür (if there had even been one), but rather responded warmly, promised the Jalayirid he might settle anywhere in Mamluk territory, and apparently was so pleased with this development that he privately considered giving him the city of Hama as a grant (*iqṭāʿ*). When Sulṭān-Aḥmad reached Aleppo, Barquq demonstrated his esteem for his guest by dispatching a high-ranking commander to escort him to Cairo in style.[43] This allowed Barquq both to emphasize his own role as a kingly patron, and to oppose Temür.

Temür also sent a letter and robe of honor from Baghdad to the Beduin Nuʿayr who had helped Sulṭān-Aḥmad.[44] This time Temür opposed Barquq

when a high Ottoman official (allegedly the vizier) stopped in Damascus while on the pilgrimage in 1395–96/798 and sent messengers to Cairo. See Ibn Qāḍī Shuhbah, *Taʾrīkh*, III:584–85, 605.

41 The messenger arrived in Cairo on 28 August/19 Shawwāl. See Ibn al-Furāt, *Duwal*, IX:343, whence Ibn Qāḍī Shuhbah, *Taʾrīkh*, III:472; also Maqrīzī, *Sulūk*, III:787–88; Ibn Duqmāq, *Jawhar*, 287; and see Ilisch, "Artuqidenherrschaft," 136.

42 Mamluk authors claim Sulṭān-Aḥmad put on Temür's robe and minted coins, but one Persian author disagrees entirely. See Ibn al-Furāt, *Duwal*, IX:343; Ibn Duqmāq, *Jawhar*, 287; Maqrīzī, *Sulūk*, III:788; Ibn Qāḍī Shuhbah, *Taʾrīkh*, III:472–73; Mīrkhwānd, *Rawḍah*, VI:1:4793; also ʿAzzāwī, *Tarīkh al-ʿIrāq*, II:204–05.

43 For this part of Temür's campaign see Roemer, "Tīmūr in Iran," 64–65; Manz, *Rule*, 72. For Sulṭān-Aḥmad's family members see Barquq's letters to Temür (below) and Maqrīzī, *Sulūk*, III:788–89; Ibn Ḥajar, *Inbāʾ*, I:450–51; also Ibn al-Furāt, *Duwal*, IX:344–47; Ibn Duqmāq, *Jawhar*, 287–89; Ibn Qāḍī Shuhbah, *Taʾrīkh*, III:473–75.

44 Ibn Qāḍī Shuhbah, *Taʾrīkh*, III:479. A copy of the text was included with a letter Barquq sent to Temür in February–March/Jumādà I 796. See Qalqashandī, *Ṣubḥ*, VII:335; also below.

more openly by observing in the letter that Barquq had recently expelled Nuʿayr from Syria (which was true), and suggested that Nuʿayr avenge himself by joining Temür's forces.[45] Although the letter promised that Nuʿayr could win land and the command of men by showing allegiance to Temür, this was more an order than an invitation, since it also explained that Temür was on his way to (conquer) Egypt, and so Nuʿayr would be wise to submit voluntarily now, rather than involuntarily later. On the margin was a warning: "We have written to Sulṭān-Aḥmad that he must come to us – see what happened to him. You or one of your sons must come to us, for your own sake."[46] But Nuʿayr, too, refused Temür's demands and forwarded the letter to Barquq; this proof of loyalty then helped him reconcile with the Mamluk sultan.[47] While this was going on, Barquq welcomed another embassy from Toqtamish in June–July 1393/Shaʿbān 795.[48] During this campaign Temür also struggled militarily with Qara Yūsuf, whom he was never able to capture or kill, and who relied on Barquq as his overlord and source of moral and distant military support.[49]

In addition to plying Barquq's governors and allies, old and new, with unwanted attention, Temür sent ambassadors from Baghdad to the Mamluk sultan himself in late autumn 1393/795–96. This was a group of scholars and military men, led by one Shaykh Sāweh, who brought a letter from Temür and an assortment of kingly gifts.[50] Despite the quality of the presents, the mission was beset by trouble almost immediately. The Mamluk officials who met it suspected the ambassadors of being spies, for they were writing down notes about each stage in their journey. Then at al-Raḥbah the ambassadors ordered the governor to submit to Temür by kissing the ground before them and including Temür's titles (and presumably those of his Chingizid puppet) in the sermons in the local mosque.[51] As a result the entire mission was detained in the fort, which was unprecedented, and the letter and gifts proceeded to Cairo without them. There Barquq and his advisors heard the letter in November–December 1393/Muḥarram 796, discussed the situation

[45] Nuʿayr had supported a Mamluk rebel against Barquq earlier that year. See Ibn al-Furāt, *Duwal*, IX:333; Maqrīzī, *Sulūk*, III:782; Ibn Ḥajar, *Inbāʾ*, I:451.

[46] Qalqashandī, *Ṣubḥ*, VII:335.

[47] Nuʿayr is alleged to have put on the robe Temür sent (Ibn Qāḍī Shuhbah, *Taʾrīkh*, III:479), but this must have been a ploy, since in addition to helping Sulṭān-Aḥmad and sending Temür's letter to Barquq, Nuʿayr had the governor of Aleppo intercede for him with the Mamluk sultan, and thus regained his land grant. See Ibn al-Furāt, *Duwal*, IX:346, 378; Maqrīzī, *Sulūk*, III:789.

[48] Ibn al-Furāt, *Duwal*, IX:338; Maqrīzī, *Sulūk*, III:785; Spuler, *Goldene Horde*, 132–33.

[49] See below in this chapter.

[50] Niẓām al-Dīn Shāmī, *Ẓafarnāmah*, ed. Felix Tauer (Prague, 1937), 221; Sharaf al-Dīn ʿAlī Yazdī, *Ẓafarnāmah*, ed. Muḥammad ʿAbbāsī (Tehran, 1957), I:458 (without mentioning the gifts); Mīrkhwānd, *Rawḍah*, VI:1:4801; Ibn Qāḍī Shuhbah, *Taʾrīkh*, III:479, 502; Ibn Ḥajar, *Inbāʾ*, I:473.

[51] This appeared in the text of a letter Barquq sent to Temür; see Qalqashandī, *Ṣubḥ*, VII:340 and the discussion below.

at length and reviewed the gifts, which included eighteen slaves: nine boys and nine girls. Since diplomatic protocol required female slaves to go straight to the harem, Barquq seems to have met only with the boys in a public audience. There he discovered that eight were the Muslim children of important Baghdad officials and had been enslaved illegally, while only one was a lawful mamluk.[52] Temür's choice of these children could not have been accidental, and suggested a desire to intimidate Barquq with a warning of what could happen to his subjects if he was not careful. But by threatening Barquq in this way and sending unlawful slaves, Temür provided proof that his claim to be a worthy Muslim ruler was unsupportable.

Temür also used this mission to present his creative vision of Chingizid tradition. It is impossible to determine all of the ideology expressed here since Temür's letter has survived only in multiple, incomplete versions; nevertheless some general principles do emerge from the remaining evidence.[53] In one version of his letter, Temür discussed Mamluk relations with the Chingizid rulers of Iran (the Ilkhanids), noting that peace and cordial diplomacy had prevailed after the initial hostility. The letter continued that although this was a good situation for both sides, after the death of Abū Saʿīd no Chingizid had remained in Iran, and thus lesser kings, factionalism and anarchy had appeared. It then proclaimed creatively that a ruler from the lineage of Chingiz Khan had returned to claim the throne (of Iran), and would also wrest Islamic lands from evildoers.[54] Temür here meant his Ögedeid puppet, and blithely ignored the detail that the Ögedeids had never enjoyed rights to Ilkhanid territory. Temür demanded submission from Qāḍī Burhān al-Dīn of Sivas with a similar Ögedeid claim.[55]

Another version of Temür's letter to Barquq began with a Quranic verse on sovereignty (4:59) and a lengthy elaboration on the divine support Temür

52 For protocol on female slaves see Ibn al-ʿAbbāsī, *Āthār*, 195. Barquq handed the boys over to the chief judge for care, but there is no record of the fate of the girls. Ibn al-Furāt, *Duwal*, IX:362; Maqrīzī, *Sulūk*, III:797; Ibn Qāḍī Shuhbah, *Taʾrīkh*, III:502–03; also see Ibn Ḥajar, *Inbāʾ*, I:473–74.

53 Only two descriptions (not texts) of the letter to Barquq survive, along with a draft of a possible text. For the descriptions see Shāmī, *Ẓafarnāmah*, 221; Yazdī, *Ẓafarnāmah*, I:458. For the draft see ʿAbd al-Ḥusayn Navāʾī, *Asnād va mukātabāt-i taʾrīkhī-yi Īrān az Tīmūr tā Shāh Ismāʿīl* (Tehran, 1962), 75–79, and the partial translation and discussion in Woods, "Genealogy," 107–08; see also Manz, "Conqueror's Legacy," 25, and "Sovereignty," 111. It is difficult to date the draft: it mentions the destruction of an embassy (1393/795?), but not only does not condemn this clearly (as in Temür's letter of February 1295/Rabiʿ II 796 [see below]), but excuses the sultan for not knowing what was happening; additionally it is couched in entirely conciliatory tones. Woods provisionally dates this to 1393/795 or 1394/797 (p. 107), which I find reasonable. Navāʾī placed it in the reign of Barquq's son Faraj even though it lacks references to important later events (especially the capture of Temür's man Atlamish, see below). It could also have been used for both sultans.

54 Shāmī, *Ẓafarnāmah*, 221; Yazdī, *Ẓafarnāmah*, I:458; also a shorter version in Mīrkhwānd, *Rawḍah*, VI:1:4801.

55 For the Ögedeid version of Mongol history sent to Sivas in 1393–94/796 see Astarābādī, *Bazm*, 460; also Woods, "Genealogy," 106.

enjoyed, then went on to bemoan the evils into which Iran had fallen, and explained that Temür's task was to cleanse those lands.[56] Thereafter Temür presented an even more creative revision of Mongol history than the Ögedeid one when he explained that Chingiz Khan's youngest son Tolui, whose Ilkhanid offspring had actually controlled Iran, had usurped the territory from his older brother, Chagatai, to whom the Great Khan had really left it. This allowed Temür to claim that his own invasion of Iran was merely a restoration of Chagataid rights. Temür then referred to a historical Mamluk–Chagataid alliance in which al-Nāṣir (Muḥammad) had declared that Ilkhanid territory rightfully belonged to the Chagataids. By adding that Chagataid hostilities with the Ikhanids had kept the latter from "finishing off" the Mamluks, Temür implied that a certain amount of Mamluk gratitude was in order.[57] Temür also revealed his obsession with the Jalayirids and his desire to promote himself as a caretaker of Muslims when he explained that he had intended to reconquer Ilkhanid territory (for the Chagataids) after the death of Abū Saʿīd, but had heard about the good rule of Shaykh Uvays, and had decided not to harm the Jalayirid's Muslim subjects by leading an army among them. But once Temür realized that Shaykh Uvays's successors were evil, he set out to wrest Iran from them. Temür used a similar Chagataid revision when writing to Beyazid.[58]

Unfortunately it is unclear which of these versions of Chingizid history actually reached Barquq. But it is at least evident from Barquq's response that Temür asked about Mamluk military capabilities, vaunted the size of his own armies and demanded that the sultan hand over Sulṭān-Aḥmad.[59] Both versions of the letter closed by waxing eloquent on the friendship Temür hoped to achieve with Barquq, although the ambassadors' behavior, the callous enslavement of Muslim children as gifts and Barquq's own written response clarified that this "friendship" really meant submission.[60] The comments Temür made to other rulers also revealed his hostility. When ʿĪsà of Mardin refused to submit to Temür on the grounds that Barquq was in charge, Temür attacked Barquq's position as regional sovereign and dismissed the years of Artuqid loyalty to the Mamluks by arguing that ʿĪsà's ancestors had ruled Mardin independently for ages, and that Barquq had no claim to his loyalty: "Your forebears have [spent] hundreds of years ruling this region, and your name is on the coinage and in the sermons. What is the ruler of Egypt?"[61] Temür's hostility was even more evident, and the reasons

56 For the text see note 53 above.

57 For the citation see Navā'ī, *Asnād*, 77. Although the Mamluks exchanged embassies with the Chagataids beginning in the 1270s/670s, they were not close. See Qalqashandī, *Ṣubḥ*, VII:328–29; also Chapters 2, 4.

58 This was in 1394/796. For the text see note 33 above.

59 These points can be reconstructed from a later letter written for Barquq. See Qalqashandī, *Ṣubḥ*, VII:341.

60 Navā'ī, *Asnād*, 79; Shāmī, *Ẓafarnāmah*, 221; Yazdī, *Ẓafarnāmah*, I:458.

61 Ibn al-Furāt, *Duwal*, IX:343; Maqrīzī, *Sulūk*, III:787–88; Ibn Qāḍī Shuhbah, *Ta'rīkh*, III:472; Ibn Duqmāq, *Jawhar*, 287; also see Ilisch, "Artuqidenherrschaft," 136.

for it explicit, when he later wrote to Beyazid. In his letter Temür revealed his obsession with noble lineage, his contempt for slaves and his corresponding scorn for Barquq when he disparaged the Mamluks as "little Circassian slaves" (*ghulāmak-i charkasī*). Temür also pointed out to Beyazid that Barquq had murdered Temür's ambassadors (see below), imprisoned the Abbasid caliph (in the 1380s/780s) and killed his own (Qalawunid) master to sit on the throne (which was false), which indicated that Barquq was both disloyal and unworthy of rule.[62]

Barquq's reaction to Temür's embassy was hostile. In Cairo the sultan and his advisors decided that the ambassadors must neither enter Mamluk territory nor return to Temür, and so they were put to death in al-Raḥbah.[63] This treatment was offensive and nearly unprecedented: even antagonistic Ilkhanid embassies had traveled at least to Damascus (under heavy guard), and only Qutuz had ever actually killed ambassadors.[64] Barquq also rejected Temür's demands by lavishly welcoming the refugee Sulṭān-Aḥmad, who arrived in Cairo on 20 January 1394/17 Rabīʿ I with his entourage.[65] Sulṭān-Aḥmad's reception in Cairo was more magnificent than the ceremonies for any important man before him, and demonstrated both Barquq's high regard for the Jalayirid, and Barquq's desire to announce his opposition to Temür, whose frequent use of spies may have ensured that he heard the particulars of Sulṭān-Aḥmad's reception and understood their meaning.[66] The welcome also allowed Barquq to show off his qualities as a royal patron and host, which formed part of his understanding of proper Muslim kingship.

When Sulṭān-Aḥmad arrived in Cairo, Barquq paid his guest the unprecedented compliment of personally riding out with his commanders and armies to meet him. Sulṭān-Aḥmad was eager to express his own gratitude, and therefore dismounted to meet the senior chamberlain, who introduced the important commanders as they came to greet the guest. To thank them for

[62] For the text see note 33 above; for Temür's hostility to slavery see note 9 above. For Barquq's Qalawunid "master," Ḥājjī b. al-Ashraf Shaʿbān (who outlived Barquq), see Holt, *Crusades*, 128. The reference to the caliph meant al-Mutawakkil ʿalà Allah, for whom see note 12 above.

[63] Ibn al-Furāt, *Duwal*, IX:362; Maqrīzī, *Sulūk*, III:797; Ibn Qāḍī Shuhbah, *Taʾrīkh*, III:479, 503 (claiming the Baghdadis [i.e., the scholars] were not executed and later went to Damascus). But Temür explicitly criticized Barquq for murdering the scholars. For references in Temür's letters see discussion below and also Brinner, "Documents," 133, 135; also Shāmī, *Ẓafarnāmah*, 222; Yazdī, *Ẓafarnāmah*, II:199.

[64] Later Temürid historians likened the murder to the Khwārazm-Shāh execution of merchants from Chingiz Khan at Utrar in 1218/614–15. This equated Temür with Chingiz Khan, and Barquq with the evil Khwārazm-Shāh. Shāmī, *Ẓafarnāmah*, 221–22; Yazdī, *Ẓafarnāmah*, II:199; also see Manz, "Sovereignty," 119.

[65] The reception probably rivaled al-Nāṣir Muḥammad's 1320/720 welcome of his Golden Horde fiancée Tulunbay.

[66] Temürid spies were captured in Mamluk territory as early as July–August 1387/Rajab 789 (Ibn al-Furāt, *Duwal*, IX:14), and as late as January–February 1394/Rabīʿ I 796 (Ibn Qāḍī Shuhbah, *Taʾrīkh*, III:506; Ibn al-Furāt, *Duwal*, IX:369; Ibn Ḥajar, *Inbāʾ*, I:474; Maqrīzī, *Sulūk*, III:802).

Barquq's generosity, Sulṭān-Aḥmad embraced the highest-ranking officers, rather than letting them kiss his hand. Thereafter Barquq descended from a nearby dais, walked up to greet Sulṭān-Aḥmad personally and in turn refused to let his guest kiss the royal hand. Barquq then led Sulṭān-Aḥmad by the hand to the dais, sat with him, reassured him and promised to restore him to his throne. Then Barquq gave Sulṭān-Aḥmad a purple coat lined with ermine and decorated with wide bands of golden embroidery, as well as a horse completely caparisoned with golden tack.[67] The two men rode together into the city, chatting, until they reached the citadel. There the escort dismounted, leaving only the sultans on horseback. Barquq took leave of his guest and directed him to his lodgings, to which the commanders escorted him in a glorious procession. There Sulṭān-Aḥmad enjoyed a ceremonial banquet, to which Barquq sent a magnificent gift of money, cloth, horses and slaves. The next day Sulṭān-Aḥmad attended the reception at the citadel, where Barquq allowed him the unprecedented high honor of sitting down while the commanders were standing. Sulṭān-Aḥmad also spent time inside the palace with Barquq, and went hunting with him in Giza.[68] A short time later, Barquq honored Sulṭān-Aḥmad and linked himself personally to the Jalayirid family by marrying Sulṭān-Aḥmad's niece Tundī. This was the first time a Mamluk sultan had wedded a princess from an established dynasty since al-Nāṣir Muḥammad and the Chingizid Tulunbay in 1320/720.[69]

But despite Barquq's pointed attention to Sulṭān-Aḥmad and decisive murder of Temür's ambassadors, Temür himself had not finished making demands. Rather he displayed his capacity for ideological innovation by using the Ilkhanids as a historical model, even though elsewhere he had denounced their usurpation of Iran from the Chagataids. Thus Temür sent Barquq a new letter, which had been copied from a demand for submission written for Hülegü over 130 years earlier and dispatched to the Ayyubid al-Nāṣir Yūsuf and the Mamluk Qutuz in 1259–60/658.[70] Temür also called himself an Ilkhanid in a letter to Beyazid, gave an Ilkhanid title to a Chingizid puppet in Mazandaran and copied Ilkhanid imperial architectural styles in his own monuments.[71]

67 For the coat (Ar. *qabā'*) see Y. K. Stillman and N. A. Stillman, "Libās iii: Iran," *EI²* V:747, 748.

68 See Ibn al-Furāt, *Duwal*, IX:366–68, whence all others: Ibn Duqmāq, *Jawhar*, 289–90; Ibn Qāḍī Shuhbah, *Ta'rīkh*, III:504–06; Maqrīzī, *Sulūk*, III:799–801; Ibn Ḥajar, *Inbā'*, I:469.

69 This was the daughter of Sulṭān-Aḥmad's brother, Sulṭān-Ḥusayn. Barquq later divorced Tundī and married her to her cousin Shāh Walad b. Shāh Zādeh b. Shaykh Uvays, but this did not affect the cordiality between the two rulers. See Muḥammad al-Sakhāwī, *al-Ḍaw' al-lāmi' li-ahl al-qarn al-tāsi'*, no editor (Cairo, [n.d.]), XII:16; Maqrīzī, *Sulūk*, III:807, 832; Ibn Ḥajar, *Inbā'*, I:469.

70 It may also have gone to the caliph al-Musta'ṣim in 1258/655–56. See Brinner, "Documents," 122. This important article includes texts and source references, although Brinner conflated Temür's first ambassadors, sent from Baghdad and subsequently murdered, with this second embassy, which carried the Hülegü-era letter.

71 For the letter to Beyazid see Navā'ī, *Asnād*, 97–100; also Woods, "Genealogy," 100; Manz, 'Sovereignty," 113, 119; for the puppet see Manz, "Mongol History," 139; for the architecture see Blair, "The Imperial," 147.

The letter to Barquq arrived in Cairo on 5 February 1394/3 Rabīʿ II 796, accompanied by a sword and quiver as "gifts," which was an unmistakable challenge to war.[72] The ambassadors were not murdered this time, but were probably detained at an unspecified location. In the letter Temür warned:

> Know that we are the soldiers of God, created from his wrath, given dominion over those on whom His anger has descended ... We do not feel tenderness for the one who complains, nor do we have mercy on the tear[s] of the one who weeps, for verily God has torn mercy from our hearts ...
>
> Our hearts are like mountains and our numbers like sand ... He who makes peace with us is saved, and he who fights us regrets it ... If you submit to our authority and accept our conditions, you will have what we have. If you oppose [us] and persevere in your disobedience, then blame no one but yourselves.[73]

Temür's scribes lifted these fiery phrases directly from the letter written for Hülegü, and added a few new points. In particular Temür condemned Barquq's murder of Shaykh Sāweh with indignation rooted in Chingizid and Islamic traditions: "You have killed scholars and rebelled against the lord of heaven and earth [i.e. the Ögedeid puppet]. You have shed the blood of noble descendants of the Prophet; this, by God, is oppression ... Do not kill the two [new] envoys as you did the first ones, disobey as you always did in past years, and rebel against the lord of the worlds."[74]

One theory suggests that the use of an outdated letter reflected either laziness on the part of Temür's scribes, or a professional challenge to Barquq's chancellery.[75] But as a man deeply interested in controlling the way others perceived him, Temür was unlikely to have given his scribes such autonomy, and was rather trying to intimidate the Mamluks by raising the ancient specter of Ilkhanid aggression. Unfortunately for Temür, Barquq not only refused to be intimidated, but his chancellery caught the anachronism of the Ilkhanid text and mocked it by replying with an anachronistic response, possibly written for al-Nāṣir Yūsuf (Qutuz's only reply had been the murder of Hülegü's ambassadors).[76] In it Barquq used words copied directly from the earlier letter to trumpet his own military abilities and deride Temür's boasting:

> Our horses are like lightning and our arrows are Arab ... our hands are strong at striking and we are mentioned in the East and the West. If we kill you, then what a gain this is! If one of us is killed, then there is only an instant between him and paradise ...

[72] See Barquq's later response, Qalqashandī, *Ṣubḥ*, VII:333–34; for the date see Maqrīzī, *Sulūk*, III:803; Ibn al-Furāt, *Duwal*, IX:371.

[73] Brinner, "Documents," 128–30; also Vaṣṣāf, *Geschichte*, II:85–86 (Arabic) and I:81–83 (German) for the letter to al-Nāṣir Yūsuf; also see Chapter 2 for a slightly different version.

[74] Brinner, "Documents," 133, 135. [75] *Ibid.*, 126.

[76] It is unclear where the Mamluks acquired this text, for although it appears both in Vaṣṣāf as the response for al-Nāṣir Yūsuf, and in histories written after Temür's invasions, the Mamluk chancellery manuals themselves do not include it. See *ibid.*, 121, 123, 136.

> As for your claim that your hearts are like mountains and your armies like sand: the butcher does not care about the number of the sheep, while a little fire is enough [to burn] many logs. How many small groups have overcome large ones when God allows it?[77]

With this dramatic martial imagery, Barquq and his ideologues fully revived the outdated ideology of Guardianship first used against the early Ilkhanids. The letter also invoked the Abbasid caliph anachronistically: "And do you demand that we submit to you, after the commander of the faithful and the caliph of the Prophet of God, lord of the world? There will be no obedience to you."[78] Barquq also took the opportunity (and his scribes took the Hülegü-era wording) to categorize Temür as an unbeliever: "We have known ever since you emerged from your country that you are infidels."[79] Barquq reinforced this notion by informing his subjects of Temür's un-Islamic behavior through public announcements, and ordered them to prepare to fight the warlord.[80] Barquq's letter closed by deriding the poor diplomatic protocol displayed by Temür's chancellery staff, which was reminiscent of the insults that Muḥammad and Ghazan had traded: "Tell the scribe who wrote this letter that: your letter is like the striking of a stringed instrument or the droning of flies. 'Nay! We shall record what he says, and we shall add and add to his punishment.' (Q 19:79)"[81]

But Barquq's clearest rejection of Temür's ideology and endorsement of his own kingship appeared in another letter to the warlord, longer than the anachronistic response and composed afresh a few months later.[82] In it Barquq and his ideologues relied heavily on Mamluk history to situate Barquq as a ruler, just as Temür himself did with Chingizid history, although also like Temür, Barquq took some liberties with the history he presented. In particular Barquq's chancellery wrote the sultan's identity as a Circassian into Mamluk history in places where it did not belong, and used it to bolster his role as a divinely supported sovereign and a kingly patron and host, who had been honored with the task of serving the two holy shrines.

In the letter Barquq described the Mamluk sultans as the previous kings of Islam (*mulūk al-islām al-sālifīn*), and specified that they were all Circassians, just as he was. Since most of them had been ethnic Turks, and since this fact was well known in the Mamluk Sultanate and elsewhere, this was a rewriting of history. But by doing this, Barquq was able to state that the Circassian race (*jins*) had defeated the Mongols on numerous occasions, and had been led to victory by God and rewarded by Him with care of the two holy shrines.[83] The rest of Barquq's arguments rested within this vision of himself as a historical figure in a long and glorious line of kings, who belonged to a specific ethnic

77 *Ibid.*, 139–40. 78 *Ibid.*, 141. 79 *Ibid.*, 138.

80 This was in October–November 1393/Dhū al-Ḥijjah 795. Ibn Ḥajar, *Inbāʾ*, I:456–57; Ibn Qāḍī Shuhbah, *Taʾrīkh*, III:478–79; Maqrīzī, *Sulūk*, III:791.

81 Brinner, "Documents," 142, verse misprinted as XIX:82.

82 This was in March–April 1394/Jumādā I 796. For the text see Qalqashandī, *Ṣubḥ*, VII:332–43.

83 *Ibid.*, 333, 334, 337–38, 339, 341.

group that had been chosen by God for important religious tasks. In particular Barquq promoted his connection to the two holy shrines – bestowed on Circassians by God – although he did so unusually as servant (*khādim*), not Guardian (*ḥāmī*), even though he was acting as a Guardian when the letter was written. The letter criticized Temür for including the sword and quiver with the Hülegü-era letter, and explained that not even a Chingizid would send these items to the servant of the two holy shrines.[84] It then demanded to know whether the gesture was friendly or hostile, and warned that if hostile, Barquq was not afraid, since God was on his side. The letter also criticized Temür's (murdered) ambassadors not only for spying and for demanding submission from Barquq's governor, but for committing the latter offense when they knew that the governor represented the servant of Mecca and Medina. Barquq similarly explained his affection for Sulṭān-Aḥmad on the historical grounds that his father (Shaykh Uvays) had at one time shared the task of caring for the two holy shrines with the Mamluk sultans.[85]

Barquq also used his Circassian ethnicity to promote his position as a regional sovereign, a kingly patron of others and helpful to those in need, most specifically the Beduin Nu'ayr and Sulṭān-Aḥmad. This took place when the letter discussed the duty of a Circassian king to help any person in trouble:

> How would it be acceptable in the laws of manliness, honor and loyalty if we surrendered our guest and the person who sought help from us? – Especially since we are Circassian, which is the race of the Islamic kings of old [i.e., the Mamluks], and the servants of the two holy shrines. The histories confirm what happened [between] them [and] the Mongols. It is in our nature and the nature of our race that we refrain from handing over our guest, or a person who sought our help, to anyone. If you do not believe this, well, you have people of our race among you. Get them to tell you – we do not allow harm to come to our guests.[86]

The letter also asserted Barquq's regional sovereignty by rebuking the warlord for criticizing Qara Yūsuf.

In contrast to this positive depiction of Barquq, the letter described Temür in deeply insulting terms. It lambasted Temür for being an infidel, and pointed as evidence to Temür's treatment of Sulṭān-Aḥmad's wives, some of whom had been captured while Sulṭān-Aḥmad escaped.[87] In a lengthy section supported by numerous scriptural citations, the letter presented Temür's decision to give them to other men while they were still married to Sulṭān-Aḥmad as a flagrant violation of all schools of Islamic law, and an indication that Temür was no Muslim whatsoever. It went on to further

[84] *Ibid.*, 333.

[85] *Ibid.*, 337. Barquq's approval here may have been genuine or another rewriting of history, since it had been al-Ashraf Sha'bān who "shared" this responsibility with Shaykh Uvays, not Barquq, and Sha'bān's relationship to Shaykh Uvays was cold. See Chapter 5.

[86] *Ibid.*, 337–38. [87] See note 43 above.

condemn Temür as an infidel and an oppressor by describing his destruction of Baghdad in detail and denouncing it vehemently.

The letter also vilified Temür as a liar and a hypocrite: it pointed out that Temür had promised to treat Sulṭān-Aḥmad well, then had broken his own promise; had allowed Mamluk rebels to take refuge with him even as he asked Barquq for an alliance that included the return of dissidents, and had tried to entice Nuʿayr to join him in opposition to Barquq. To drive the point home, the letter quoted Temür's own missive – which Nuʿayr had forwarded to Cairo – as proof of Nuʿayr's loyalty to Barquq. Barquq's chancellery also scorned Temür for pretensions to grandeur by claiming that although his scribes had written Barquq's titles correctly, Temür himself had used an inappropriately lofty seal, which was disrespectful to Barquq.[88] The letter also mocked Temür's manipulation of history: it faulted Temür's grasp of the Chingizid story, criticized Temür for misunderstanding the relationship between al-Nāṣir Muḥammad and Abū Saʿīd, and taunted him by naming individual Ilkhanid rulers the Mamluks had defeated.[89] The letter further belittled its recipient by using small (third-sized) paper, and employing an insultingly low form of address, "Amīr Temür," and the unprecedented second-person ("you") which was devoid of honorifics, instead of the standard third-person ("he" or "they") and the corresponding appellations of "His Dignity," "The Seat" or "His Honor," with honorifics.[90] By contrast, Barquq was identified respectfully with the first-person plural ("we") and entitled "Servant of the Two Holy Shrines."

In addition to the ideas of kingship expressed in his correspondence and his overt patronage of Sulṭān-Aḥmad, the Mamluk sultan also responded to Temür militarily. This emphasized the sultan's roles as supreme Guardian and regional sovereign, and once again proved that Barquq actually sought to live up to the responsibilities that the later Qalawunids had only pretended to master. After extensive preparations in January–February 1394/(late) Ṣafar–Rabīʿ I 796, Barquq set out for Syria with his assembled forces, accompanied by Sulṭān-Aḥmad and his retinue. Barquq spent the spring at Damascus, moved to Aleppo in late summer, made a brief foray to the banks of the Euphrates but failed to engage Temür's forces there, and finally began the homeward journey in the autumn. He returned to Cairo in November–December 1394/Ṣafar 797, and later that month received word that Temür had left the region.[91]

While guarding his territories and waiting for Temür, Barquq spent his time in Syria strengthening connections to his governors and allies. In

[88] It read, "There is salvation in righteousness" (Per. *rāstī rastī*, lit. "You have done right and you are saved"). Qalqashandī, *Ṣubḥ*, VII:333; I thank John Woods for both translations.

[89] *Ibid.*, 333, 338, 339.

[90] For the paper see *ibid.*, 332; the form of address appears throughout the letter. See also Chapter 5 note 5.

[91] See Ibn al-Furāt, *Duwal*, IX:362–64, 380–81, 382; similar references are scattered throughout all other Mamluk sources.

Damascus he finalized his agreement with Qāḍī Burhān al-Dīn, and received notice from Beyazid that he had gathered a vast army and was awaiting Barquq's orders.[92] Barquq welcomed new ambassadors from Toqtamish, who expressed their hope for cooperation against Temür, and met with the Doğerid Sālim, who had fled Temür and now sought the sultan's help against him.[93] At the same time Barquq underscored his own regional sovereignty and his continued support for Sulṭān-Aḥmad by making Sulṭān-Aḥmad his governor in Baghdad, complete with a sword, robe of honor and appointment decree, and sent him back in May/Rajab to reconquer his city from Temür's governor. News arrived in July–August/Shawwāl that Sulṭān-Aḥmad had succeeded, and was having the sermons performed in Barquq's name.[94] Unfortunately Barquq did not manage to save ʿĪsà of Mardin: Temür's siege of the city began just as Barquq left Cairo, and so ʿĪsà had submitted to a humiliating captivity. He was replaced by his son-in-law, al-Ṣāliḥ Aḥmad b. Iskandar (r. 1394–96/796–98), who took it upon himself to reestablish a relationship with Cairo at the first opportunity. Aḥmad therefore wrote to Barquq in spring 1395/mid-797 and asked to be reappointed as a Mamluk governor, which Barquq granted.[95] Later that year Barquq received an embassy from another longstanding governor, Qara Yūsuf, who sent news of his own battles with Temürid forces; at the same time, however, a more disappointing report came detailing Toqtamish's defeat by Temür and subsequent flight.[96]

Some of Barquq's governors and allies also sought to prove their loyalty and ensure Barquq's continued protection by sending him not only news and letters, but men: when in January–February 1394/Rabīʿ I 796 the Doğerid Sālim captured a Mongol called Dawlat Khwājā in Anatolia, he sent him to the governor of Aleppo, who forwarded him to Cairo just as Barquq was completing his campaign preparations. There Dawlat Khwājā was imprisoned and tortured for timely information about Temür's movements, troops and spies.[97] Later in November–December 1395/Ṣafar 798, after Temür had

[92] For Qāḍī Burhān al-Dīn see Astarābādī, *Bazm*, 456–59; Ibn al-Furāt, *Duwal*, IX:386, whence Maqrīzī, *Sulūk*, III:817; Ibn ʿArabshāh, *ʿAjāʾib*, 152–55, and Sanders, *Tamerlane*, 88–91; Ibn Ḥajar, *Inbāʾ*, I:473. For Beyazid see Ibn al-Furāt, *Duwal*, IX:382, 386; Maqrīzī, *Sulūk*, III:813, 817; Ibn Qāḍī Shuhbah, *Taʾrikh*, III:517, IX:382, 386; Ibn Duqmāq, *Jawhar*, 291.

[93] For Sālim the Doğerid see Ibn al-Furāt, *Duwal*, IX:382; Ibn Qāḍī Shuhbah, *Taʾrīkh*, III:513; for Toqtamish see Ibn al-Furāt, *Duwal*, IX:381–82; Maqrīzī, *Sulūk*, III:813; Ibn Qāḍī Shuhbah, *Taʾrīkh*, III:512; Ibn Ḥajar, *Inbāʾ*, I:471.

[94] Ibn al-Furāt, *Duwal*, IX:383; Maqrīzī, *Sulūk*, III:814–15, 817; Ibn Qāḍī Shuhbah, *Taʾrīkh*, III:515–17; Ibn Duqmāq, *Jawhar*, 291–92.

[95] See Ilisch, "Artuqidenherrschaft," 137–38, 141.

[96] Separate embassies from Qara Yūsuf and Toqtamish arrived in September–October 1395/Dhū al-Ḥijjah (Ibn al-Furāt, *Duwal*, IX:416; Maqrīzī, *Sulūk*, III:842–43; Ibn Qāḍī Shuhbah, *Taʾrīkh*, III:556–67); also see Spuler, *Goldene Horde*, 133–34; Devin DeWeese, "Toḳtamish," *EI*^{2} X:562–63.

[97] Ibn al-Furāt, *Duwal*, IX:369, whence Ibn Qāḍī Shuhbah, *Taʾrīkh*, III:506, and Maqrīzī, *Sulūk*, III:802; also Ibn Ḥajar, *Inbāʾ*, I:474.

left the region to his son Mīrānshāh, Qara Yūsuf ambushed the hunting expedition of a Mongol named Atlamısh whom Temür had left holding a fort near Tabriz, and captured him and sent him to Barquq as well.[98] Atlamısh was Temür's milk brother (*kokaltash*[99]), and his capture by Qara Yūsuf and imprisonment in Cairo became a central and sore point in Temür's relationship to the Mamluks, since he wrote repeatedly to Cairo and demanded Atlamısh, but Barquq always refused.[100] Certainly Qara Yūsuf benefited from his loyalty, for when Mīrānshāh drove him out of Mosul in 1396–97/799, he was able to take refuge in Mamluk Syria, from which Barquq seems to have reestablished him in Edessa and possibly Mosul when he sent out two armies to guard against Mīrānshāh in autumn 1398/late 800.[101] Similarly, although the Artuqid relationship with Cairo lapsed for two years after Temür reinstated ʿĪsà in July–August 1396/Shawwāl 798, by April–May 1398/Shaʿbān 800 ʿĪsà felt safe enough to petition Barquq for a pardon and the right to be a governor once again.[102]

Temür's third campaign: 1399–1404/801–07

When Temür led his third and final campaign towards Iran, he faced a radically different situation. His son Mīrānshāh had attempted to assert independent authority in an episode the historians euphemized as a fit of madness.[103] Among Temür's opponents, two rulers had died: Qāḍī Burhān al-Dīn of Sivas in June–July 1398/Shawwāl 800 and, more significantly, Barquq in June 1399/Shawwāl 801. Thereafter Beyazid had begun to expand into eastern Anatolia at the expense of his Türkmen rivals, including the Mamluks' Dulqadirid governors, and the Mamluks themselves. But the Mamluks were slow to respond, since in Egypt the Sultanate had passed nominally to Barquq's ten-year-old son al-Nāṣir Faraj and actually to his advisors, who were soon caught up with factional struggle in Cairo and rebellion in Syria.[104] Meanwhile Temür had heard of his son's rebellion and Barquq's death while campaigning in India, and had decided to return to the

98 Yazdī, *Ẓafarnāmah*, II:200; Ibn Ḥajar, *Inbāʾ*, I:509; Ibn al-Furāt, *Duwal*, IX:430 whence Maqrīzī, *Sulūk*, III:851 and Ibn Qāḍī Shuhbah, *Taʾrīkh*, III:574.
99 I.e., a slave. I thank John Woods for pointing this out.
100 In 1396–97/799 Temür sent his first request for Atlamısh and a second person (Dawlat Khwājā?), but Barquq only let them write a censored letter telling how well they were treated. Some historians claim that Atlamısh was well housed and fed (Ibn al-Furāt, *Duwal*, IX:430, 453, whence Ibn Qāḍī Shuhbah, *Taʾrīkh*, III:574), but others believed that Barquq locked Atlamısh up like a criminal (Yazdī, *Ẓafarnāmah*, II:200; Mīrkhwānd, *Rawḍah*, VI:1:4962). Barquq offered to trade Atlamısh for some of his own commanders (captive with Temür), but no exchange was made.
101 See Ilisch, "Artuqidenherrschaft," 143–44; for the campaigns see Maqrīzī, *Sulūk*, III:880, 887; Ibn al-Furāt, *Duwal*, IX:467; Ibn Qāḍī Shuhbah, *Taʾrīkh*, III:620–22.
102 Ilisch, "Artuqidenherrschaft," 143–44.
103 Roemer, "Tīmūr in Iran," 74–75; Manz, *Rule*, 72–73.
104 Maqrīzī, *Sulūk*, III:982–1016; Ibn Ḥajar, *Inbāʾ*, II:94–103.

west. But despite increasingly frequent reports of his approach, the Mamluk commanders demonstrated a collective failure to achieve Barquq's formidable breadth of vision, and focused shortsightedly on internal politics, rather than on the very real danger Temür posed.

During his absence from the region Temür's own ideology had not changed, and although evidence for Temür's proclamations to Faraj is scant, certainly elsewhere he continued to combine Mongol and Islamic norms with ease.[105] Temür also retained his mixture of righteous anger and deep contempt for the Mamluk sultan, for even after the free-born Faraj came to the throne, Temür viewed him as the son of a slave and therefore unfit to rule. Temür also resented the Mamluks for keeping Atlamısh despite his own demands for him. After gaining the upper hand over Faraj militarily, therefore, Temür forced him to become a tribute-paying governor, which was an unprecedented and deeply humiliating event in the history of the Sultanate, and which destroyed Mamluk claims to legitimate rule.

The beginning of Faraj's reign represented a thin time ideologically, for the commanders paid no attention to questions of kingship, and Faraj himself was too young to develop an independent vision. Faraj's early interactions with Temür were few, and the record of them is scant, thus it is impossible to determine whether Faraj's chancellery expressed the creative ideas of Circassian pride, kingly patronage or the older Guardianship. Later Faraj's administration did use the ideological gold standard, dynasty, since Faraj was Barquq's son; it also invoked the Abbasid caliph anachronistically and maintained Barquq's favorite title of "Servant of the Two Holy Shrines."[106] But certainly one important change in Mamluk kingship, albeit a negative one, did emerge even early in Faraj's reign: the sultan lost his claim to being a regional sovereign and patron to other rulers. This first appeared when the Mamluk commanders working in Faraj's name failed to help the Dulqadirids or their own city of Malatya against the Ottoman aggressor.[107] More ominously, when Temür drove Qara Yūsuf and Sulṭān-Aḥmad out of their territory again in summer 1400/802, they fled to the Euphrates and wrote to Faraj asking permission to enter Syria. But in marked contrast to Barquq's constant patronage, Faraj's chancellery sent an equivocal response, asking them to wait while the sultan and the commanders considered the situation. During the delay the governor of Aleppo took it upon himself to attack the petitioners, which itself was a testament to the weakness in Cairo. Qara Yūsuf and Sulṭān-Aḥmad were therefore forced to fight, and after defeating the

[105] Temür's letters to Faraj have not survived, but we know that to Beyazid Temür both described himself as an Ilkhanid and used the norm of Islamically sanctioned warfare (*ghazā'*). Woods, "Genealogy," 100, 109; Manz, "Sovereignty," 113, and "Conqueror's Legacy," 26.

[106] For Faraj's inscriptions see *CIA*, 316–33.

[107] Maqrīzī, *Sulūk*, III:965, 971–72, 978, whence Ibn Qāḍī Shuhbah, *Ta'rīkh*, IV:23, 29, 64–65.

governor, fled to Ottoman territory for asylum.[108] The subordination of the Artuqid ʿĪsà to Cairo may also have lapsed during this period.[109] Nor, as Temür came closer in late summer 1400/early 803, did the Mamluks revive their position of patronage. Thus when Beyazid stopped menacing Dulqadirid and Mamluk cities and sent an ambassador to Cairo in August–September/Muḥarram to arrange an alliance, just as he had done with Barquq, the Mamluk commanders privately mocked his request among themselves: "Now he becomes our friend! [But] when our master al-Ẓāhir Barquq died, he attacked our lands and took Malatya from us. He is not our friend. Let him fight for his lands, and we will fight for our lands and people."[110] It is unlikely that their official response was much warmer, and no alliance seems to have been made.[111]

Meanwhile Temür advanced into Anatolia and seized Malatya and Bahasna, causing the Mamluks finally to dispatch a commander named Asanbugha in September/early Ṣafar to muster the Syrian armies at Aleppo. In Egypt forces began to prepare in October–November/Rabīʿ I.[112] From Malatya, Temür sent out letters to major Mamluk cities, similar to those Ghazan had sent to the Syrian populace a century earlier.[113] Temür's letters were addressed to shaykhs, commanders and judges, and sought to justify his invasion by listing offenses like Barquq's murder of the 1393–94/795 ambassadors and his repeated failure to return Atlamısh to Temür. This resembled Ghazan's condemnation of Muḥammad for the raid on Mardin in 1299/698; also like Ghazan, Temür warned that if Faraj did not capitulate (and in this case, send Atlamısh), he would be responsible for Muslim bloodshed. Temür's letters were meant to frighten the Syrians, for they emphasized Temür's destructive exploits in Anatolia, and added terrifying details from his campaigns in India and Georgia. One letter stated that Temür was on his way to capture Egypt and establish the coins and sermons in his (and his Chingizid puppet's) name; it also asserted Temür's desire to control Islamic symbols of legitimacy by stating his intention to become the one to appoint the caliph.[114]

108 Maqrīzī, *Sulūk*, III:1020–21, 1023; Ibn Ḥajar, *Inbāʾ*, II:108–09; Ibn Qāḍī Shuhbah, *Taʾrīkh*, IV:100–01, 105.

109 Ilisch, "Artuqidenherrschaft," 144–46.

110 Yūsuf Ibn Taghrībirdī, *al-Nujūm al-zāhirah fī mulūk Miṣr wa al-Qāhirah*, (various editors) (Cairo, 1929–72), XII:217.

111 Maqrīzī reports tersely only that the ambassadors went back with a response in *Sulūk*, III:1027; Ibn Qāḍī Shuhbah, *Taʾrīkh*, IV:149–50.

112 Maqrīzī, *Sulūk*, III:1030–31.

113 Shāmī, *Ẓafarnāmah*, 222; Ibn ʿArabshāh, *ʿAjāʾib*, 197–99; Sanders, *Tamerlane*, 119–20. One arrived in Aleppo and Damascus in September–October/Ṣafar (described in Ibn Ḥajar, *Inbāʾ*, II:133; Ibn Qāḍī Shuhbah, *Taʾrīkh*, IV:148, specifying that the letter was in Persian (*ʿajamī*); also Ibn Taghrībirdī, *Nujūm*, XII:219–20). Another reached Cairo in October–November/Rabīʿ I; for this text see Maqrīzī, *Sulūk*, III:1031.

114 Maqrīzī, *Sulūk*, III:1031; for the caliph see Ibn ʿArabshāh, who also specified coinage for both Sulṭān-Maḥmūd Khan and Temür (the Mamluk historians omitted the khan). Ibn ʿArabshāh, *ʿAjāʾib*, 197–98; Sanders, *Tamerlane*, 119.

Although another implied that Temür did not want to fight the Mamluks, and would retreat and forgive the murder of his embassy in exchange for Atlamısh, this message may have been an attempt to lull the Syrians.[115] Temür's desire to justify his actions to the Mamluk populace also appeared later when he had an inscription carved into the wall of a mosque in the Mamluk city of Hama, which proclaimed his own divine support, and referred once again to the Mamluk sins of killing Temür's envoys and imprisoning his friends.[116]

But Temür's declarations were not well received: in Damascus, the governor, Sūdūn, made the bold and belligerent decision to decapitate the letter carrier publicly.[117] This was probably a conscious imitation of Barquq's execution of the embassy of 1393–94/795, for Sūdūn was Barquq's relative from Circassia and had risen to a high position under family patronage.[118] But Sūdūn soon suffered terribly for his emulation of Barquq, for in October–November/Rabīʿ I Temür descended on Aleppo, where all the Mamluk governors had gathered, and captured the city and the governors themselves, Sūdūn among them, after only brief resistance.[119] Once in captivity Sūdūn received the treatment that Temür surely would have liked to inflict on Barquq: Sūdūn was tortured, and died a few weeks later, possibly violently. He was buried outside Damascus, still in his chains.[120] At Aleppo Temür also seized Faraj's reconnaissance man Asanbugha and sent him back to Cairo with a demand for submission.[121] In addition Temür had a victory letter composed in which he tried to forestall further resistance by both

[115] Or this version may have some truth in it, since Temür's amirs were unenthusiastic about fighting the Mamluks. Shāmī, *Ẓafarnāmah*, 222.

[116] This was in November–December/Rabiʿ II. It said, "The reason for inscribing these lines was that God gave us conquest of the lands and kingdoms until we reached Iraq and Baghdad. We became neighbors to the sultan of Egypt. Then we corresponded with him and sent our envoy to him with [different] types of rarities and gifts. But he killed our envoys without a reason. We had intended in that to establish friendship between and from both sides. A while later some Türkmen [Qara Yūsuf] captured some people from our side [Atlamısh], and sent them to the sultan of Egypt, Barquq. He imprisoned them and treated them badly. Thus we had to head in this direction to save our imprisoned men from the hands of those who went against us. For this reason we descended on Hama on 20 Rabīʿ II 803/[8 December 1400]." Ibn ʿArabshāh, *ʿAjāʾib*, 227; Sanders, *Tamerlane*, 135; Ibn Ḥajar, *Inbāʾ*, II:139–40; also see Aubin, "Les Villes," 96–97.

[117] Ibn ʿArabshāh, *ʿAjāʾib*, 199; Sanders, *Tamerlane*, 120.

[118] See Ibn Taghrībirdī, *Manhal*, VI:111–15.

[119] Ibn Qāḍī Shuhbah, *Taʾrīkh*, IV:151–55; Maqrīzī, *Sulūk*, III:1031–34; Ibn Ḥajar, *Inbāʾ*, II:134–36; Ibn Taghrībirdī, *Nujūm*, XII:221–24; Ibn ʿArabshāh, *ʿAjāʾib*, 199–219; Sanders, *Tamerlane*, 119–31; Shāmī, *Ẓafarnāmah*, 224–28 and translated by Lewis in *Islam*, 104–09; Yazdī, *Ẓafarnāmah*, II:207–21. Also see Aubin, "Les Villes," 95–122, esp. 96–97.

[120] The cause of death is unknown. Ibn ʿArabshāh claimed stomach illness, but Ibn Taghrībirdī, who reported the torture and burial in chains, identified the possible causes of death as torture, throat-cutting (Ar. *dhabḥ*) or being crushed by an elephant (!). See Ibn ʿArabshāh, *ʿAjāʾib*, 222, 231; Sanders, *Tamerlane*, 132, 135; Ibn Taghrībirdī, *Manhal*, VI:115.

[121] Ibn Qāḍī Shuhbah, *Taʾrīkh*, IV:157, 162; Walter J. Fischel, "A New Latin Source on Tamerlane's Conquest of Damascus (1400/1401) (B. de Mignanelli's 'Vita Tamerlani' (1416)," *Oriens* 9 (1956), 212.

promising to pardon the Syrians, and terrifying them with a description of events at Aleppo.[122]

Temür continued south, capturing the smaller Syrian cities, while the Mamluk sultan, commanders and remaining armies set out from Egypt and reached Damascus on 23 December/6 Jumādà I, shortly before Temür.[123] Once camped outside the city the two armies skirmished, fought and exchanged messengers.[124] Here the Temürid and Mamluk stories vary: the Temürid historians claim that Faraj sent envoys and Assassin(s) to Temür, who caught them, executed the Assassin(s), mutilated the envoys and sent them back.[125] The Mamluk historians ignore this incident, but point out that some of Temür's men defected to the Mamluk sultan and warned him about Temür's craftiness.[126] Despite these discrepancies, it is clear that Temür sent to Faraj demanding Atlamısh's return and pointing out that blame for past events (Aleppo) should fall on the Mamluks for refusing to honor his earlier requests or enter into relations.[127] Temür also ordered Faraj to submit to his sovereignty and demonstrate it in coins and sermons.[128] But the Mamluks refused to negotiate, and the skirmishes and battles continued.

It is unclear what the outcome of this standoff would have been, had not the Mamluk commanders then made an astonishingly poor decision. Panicking about a possible coup in Cairo, they suddenly seized the young sultan and headed for Egypt at night on 6 January 1401/20 Jumādà I, leaving the remaining Mamluk armies to flee in disarray the next morning.[129] The Temürid forces awoke to find their enemies gone or leaving, and immediately plundered their camp. Perhaps realizing the damage this flight had caused, Faraj's chancellery composed a warlike missive to Temür shortly thereafter, which simultaneously explained the sultan's departure and belittled Temür by stating that a man with two illnesses in his body will cure the more dangerous one first. Thus, trouble from a rebellious mamluk (the greater illness) had drawn the sultan back to Cairo, leaving Temür (the lesser illness) behind.[130] It is unclear who took this message to Damascus, but it did no good whatsoever, and shortly thereafter the city fell to the warlord. Temür remained there for

122 Aubin, "Les Villes," 96, citing MS Bibliothèque Nationale Arabe 3423, fol. 399a.

123 Walter J. Fischel, *Ibn Khaldūn and Tamerlane: Their Historic Meeting in Damascus, 1401 AD (803 AH): A Study Based on Arabic Manuscripts of Ibn Khaldūn's "Autobiography," with a Translation into English, and a Commentary* (Berkeley and Los Angeles, 1962), 30 and notes 15–16 on 55–56.

124 For skirmishes and battles see Fischel, *Ibn Khaldūn*, 30 and notes 20–21 on 57–59.

125 Yazdī, *Ẓafarnāmah*, II:226–27, whence Mīrkhwānd, *Rawḍah*, VI:1:4976–77; Shāmī omits the mutilation, *Ẓafarnāmah*, 230.

126 Maqrīzī, *Sulūk*, III:1042; Ibn ʿArabshāh, *ʿAjāʾib*, 243; Sanders, *Tamerlane*, 140; Naṭanzī/Istakhrī, *Muntakhab*, 278–79.

127 Shāmī, *Ẓafarnāmah*, 231; Yazdī, *Ẓafarnāmah*, II:228–30; Ibn Ḥajar, *Inbāʾ*, II:137; Maqrīzī, *Sulūk*, III:1042; Ibn Taghrībirdī, *Nujūm*, XII:235; Qalqashandī, *Ṣubḥ*, VII:330.

128 Yazdī, *Ẓafarnāmah*, II:229; Mīrkhwānd, *Rawḍah*, VI:1:4978–79.

129 Fischel, *Ibn Khaldūn*, 30 and notes 22–26 on 59–62.

130 Ibn ʿArabshāh, *ʿAjāʾib*, 276–279; Sanders, *Tamerlane*, 155.

nearly three months, during which Friday prayers were read in his name and the name of his Ögedeid puppet. The Damascenes surrendered and were granted an amnesty, but paid a high ransom, which was extracted painfully through torture and confiscation over a period of weeks.[131]

While in Damascus Temür reopened negotiations for Atlamısh, to which the Mamluks responded by dispatching a letter with a commander named Baysaq.[132] Knowing they were in a new position of weakness, the Mamluks demonstrated a hasty respect for Temür by producing a letter penned in good calligraphy and plenty of gold ink on two-thirds-sized paper, that is, twice as large as those written for Barquq.[133] Temür must have enjoyed his new position of strength and the humiliation of his adversaries, for he took pains to treat Baysaq badly. When during the interview Baysaq failed to explain the meaning of his own name to Temür's satisfaction, Temür abused him, denounced Faraj for sending an ignoramus, then condescendingly allowed that such sophisticated matters of diplomacy were beyond Faraj's limited mental capacity. To further demoralize Baysaq and ensure that the Mamluks in Cairo were disheartened as well, Temür forced Baysaq to tour the devastated city of Damascus before sending him back to Egypt and himself departing for Diyarbakir in March–April/Shaʿbān.[134]

The conquest of Damascus was a turning point for Temür, for it paved the way for him to make the Mamluk sultan his governor. This struck a crushing blow to Mamluk ideas of kingship: the notion of Guardianship that Barquq had so effectively revived could no longer be maintained after the humiliating falls of Aleppo and Damascus, while the regional supremacy of the Mamluk sultan, carelessly discarded during Faraj's early reign, was clearly a fantasy since the Mamluks could not even protect their own territory, let alone that of outlying rulers. Even the sultan's own sovereignty had crumbled, since he was now reduced to submitting to Temür. As a result, and as shown in Faraj's newly obsequious letters, the Mamluk sultan appeared to have no justifications for independent rule at all.

But although the Mamluks could not keep their sultan from humiliation, Temür did not demand full submission and tribute immediately. The Mamluks therefore made an unsuccessful attempt to revive their discarded position of regional sovereignty after Temür left their territory when they met with an Ottoman delegation bearing lavish gifts in July–August 1401/Dhū al-Ḥijjah 803, which Beyazid had sent despite the Mamluks' earlier cold

[131] Aubin, "Les Villes," 98–120; Stefan Heidemann, "Tīmūr's Campmint during the Siege of Damascus in 803/1401," in *Matériaux pour l'Histoire Économique du Monde Iranien* 21 (1999), 179–206.

[132] Temür offered to return captured military and civilian officials and leave Damascus. Maqrīzī, *Sulūk*, III:1054; Ibn Qāḍī Shuhbah, *Taʾrīkh*, IV:179; Ibn Taghrībirdī, *Nujūm*, XII:249; also see Fischel, *Ibn Khaldūn*, 44 and notes 194–95 on 107–09.

[133] Qalqashandī, *Ṣubḥ*, VII:343–44.

[134] Maqrīzī, *Sulūk*, III:1054; Ibn Qāḍī Shuhbah, *Taʾrīkh*, IV:179; Ibn Taghrībirdī, *Nujūm*, XII:249–50; Ibn ʿArabshāh, *ʿAjāʾib*, 279–80; Sanders, *Tamerlane*, 156–57.

reception. Nevertheless the two sides did not come to an agreement.[135] Similarly the Mamluks themselves contacted their spurned governor, Qara Yūsuf, also in July–August/Dhū al-Ḥijjah, and discussed resuming relations and finding a place for him to settle. As in the Ottoman case, however, no real alliance emerged.[136]

A year later Temür defeated the Ottoman armies and captured Beyazid at the battle of Ankara on 27 July 1402/26 Dhū al-Ḥijjah 804. Afterwards Temür sent the news to Faraj from Izmir, followed some months later by an official embassy, which reached Cairo in late December 1402/early Jumādà II 805.[137] Now the time had come for Temür to humble the Mamluk sultan once and for all. To this end the ambassadors brought a gilded flag with Temür's name on it, which visibly demonstrated Temür's lordship over Faraj, since rulers commonly sent flags to their governors (and not the other way around) – the later Qalawunids had routinely dispatched sultanic and caliphal banners to subordinates.[138] To further demonstrate his power, Temür ordered the Mamluks to deliver Atlamısh to him, after which he would return to Samarqand.[139] In an open acknowledgment of their own weakness, the Mamluks at last not only permitted their captive of almost ten years to depart, but sent with him money, cloth and supplies, as well as a magnificent robe and a horse with golden tack.[140]

The text of the response written for Faraj demonstrated that the sultan, his advisors and his chancellery had abandoned previous concepts of Mamluk kingship. It bore no traces of regional supremacy, sovereignty or Guardianship, and relied ideologically only on an unimpressive reference to the Abbasid caliph. Stylistically the letter underscored the Mamluks' new forced subservience to Temür by employing the protocol once reserved for Mongol rulers: it referred to Temür primarily in the third person with the kingly appellation "His Lofty, Noble Dignity (*al-maqām al-sharīf al-ʿālī*)" rather than in the second person as "Amir Temür," and honored him with courtesies like "may his greatness be increased," which had never appeared in Barquq's letters.[141] The titles used for Temür were extensive and elevated, and consistently included "Imperial Son-in-Law" (*kūrkān* from *küregen*), as well as

135 Maqrīzī, *Sulūk*, III:1069; Fischel, *Ibn Khaldūn*, 44 and notes 190–93 on 107.
136 Maqrīzī, *Sulūk*, III:1088; Ibn Qāḍī Shuhbah, *Taʾrīkh*, IV:272.
137 Maqrīzī, *Sulūk*, III:1098–99; Qalqashandī, *Ṣubḥ*, VII:344; Yazdī, *Ẓafarnāmah*, II:330–31; Mīrkhwānd, *Rawḍah*, VI:1:5047.
138 Ibn Ḥajar, *Inbāʾ*, II:229.
139 Temür had actually sent three demands for Atlamısh after Damascus: first through the reinstated ʿĪsà of Mardin (letter dated 13 June 1402/12 Dhū al-Qaʿdah 804); second from Izmir, dated 11 September (1402)/12 Ṣafar (805), and a third, also from Anatolia, dated 29 September (1402)/1 Rabīʿ I (805). See Qalqashandī, *Ṣubḥ*, VII:346–47; also Maqrīzī, *Sulūk*, III:1098; Yazdī, *Ẓafarnāmah*, II:330–31, 356; Mīrkhwānd, *Rawḍah*, VI:1:5039, 5047, 5065.
140 Ibn Qāḍī Shuhbah, *Taʾrīkh*, IV:301–02; Maqrīzī, *Sulūk*, III:1098–99.
141 Qalqashandī, *Ṣubḥ*, VII:343–44; for the text see 344–49.

the mystical title "Spiritual Pole of Islam and Believers (*quṭb al-islām wa al-muslimīn*)."[142]

The letter opened with blessings on the Prophet, whom it credited with settling disputes between two great groups of his followers. This was an allusion to Temür's followers and the Mamluks, and unlike Barquq's denunciations of Temür as an unbeliever, indicated that the Mamluks now acknowledged Temür as a Muslim.[143] Thereafter Faraj apologized for delaying Atlamısh – albeit slyly by claiming that it had been because of the terrible news from Damascus – then addressed Temür's peace proposal. Here Temür must have been deliberately imitating older Mongol requests for "peace" that really meant subjugation, since he specified that Faraj should send a person close to himself to arrange it. But whereas Barquq had responded to similar proposals by blasting Temür as a liar who said peace but did not mean it, here his powerless son meekly acquiesced in the choice of an ambassador named Aḥmad b. Gh-l-bak, whom the letter explicitly identified as a relative of both Barquq and Faraj.[144]

Faraj's letter then related that the sultan had met with the caliph, judges, senior commanders and heads of state to discuss a peace, and after deliberation, had agreed to arrange one.[145] This phrasing allowed Faraj's chancellery to pretend that the sultan had had a choice in the matter, and drew on the tarnished ideological glory of the Abbasid caliph, for what little it was worth. The Mamluk letter promised that the agreement had been ratified, and that Atlamısh could vouch for it. The terms stipulated that both sides would maintain the bond of affection, fight the enemies and befriend the friends of the other, treat representatives of the other side with honor, and capture escapees and send them back in chains. Two copies of the treaty accompanied the letter: one signed by Faraj, and a blank one for Temür to sign and return.[146] Then, in a point that was demeaning to Barquq's memory and surely painful for the sultan personally, the letter grovelingly assured Temür that Faraj was happy to accept him as a father in place of Barquq, and to rely on Temür in the future. Regardless of whatever parental imagery Temür had used to elicit this response, this most likely had been an attempt to humiliate the adolescent sultan while pretending to be kind. Certainly Temür considered Faraj to be unworthy of even a fictitious family connection to himself, for in a letter to Beyazid written before the battle of Ankara Temür had explained that he opposed calling Faraj his "son" because Faraj was a slave born of a slave (*ghulām*, *ghulāmzādah*), to whom a family link (*waṣlat*) was inappropriate.[147] Also humiliating was Faraj's signature in gold with its cravenly fawning sentiment: "The one longing [for your presence], Faraj b.

[142] *Ibid.*, 345, 350, 351. [143] *Ibid.*, 344.
[144] I can find no other evidence to support this claim. *Ibid.*, 349.
[145] *Ibid.*, 347. [146] For the treaty see *ibid.*, XIV:115–20.
[147] Navā'ī, *Asnād*, 104–11; there is also an unpublished translation by John E. Woods.

Barquq (*al-mushtāq Faraj b. Barqūq*)."[148] When Faraj's ambassadors reached Temür they groveled before him, promised that sermons and coins in Mamluk territory now included his name, and told him that Faraj would send him tax monies.[149]

Temür's final embassy to Faraj drove the last nail into the coffin of Mamluk kingship and flaunted Temür's position as an overlord and sovereign. Nevertheless the Mamluk commanders were at first reluctant to admit that their sultan was now someone else's tribute-paying governor. Thus when the embassy arrived in July–August 1403/Muḥarram 806, the chamberlain and some commanders went to meet it outside the city in order to honor Temür properly, but the sultan did not go. Nevertheless the Mamluks could not match Temür's ability to manipulate ceremonies to his own ideological advantage, even from afar, for the embassy boasted an elephant, whose rider brandished two green flags aloft during the procession into the city.[150] Unlike the Mamluk yellow sultanic flags, these represented Temür himself, and like the banner he had sent in 1402/805, probably bore his emblazoned name, and therefore demonstrated his sovereignty to every onlooker on the parade route.

A few days after this dramatic entrance, the ambassadors met with the sultan in a strained formal reception. There the letter was read aloud, and the ambassadors presented the adolescent sultan with a robe of honor made expressly for him, along with the proper accessories and a jeweled headpiece (*tāj*). By putting on this regalia, Faraj would signal his formal subordination to Temür and his acceptance of a position as Temür's governor in Egypt and Syria.[151] At first, however, the Mamluk commanders resisted Temür's proclamation of sovereignty by preventing Faraj from donning the garment, refusing to give robes to Temür's ambassadors and sending them back to their lodgings to stay there incommunicado. However, the commanders must have realized that their defiance could only lead to trouble, for ultimately they relented, provided the ambassadors with robes and stipends, and let them move about the city.[152] (It is unrecorded, however, whether Faraj ever put on his robe.)

Temür's letter demonstrated a mixture of practicality and cruelty.[153] It announced that the Mamluk envoys, gifts and Atlamısh had arrived safely, then reminded the Mamluks that the previous trouble between them had been

148 Qalqashandī, *Ṣubḥ*, VII:344.
149 Shāmī, *Ẓafarnāmah*, 274–75; Yazdī *Ẓafarnāmah*, II:356–57; Mīrkhwānd, *Rawḍah*, VI:1:5065–66.
150 Ibn Ḥajar, *Inbāʾ*, II:256; Maqrīzī, *Sulūk*, III:1111; Ibn Qāḍī Shuhbah, *Taʾrīkh*, IV:312.
151 For the crown see Ibn Qāḍī Shuhbah, *Taʾrīkh*, IV:312; Shāmī, *Ẓafarnāmah*, 275; Yazdī, *Ẓafarnāmah*, II:357; Mīrkhwānd, *Rawḍah*, VI:1:5066; for the robe see Ibn Ḥajar, *Inbāʾ*, II:256.
152 Ibn Ḥajar, *Inbāʾ*, II:256; Maqrīzī, *Sulūk*, III:1111–12.
153 No text remains, but Temür's points can be reconstructed from Faraj's response. Qalqashandī, *Ṣubḥ*, VII:350–55.

Barquq's fault, which they were not to forget, and which must have grieved Faraj. (Faraj's only official consolation was his own chancellery's respectful designation of Barquq in letters as "The Martyr.") Temür then demonstrated his position as a sovereign by promising to uphold the peace, support the Mamluks in need and send them armies when requested, just as the Mamluks had once promised their own governors. Worst of all, Temür ordered Faraj to surrender several forts in Anatolia, which would destroy the northern Mamluk frontier, reduce the tax yield to Cairo and guarantee Temür easy access to Anatolia and the Mamluk Sultanate.[154] Finally, Temür seems to have suggested that Faraj marry a daughter of one of the "kings of the east" so that their friendship might be complete. Considering Temür's veiled contempt for Faraj, this proposal may have had some other cruel significance, but if so it never emerged fully because the Mamluk commanders rejected it.[155]

The response for Faraj showed his lowered status even more clearly than the one written in 1402–03/805.[156] After summarizing Temür's own letter, it expressed delight that Atlamısh had arrived safely, and assured Temür that the Mamluk envoys had appreciated his superior hospitality. It promised that Temür's own ambassadors were being well treated, reiterated the terms of the peace agreement and told Temür that Faraj had surrendered the forts of Elbistan, Malatya, Karkar, Kakhta (Kahta), Qalʿat al-Rūm (Hromgla) and al-Bīrah to Temür's governors. The letter assured Temür that the Mamluk sultan would no longer collect taxes from those lands, and even offered to surrender Damascus and Aleppo if Temür asked.

Despite the initial hostility they encountered, Temür's ambassadors remained in Mamluk territory until September–October/Rabīʿ I, at which point they began their preparations to leave, but then were delayed by heavy rain.[157] Going with them were elaborate gifts for Temür, which included a giraffe, and the tribute Faraj owed as a humiliated governor.[158] As the embassy was waiting to leave, a curious epilogue to Temür's struggles with

154 *Ibid.*, 351–54. 155 Ibn Ḥajar, *Inbāʾ*, II:257.

156 For the text see Qalqashandī, *Ṣubḥ*, VII:350–55.

157 The sources are unclear about the chronology. Temür's envoys received departure robes in September–October 1403/Rabīʿ I, but their giraffe went to Damascus ahead of them (Ibn Qāḍī Shuhbah, *Taʾrīkh*, IV:349). The ambassadors were then delayed until January–February 1404/Rajab, received additional departure robes in that month, left in February–March/Shaʿbān and reached Aleppo by April–May/Shawwāl, passing Temür's second envoy on the way. See Ibn Qāḍī Shuhbah, *Taʾrīkh*, IV:349, 351, 352, 356–57, 358, 365, 395; Ibn Ḥajar, *Inbāʾ*, II:261, 262, 264; Maqrīzī, *Sulūk*, III:1117, 1120, 1123.

158 Ibn ʿArabshāh refers to the arrival of the embassy in Samarqand with its memorable giraffe, and describes the ambassadors presenting tribute (*al-ḥaml wa al-taqādum*, sing. *taqdimah*) to Temür. Ibn ʿArabshāh, *ʿAjāʾib*, 380. This terminology specifically indicated tribute, not diplomatic gifts (*hadīyah* or *hadāyā*; *tuḥuf* ["rarities"]). Sanders did not realize the significance of the Arabic technical terms, which he translated as "various gifts" in *Tamerlane*, 220. For other references to the giraffe see Ibn Qāḍī Shuhbah, *Taʾrīkh*, IV:349, 351; Ibn Ḥajar, *Inbāʾ*, II:264; Yazdī, *Ẓafarnāmah*, II:425; Mīrkhwānd, *Rawḍah*, VI:1:5116; González de Clavijo, *Embassy*, 86.

Sulṭān-Aḥmad and Qara Yūsuf took place, which underscored how far Faraj had fallen from the former sovereignty of the Mamluk sultans. In September–October/Rabīʿ I, news came from Aleppo that Sulṭān-Aḥmad had arrived and wanted to apologize for fighting with the Mamluk governor in 1400/802, but he was rebuffed, and so he headed for Anatolia. Shortly thereafter, however, the governor of Syria, Shaykh al-Muḥammadī, sent news that he had welcomed Qara Yūsuf into his home, then received Sulṭān-Aḥmad. The commanders quickly ordered Shaykh to seize and chain both men according to the agreement with Temür, which Shaykh did.[159] In addition to waiting for the weather to improve, the Mamluks wanted to resolve the situation in Damascus before sending the envoys back to Temür. They thus added to their letter an explanation that Faraj had delayed the ambassadors only to clear up the matter of Sulṭān-Aḥmad and Qara Yūsuf, assured Temür that the two were incarcerated in Damascus and promised that the envoys would explain everything.[160] Nevertheless, because of the delay a second envoy soon arrived from Temür, wanting to know where the first ambassadors were.[161] But although thereafter the Mamluk commanders ordered Shaykh to execute his prisoners, he refused, preferring to free them and use their support in an unsuccessful bid for power.[162] Then after Temür's death in 1405/807, Faraj's humiliating stint as a governor was mercifully forgotten, and the Mamluk administration slowly began to rebuild its concepts of kingship.

159 Shaykh received Qara Yūsuf in October–November/Rabīʿ II and Sulṭān-Aḥmad in December 1403–January 1404/Jumādà II, then arrested them in January–February/Rajab. Maqrīzī, *Sulūk*, III:1116, 1118–19, 1120; Ibn Qāḍī Shuhbah, *Taʾrīkh*, IV:347–48; Ibn Ḥajar, *Inbāʾ*, II:263–64.

160 Qalqashandī, *Ṣubḥ*, VII:355.

161 He arrived in March–May/Ramaḍān-Shawwāl, and was sent back in July–August/Muḥarram 807. Maqrīzī, *Sulūk*, III:1123; Ibn Qāḍī Shuhbah, *Taʾrīkh*, IV:358, 395–96; Ibn Ḥajar, *Inbāʾ*, II:264.

162 Ibn Ḥajar, *Inbāʾ*, II:264. For Shaykh's bid for power see the events of 1404–05/807 in Maqrīzī, *Sulūk*, III:1130–68; also see Sümer, "Ḳarā-Ḳoyunlu," 586.

Epilogue

Temür's career was a watershed both for Mongol influence on models of kingship, and for Mamluk proclamations of sovereignty. In neither case was this the end of an era, for Chingizid legitimacy continued to influence rulers in their ideological choices, while the Mamluks eventually managed to rebuild their statements of kingship from the ground up. Nevertheless, the years after Temür's death saw the beginning of a new phase in ideology, for his experiments not only showed the way for other creative responses to the Chingizid legacy, but Temür's own legacy began to grow, and ultimately affected notions of legitimacy as powerfully as did the Chingizid model.[1] At the same time the Mamluks returned to their own time-tested ideas of kingship. Ironically, now that the Chingizid model was moving from monolithic status to something that Turkic rulers could slowly rival or adapt, Mamluk ideology began to appear as one set of ideas among many, and therefore seemed far less weak and anachronistic, while the question of Mamluk slavery – so intolerable to Chingizids or to the revivalist Temür – appears to have faded in importance among the Temürid successors.

After Temür's death Turkic rulers continued to experiment with understandings of legitimate rule, and now responded not only to the Chingizids, but eventually to Temür's life and career as well. One way Turkic rulers did this was by using their own heroic ancestors to rival Chingiz Khan and the golden family. Foremost among these martial ancestors was naturally Temür himself, whose aura and reputation soon established his descendants as a dynasty worthy of rule. Temür's son Shāh Rukh (r. 1409–47/811–50) thus drew on his father's example in 1434/838 by sending the Mamluk sultan Barsbay (r. 1422–38/825–41) an appointment robe and a demand that Barsbay become his governor, although Barsbay's response did not acknowledge Temür's legacy in any positive way, since he ferociously asserted renewed Mamluk independence by having the robe torn to shreds and the

[1] Manz, "Family and Ruler," 57–78.

ambassador dunked in a pond until he nearly died.[2] Other noble non-Chingizid forebears used for purposes of legitimacy included members of the Seljuk-era Oghuz confederation, who were invoked by the Turkic Qara Qoyunlu, Ottomans and Aq Qoyunlu, most successfully among these last with the heroic figure of Bayandur Khan.[3] All of these grand dynastic elaborations were far more convincing than the earlier experiments of the Chobanids and Jalayirids. In addition the notion of the "Lord of the Auspicious Conjunction (*ṣāḥib qirān*)" or undefeated sovereign also gained force in the years after Temür, especially since both Chingiz Khan and Temür were posthumously considered to be examples of these rare figures.[4]

At the same time, special religious claims for legitimacy grew increasingly popular as nomadic rulers searched for new ways to respond to the Chingizid and growing Temürid models of kingship. A few rulers still appealed anachronistically to the power of the Abbasid caliph to confer legitimacy, as when the Temürid Pīr Muḥammad b. ʻUmar Shaykh (d. 1407/809) considered seeking a diploma granting him rule from the Abbasid caliph in Cairo, or when the Mamluk sultan Qaytbay (r. 1468–96/872–901) tried to use an Abbasid decree to appoint the Ottoman Beyazid II (r. 1481–1512/886–918) as a Mamluk governor in 1485/890.[5] But in addition to this older model, rulers after Temür like the Aq Qoyunlu Uzun Ḥasan (r. 1457–78/861–82) began to use the Islamic concept of the "Centennial Renewer (*mujaddid*)" at which both Ghazan and al-Nāṣir Muḥammad had once hinted, while many rulers appeared as divinely supported (*mu'ayyad min 'inda Allah*) in the works of scholars, thinkers and ideologues.[6] Shāh Ismāʻīl (r. 1501–24/907–30) of the Safavid dynasty claimed variously descent from ʻAlī and Fāṭimah, spiritual leadership of the Safavid mystic order, status as the "Rightly Guided One (*mahdī*)" or even divinity to justify himself.[7] At the same time the support of law remained particularly important as a way for nomadic rulers to promote their legitimacy, although the tension between Islamic law and dynastic law proved to be difficult to reconcile well into the sixteenth century.[8]

In contrast to this lively period of experimentation among Turkic rulers of nomadic origins, among the Mamluks the years following Temür's death were a period of slow and conservative ideological revival. For the first fifteen of those years the Mamluks were primarily occupied with internal struggles,

2 Holt, *Crusades*, 188–89; Anne F. Broadbridge, "Mamluk–Ottoman Relations from 1414–53," unpublished paper, 22–23. For the most complete work on Barsbay see Aḥmad Darrag, *L'Égypte sous le règne de Barsbāy, 825–841/1422–1438* (Damascus, 1961), esp. 363–402.

3 Fleischer, *Bureaucrat*, 273, 276, 286–87; Woods, *Aqquyunlu*, 25–29, esp. 27.

4 See Chapter 2 for Abaqa's interest in the "Ṣāhib Qirān" title; also see Fleischer, *Bureaucrat*, 279–80.

5 For Pīr Muḥammad see Manz, "Conqueror's Legacy," 34–35; for Qaytbay and Beyazid II (who rejected the offer) see Carl F. Petry, *Twilight of Majesty: The Reigns of the Mamlūk Sultans al-Ashrāf Qāytbāy and Qānsūh al-Ghawrī in Egypt* (Seattle, 1993), 93–94; Holt, *Crusades*, 197.

6 Woods, *Aqquyunlu*, 100–06, esp. 104–05.

7 H. R. Roemer, "The Safavid Period," *CHIr* VI:189–350, esp. 209–11, 214–15, 216.

8 See Fleischer, *Bureaucrat*, 286–92; McChesney, "Zamzam Water," entire.

thus it was not until after the sultan al-Mu'ayyad Shaykh (r. 1412–21/814–24) had subdued his rivals at home that he could proclaim Mamluk kingship to the outside world once again. This Shaykh did by reestablishing a relationship of patronage over the new Ottoman ruler Mehmed I in 1414/817, then mounting an expedition with his own son in 1417/820 and sending the same son independently in 1419/822 to reassert Mamluk sovereignty over eastern Anatolia. In an ambitious statement, Shaykh was proclaimed sultan in the once Seljuk and now Qaramanid capital of Kayseri in 1419/822, but this claim was just as ephemeral as Baybars's had been almost 150 years earlier.[9]

Thereafter the sultan Barsbay restored the cornerstone of Mamluk ideology by acting as a Guardian of Islam and a holy warrior when his forces undertook three naval campaigns to Cyprus in the late 1420s/820s. Unlike earlier times, however, Mamluk jihad in the period after Temür tended to target Christians, not 'infidel' nomads, which had been outdated as an ideology even when Barquq used it against Temür. Thus when Shāh Rukh demanded Barsbay's submission, for example, Barsbay does not seem to have called Shāh Rukh's credentials as a Muslim into question (nor did Shāh Rukh insult Barsbay's slave origin). But Barsbay has been described as the last effective Mamluk leader of jihad against any target, even though later sultans made some attempts as well, and soon the Ottomans far surpassed the Mamluk record of holy struggle.[10]

Once the Mamluks were in a position to do so, they also resumed their jealous monopoly over the pilgrimage ceremonies in the Hijaz. Thus Barsbay and Shāh Rukh engaged not only in their showdown over sovereignty, but in a contest over the purely Islamic kingly ideal of sending the curtains for the Ka'aba to Mecca. When not demanding Barsbay's submission, Shāh Rukh spent his diplomatic energy asking for permission to provide curtains, which Barsbay repeatedly refused.[11] Only after Barsbay's death did the far more conciliatory sultan Jaqmaq (r. 1438–53/842–57) permit Shāh Rukh to send a single set of curtains for one year, but even this was seen as an affront to the honor of the Mamluk sultan, and incited a riot in Cairo.[12] Thereafter the Mamluks continued to defend their sovereignty over Mecca and Medina: a later challenge came from Uzun Ḥasan, who sent several palanquins, then had his name briefly inserted into the sermons in 1473/877, which provoked Mamluk fury.[13]

Thus both the Mamluks with their antiquated notions and the Chingizid model against which they fashioned them survived Temür's unique ideology and the devastating campaigns that accompanied it. Nevertheless Temür had done his work well enough that neither survived unchanged, and his death ushered in a new phase in definitions of kingship among Muslim Mamluks, Mongols and Turks.

[9] For the Ottomans see Broadbridge, "Relations," 4; for the Anatolian campaigns see Holt, *Crusades*, 182–83.

[10] For Barsbay see Holt, *Crusades*, 184; for the Ottomans see Broadbridge, "Relations," 15–16.

[11] Darrag, *Barṣbāy*, 381–85. [12] See Holt, *Crusades*, 188–90.

[13] Jomier, *Maḥmal*, 50–53; Woods, *Aqquyunlu*, 107–08.

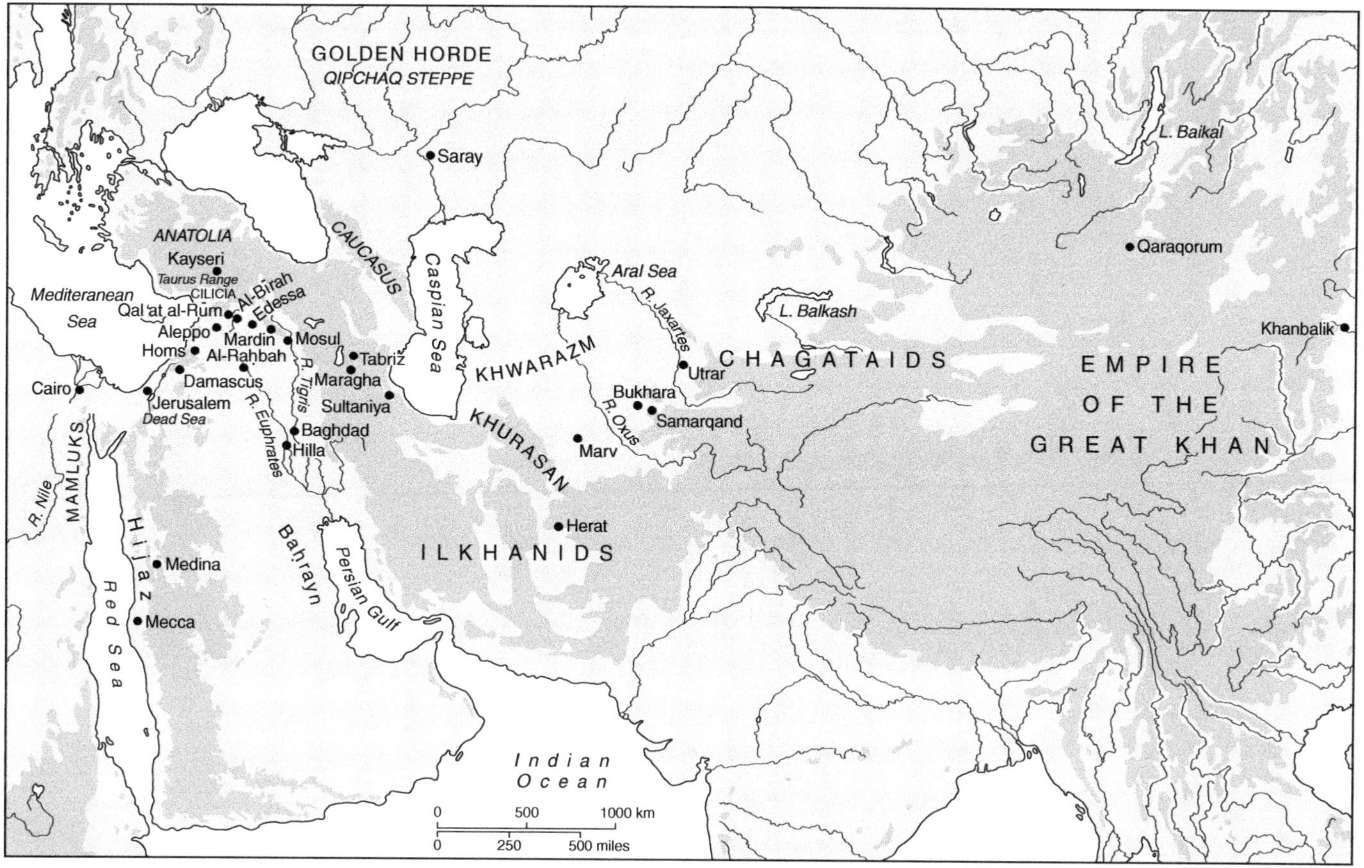

Map 1. The Mongol and Turkic world

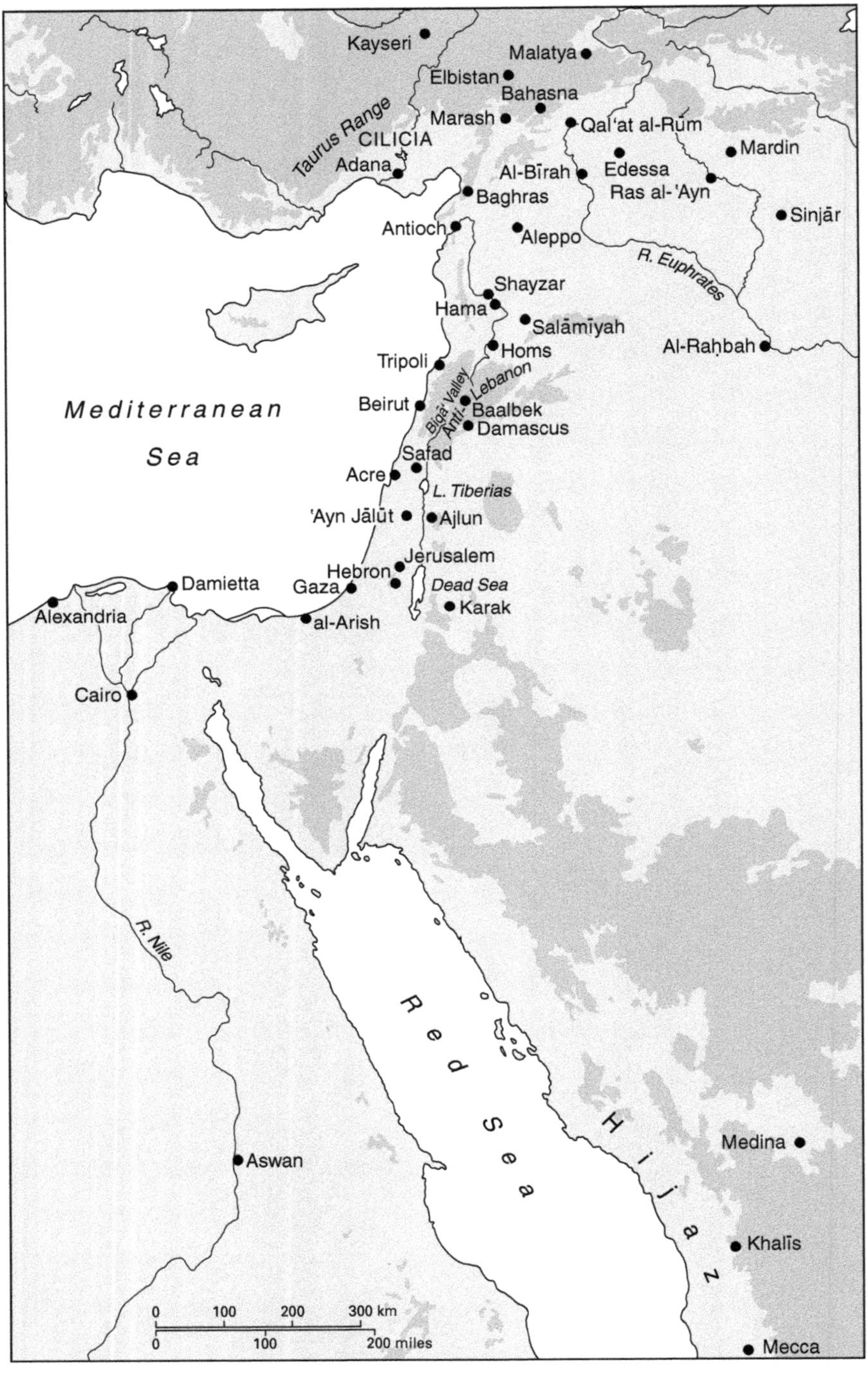

Map 2. The Mamluk Sultanate

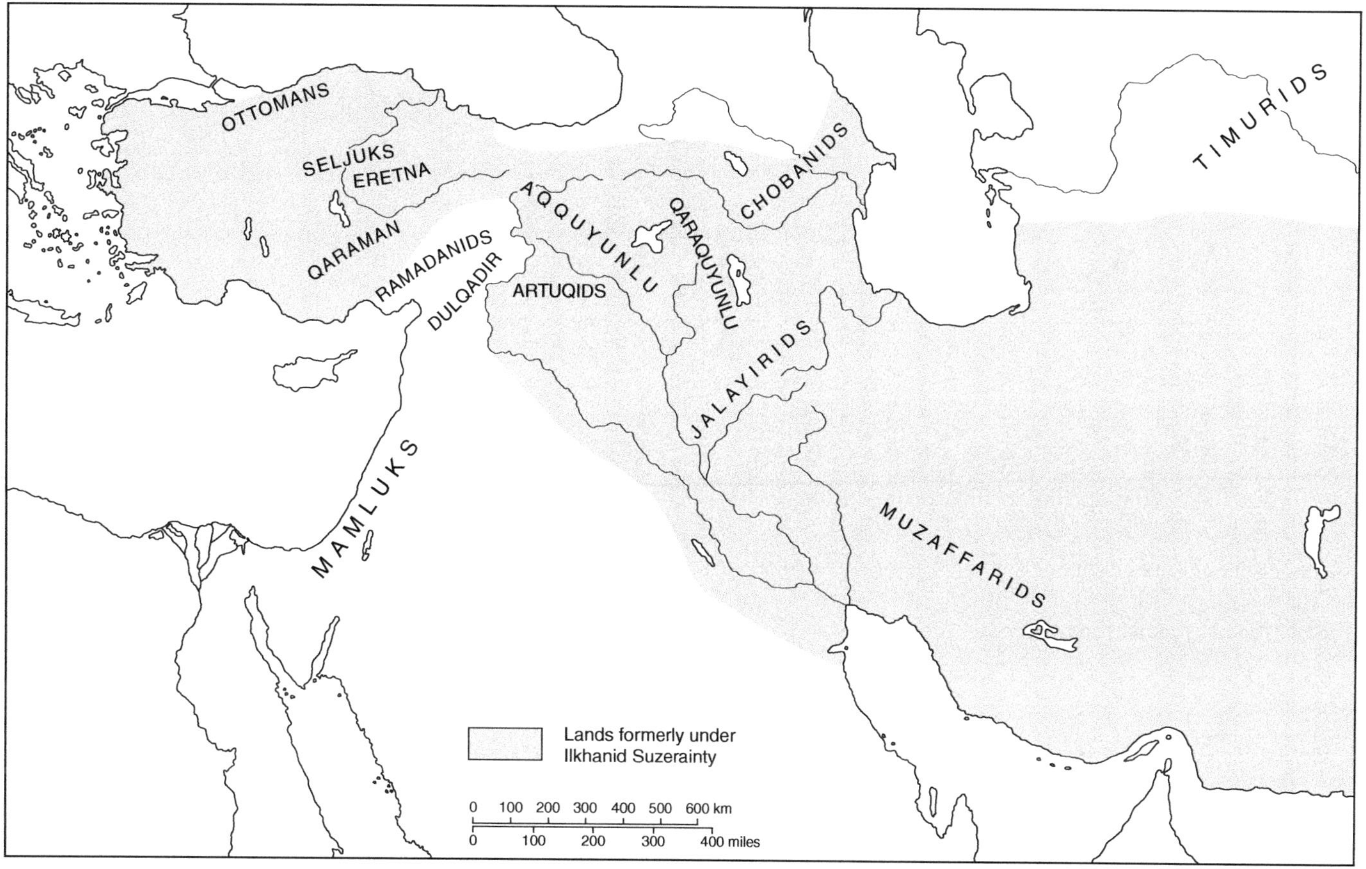

Map 3. The post-Ilkhanid world

Table 1. *Mamluk sultans, 1259–1405/657–807*

1259/657	al-Muẓaffar Qutuz
1260/658	al-Ẓāhir Baybars
1277/676	al-Saʿīd Berke Khan b. Baybars
1279/678	al-ʿĀdil Sulamish b. Baybars
1279/678	al-Manṣūr Qalawun
1290/689	al-Ashraf Khalīl b. Qalawun
1293/693	al-Nāṣir Muḥammad b. Qalawun (first reign)
1294/694	al-ʿĀdil Kitbugha
1296/696	al-Manṣūr Lajin
1299/698	al-Nāṣir Muḥammad b. Qalawun (second reign)
1309/708	al-Muẓaffar Baybars
1310/709	al-Nāṣir Muḥammad b. Qalawun (third reign)
1341/741	al-Manṣūr Abū Bakr b. Muḥammad
1341/742	al-Ashraf Kujuk b. Muḥammad
1342/742	al-Nāṣir Aḥmad b. Muḥammad
1342/743	al-Ṣāliḥ Ismāʿīl b. Muḥammad
1345/746	al-Kāmil Shaʿbān b. Muḥammad
1346/747	al-Muẓaffar Ḥājjī b. Muḥammad
1347/748	al-Nāṣir Ḥasan b. Muḥammad (first reign)
1351/752	al-Ṣāliḥ Ṣāliḥ b. Muḥammad
1354/755	al-Nāṣir Ḥasan b. Muḥammad (second reign)
1361/762	al-Manṣūr Muḥammad b. Ḥājjī b. Muḥammad
1363/764	al-Ashraf Shaʿbān b. Ḥusayn b. Muḥammad
1377/778	al-Manṣūr ʿAlī b. Shaʿbān b. Ḥusayn
1381/783	al-Ṣāliḥ Ḥājjī b. Shaʿbān b. Ḥusayn (first reign)
1382/784	al-Ẓāhir Barquq (first reign)
1389/791	al-Ṣāliḥ Ḥājjī b. Shaʿbān b. Ḥusayn (second reign)
1390/792	al-Ẓāhir Barquq (second reign)
1399/801	al-Nāṣir Faraj b. Barquq

Table 2. *Chingiz Khan and his descendants*

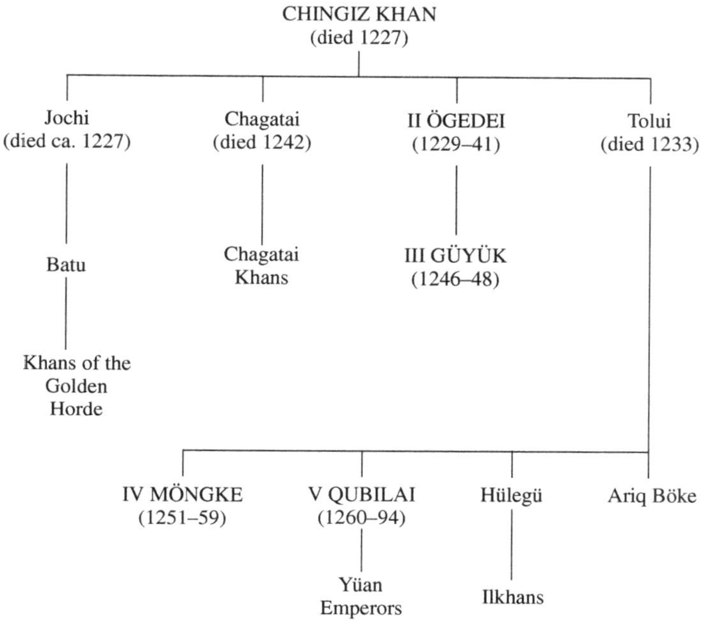

Table 3. *The Ilkhanids*

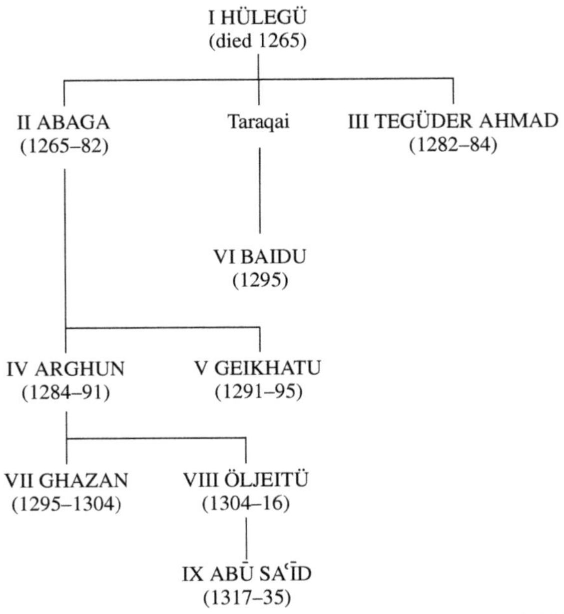

Table 4. *The Golden Horde*

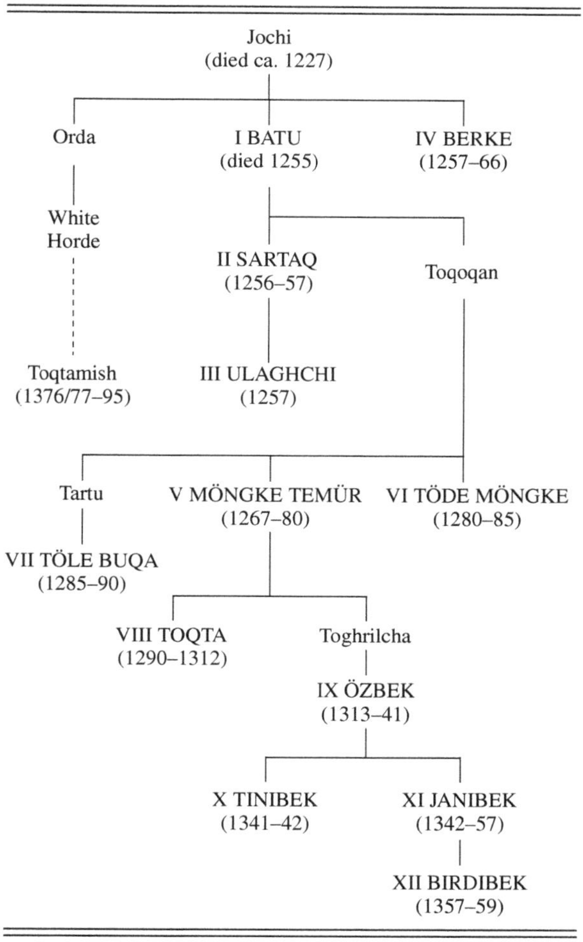

Bibliography

Arabic sources

Abū al-Fidāʾ, Ismāʿīl. *The Memoirs of a Syrian Prince: Abūʾl-Fidāʾ, Sultan of Ḥamāh (672–732/1273–1331)*. Tr. and ed. P. M. Holt. Wiesbaden, 1983.

Abū Shāmah, ʿAbd al-Raḥmān. *Tarājim rijāl al-qarnayn al-sādis wa al-sābiʿ al-maʿrūf bi-al-dhayl ʿalà al-rawḍatayn*. Ed. Muḥammad Zāhid b. al-Ḥasan al-Kawtharī. Cairo, 1947.

al-ʿAynī, Maḥmūd. *ʿIqd al-jumān fī taʾrīkh ahl al-zamān*. Ed. Muḥammad Muḥammad Amīn. Cairo, 1987–92.

— "ʿIqd al-Jumān fī taʾrīkh ahl al-zamān." Istanbul, Topkapi Library, MS Ahmed III 2912/4.

Baybars al-Dawādār al-Manṣūrī. *Kitāb al-tuḥfah al-mulūkīyah fī al-dawlah al-turkīyah*. Ed. ʿAbd al-Ḥamīd Ṣāliḥ Ḥamdān. Cairo, 1987.

— *Zubdat al-fikrah fī taʾrīkh al-hijrah*. Ed. Donald S. Richards. Beirut, 1998.

al-Dhahabī, Muḥammad. *Kitāb duwal al-Islām*. Ed. Fāhim Muḥammad Shaltūt and Muḥammad Muṣṭafà Ibrāhīm. Qatar, 1988.

— "Taʾrīkh al-Islām wa ṭabaqāt al-mashāhīr wa al-aʿlām." Dār al-Kutub, Cairo. MSS 10680, 10682, 10697.

al-Fakhrī, Baktāsh. *Taʾrīkh salāṭīn al-mamālīk* or *Beiträge zur Geschichte der Mamlukensultane*. Ed. K. V. Zettersteen. Leiden, 1919.

al-Fākihī. *Kitāb al-muntaqà fī akhbār umm al-qurà*, in *Die Chroniken der Stadt Mekka*. Ed. Ferdinand Wüstenfeld. Leipzig, 1857–61, repr. Beirut, 1964.

al-Fāsī, Muḥammad. *al-ʿIqd al-thamīn fī taʾrīkh al-balad al-amīn*. [Cairo,] 1958.

— *Shifāʾ al-gharām bi-akhbār al-balad al-ḥarām*, in *Die Chroniken der Stadt Mekka*. Ed. Ferdinand Wüstenfeld. Leipzig, 1857–61, repr. Beirut, 1964.

Fischel, Walter J. *Ibn Khaldūn and Tamerlane: Their Historic Meeting in Damascus, 1401 AD (803 AH): A Study Based on Arabic Manuscripts of Ibn Khaldūn's "Autobiography," with a Translation into English, and a Commentary*. Berkeley and Los Angeles, 1962.

al-Ḥalabī, Shihāb al-Dīn Maḥmūd. *Ḥusn al-tawassul ilà ṣināʿat al-tarassul*. Ed. Akram ʿUthmān Yūsuf. Baghdad, 1980.

Ibn al-ʿAbbāsī, Ḥasan. *Āthār al-uwal fī tartīb al-duwal*. Ed. ʿAbd al-Raḥmān ʿUmayrah. Beirut, 1989.

Ibn ʿAbd al-Ẓāhir, Muḥyī al-Dīn. *al-Alṭāf al-khafīyah min al-sīrah al-sharīfah al-sulṭānīyah al-Ashrafīyah*. Ed. Axel Moberg as *Ur ʿAbd Allah B. ʿAbd Ez-Zahir's*

Biograhi Över Sultanen El-Melik El-Asraf Halil. Arabisk Täxt med Översättning Inledning Ock Anmärkningar Utjiven. Lund, 1902.

— *al-Rawḍ al-ẓāhir fī sīrat al-Malik al-Ẓāhir*. Ed. ʿAbd al-ʿAzīz Khuwayṭir. Riyadh, 1976.

— *Tashrīf al-ayyām wa al-ʿuṣūr fī sīrat al-Malik al-Manṣūr*. Ed. Murād Kāmil. Cairo, 1961.

Ibn ʿArabshāh, Aḥmad. *ʿAjāʾib al-maqdūr fī nawāʾib Tīmūr*. Ed. Aḥmad Fāʾiz al-Ḥumṣī. Beirut, 1987.

— *Tamerlane or Timur the Great Amir*. Tr. J. H. Sanders. Lahore, 1936, repr. 1976.

Ibn Baṭṭūṭah, ʿAbdallah. *The Travels of Ibn Baṭṭūṭa, AD 1325–1354*. Tr. with revision and notes from the Arabic text edited by C. Defrémery and B. R. Sanguinetti by H. A. R. Gibb. Cambridge and London, 1958–2000. Hakluyt Society 2nd series.

Ibn al-Dawādārī. *Kanz al-durar wa jāmiʿ al-ghurar*. Vol. VIII, ed. Ulrich Haarmann. Cairo, 1971; vol. IX, ed. Hans Robert Roemer. Cairo, 1960.

Ibn Duqmāq, Ibrāhīm. *al-Jawhar al-thamīn fī siyar al-mulūk wa al-salāṭīn*. Ed. Muḥammad ʿIzz al-Dīn ʿAlī. Beirut, 1985.

Ibn al-Furāt, Muḥammad. "Taʾrīkh al-duwal wa al-mulūk." Dār al-Kutub, Cairo. MSS 54251, 36310.

— *Taʾrīkh Ibn al-Furāt* or *Taʾrīkh al-duwal wa al-mulūk*. Ed. Costantine K. Zurayk. Beirut, [1936–42].

[Pseudo] Ibn al-Fuwaṭī. *al-Ḥawādith al-jāmiʿah wa al-tajārib al-nāfiʿah fī al-miʾah al-sābiʿah*. Ed. Mahdī al-Najum. Beirut, 2003.

Ibn Ḥabīb, al-Ḥasan. *Tadhkirat al-nabīh fī ayyām al-Manṣūr wa banīhi*. Eds. Muḥammad Muḥammad Amīn and Saʿīd ʿĀshūr. Cairo, 1976.

Ibn Ḥajar al-ʿAsqalānī, Aḥmad. *al-Durar al-kāminah fī aʿyān al-miʾah al-thāminah*. [No Ed.] Beirut, 1993.

— *Inbāʾ al-ghumr bi-abnāʾ al-ʿumr*. Ed. Ḥasan Ḥabashī. Cairo, 1969.

Ibn al-ʿIbrī/Bar Hebraeus, Gregorius Abū al-Faraj. *The Chronography of Gregory Abūʾl-Faraj, the Son of Aaron, the Hebrew Physician, Commonly Known as Bar Hebraeus*. Tr. E. A. W. Budge. London, 1932.

— *Taʾrīkh mukhtaṣar al-duwal*. Ed. Father Anton Ṣalaḥānī. Beirut, 1958.

Ibn Jamāʿah, Badr al-Dīn Muḥammad. "Kitāb taḥrīr al-aḥkām fī tadbīr ahl al-islām." Ed. Hans Kofler as "Handbuch des islamischen Staats- und Verwaltungsrechtes von Badr al-Dīn Ibn Gamāʿah." *Islamica* 6 (1934): 347–414.

Ibn Kathīr, Ismāʿīl. *al-Bidāyah wa al-nihāyah fī al-taʾrīkh*. Ed. Maktab Taḥqīq al-Turāth. Beirut, 1993.

Ibn al-Nafīs. *The Theologus Autodidacticus of Ibn al-Nafīs*. Eds. Max Mayerhof and Joseph Schacht. Oxford, 1968.

Ibn Nāẓir al-Jaysh. *Kitāb tathqīf al-taʿrīf bi-al-muṣṭalaḥ al-sharīf*. Ed. Rudolf Veselý. Cairo, 1987.

Ibn Qāḍī Shuhbah, Abū Bakr. *taʾrīkh Ibn Qāḍī Shuhbah*. Ed. ʿAdnān Darwīsh. Damascus, 1977–.

Ibn Shaddād, Muḥammad b. ʿAlī. *Taʾrīkh al-Malik al-Ẓāhir*. Ed. Aḥmad Ḥuṭayṭ. Wiesbaden, 1983.

Ibn Taghrībirdī, Yūsuf. *History of Egypt, 1382–1469 AD*. Tr. William Popper. Berkeley, 1954–.

— *al-Manhal al-ṣāfī wa al-mustawfà baʿada al-wāfī*. Eds. Muḥammad Muḥammad Amīn and Saʿīd ʿĀshūr. Cairo, 1984–.

— *al-Nujūm al-zāhirah fī mulūk Miṣr wa al-Qāhirah*. [Various editors]. Cairo, 1929–72.

Ibn Tiqtaqah, Muḥammad. *al-Fakhrī fī al-adab al-sulṭānīyah wa al-duwal al-islāmīyah.* Tr. C. E. J. Whitting as *Al-Fakhri: On the Systems of Government and the Moslem Dynasties*. London, 1948.

Ibn al-Wardī, ʿUmar. *Taʾrīkh Ibn al-Wardī.* Ed. Muḥammad Mahdī al-Sayyid Ḥasan al-Khurāsānī. Najaf, 1969.

Ibn Wāṣil, Muḥammad. "Taʾrīkh al-wāṣilīn min akhbār al-khulafāʾ wa al-mulūk wa al-salāṭīn." Dār al-Kutub, Cairo, MSS 40340 and 40477.

al-Jazarī, Muḥammad. *Taʾrīkh ḥawādith al-zamān wa anbāʾihi wa wafāyāt al-akābir wa al-aʿyān min abnāʾihi* or *Taʾrīkh al-Jazarī.* Ed. ʿUmar ʿAbd al-Salām Tadmurī. Sidon and Beirut, 1998.

al-Kātib al-Baghdādī, Ghiyāth al-Dīn. *al-Taʾrīkh al-Ghiyāthī: al-faṣl al-khāmis min sanat 656–891/1258–1486.* Ed. Ṭāriq Nāfiʿ al-Ḥamdānī. Baghdad, 1975.

al-Maqrīzī, Aḥmad. *Kitāb al-sulūk li-maʿrifat duwal al-mulūk.* Ed. Muḥammad Muḥammad Amīn and Saʿīd ʿĀshūr. Cairo, 1956–73.

Mufaḍḍal Ibn Abī al-Faḍāʾil. *Ägypten und Syrien zwischen 1317 und 1341 in der Chronik des Mufaḍḍal b. Abī l-Faḍāʾil.* Ed. and tr. S. Kortantamer. Freiburg im Breisgau, 1973.

— *Kitāb al-nahj al-sadīd wa al-durr al-farīd fīmā baʿda taʾrīkh Ibn al-ʿAmīd.* Ed. and tr. E. Blochet. Paris, 1911, 1920, 1932.

al-Nuwayrī, Aḥmad. *Nihāyat al-arab fī funūn al-adab.* Ed. Fahīm Muḥammad ʿAlawī Shaltūt. Cairo, 1998. Vol. XXXII.

— *Nihāyat al-arab fī funūn al-adab.* Ed. Muṣṭafà Hijāzī. Cairo, 1997. Vol. XXXIII.

— *Nihāyat al-arab fī funūn al-adab.* Ed. Saʿīd ʿĀshūr. Cairo, 1985–92. Vols. XXVII, XXIX, XXX, XXXI.

al-Qalqashandī, Aḥmad. *Ṣubḥ al-aʿshā fī ṣināʿat al-inshāʾ.* Ed. Muḥammad Ḥusayn Shams al-Dīn. Beirut, 1987.

al-Ṣafadī, Khalīl. *Aʿyān al-ʿaṣr wa aʿwān al-naṣr.* Ed. ʿAlī Abū Zayd. Beirut and Damascus, 1998.

— *al-Wāfī bi-al-wafāyāt or Das biographische Lexicon des Ṣalāḥuddīn Halīl ibn Aibak aṣ-Ṣafadī.* Ed. Hellmut Ritter et al. Wiesbaden, 1962–.

al-Sakhāwī, Muḥammad. *al-Ḍawʾ al-lāmiʿ li-ahl al-qarn al-tāsiʿ.* Cairo, [n.d.].

al-Samhūdī, ʿAlī. *Wafāʾ al-wafāʾ bi-akhbār dār al-muṣṭafà.* Ed. Muḥammad Muḥyī al-Dīn ʿAbd al-Ḥamīd. [Cairo,] Egypt, 1954.

Shāfiʿ b. ʿAlī. *al-Faḍl al-maʾthūr min sīrat al-Malik al-Manṣūr.* Ed. ʿUmar ʿAbd al-Salām Tadmurī. Beirut, 1998.

— *Ḥusn al-manāqib al-sirrīyah al-muntazaʿah min al-sīrah al-Ẓāhirīyah.* Ed. ʿAbd al-ʿAzīz Khuwayṭir. Riyadh, 1989.

al-Shujāʿī. *Taʾrīkh al-Malik al-Nāṣir Muḥammad b. Qalāwūn al-Ṣāliḥī wa Awlādihi.* Ed. Barbara Schäfer. Wiesbaden, 1977.

al-Ṣuqāʿī, Faḍlallah. *Tālī kitāb wafāyāt al-aʿyān.* Ed. and tr. Jacqueline Sublet. Damascus, 1974.

al-Suyūṭī, ʿAbd al-Raḥmān. *History of the Caliphs.* Tr. Henry Sullivan Jarrett. Amsterdam, 1970.

— *Taʾrīkh al-khulafāʾ.* Ed. Muḥammad Muḥyī al-Dīn ʿAbd al-Ḥamīd. Saida and Beirut, 1997.

al-ʿUmarī, Aḥmad b. Faḍlallah. *Das mongolische Weltreich: al-ʿUmarī's Darstellung der mongolischen Reiche in seinem Werke Masālik al-abṣār fī mamālik al-amṣār.* Ed. and tr. Klaus Lech. Wiesbaden, 1968.

— *al-Taʿrīf bi-al-muṣṭalaḥ al-sharīf.* Ed. Samir al-Droubi. Karak, 1992.

al-Yūnīnī, Mūsà. *Dhayl mir'āt al-zamān*. Hyderabad, 1954–61.
— *Dhayl mir'āt al-zamān*. Ed. and tr. Li Guo as *Early Mamluk Syrian Historiography: al-Yūnīnī's Dhayl mir'āt al-zamān*. Leiden, 1998.
al-Yūsufī, Mūsà. *Nuzhat al-nāẓir fī sīrat al-Malik al-Nāṣir*. Ed. Aḥmad Ḥuṭayṭ. Beirut, 1986.
Author Z. *Ta'rīkh salāṭīn al-mamālīk* or *Beiträge zur Geschichte der mamlukensultane*. Ed. K. V. Zettersteen. Leiden, 1919.

Persian sources

Ahrī, Abū Bakr. *Ta'rīkh-i Shaikh Uwais (History of Shaikh Uways): An Important Source for the History of Ādharbaijān in the Fourteenth Century*. Tr. J. B. van Loon. The Hague, 1954.
al-Aqsarā'ī, Karīm al-Dīn Maḥmūd. *Müsâmeret ül-ahbâr: Mogollar zamaninda Türkiye Selçuklari Tarihi*. Ed. Osman Turan. Ankara, 1944.
Astarābādī, 'Azīz. *Bazm wa razm*. Ed. Köprülü Zadeh Mehmet Fuat. Istanbul, 1928.
Āyatī, 'Abd al-Muḥammad. *Taḥrīr-i ta'rīkh-i Vaṣṣāf*. [Tehran], 1993–94.
Banākatī, Davud. *Ta'rīkh-i Banākatī* or *Rawḍ al-albāb fī tawārīkh al-akābir wa al-ansāb*. Ed. Ja'far Shi'ār. Tehran, 1969.
Ḥāfiẓ Abrū, 'Abdallah Khwāfī. *Dhayl-i jāmi' al-tawārīkh-i Rashīdī*. Ed. Khānbābā Bāyānī. Tehran, 1971.
Juvaynī, 'Alā' al-Dīn 'Aṭā' Malik. *Ta'rīkh-i Jahān Gushā*. Tr. J. A. Boyle as *The History of the World-Conqueror*. Seattle, 1997.
Mīrkhwānd, aka Muḥammad b. Khwāndamīr. *Rawḍat al-ṣafā' fī sīrat al-anbiyā' wa al-mulūk wa al-khulafā'*. Ed. Jamshīd Kayānfar. Tehran, 2001–02.
Nakhjavānī, Muḥammad. *Dastūr al-kātib fi ta'yīn al-marātib*. Ed. A. A. Alizade. Moscow, 1964–76.
Naṭanzī, Mu'īn al-Dīn. *Muntakhab al-tawārikh-i mu'īnī*. Ed. Jean Aubin. Tehran, 1957.
— *Muntakhab al-tawārikh-i mu'īnī*. Ed. Parvīn Istakhrī. Tehran, 2004.
Qāshānī, Abū al-Qāsim 'Abdallah. *Ta'rīkh-i pādshāh-i sa'īd Ghiyāth al-Dunyā wa al-Dīn Uljaytu Sulṭān Muḥammad*. Ed. M. Hambly. Tehran, 1969.
Qazvīnī, Ḥamdallah Mustawfī. *The Geographical Part of the Nuzhat al-Qulūb*. Tr. G. Le Strange. Leiden, 1919.
— *Ta'rīkh-i guzīdah*. Ed. 'Abd al-Ḥusayn Navā'ī. Tehran, 1362.
Qazvīnī, Zayn al-Dīn b. Ḥamdallah. *Dhayl-i ta'rīkh-i guzīdah*. Ed. Iraj Afshar. Tehran, 1993–94.
Rashīd al-Dīn, Faḍlallah. *Histoire des Mongols de la Perse*. Ed. and tr. E. Quatremère. Amsterdam, 1886, repr. 1968.
— *Jāmi' al-tawārīkh*. Ed. Muḥammad Rawshan and Mustafā Musavī. Tehran, 1994.
— *The Successors of Genghis Khan*. Tr. J. A. Boyle. New York, 1971.
Samarqandī, 'Abd al-Razzāq. *Maṭla'-i Sa'dayn va majma'-yi baḥrayn*. Ed. 'Abd al-Ḥusayn Navā'ī. Tehran, 1993.
Shāmī, Niẓām al-Dīn. *Ẓafarnāmah: Ta'rīkh-i futūḥāt-i amīr Tīmūr Kurkānī*. Ed. Felix Tauer. Prague, 1937.
Vaṣṣāf al-Ḥaẓrah, 'Abd Allah. *Tajzīyat al-amṣār wa tazjīyat al-a'ṣār*. Ed. Joseph Hammer-Purghstall as *Geschichte Vaṣṣāf's: persisch herausegegeben und deutsch übersetz*. Vienna, 1856.

— *Ta'rīkh-i Vaṣṣāf al-Ḥazrah*. Tehran, 1956. (Also see Āyatī.)
Yazdī, Sharaf al-Dīn ʿAlī. *Ẓafarnāmah*. Ed. Muḥammad ʿAbbāsī. Tehran, 1957–58.

Other sources

The Chronicle of Novgorod. Ed. and tr. Robert Michell and Neill Forbes. London, 1914; repr. New York, 1970.
Feridun Beg. *Mecmu'at-i munshe'at-i selatin* [n.p.], [1848–49].
González de Clavijo, Ruy. *Narrative of the Embassy of Ruy González de Clavijo to the Court of Timour at Samarcand, AD 1403–6*. Tr. Clements R. Markham. Hakluyt Society 1st series. Vol. XXVI. London, 1859.
Grigor of Akner. "History of the Nation of the Archers (the Mongols)." Ed. and tr. Robert P. Blake and Richard N. Frye. *HJAS* 12:3/4 (December 1949): 269–399.
Polo, Marco. *The Description of the World*. Ed. A. C. Moule and Paul Pelliot. London, 1938, repr. New York, 1976.

Modern studies

Afsaruddin, Asma. *Excellence and Precedence: Medieval Islamic Discourse on Legitimate Leadership*. Leiden, 2002.
Afshar, Iraj. "Manuscript and Paper Sizes Cited in Persian and Arabic Texts." *Maqālāt va dirāsāt muhdà ilà al-duktūr Ṣalāḥ al-Dīn al-Munajjid / Essays in Honour of Ṣalāḥ al-Dīn al-Munajjid*. London, 2002. 659–73.
Ahmed, Nazir. "Diplomatic Relations between the Sultans of Delhi and the Il-Khans of Iran." *Islamic Heritage in South Asian Subcontinent*. Jaipur, 1998 (2000). 60–75.
Aigle, Denise. "Le Grand *jasaq* de Gengis-Khan, l'empire, la culture mongole et la *sharīʿa*." *JESHO* 47:1 (2004). 31–79.
— "Le Soufism sunnite en Fars: Šayḫ Amīn al-Dīn Balyānī." *Domination*. 231–60.
Album, S. "Studies in Ilkhanid History and Numismatics I: A Late Ilkhanid Hoard (743/1341)." *Studia Iranica* 13:1 (1984): 49–116.
— "Studies in Ilkhanid History and Numismatics II: A Late Ilkhanid Hoard (741/1340) as Evidence for the History of Diyar Bakr." *Studia Iranica* 14:1 (1985): 45–76.
— *Sylloge of Islamic Coins in the Ashmolean*. Vol. IX. Oxford, 2001.
Allouche, Adel. "Tegüder's Ultimatum to Qalawun." *IJMES* 22 (1990): 437–46.
Allsen, Thomas T. "Biography of a Cultural Broker, Bolad Ch'eng-Hsiang in China and Iran." *Court*, 7–22.
— "Changing Forms of Legitimation in Mongol Iran." *Rulers from the Steppe: State Formation on the Eurasian Periphery. Proceedings of the Soviet–American Academic Symposia in Conjunction with the Museum Exhibition: "Nomads: Masters of the Eurasian Steppe."* Eds. Gary Seaman and Daniel Marks. Vol. II. Los Angeles, 1991.
— *Commodity and Exchange in the Mongol Empire: A Cultural History of Islamic Textiles*. Cambridge, 1997.
— *Mongol Imperialism: The Policies of the Grand Qan Möngke in China, Russia and the Islamic Lands 1251–59*. Berkeley and Los Angeles, 1987.
— "Robing in the Mongolian Empire." *Robes and Honor: The Medieval World of Investiture*. Ed. Stewart Gordon. New York, 2001. 305–13.

Amitai, Reuven. "The Conversion of Tegüder Ilkhan to Islam." *JSAI* 25 (2001): 15–43.
— "Evidence for the Early Use of the Title *Īlkhān* among the Mongols." *JRAS* 3rd series 1:3 (1991): 353–61.
— "The Mongol Occupation of Damascus in 1300: A Study of Mamluk Loyalties." *The Mamluks in Egyptian Politics and Society*. Eds. Michael Winter and Amalia Levanoni. Leiden, 2004. 21–41.
— "al-Nuwayrī as a Historian of the Mongols." *The Historiography of Islamic Egypt (c. 950–1800)*. Ed. Hugh Kennedy. Leiden, 2001. 23–36.
— "The Resolution of the Mongol–Mamluk War." *Mongols, Turks and Others: Eurasian Nomads and the Sedentary World*. Eds. Reuven Amitai and Michal Biran. Leiden and Boston, 2005. 359–90.
— "Whither the Ilkhanid Army? Ghazan's First Campaign into Syria (1299–1300)." *Warfare in Inner Asian History, 500–1800*. Ed. N. Di Cosmo. Leiden, 2002. 221–64.
Amitai-Preiss, Reuven. "An Exchange of Letters in Arabic between Abaγa Īlkhān and Sultan Baybars (AH 667/AD 1268–69)." *CAJ* 38:1 (1994): 11–33.
— "Ghazan, Islam and Mongol Tradition: A View from the Mamlūk Sultanate." *BSOAS* 59:1 (1996): 1–10.
— "Mongol Imperial Ideology and the Ilkhanid War against the Mamluks." *Mongol Empire*. 57–72.
— *Mongols and Mamluks: The Mamluk–Īlkhānid War, 1260–1281*. Cambridge, 1995.
— "Sufis and Shamans: Some Remarks on the Islamization of the Mongols in the Ilkhanate." *JESHO* 42:1 (1999): 27–46.
Andrews, Peter Alford. *Felt Tents and Pavilions: The Nomadic Tradition and its Interaction with Princely Tentage*. London, 1999.
— "Miẓalla: 4. In the Persian, Indian and Turkish Lands." *EI²* VII:192–94.
ʿAnkawi, ʿAbdullah. "The Pilgrimage to Mecca in Mamlūk Times." *Arabian Studies* 1 (1974): 146–70.
Artuk, Ibrahim and Artuk, Cevriye. *İstanbul Arkeoloji Müzeleri Teşirdeki İslâmî Sikkeler Kataloğu*. Istanbul, 1970–74.
Ashtor, Eliyahu. "L'Inquisition dans l'état mamlouk." *Rivista degli Studi Orientali* 25 (1950): 11–26.
Aubin, Jean. "Comment Tamerlan prenait les villes." *SI* 19 (1963): 83–122.
— *Émirs mongols et vizirs persans dans les remous de l'acculturation*. Paris, 1995.
Ayalon, David. "The Auxiliary Forces of the Mamluk Sultanate." *Der Islam* 65 (1988): 13–37. Reprinted in *Islam and the Abode of War: Military Slaves and Islamic Adversaries*. London, 1994.
— *L'Esclavage du mamelouk*. Jerusalem: 1951. Reprinted in *The Mamluk Military Society: Collected Studies*. London, 1979.
— "The Great *Yāsa* of Chingiz Khān: A Reexamination." *SI* 33 (1971): 97–140; 34 (1971): 151–80; 36 (1972): 113–58; 38 (1973): 107–56. Reprinted in *Outsiders in the Lands of Islam: Mamluks, Mongols and Eunuchs*. London, 1988.
— "The Wafidiya in the Mamluk Kingdom." *Islamic Culture* 25 (January–October 1951): 89–104. Reprinted in *Studies on the Mamlūks of Egypt (1250–1517)*. London, 1977.
al-ʿAzzāwī, ʿAbbas. *Taʾrīkh al-ʿIrāq bayna Iḥtilālayn: Ḥukūmat al-Jalāyirīyah*. Baghdad, 1935–49.
Babinger, Franz. "Ramaḍān-Oghullarī." *EI²* VIII:418–19.

Baldick, Julian. *Animal and Shaman: Ancient Religions of Central Asia*. New York, 2000.

Balog, Paul. *The Coinage of the Mamlūk Sultans of Egypt and Syria*. New York, 1964.

Bausani, A. "Religion Under the Mongols." *CHIr* V:538–49.

Beffa, Marie-Lise. "*Le Concept de* tänggäri *«ciel» dans l'*Histoire secrète des Mongols." *Études Mongoles et Siberiennes* 24 (1993): 215–36.

Behrens-Abouseif, Doris. "The Citadel of Cairo: Stage for Mamluk Ceremonial." *AI* 24 (1988): 25–79.

— "The Mahmal Tradition and the Pilgrimage of the Ladies of the Mamluk Court." *Mamluk Studies Review* 1 (1997): 92–93.

— "Qāytbāy's *Madrasahs* and the Evolution of Haram Architecture." *Mamluk Studies Review* 3 (1999): 129–47.

Berchem, Max van. *Amida: matériaux pour l'épigraphie et l'histoire musulmanes du Diyar-Bekr*. Paris, 1910.

— *Matériaux pour un corpus inscriptionum arabicarum*. Paris, 1894. Vol. XIX.

Berend, Nora. *At the Gate of Christendom: Jews, Muslims and "Pagans" in Medieval Hungary, c. 1000–c. 1300*. Cambridge, 2001.

Biran, Michal. "The Chaghadaids and Islam: The Conversion of Tarmashirin Khan (1331—34)." *JAOS* 122:4 (October–December 2002): 742–52.

— *Qaidu and the Rise of the Independent Mongol State in Central Asia*. Richmond, Surrey, 1997.

Blair, Sheila. "The Coins of the Later Ilkhanids: A Typological Analysis." *JESHO* 25 (October 1983): 295–317.

— "The Epigraphic Program of the Tomb of Uljaytu at Sultaniyya: Meaning in Mongol Architecture." *Islamic Art* 2 (1987): 43–96.

— "The Mongol Capital of Sulṭāniyya, 'The Imperial.'" *Iran* 24 (1986): 139–51.

— "Patterns of Patronage and Production in Ilkhanid Iran: The Case of Rashīd al-Dīn." *Court*. 39–62.

— "The Religious Art of the Ilkhanids." *Legacy*. 104–33.

Bloom, Jonathan M. *Paper Before Print: The History and Impact of Paper in the Islamic World*. New Haven and London, 2001.

Boyle, J. A. "Political and Dynastic History of the Īl-Khāns." *CHIr* V:303–421.

— "Turkish and Mongol Shamanism in the Middle Ages." *Folklore* 83 (1972), 177–93. Reprinted in *The Mongol World Empire, 1206–1370*. London, 1977.

Broadbridge, Anne F. "Apostasy Trials in Eighth/Fourteenth Century Egypt: A Case Study." *The History and Historiography of Central Asia: A Festschrift for John E. Woods*. Eds. Judith Pfeiffer and Sholeh A. Quinn with Ernest Tucker. Wiesbaden, 2006: 363–82.

— "Mamluk Legitimacy and the Mongols: The Reigns of Baybars and Qalāwūn." *Mamluk Studies Review* 5 (2001): 91–118.

Brinner, William M. "Some Ayyūbid and Mamlūk Documents from Non-Archival Sources." *Israel Oriental Society* 2 (1972): 117–43.

Cahen, Claude. "Artuḳids." *EI²* I:662–67.

— "Eretna." *EI²* II:705–07.

— *The Formation of Turkey: The Seljukid Sultanate of Rūm: Eleventh to Fourteenth Century*. Tr. and ed. P. M. Holt. Harlow, 2001.

— "Futuwwa." *EI²* II:961–69.

Calmard, Jean. "Le Chiisme imamite sous les Ilkhans." *Domination*. 261–92.

Canard, M. "Une lettre du Sultan Malik Nâṣir Ḥasan à Jean VI Cantacuzène (750/1349)." *Annales de l'Institut d'Études Orientales* 3 (Paris, 1939): 27–52.
— "Un traité entre Byzance et l'Égypte au XIIIe siècle et les relations diplomatiques de Michel VIII Paléologue avec les sultans mamlûks Baibars et Qalâ'ûn." *Mélanges Gaudefroy-Demombynes* (Cairo, 1935–45): 197–224.
Clauson, Sir Gerard. *An Etymological Dictionary of Pre-Thirteenth Century Turkish.* Oxford, 1972.
Cleaves, Francis Woodman. "The Anonymous Scribal Note Pertaining to the *Bičig* of Ötemiş." *HJAS* 16 (1953): 478–86.
— "A Chancellery Practice of the Mongols in the Thirteenth and Fourteenth Centuries." *HJAS* 14 (1951): 493–526.
— "The Mongolian Documents in the Musée de Téhéran." *HJAS* 16 (1953): 1–107.
— *The Secret History of the Mongols.* Cambridge, MA, 1982.
Combe, Étienne; Sauvaget, Jean; Wiet, Gaston et al. *RCEA.*
Darrag, Aḥmad. *L'Égypte sous le règne de Barṣbāy, 825–841/1422–1438.* Damascus, 1961.
DeWeese, Devin. *Islamization and Native Religion in the Golden Horde: Baba Tükles and Conversion to Islam in Historical and Epic Tradition.* University Park, PA, 1994.
— "Toḳtamish." *EI²* X: 560–63.
D'Ohsson, Baron Constantin. *Histoire des Mongols, depuis Tchinguiz-Khan jusqu'à Timour Bey, ou Tamerlan.* Amsterdam and The Hague, 1835.
Donzel, E. van. "Mudjaddid." *EI²* VII:290.
Edbury, Peter. *The Kingdom of Cyprus and the Crusades, 1191–1374.* Cambridge, 1991.
Escovitz, Joseph H. *The Office of Qâḍî al-Quḍât in Cairo under the Baḥrî Mamlûks.* Berlin, 1984.
Fischel, Walter J. "A New Latin Source on Tamerlane's Conquest of Damascus (1400/1401) (B. de Mignanelli's 'Vita Tamerlani' (1416)." *Oriens* 9 (1956): 201–32.
Fleischer, Cornell H. *Bureaucrat and Intellectual in the Ottoman Empire.* Princeton, 1986.
Golden, P. B. "I Will Give the People unto Thee": The Činggisid Conquests and their Aftermath in the Turkic World." *JRAS* 3rd series, 10:1 (April 2000): 21–41.
Halperin, Charles J. "The Kipchak Connection: The Ilkhans, the Mamluks and Ayn Jalut." *BSOAS* 63 (2000): 229–45.
— *Russia and the Golden Horde: The Mongol Impact on Medieval Russian History.* Bloomington, 1985.
Hamayon, Roberte. *La Chasse à l'âme: esquisse d'une théorie du chamanisme sibérien.* Nanterre, 1990.
Hambis, L. "La Lettre mongole du Gouverneur de Karak." *Acta Orientalia Academiae Scientiarum Hungaricae* 15 (1962): 143–46.
Heidemann, Stefan. *Das Allepiner Kalifat (AD 1261): vom Ende des Kalifates in Baghdad über Aleppo zu den Restaurationen in Kairo.* Leiden, 1994.
— "Tīmūr's Campmint during the Siege of Damascus in 803/1401." *Matériaux pour l'Histoire Économique du Monde Iranien* 21 (1999): 179–206.
Hein, Horst. "Hülägüs Unterwerfungsbriefe an die Machthaber Syriens und Ägyptens." *ZDMG* 150:2 (2000): 425–60.

Herrmann, Gottfried and Doerfer, Gerhard. "Ein Erlass des Ǧalāyiriden Solṭān Ḥoseyn aus dem Jahr 780/1378." *Erkenntnisse und Meinungen* 1 (1973): 135–63.

— "Ein persich-mongolischer Erlaß aus dem Jahr 725/1325." *ZDMG* 125:2 (1975): 317–46.

— "Ein persich-mongolischer Erlass des Ǧalāyeriden Šeyḫ Oveys." *CAJ* 19 (1975): 1–88.

Hillenbrand, Robert. "The Arts of the Book in Ilkhanid Iran." *Legacy*. 134–67.

Hodgson, Marshall. *The Venture of Islam*. Chicago, 1974.

Holt, Peter Malcolm. *The Age of the Crusades: The Near East from the Eleventh Century to 1517*. London and New York, 1986.

— "The Īlkhān Aḥmad's Embassies to Qalāwūn: Two Contemporary Accounts." *BSOAS* 49 (1986): 128–32.

— "The Position and Power of the Mamlūk Sultan." *BSOAS* 38 (1975): 237–49.

— "Some Observations on the ʿAbbāsid Caliphate of Cairo." *BSOAS* 47 (1984): 501–07.

— "The Structure of Government in the Mamluk Sultanate." *The Eastern Mediterranean Lands in the Period of the Crusades*. Ed. P. M. Holt. Warminster, England, 1977. 44–61.

Horst, Heribert. "Eine Gesandtschaft des Mamlūken al-Malik al-Nāṣir am Īlhān-Hof in Persien." *Der Orient in der Forschung: Festschrift für Otto Speis zum 5 April 1966*. Wiesbaden, 1967. 348–70.

Howorth, Sir Henry H. *History of the Mongols from the 9th to the 19th Century, III: Mongols of Persia*. London, 1876–1927.

Humphreys, R. Stephen. "The Expressive Intent of the Mamluk Architecture of Cairo: A Preliminary Essay." *SI* 35 (1972): 69–119.

— *From Saladin to the Mongols: The Ayyubids of Damascus, 1193–1260* (Albany, 1977).

Ilisch, Ludger. "Geschichte der Artuqidenherrschaft von Mardin zwischen Mamluken un Mongolen 1260–1410 AD." Ph.D. dissertation. Westfälischen Wilhelms-Universität zu Münster. 1984.

Inalcık, Halil. "Osmanlılar'da saltanat veraseti usulü ve Türk hâkimiyet telâkkisiyle ilgisi." *Siyasal Bilgiler Fakültesi Dergisi* 14 (1956): 69–94. Translated as "The Ottoman Succession and its Relations to the Turkish Concept of Sovereignty." *The Middle East and the Balkans under the Ottoman Empire: Essays on Economy and Society*. Bloomington, 1993. 37–63.

— *The Ottoman Empire: The Classical Age, 1300–1600*. Tr. Norman Itzkowitz and Colin Imber. New Rochelle, NY, 1973.

— "Suleiman the Lawgiver and Ottoman Law." *Archivum Ottomanicum* 1 (1969): 105–38.

Irwin, Robert. *The Middle East in the Middle Ages: The Early Mamluk Sultanate 1250–1382*. Carbondale, 1986.

— "What the Partridge Told the Eagle: A Neglected Arabic Source on Chinggis Khan and the Early History of the Mongols." *Mongol Empire*. 1–11.

Jackson, Peter. "Aḥmad Takudar." *EIr* I:661–62.

— "The Dissolution of the Mongol Empire." *CAJ* 22:3–4 (1978): 186–244.

— "The Mongols and the Faith of the Conquered." *Mongols, Turks and Others: Eurasian Nomads and the Sedentary World*. Eds. Reuven Amitai and Michal Biran. Leiden and Boston, 2005. 245–90.

— *The Mongols and the West, 1221–1410*. Harlow, 2005.

James, David. *Qur'āns of the Mamlūks*. New York, 1988.

Jomier, Jacques. *Le Maḥmal et la caravane égyptienne des pèlerins de la Mecque (XIIIe–XXe siècles)*. Cairo, 1953.

Kara, G. "Part Three: Mongol Writing Systems." *History of Civilizations of Central Asia* IV:2. Eds. C. E. Bosworth and M. S. Asimov. Paris, 1992–. 335–37.

Khazanov, Anatoly M. "Muḥammad and Jenghiz Khan Compared: The Religious Factor in World Empire Building." *Comparative Studies in Society and History* 35 (1993): 461–79.

Koca, Salim. "Anatolian Turkish Beyliks." *The Turks, II: Middle Ages*. Eds. Hasan Celal Güzel et al. Ankara, 2002. 507–53.

Komaroff, Linda. "The Epigraphy of Timurid Coinage: Some Preliminary Remarks." *Museum Notes* 31 (1986): 207–32.

Kramarovsky, Mark G. "The Culture of the Golden Horde and the Problem of the 'Mongol Legacy.'" *Rulers from the Steppe: State Formation on the Eurasian Periphery*. Eds. Gary Seaman and Daniel Marks. Los Angeles, 1991. 255–66.

Krawulsky, Dorothea. *Mongolen und Ilkhane, Ideologie und Geschichte: 5 Studien*. Tübingen, 1989.

Kruk, Remke. "History and Apocalypse: Ibn al-Nafîs' Justification of Mamluk Rule." *Der Islam* 72 (1995): 324–37.

Lambton, A. K. S. "Justice in the Medieval Persian Theory of Kingship." *SI* 17 (1962). 91–119. Reprinted in *Theory and Practice in Medieval Persia*. London, 1980.

Lane-Poole, Stanley. *Catalogue of Oriental Coins in the British Museum*. London, 1875–90. Reprinted Bologna, 1967.

Langdon, John S. "Byzantium's Initial Encounter with the Chinggisids: An Introduction to the Byzantino-Mongolica." *Viator* 29 (1998): 95–139.

Lavoix, Henri. *Catalogue des monnaies musulmanes de la Bibliothèque nationale*. Paris, 1896.

Levanoni, Amalia. *A Turning Point in Mamluk History: The Third Reign of al-Nāṣir Muḥammad Ibn Qalawun (1310–1341)*. Leiden, 1995.

Lewis, Bernard, ed. and tr. *Islam: From the Prophet Muḥammad to the Capture of Constantinople*, vol. I: *Politics and War*. New York, 1987.

Lippard, Bruce G. "The Mongols and Byzantium, 1243–1341." Ph.D. dissertation. Department of Uralic and Altaic Studies, Indiana University. 1983.

Little, Donald Presgrave. *An Introduction to Mamlūk Historiography: An Analysis of Arabic Annalistic and Biographical Sources for the Reign of al-Malik an-Nāṣir Muḥammad ibn Qalā'ūn*. Montreal, 1970.

— "Notes on Aitamiš, a Mongol Mamlūk." *Die islamische Welt zwischen Mittelalter und Neuzeit: Festschrift für Hans Robert Roemer zum 65. Geburtstag*. Eds. Ulrich Haarmann and Peter Bachmann. Wiesbaden, 1979. 387–401. Reprinted in *History and Historiography of the Mamlūks*. London, 1986.

Lockhart, Laurence. "The Relations between Edward I and Edward II of England and the Mongol Īl-Khāns of Persia." *Iran* 6 (1968): 23–31.

Lowry, Heath W. *The Nature of the Ottoman State*. New York, 2003.

McChesney, R. D. "Zamzam Water on a White Felt Carpet: Adapting Mongol Ways in Muslim Central Asia, 1550–1650." *Technology*. 63–80.

McCormick, Michael. *Eternal Victory: Triumphal Rulership in Late Antiquity, Byzantium and the Early Medieval West*. Cambridge, 1986.

Madelung, Wilferd. "Mahdī." *EI²* V:1230–38.
— "A Treatise on the Imamate Dedicated to Sultan Baybars I." *Proceedings of the 14th Congress of the Union Européenne des Arabisants et Islamisants* I. Ed. A. Fodor. Budapest, 1995. 91–102.
Manz, Beatrice Forbes. "Family and Ruler in Timurid Historiography." *Studies on Central Asian History in Honor of Yuri Bregel.* Ed. Devin DeWeese. Bloomington, IN, 2001. 57–78.
— "Mongol History Rewritten and Relived." *Revue des Mondes Musulmans et de la Méditerranée* 89–90 (2000): 129–49.
— *The Rise and Rule of Tamerlane.* Cambridge, 1989.
— "Tamerlane and the Symbolism of Sovereignty." *Iranian Studies* 21:1–2 (1988): 105–22.
— "Temür and the Problem of a Conqueror's Legacy." *JRAS* 3rd series 1 (April 1998): 21–41.
Martin, Janet. "The Land of Darkness and the Golden Horde: The Fur Trade under the Mongols, XIII–XIVth Centuries." *Cahiers du Monde Russe et Soviétique* 19:4 (1978): 401–21.
Massé, Henri. "Ordonnance rendue par le prince ilkanien Aḥmad Jalair en faveur du Cheikh Sadr od-Dîn (1305–1392)." *JA* 230 (1938): 465–68.
Masson-Smith, John. "Djalāyir, Djalāyirids." *EI²* II:401.
Masuya, Tomoko. "Ilkhanid Courtly Life." *Legacy.* 74–103.
Mayer, L. A. *Mamluk Costume: A Survey.* Geneva, 1952.
Melville, Charles. "Abū Saʿīd and the Revolt of the Amirs in 1319." *Domination.* 89–120.
— "The Chinese-Uighur Calendar of the Mongol Period." *Iran* 32 (1994): 83–98.
— *The Fall of Amir Chupan and the Decline of the Ilkhanate, 1327–1337: A Decade of Discord in Mongol Iran.* Bloomington, IN, 1999.
— "*Pādshāh-i Islām:* The Conversion of Sultan Maḥmūd Ghāzān Khān." *Pembroke Papers* 1 (1990): 159–77.
— "'Sometimes by the Sword, Sometimes by the Dagger': The Role of the Ismaʿilis in Mamlūk–Mongol Relations in the 8th/14th Century." *Mediaeval Ismaʿili History and Thought.* Ed. Farhad Daftary. Cambridge, 1996. 247–63.
— "Wolf or Shepherd? Amir Chupan's Attitude to Government." *Court.* 79–93.
— "'The Year of the Elephant': Mamluk–Mongol Rivalry in the Hejaz in the Reign of Abū Saʿīd (1317–1335)." *Studia Iranica* 21:2 (1992): 197–214.
Melville, Charles and Zaryab, Abbas. "Chobanids." *EIr* V:496–502.
Meserve, Ruth I. "The Uses of Blood in Traditional Inner Asian Societies." *Technology.* 35–50.
Meyvaert, Paul. "An Unknown Letter of Hulagu, Il-Khan of Persia, to King Louis IX of France." *Viator* 11 (1980): 246–61.
Mordtmann, J. H. and Ménage, V. L. "Dhuʾ l-Ḳadr." *EI²* II:239–40.
Morgan, D. O. "The 'Great *Yasa* of Chinggis Khan' Revisited." *Mongols, Turks and Others: Eurasian Nomads and the Sedentary World.* Eds. Reuven Amitai and Michal Biran. Leiden and Boston, 2005. 291–308.
— "The 'Great Yāsā of Chingiz Khān' and Mongol Law in the Īlkhānate." *BSOAS* 49 (1986): 163–76.
— *The Mongols.* Oxford, 1986.
— "The Mongols and the Eastern Mediterranean." *Latins and Greeks in the Eastern Mediterranean after 1204.* Eds. Benjamin Arbel et al. London, 1989. 198–211.

— "The Mongols in Syria, 1260–1300." *Crusade and Settlement: Papers Read at the First Conference of the Society for the Study of the Crusades and the Latin East and Presented to R. C. Smail.* Ed. Peter W. Edbury. Cardiff, UK and Atlantic Highlands, NJ, 1985. 231–35.

— "Öldjeytu." *EI*[2] VIII:168–69.

Mostaert, Antoine and Cleaves, Francis Woodman. *Les Lettres de 1289 et 1305 des Ilkhans Arγun et Öljeitü à Philippe le Bel.* Cambridge, MA, 1962.

— "Trois documents mongols des archives secrètes vaticanes." *HJAS* 15 (1952): 478–85.

Navā'ī, 'Abd al-Ḥusayn. *Asnād va mukātabāt-i ta'rīkhī-yi Īrān az Tīmūr tā Shāh Ismā'īl.* Tehran, 1962.

Nielsen, Jørgen S. *Secular Justice in an Islamic State: Maẓālim under the Baḥrī Mamlūks, 662/1264–789/1387.* Leiden, 1985.

Northrup, Linda. "The Baḥrī Mamlūk Sultanate, 1250–1390." *The Cambridge History of Egypt.* Ed. Carl F. Petry. Cambridge, 1998. I:242–89.

— *From Slave to Sultan: The Career of al-Manṣūr Qalāwūn and the Consolidation of Mamluk Rule in Egypt and Syria (678–689 AH/1279–1290 AD).* Stuttgart, 1998.

O'Kane, Bernard. "Monumentality in Mamluk and Mongol Art and Architecture." *Art History* 19:4 (December 1996): 499–522.

Ota, Keiko. "The Meccan Sharifate and its Diplomatic Relations in the Bahri Mamluk Period." *Annals of Japan Association for Middle East Studies* 17:1 (2002): 1–20.

Papazian, A. D. "Deux nouveaux iarlyks d'Ilkhans." *Banber Matenadarani* 6 (1962): 379–401.

Petry, Carl F. "Robing Ceremonials in Late Mamluk Egypt: Hallowed Traditions, Shifting Protocols." *Robes and Honor: The Medieval World of Investiture.* Ed. Stewart Gordon. New York, 2001. 353–77.

— *Twilight of Majesty: The Reigns of the Mamlūk Sultans al-Ashrāf Qāytbāy and Qānsūh al-Ghawrī in Egypt.* Seattle, 1993.

Pfeiffer, Judith. "Conversion Versions: Sultan Öljeytü's Conversion to Shi'ism (709/1309) in Muslim Narrative Sources." *Mongolian Studies* 22 (1999): 35–67.

— *Twelver Shī'ism in Mongol Iran.* Istanbul, 1999.

Rabbat, Nasser. "The Changing Concept of *Mamlūk* in the Mamluk Sultanate in Egypt and Syria." *Slave Elites in the Middle East and Africa: A Comparative Study.* Eds. Miura Toru and John Edwards Philips. London and New York, 2000. 81–98.

— *The Citadel of Cairo: A New Interpretation of Royal Mamluk Architecture.* Leiden and New York, 1995.

— "The Ideological Significance of the *Dār al-Adl* in the Medieval Islamic Orient." *IJMES* 27 (1995): 3–28.

Rabino, H. L. "Coins of the Jalā'ir, Ḳara Ḳoyūnlū, Musha'sha', and Āḳ Ḳoyūnlū Dynasties." *Numismatic Chronicle* 6th series, 10 (1950). 94–139.

de Rachewiltz, I. "Some Reflections on Činggis Qan's *J̌asaγ*." *East Asian History* 6 (1993). 91–104.

— "Some Remarks on the Ideological Foundations of Chingis Khan's Empire." *Papers on Far Eastern History* 7 (1973): 21–36.

Raff, Thomas. *Remarks on an Anti-Mongol Fatwà by Ibn Taīmiya.* Leiden, 1973.

Ratchnevsky, Paul. *Genghis Khan: His Life and Legacy.* Tr. and ed. Thomas Nivison Haining. Oxford, 1991.

Richard, Jean. "D'Älğigidäi à Ġazan: la continuité d'une politique franque chez les Mongols d'Iran." *Domination.* 57–69.

Roemer, H. R. "The Jalayirids, Muzaffarids and Sarbadārs." *CHIr* VI:1–41.

— "The Safavid Period." *CHIr* VI:189–350.

— "Tīmūr in Iran." *CHIr* VI:42–97.

Roux, Jean-Paul. *La Religion des Turcs et des Mongols*. Paris, 1984.

Sabra, Adam. *Poverty and Charity in Medieval Islam: Mamluk Egypt, 1250–1517*. Cambridge, 2000.

Saunders, J. J. *The History of the Mongol Conquests*. London, 1971.

Schamiloglu, Uli. "The Golden Horde." *The Turks*, II: *Middle Ages*. Eds. Hasan Celal Güzel et al. Ankara, 2002. 819–34.

Sela, Ron. *Ritual and Authority in Central Asia: The Khan's Inauguration Ceremony*. Bloomington, IN, 2003.

Shoshan, Boaz. *Popular Culture in Medieval Cairo*. Cambridge, 1993.

Shukurov, Rustam. "Turkoman and Byzantine Self-Identity: Some Reflections on the Logic of the Title-Making in Twelfth- and Thirteenth-Century Anatolia." *Eastern Approaches to Byzantium*. Ed. Antony Eastmond. Aldershot, 2001. 259–76.

Sinor, D. "Diplomatic Practices in Medieval Inner Asia." *The Islamic World from Classical to Modern Times*. Eds. C. E. Bosworth et al. Princeton, 1989. 337–55.

— "Language Situation and Scripts, Part Two: Old Turkic and Middle Turkic Languages." *History of Civilizations of Central Asia*. Eds. C. E. Bosworth and M. S. Asimov. Paris, 1992–. IV:2:331–33.

— "Les Relations entre les Mongols et l'Europe jusqu'à la mort d'Arghoun et de Béla IV." *Cahiers d'Histoire Mondiale* 3:1 (1956): 39–62.

Sivan, Emmanuel. *L'Islam et la croisade: idéologie et propagande dans les réactions musulmanes aux croisades*. Paris, 1968.

de Somogyi, Joseph. "Adh-Dhahabī's Record of the Destruction of Damascus by the Mongols in 699–700/1299–1301." *Ignace Goldziher Memorial Volume*. Ed. D. S. Loewinger. Budapest, 1948–58. 353–86.

Soudavar, Abolala. "The Saga of Abū-Saʿīd Bahādor Khān: The Abū-Saʿīdnāmé." *Court*. 95–218.

Spuler, Bertold. *Die Goldene Horde: die Mongolen in Russland 1223–1502*. Weisbaden, 1965.

— *Die Mongolen in Iran: Politik, Verwaltung und Kultur in der Ilchanenzeit (1220–1350)*, 4th edn. Leiden, 1988.

— *The Mongols in History*. Tr. Geoffrey Wheeler. London, 1971.

Stewart, Angus Donal. *The Armenian Kingdom and the Mamluks: War and Diplomacy during the Reigns of Hetʿum II (1289–1307)*. Leiden, 2001.

Stillman, N. A. "Khilʿa." *EI²* V:6–7.

Stillman, Y. K. and Stillman, N. A. "Libās iii: Iran." *EI²* V:747–50.

Sümer, Faruk. "Döger." *EI²* II:613–14.

— "Ḳarā-Ḳoyunlu." *EI²* IV:584–88.

— "Ḳarāmān-Oghullari." *EI²* IV:619–25.

Taeschner, Fr. "[Futuwwa] Post-Mongol Period." *EI²* II:966–69.

Titley, Norah M. *Persian Miniature Painting and its Influence on the Art of Turkey and India*. Austin, TX, 1983.

Thorau, Peter. *The Lion of Egypt: Sultan Baybars I and the Near East in the Thirteenth Century*. Tr. P. M. Holt. London and New York, 1992.

Togan, [A.] Zeki Velidi. "Timurs Osteuropapolitik." *ZDMG* 108 (1958): 279–98.

Vernadsky, George. *The Mongols and Russia*. New Haven, 1953.
Voegelin, Eric. "The Mongol Orders of Submission to European Powers, 1245–1255." *Byzantion* 15 (1940–41): 378–413.
Walker, Bethany. "The Social Implications of Textile Development in Fourteenth-Century Egypt." *Mamluk Studies Review* 4 (2000): 167–217.
Wiederhold, Lutz. "Legal-Religious Elite, Temporal Authority and the Caliphate in Mamluk Society: Conclusions Drawn from the Examination of a 'Zahiri Revolt' in Damascus in 1386." *IJMES* 31 (1999): 203–35.
Woods, John E. *The Aqquyunlu: Clan, Confederation, Empire*. Salt Lake City, 1999.
— "Timur's Genealogy." *Intellectual Studies on Islam: Essays Written in Honor of Martin B. Dickson*. Eds. Michel M. Mazzaoui and Vera B. Moreen. Salt Lake City, 1990. 85–125.
Yang, Lien-Sheng. "Hostages in Chinese History." *Studies in Chinese Institutional History*. Cambridge, 1961. 43–57.
Yapı Kredi Bank. *Ak Akçe: Moğol ve Ilhanlı Sikkeleri/Mongol and Ilkhanid Coins*. Istanbul, 1992.
Zakirov, S. *Diplomaticheskie Otnosheniia Zolotoi Ordy s Egiptom (XIII–XIV vv.)*. Moscow, 1966.

Index

Abaji (Ilkhanid envoy) 122, 123
Abaqa (Ilkhanid ruler) 32–37, 44
  canvassing of Christian aid 32
  death 39
  divine support 33, 34
  and Golden Horde 59
  military activities 38–39, 60, 61
  see also under ambassadors; letter(s); oral message(s)
Abu Bakr, al-Mansur (Qalawunid sultan) 145
Abu Numayyad Sharifs 97–98, 102
Abu Sa'id (Ilkhanid ruler) 4–5, 9, 99–100, 101
  (acceptance of) place in Muslim hierarchy 103, 105, 110–111, 125–128
  assumption of personal rule 117
  complicity in murder 129–131
  death (and aftermath) 138, 139, 151, 178
  dynastic consciousness 100–101
  ideology 99–100
  as patron of religion 100, 102–103
  and the pilgrimage 106, 128
  poetry 128
  response to death of Temürtash 123–124
  see also ambassadors; letters; marriage alliances; Muhammad, al-Nasir; titles
Ahmad, al-Mansur (Artuqid ruler) 152, 164
Ahmad, al-Nasir (Qalawunid sultan) 154
Ahmad, al-Salih (Artuqid ruler) 186
Ahmad b. Taymiyah 66, 86, 115
Akhijuq 162
al-Hakim bi-amr Allah (Abbasid caliph) 42, 47–48, 52–53, 55, 56, 62–63, 68, 84
  and *futuwah* 54
  sermons 47–48
  suppression 42
'Ala' al-Din (Qaramanid ruler) 154
'Ali, al-Salih (Qalawunid heir) 39, 44
'Ali (caliph) 76–77, 80
'Ali b. Berke Khan 89
'Ali b. Fadlallah, 'Ala' al-Din 148
'Ali Padshah (Ilkhanid governor) 139–141
'Ali Shah (Ilkhanid vizier) 102
ambassadors/envoys *see also* letter(s)
  arrogant behavior 107–109
  formal audience 24
  humiliation 37, 90, 195
  immunity 25, 89
  imprisonment 88, 89
  lodging 23–24, 108
  murder/execution 25, 30, 34, 180, 182, 190
  provisioning 21
  punishment(s) 24, 198–199
  purification 36
  reception 20–24, 43, 44, 87, 107–109, 123–124, 182
  Anatolian
    Sülemish to Mamluks 70, 72
    to Baybars 37
    to Khalil 46
    to Lajin 70
    to Muhammad 72, 144
  Artuqid 151
    Ahmad to Barquq 186
    Isa to Barquq 153, 172, 173, 176, 187
    Isa to Faraj 193
    Isa to Temür 179
    Salih to Qalawunids 4, 151, 152
  Byzantine
    Andronicus II to Ghazan 87
  Chobanid 160
    Choban to Muhammad 114, 117, 121
    Hasan to Isma'il 159
    Malik Ashraf to Hasan and Salih 160
  Golden Horde
    Berke to Baybars 54, 55–56
    Janibek to Hasan 161–162
    Möngke Temür to Baybars 59, 60–61
    Noqai to Baybars 59–60
    Özbek to Muhammad 131–132, 134, 137
    Töde Möngke to Qalawun 62
    Toqta to Ghazan 87
    Toqta to Muhammad 131
    Toqtamish to Barquq 172, 177, 186

Ilkhanid 21, 111, 129
Abaqa to Baybars 32–37
Abaqa to European monarchs 32
Arghun to European monarchs 44
Abu Sa'id to Muhammad 104–110, 111–113, 121–122, 124, 128–129
Choban to Muhammad 114–115, 117
Geikhatu to Khalil 48–49
Ghazan to Boniface VIII 85
Ghazan to governor of Aleppo 93
Ghazan to European monarchs 87
Ghazan to Muhammad 73, 81, 87, 90
Hülegü to Byzantines 54–55
Hülegü to Qutuz 28–30
Musa to Muhammad 140
Öljeitü to European monarchs 95
Öljeitü to Muhammad 95
Sülemish to Lajin/Muhammad 70, 72
Tegüder to Qalawun 39–40, 43
Temürtash to Muhammad 117–118
Jalayirid 141
Shaykh Hasan to Muhammad 141, 142, 144
Shaykh Uvays to Mamluks 163, 164
Sultan-Ahmad to Barquq 172, 176, 186
Sultan-Ahmad to Faraj 188, 197
Sultan-Ahmad to Mamluks 167
Sultan-Husayn to Mamluks 167
Mamluk
Barquq to Beyazid 175
Barquq to Temür 182, 183
Baybars to Abaqa 34, 37
Baybars to Berke 52, 53–55, 56
Baybars to Noqai 56
Faraj to Beyazid 192
Faraj to Temür 192, 195, 196
Hasan to Janibek 162
Hasan to John Cantacuzenus 147
Lajin to Sülemish 70
Muhammad to Abu Sa'id 111–113, 123–124
Muhammad to Eretna 143–144
Muhammad to Ghazan 85, 87–90, 108
Muhammad to Musa 140–141
Muhammad to Özbek 132–133, 134–135, 136, 137
Muhammad to Sülemish 70–71
Qalawun to Tegüder 40–42
to Qara Qoyonlu 152
Sha'ban to Mahmud 147, 152–153
Sha'ban to Mehmed Bulaq 147
to Shaykh Hasan 160
Nu'ayr to Barquq 177
Ögedeid
Qaidu to Mamluks 62
Ottoman
Beyazid to Barquq 175, 186
Beyazid to Faraj 189, 192–193
Murat to Barquq 172–173
Papal
Boniface VIII to/from Ghazan 85
Clement V to/from Öljeitü 95, 96
Qadi Burhan al-Din to Barquq 174
Temürid
to Barquq 171, 177–178, 182, 184, 187
to Beyazid 179–180, 181, 188, 194
to Faraj 193, 195–197
to 'Isa 176, 179
to Nu'ayr 176
to Qadi Burhan al-Din 174, 178
to Sultan-Ahmad 176
Anatolia 41–42, 46, 72, 117–118, 143–144, 153–156
Baybars's battle for 37–38
cession to Temür 196
Mamluk problems in 154–156
Andronicus II, Byzantine emperor 87
Anushirvan Khan (Ilkhanid puppet) 159
apostasy, apostate 12, 77, 120, 138
Aq Qoyunlu 9, 199
Uzun Hasan 199, 200
Aqqush al-Afram (Mamluk governor) 96
Aqqush al-Mas'udi, Faris al-Din (Mamluk envoy) 56–58
Ardakin (wife of Khalil) 50
Arghun, Sayf al-Din (viceregent under Muhammad) 133
Arghun (Ilkhanid ruler) 44, 47, 65–66
death 44, 46
as Lord of the Auspicious Conjunction 44
see also under ambassadors; letter(s)
Arjuwash (Mamluk commander) 73
Arpa (Mongol prince) 139
Artuqids 151–153
relations with Mamluks 151–153, 163, 172, 173, 176, 186, 187, 193
see also Ahmad, al-Mansur; Ahmad, al-Salih; Dawud, al-Muzaffar; Ghazi, al-Mansur; 'Isa, al-Zahir; Mahmud, al-Salih; Salih, al-Salih
Asanbugha (Mamluk commander) 189, 190
Assassins 101–102, 109
Atlamish (Temürid captive with Mamluks) 186–187, 191, 192, 193
Aturji (Mamluk envoy) 132–133
Auspicious Conjunction, Lord of 44, 169–170, 199
see also Arghun; Temür
Aybak al-Afram (Mamluk commander) 90–91
see also Ghazan: decree to Aybak
'Ayn Jalut, battle of 27, 30, 35

Aytamish al-Muhammadi (Mamluk commander and envoy) 107, 109, 118, 121–122, 123–124, 128
Ayyubid(s) 10, 12

Baghdad, destruction of *see* Hülegü
Baghdad Khatun (daughter of Choban) 123–124, 125
Baiju Noyan (Mongol commander) 70
Baktimur al-Saqi (Mamluk commander) 133
Baktimur al-Silahdar (Mamluk rebel) 70, 73, 78–79, 96
banner(s) 23
  black (caliphal) 15, 62–63
  black (used by Ghazan) 65–66, 118
  Ilkhanid 105
  Mamluk, sultanic 46, 103–104, 159
  Temürid 193, 195
Barquq, al-Zahir (Mamluk sultan) 5, 150, 168, 181, 184, 190
  Circassian identity 183–184
  dealings with lesser rulers 172–173, 174–175, 180–181
  death 187
  divine support 183
  dynastic ambitions 170
  ideology 170–171, 183
  as innovative thinker 171
  military activities 183–187
  post-mortem humiliation 194, 195–196
Barsbay, al-Ashraf (Mamluk sultan) 198–199, 200
Barsbugha 129–130
Bayandur Khan 199
Baybars al-Jashnakir, al-Muzaffar (Mamluk commander and sultan) 91
Baybars al-Mansuri (historian) 92–93
Baybars, al-Zahir (Mamluk sultan) 10, 13, 30–38, 58
  alliance with Berke 58
  alliance with Möngke Temür 36, 60–61
  ascension to power 31
  and caliphate 14–15, 31, 52–53, 150
  correspondence 31–32 (*see also under* letter(s))
  dealings with Golden Horde 51–58, 59–60
  dealings with Ilkhanids 32–37
  death 37–38
  divine support 30
  dynastic ambitions 31, 38
  and *futuwah* 54
  ideology 38, 62–63
  military achievements 37–38
  as model for Khalil 45–46, 48–49
  as model for Qalawun 38
  ostentation 61
  as patron of neighboring rulers 31–32
  pilgrimage 35
  son of *see* Muhammad Berke Khan
Baysaq (Mamluk commander) 192
Beduin people 103–104, 176–177
Béla IV of Hungary 29
Berke (Golden Horde khan) 10, 21, 27–28, 51–58
  and *futuwah* 54
  see also ambassadors; Baybars: alliance with; conversion(s); Hülegü; letter(s)
Beyazid I (Ottoman ruler) 150, 175, 179–180, 185–186, 187, 189, 192–193
  see also ambassadors: Ottoman; letter: Ottoman
Beyazid II (Ottoman ruler) 199
Birdibek (Golden Horde khan) 162
blood, (taboo on) shedding of 25, 30, 123
  see also execution
Bolad Agha (Mongol notable) 66
Boniface VIII (Pope), letters to/from Ghazan 85
Börte (wife of Chingiz Khan) 7
Broadbridge, Anne F. 58

caliph/caliphate (Abbasid)
  allegiance to 42, 45, 84, 183, 199
  appearance on coins 88
  black, as official color 15
  decline/suppression of role 42, 171
  house arrest 15, 62–63
  legitimacy 68–70
  legitimating role 15, 62–63
  political role 150
  as rallying point 56
  role in Islamic ideology 14–15, 99–100, 149–150
  see also banner(s); coins; *titles of caliphs*
candles, provision for holy cities 164
carrier pigeons 77
Centennial Renewer (Mujaddid) 199
  see also Ghazan; Muhammad, al-Nasir
Chagatai (son of Chingiz Khan) 7
Chagataid(s), Temür as Reviver of 9, 169, 179
chancellery
  Ilkhanid 20
  Jalayirid 157
  Mamluk 82, 148, 191
chancellery/ies
  role in letter production 17, 20
Chingiz Khan 1, 6–7, 13, 67
  death 7–8
  descendants 179
  dynasty 7–8
  law, decrees of (*yasa*) 35, 53–54, 62
  royal authority founded on 8, 79
  senior wife *see* Börte
Chingizid dynasty/traditions
  (alleged) protection 9–10

coronation rituals 146
importance to later rulers 66–67, 74, 130, 156–157, 161, 168–170
(projected) marriage alliances 106–107, 109, 133–134
see also ideology(ies): Chingizid-Mongol
Choban (Ilkhanid viceregent) 4, 99, 101, 108, 109–110, 114–117, 118, 156
buildings/architecture (in Hijaz) 115–116, 125
burial 125
death 117, 121, 123
dynastic consciousness 100–101
as patron of religion 100, 114–115, 116
Chobanid dynasty 11, 156, 157–162
ideology 159–160
relations with Mamluks 160–162
see also Hasan b. Temürtash; Malik Ashraf
Circassian race/identity *see* Barquq
Clement IV, Pope 32
Clement V, Pope 95–96
see also ambassadors; letter(s)
clothing, ceremonial significance 54
see also robe(s)
coins
Golden Horde 62
Ilkhanid 64–65, 66
indicating submission 88
rebel/seditious 118
Jalayirid 157, 164
Mamluk 52, 144, 171
Abbasid presence/absence 149–150
indicating submission 195
conversion(s) (to Islam) 52
(allegedly) false 83 (*see also* Ghazan: conversion: Mamluk responses to)
precedence in 40, *see also* Islam: seniority within
Golden Horde
Berke 53
Noqai 59–60
Özbek 99
Töde Möngke 62
Ilkhanids 4, 64, 66
Ghazan 64, 65, 66, 75, 77
Öljeitü 94
Tegüder 39, 40
see also Islam: seniority within; *names of converts especially* Ghazan, Tegüder
curtains, provision for holy places 102–103, 200

Damascus, occupations/battles for 73, 74–80, 191–192
see also Ghazan: military campaigns; Temür: military campaigns: third
Dawlat Khan (Ilkhanid ambassador) 35–36
Dawlat Khwaja 186
Dawud, al-Muzaffar (Artuqid ruler) 153
defection(s) 70–72, 89
attempts to induce 80
Dilshad Khatun (wife of Abu Sa'id) 138, 156
Dimashq Khwaja (son of Choban) 110, 115, 123
diplomacy 16–26
analysis 16
ideological models expressed through 26
see also ambassadors; letter(s); oral message(s); protocol
dissidents *see* defection(s)
divine favor/support
Turkic 9
see also Abaqa; Barquq; Baybars; Ghazan; Hülegü; Lajin; Muhammad, al-Nasir; Temür
divine mandate 6, 7, 13, 17, 27, 34, 157, 169
Dogerids 149, 151, 153, 186
Dulqadirids 149, 155
see also Qaraja
dynasty (concept) *see* lineage

Edward I of England 32, 87, 95–96
Edward II of England 96
Elbistan, battle of 37
elephant(s) 128, 195
Enduring Sky, cult of 1, 6–7, 66, 94
envoys *see* ambassadors
Eretna 143–144, 148, 153, 154–155
see also ambassadors: Anatolian
execution, methods of 24, 25, 123, 190
see also ambassadors

Faraj, al-Nasir (Mamluk sultan) 5, 168
accession 187–188
dealings with Temür 191, 193–197
(lack of) ideology 188
Fedor Rostislavovich, Grand Duke 134
futuwah 49, 54
see also al-Hakim; Baybars; Berke; Khalil; al-Mustansir

Geikhatu 45–46
military activities 48–49
relation with Mamluks *see* Khalil
see also under ambassadors
Genghis Khan *see* Chingiz Khan
Ghazan 13, 20
(alleged) hypocrisy *see* conversion *below; see also under* hypocrite(s)
behavior of soldiers under 76
see also banner(s)
buildings, tomb 64–65
as Centennial Renewer 10–11, 65–66, 77, 113
see also Centennial Renewer
conversion 64, 66, 75, 77

Ghazan (cont.)
Mamluk responses to 78, 80, 83, 84, 86
see also conversion
dealings with Damascenes 74–76
dealings with Mamluks 70–93, 189
see also under Muhammad, al-Nasir
death 94
decree to Aybak 90–93
diplomatic activity 87
divine favor 76, 79, 81, 82, 84
historical awareness 80
ideology 74–80, 91–92
impact of arguments 92–93
marriage 67
military campaigns 65–66, 72–73
first 73–80
second 80, 82, 83–84
third 87, 90–93
see also Damascus; Syria
pictorial representations 70
pilgrimage 78
(proposed) alliances 85
reforms 64
religious outlook 67–70
self-characterization 92
see also ambassadors; banner(s); Boniface VIII; Guardianship; letter(s)
Ghazi, al-Mansur (Artuqid ruler) 83
al-Ghutamī (Mamluk Commander) 93
gift(s) 22–23
Golden Horde 132
Ilkhanid 79, 105–106, 111
Mamluk 54, 56, 61, 181
symbolism 33
of weaponry 36–37, 88, 182, 184
withheld 23
Gleb Vasil'kovich, Prince 134
golden dynasty/family *see* Chingizid dynasty
Golden Horde 2, 27–28
military alliance with Mamluks 136
relations with Mamluks 4, 23, 36, 50–63, 131–137
see also names of khans; conversion(s)
governors
Ilkhanid, criticized for oppression 41–42
Mamluk
over Syria 77–79
for Temür 192
Turkic, Mongol for Mamluks 148–150
financial contributions 149
visits to court 149
Guardianship (of Islam)
and holy cities 15–16, 183–184
in Ilkhanid ideology 66, 74, 76
loss of ideological significance 145–146
in Mamluk ideology 45, 46, 64, 70–71, 88, 138–139, 140, 143, 168
in Temürid ideology 170–171
see also ideology
Güyük, Great Khan 8

Hajji-Taghay (Ilkhanid commander) 139, 142–143, 144–145
al-Hakkari, 'Ala' al-Din, 49
Hasan, al-Nasir (Qalawunid sultan) 147, 151–152, 160, 163
Hasan b. Temürtash (Chobanid ruler) 157, 159
Henry II of Cyprus 73
heresy *see* apostasy
Het'um I of Armenia 13, 33
Het'um II of Armenia 48, 76–77
hierarchy/ies *see* conversion; Islam: seniority
Hodgson, Marshall 8–9
holy cities
responsibility for 40, 87, 97–98, 100, 146 (*see also* Guardianship; Jerusalem; Mecca; Medina)
expenditure on 116
rivalry over 102–104, 115–117, 125, 164–167
homosexuality 89
Homs, battle of 27, 39
Hromgla, capture of 48
Hulawun *see* Hülegü
Hülegü 8, 10, 27–28, 51
and Baybars 31–32
and Byzantines 54–55
and caliph(ate) 9, 14–15
and Civil War/Berke [Golden Horde] 51, 53–54, 55–56
death 32
disdain for slaves *see* slaves: Ilkhanid attacks on
divine support 29
military activities 52
pictorial representations 70
and Qutuz 28–30
sack of Baghdad 27–28, 47, 52–53
see also ambassadors; letter(s)
hypocrite(s)/hypocrisy, accusations of *see* conversion(s); Ghazan; Muhammad, al-Nasir: (reputation for) lies/duplicity; Temür: (alleged) lies/hypocrisy

Ibn 'Abd al-Zahir (Mamluk historian) 42
Ibn al-Sukkari, 'Imad al-Din (Mamluk envoy) 87–90, 95
Ibn 'Arabshah 20
Ibn Tiqtaqah 69
Ibrahim b. Qutlughtimur 150
Ibrahim Shah 144–145
ideology(ies) of rule, of kingship
defined 6

development 4–5
divergence from 6
models
Chingizid-Mongol 1, 6–9, 34, 79, 200
of Guardianship 14, 15–16
Islamic 2–3, 10–11, 35, 51, 64, 71, 74, 77–78, 91, 161–162, 170, 199
Islamic and Chingizid fusion 2–3, 11, 16, 39–42, 146–147, 162–163, 167, 188
Mamluk 4–5, 12–16, 83, 90, 138–139, 167, 183–184, 188–189, 198, 199–200
new developments 99–100, 110–111, 167
Ottoman 175
post-Temürid 198–200
Qalawunid 146
Temürid 9, 11, 168–170, 178–180, 188
Turkic 148
Turko-Mongol/post-Mongol 9–10, 198–199
mutual intolerance 6
see also Guardianship; *names of rulers, names of dynasties*
Ilkhanids 2, 27–28
ideology 4–5
internal rivalries 139–145, 146–147
relations with Mamluks 16, 20–21, 28–50, 72–73, 99–101
relations with Qaramanids 153
see also conversion(s); ideology; *names of leaders*
imperial *su* (fortune) 7
ink, colors 17, 20, 87–88, 113, 135, 157, 194–195
ʿIsa al-Zahir (Artuqid ruler) 153, 172, 173, 176, 179, 186, 187, 189
Islam
(alleged) betrayal of ideals 77
(calls for) unity 43, 62–63, 140
regional supremacy 4, 98
seniority within 42, 51, 62–63, 64, 83 (*see also* Muhammad, al-Nasir)
see also conversion(s); Guardianship; holy cities; ideology; *names of Muslim rulers*
Ismaʾil, al-Salih (Qalawunid sultan) 159
Ismaʾil Safavi, Shah 11, 199

Jalayirids 152, 156–157, 162–167, 179
see also Shaykh Hasan; Shaykh Uvays; Sultan-Ahmad; Sultan-Husayn; Tundi
Mamluk relations with 163–167
see also under ambassadors; letter(s)
James I of Aragon 32
Janibek (Golden Horde khan) 161–162
see also under ambassadors; letter(s)
Jaqmaq, al-Zahir (Mamluk sultan) 200
Jelu Khan (son of Choban) 125
Jerusalem 15, 73, 84, 113, 116, 135
jihad 14, 47, 200
Jochi (son of Chingiz Khan) 7, 27
John VI Cantacuzenus, Byzantine emperor 147
Juban, Sayf al-Din (Mamluk commander) 107

Kamal al-Din b. Yunus of Mosul (Ilkhanid envoy) 81
Kanuni Suleiman 'the Lawgiver' (Ottoman sultan) 11
Kay Kawus, ʿIzz al-Din (Seljuk sultan) 31, 54, 55
Kay Khusraw III (Seljuk sultan) 32
Khalil, al-Ashraf (Qalawunid sultan) 44–50, 90
and Anatolians 153–154
and Baybars 45–46, 48–49
buildings/architecture 50
and caliph 45, 150
ceremonies 47–48
death 50, 63, 64
dynastic ambitions 50
and *futuwah* 49
and Geikhatu 45–46, 48–49
and Golden Horde 63
ideology 45, 47–48, 49–50
military capabilities/achievements 44–45, 46–48
relations with neighboring rulers 49–50
as Reviver of the Abbasid State 45
titles, inscriptions of 45
Khusraw I (Sassanian emperor) 159
Khwaja Marjan (Ilkhanid governor) 163–164
kingship, (un)fitness for 74, 75–76, 81–82
ignorance and 80, 91–92
see also ideology
Kitbugha, al-Mansur (Mamluk sultan) 35, 45, 64
Konchak (Golden Horde princess) 134
Kublai Khan *see* Qubilai
Kurds 49–50
Kusharbak, Sayf al-Din (Mamluk ambassador) 53, 55

Lajin, al-Mansur (Mamluk sultan) 64, 70–71
Laszlo IV of Hungary 134
legitimacy, importance of 1
letter(s) 16–20 *see also* ambassadors
in Arabic 19–20
dating 19, 76
forgeries 86
layout 20, 92
in Mongolian 19–20
seals 19, 157
surviving examples 19–20
Anatolian
Sülemish to Mamluks 70, 72

letter(s) (cont.)
Golden Horde 20
Berke to Baybars 55
Noqai to Baybars 59–60
Özbek to Muhammad 136
Töde Möngke to Qalawun 62
Toqta to Muhammad 131
Ilkhanid
Abaqa to Baybars 34–35
Abaqa to European monarchs 32
Ghazan to Boniface VIII 85
Ghazan to governor of Aleppo 93
Ghazan to Muhammad 80–82
Ghazan to Syrians 74–80
Hülegü to Qutuz/Yusuf 13, 28–30, 181
Öljeitü to Philip IV 95–96
Tegüder to Qalawun 39–42, 43–44
Jalayirid 157, 163
Shaykh Uvays to Mamluks 163
Mamluk 17
Barquq to Temür 179, 182–183, 187, 194
Baybars to Abaqa 34–35
Baybars to Berke 51, 53, 54
Baybars to Möngke Temür 59
Baybars to Noqai 56–58, 60
Faraj to Temür 191–192, 193–195, 196
Hasan to Janibek 162
Hasan to John Cantacuzenus 147
Lajin to Sülemish 70
Muhammad to Abu Sa'id 113–114
Muhammad to Eretna 143–144
Muhammad to Ghazan 82–85, 87–88, 91–92
Muhammad to Musa 140–141
Muhammad to Özbek 132–133, 134–135, 136, 137
Muhammad to Sülemish 70–71
Qalawun to Tegüder 40–44
Qalawunids 147–148
to Qara Qoyunlu 152
Sha'ban to Mahmud 147, 152–153
Shaʿban to Mehmed Bulaq 147
to Shaykh Hasan 160
to Shaykh Uvays 163
Sunqur to Abaqa 38–39
Mongol
to Bela IV 29
Ottoman 175–176
papal
Boniface VIII to/from Ghazan 85
Clement V to/from Öljeitü 95, 96
Qadi Burhan al-Din to Barquq 174
Temürid
to Barquq 171–172, 174, 177–179, 180, 181–182
to Beduins 176–177
to Beyazid 179–180, 181, 188, 194
to Faraj 195–196
to ʿIsa 176, 179
to Mamluk cities 189–190
to Nuʿayr 176
to Qadi Burhan al-Din 174, 178
to Sultan-Ahmad 176
see also ink; paper
Lewon, Prince 33
lightning/thunder(storms) 25
lineage
Ilkhanid-Chingizid 100–101
increasing ideological significance 146, 188
(Mamluk) lack of 12 *see also* slaves/slavery: Ilkhanid attacks on Mamluk; Temür's attacks on Mamluk
role in ideology of kingship 12
Lippard, Bruce G. 55
Lord of the Auspicious Conjunction *see* Auspicious Conjunction, Lord of
Louis IX of France 32
Lu'lu'id dynasty 31

McCormick, Michael 16
Mahdi ('Rightly Guided One'), Temürtash claimed as 118, 120
Mahmud, al-Salih (Artuqid ruler) 147–148, 152–153
Mahmud al-Halabi (author) 71
Mahmud (Qaramanid ruler) 49
Malik Ashraf (Chobanid ruler) 151, 155, 159–162
Mamluk Sultanate 2–3
alliances 10
ethnic/religious composition 2
internal divisions 145, 150
military blunders 191–192
Mongol criticisms of 77–78, 79–80, 91, 170 (*see also* slaves)
regional sovereignty 5
relations with Mongols 12–14
relations with neighboring/client states 27, 149–150
relocation of population *see under* Syria
submission to Temür 193–197
system of succession 78, 79
see also ideology; *names of sultans*
Mamluk sultan(s)
ethnicity 183–184
ideological role 14–16
as religious senior 188–189 *see also* Muhammad, al-Nasir; Qalawun
Mardin, Mamluk raid on 72, 81–82, 83–84
Maria, Princess (wife of Abaqa) 32
Marj al-Suffar, battle of 90
marriage alliances (proposed) 4, 134, 181, 196
Muhammad/Abu Saʿid or Chobanids 107, 109–110, 124, 129
Muhammad/later Ilkhanids 142–143
Muhammad/Özbek 132–134, 137

marriage laws 67
Mecca
buildings/restoration schemes 115–117
see also under Choban; Muhammad, al-Nasir
unrest 128
see also holy cities; Islam: seniority within; pilgrimage(s)
Medina 15–16, 115, 125, 128, 129, 175, 184
Mehmed Bulaq (Golden Horde khan) 147–148
Mehmed I (Ottoman sultan) 200
Melville, Charles 114
merchants, treatment of 40, 41
Michael VIII Palaeologus, Byzantine emperor 32, 51, 54–55
Miranshah (son of Temür) 186–187
rebellion 187–188
Misr Khwaja (Qara Qoyunlu) 172
Möngke, Great Khan 8, 27, 28
Möngke Temür (brother of Abaqa) 39
Möngke Temür (Golden Horde khan)
death 62
and Mamluks 36, 59, 60–61
and medicines 61
and Qaidu 62
see also under ambassadors
Mongolian (language) *see* Mongols: languages
Mongols 1–2
(calls for) unity 40, 78
civil war 1, 28
conversion to Islam 10
impact on non-Mongol world 8–10, 27
languages 19–20
Mamluks who were 13
religious beliefs 25
treatises on 8–9
Muhammad, al-Nasir (Qalawunid sultan) 4–5, 63, 179, 180
accession/early reign 64, 72, 82
as (Centennial) Renewer of Religion 113
attempted assassination 130
buildings/architecture 23
in holy cities 113, 125, 129, 164
circumcision 50
complicity in murder 129–130 (*see also* Abu Saʿid; Temürtash)
daughters (and marriage) 109–110 (*see also* marriage alliances)
dealings with ambassadors 23, 106–107, 109
death 145
dynastic position 101, 111–113
fitness to rule 74, 75
and Ghazan 80–85
and the Ilkhanid successors 139–145
Ilkhanid views of 81–82, 91–92, 99, 130–131, 189
and Öljeitü 96–98
personality 99, 100, 130–131
and the pilgrimage 100, 102–104, 116, 128, 129
relations with Abu Saʿid 101–114, 117, 125–128
relations with Choban 114–115, 116–117, 124–125
relations with Golden Horde 131–137
relations with regional leaders 118, 143, 153–155
religious/political supremacy 100, 110–111, 129, 131, 135, 138–139, 144
(reputation for) lies/duplicity 109–110, 117, 122, 123–124, 130–131, 136–137, 138–139
and Temürtash 117–122, 159
wives *see* Tughay; Tulunbay
see also ambassadors; coins; Guardianship; holy cities; letter(s); marriage alliances; titles
Muhammad b. Yolqutluq (Ilkhanid ruler) 139, 141–142
Muhammad Beg (Ilkhanid commander) 141
Muhammad Berke Khan (Baybars's son) 31
circumcision 56
wedding 61
Muhammad II (Khwarazm-Shah) 29
Muhammad (the Prophet) 51, 77
descendants 67–68, 74, 111
Mujaddid *see* Centennial Renewer; Ghazan; Muhammad, al-Nasir
Mukhlis al-Din (Anatolian ambassador) 70
Murad I (Ottoman sultan) 172–173
Musa Khan (Ilkhanid successor) 139, 140–142, 144
Musa (nephew of Khalil), circumcision 50
Muslims *see* Islam
al-Mustansir (Abbasid caliph) 53
and *futuwah* 54
inauguration 31, 52
al-Mustaʾsim (Abbasid caliph) 181
execution 9, 69
al-Mutawakkil ʿala Allah (Abbasid caliph) 150

Nasir al-Din ʿAli Khwaja (Ilkhanid ambassador) 81
Noqai (Golden Horde) 55, 56–58, 59–60, 62, 78
see also ambassadors; conversion(s); letter(s)
Nuʿayr (Beduin leader) 176–177, 184, 185
see also ambassadors; letter(s)

Ögedei (Great Khan) 7
Ögedeid(s) 169, 178

Öljeitü (Ilkhanid ruler) 94–96, 105
buildings/tomb 65, 67
diplomacy 96
pictorial representations 95
religious outlook 66, 67–68, 94–95, 101
see also under ambassadors; conversion(s); letter(s); Muhammad, al-Nasir
oral message(s) 16–17
Abaqa to Baybars 33–34
Baybars to Abaqa 36
Tegüder to Qalawun 41
Osman (Ottoman ruler) 11
Ottomans *see* ambassadors; letter(s); *names of leaders*
Özbek (Golden Horde khan) 99
and Muhammad 4, 131–137
titles 135
see also ambassadors; conversion(s); letter(s); marriage alliances; Shaykh Nuʿman; Tulunbay

palanquin, ceremonial significances 102–104
paper, size/quality of 17–19, 54, 113, 135, 139, 140, 141, 143–144, 149, 162, 163, 175, 185, 192
parasol, ceremonial significance 43, 108
Parvanah, the, Muʿin al-Din 32, 36, 37–38
peace
agreement of 1323/723 99–100, 109–110, 131, 151
background 101–104
negotiations 104–110
guarantee of 75–77
Mongol, in 1304/704 78, 94
as submission 194
negotiations 194–196
Philip IV of France 95–96
pilgrimage(s) 62, 100
ceremonies 200
see also Abu Saʿid; Baybars; Ghazan; Guardianship: and holy cities; Muhammad, al-Nasir; Shaʿban
Pir Husayn 144–145
Pir Muhammad b. Umar Shaykh (Temürid prince) 199
propaganda, Mamluk 86, 90–93
protocol, diplomatic
(alleged) ignorance of 74, 81–82, 84–85, 91–92
in dealings with ambassadors 20–26
and letter production 17
Mongol/Turkic 24–25
psychological warfare *see* warfare, psychological

Qadi Burhan al-Din (ruler of Sivas) 174–175, 178, 185–186, 187
Qaidu (Ögedeid khan) 60, 61–62, 78
Qalawun, al-Mansur (Mamluk sultan) 12, 61–63, 90
ancestry 75
banners 63
and Baybars 38
buildings/architecture 40
and caliph 42, 150
death 44, 46
dynastic ambitions 38–39
and Golden Horde 61–63
ideology 41–42, 61, 64, 83, 100
and Khalil 44–45
as model for Muhammad 113
and Tegüder 39–44, 82
as warrior for the faith 47
see also ambassadors; letter(s)
Qara Muhammad (Qara Qoyunlu leader) 172–173
Qara Qoyunlu 152, 199
see also Misr Khwaja; Qara Muhammad; Qara Yusuf
Qara Yusuf (Qara Qoyunlu leader) 173, 177, 184, 186–187, 188–189, 193, 196–197
Qaraja (Dulqadirid governor for the Mamluks) 155
Qaramanid(s) 153–154
Qarasunqur (Mamluk rebel) 96, 101–102, 105, 110, 121, 122, 124
Qaytbay, al-Ashraf (Mamluk sultan) 199
Qilich Arslan IV (Seljuk sultan) 31, 32
Qipchaq (Mamluk governor and rebel) 70, 73, 78–79, 96
Qipchaq(s) 13, 29, 34
Qonqqurtai, (Ilkhanid governor) 41–42
Qubilai (Great Khan) 8, 35, 64
Quran, presentation copies 105, 166
Qurt b. Umar 150
Qutlughshah 90
Qutuz, al-Muzaffar (Mamluk sultan) 34, 180
death 30, 31
and Hülegü 13, 28–30, 181, 182
see also ambassadors; letter(s)

Ramadanids 149, 153
Rashid al-Din (Ilkhanid vizier) 64, 66, 68–69
refugees, treatment of 52
Renewer of Religion *see* Centennial Renewer; Ghazan; Muhammad, al-Nasir
Rightly Guided One *see* Mahdi
robe(s) of honor
for ambassadors 22–23
for vassals 176, 195
withheld 23, 134

Saʿd al-Dawlah (Ilkhanid vizier) 44
Salih, al-Salih (Artuqid ruler) 151–152, 160, 163

Salim (Dogerid leader) 186
al-Sallami, Majd al-Din Isma'il 104–106, 109, 110
Samaghar (Ilkhanid governor) 35–36
Sanjar (Seljuk sultan) 65
Sassanian dynasty 157–159
Sati Beg (sister of Abu Sa'id) 138, 139
Seljuks 10, 37–38, 148
seniority *see* Islam
Sha'ban, al-Ashraf (Qalawunid sultan) 147, 152–153, 184
  ancestry 147
  death 150, 167
  pilgrimage 167
  relations with Jalayirids 164–167
  see also ambassadors; letter(s); *tughrah*
Shah Rukh (son of Temür) 198–199, 200
Shahinshah (Chobanid envoy) 121
Shahnamah, Great Mongol 70
shamanistic practices 24, 66–67
Shaykh 'Abd al-Rahman (Ilkhanid envoy) 42–44
Shaykh al-Muhammadi *see* Shaykh, al-Mu'ayyad (Mamluk sultan) 197
Shaykh Edebali 11
Shaykh Hasan Jalayir 139, 141–143, 144–145, 156–157, 160
  descendants *see* Jalayirids
Shaykh Ibrahim (Ilkhanid envoy) 128–129
Shaykh Nu'man (Golden Horde envoy) 133, 135, 137
Shaykh Saweh (Temürid envoy) 177, 182
Shaykh Uvays (Jalayirid ruler) 156, 157, 161, 162–167, 184
Shaykh, al-Mu'ayyad (Mamluk sultan) 10, 197, 200
Shiism 67–70, 80, 94
signature, royal *see tughrah*
slaves/slavery
  as gifts 177–178
  Ilkhanid attacks on Mamluk 12, 13, 29–30, 75, 101
  Mamluk slavery as a problem 12
  protocol 178
  Temür's attacks on Mamluk 13, 170, 179–180
snow/ice *see* water
sources 3–4
  Arabic bias 3–4
  non-diplomatic 4
  problems in 145
spies, capture of 40, 180
steppe traditions 94
submission *see* vassals
Sudun (Mamluk governor) 190
Sülemish (Ilkhanid rebel) 70–72, 77–78, 80, 144
  see also under ambassadors; letter(s)
Sultan-Ahmad (Jalayirid) 150, 167, 172
  dealings/conflicts with Temür 176, 185, 188–189, 196–197
  reception in Cairo 180
  relations with Barquq 180–181, 184, 186
  see also under ambassadors; Jalayirids; letter(s)
Sultan-Ahmad (Jalayirid ruler) 21
Sultan-Husayn (Jalayirid) 157, 167
  see also under ambassadors; Jalayirids
Sunni Islam 101
Sunqur al-Ashqar (Mamluk commander) 33–34, 37, 38–39, 128
Suyurghatmish Khan (Temürid puppet) 171
Syria
  Ilkhanid invasions 96 *see also* Ghazan: military campaigns
  population relocation to Ilkhanate 80
  rebellions 154, 155
  Temürid invasion *see* Temür: military campaigns: third
  see also letter(s)

taboo *see* blood; water
Taghay Temür (Ilkhanid ruler) 139
Tankiz (Mamluk governor) 107–109, 119
Tarmashirin (Chagatayid khan) 135
tax revenue, demands/promises of 87, 88, 195
Tayirbugha ([former] Ilkhanid governor) 111
Tegüder Ahmad (Ilkhanid ruler) 39–44
  arguments for legitimacy 39–40
  conversion 39, 40–41
    doubts of genuineness 42–43
  death 43–44
  demand for submission 39–40
  good works 40
  and Islamic law 62
  and Qalawun 82, 83; *see also under* ambassadors; letter(s)
Temüjin *see* Chingiz Khan
Temür 2, 16, 78
  acknowledged as Muslim 194–195
  (alleged) lies/hypocrisy 185
  children 169
  death 3, 197
  divine support 169, 190
  dynasty 198–199
  empire 1, 5
  historical importance 3, 198, 200
  as Lord of the Auspicious Conjunction 169
  Mamluk criticisms of 183, 184–185
  military campaigns 29, 168, 170–171
    first (three-year in Iran) 171–173
    second (five-year in Iran) 174–187
    third (seven-year in Iran) 187–197

Temür (cont.)
  and peace initiatives 94
  relations with Barquq 13, 174–186
  relations with Faraj 188
  see also ambassadors; Chagataid(s); ideology; letter(s); slaves
Temürbugha al-Marghinani 124
Temürtash (Ilkhanid rebel) 117–122, 125, 136, 156
  decapitated head 123–124
  followers 120–121
  impersonation 159
  imprisonment/death 121–123, 130
  political ambitions 117–118, 120, 144
  relations with Muhammad 118–121
titles
  appearance in letters 17, 20
  belittling use/withholding 185
  Golden Horde
    Özbek 135
  Ilkhanid 146
    Abu Saʿid 113–114
  Jalayirid 156, 162–163
  Mamluk 45, 52
    Khalil 49–50
    lesser rulers 139, 141–142, 143–144, 149
    Muhammad 113
    Shaʿban 166
  Temürid 193–194
  Turkic/Seljuk 148
Töde Möngke (Golden Horde khan) 62–63
  see also ambassadors; letter(s)
Töle Buqa (Golden Horde khan) 63
  see also ambassadors; letter(s)
tolerance (religious), expressions of 76–77
Tolui (son of Chingiz Khan) 7, 179
Toqta (Golden Horde khan) 78, 131
  see also ambassadors
Toqtamish (Golden Horde khan) 170, 172, 177, 186
  see also ambassadors; letter(s)
Tughay (Turkish wife of Muhammad) 104
tughrah (royal signature) 166–167
Tulunbay (Chingizid wife of Muhammad) 107, 132–134, 180
  death 137
  divorce 136–137
Tundi (Jalayirid wife of Barquq) 181
Tuqsuba (Mamluk envoy) 134–135
Türkmen 149, 150, 153–156
  see also Dogerids; Dulqadirids; Qara Qoyunlu; Qaramanid(s); Ramadanids

unity *see* Islam; Mongols
Uruj, Sayf al-Din (Mamluk envoy) 121
Uzdamir al-Mujiri, Husam al-Din (Mamluk envoy) 87–90, 95, 108

vassals/vassalage 58
  demands for 28–30, 33, 34, 78, 81–82, 87, 176
  rejection of 41
vice, combating of 104

Wadi al-Khaznadar, battle of 73, 76, 80, 81–82, 84, 89, 90, 91
warfare, psychological 32
water, spiritual significance 24–25, 116

Yasaʾur (Mongol dissident) 129–131
Yuri Danilovich, Prince 134
Yusuf, al-Nasir (Ayyubid sultan) 181, 182

Zoroastrianism 11
Zubaydah, Queen 116

Cambridge Studies in Islamic Civilization

Other titles in the series

Popular Culture in Medieval Cairo
Boaz Shoshan

Early Philosophical Shiism
The Ismaili Neoplatonism of Abū Yaʿqūb al-Sijistāni
Paul E. Walker

Indian Merchants and Eurasian Trade, 1600–1750
Stephen Frederic Dale

Palestinian Peasants and Ottoman Officials
Rural Administration around Sixteenth-century Jerusalem
Amy Singer

Arabic Historical Thought in the Classical Period
Tarif Khalidi

Mongols and Mamluks
The Mamluk–Īlkhānid War, 1260–1281
Reuven Amitai-Preiss

Hierarchy and Egalitarianism in Islamic Thought
Louise Marlow

The Politics of Households in Ottoman Egypt
The Rise of the Qazdağlis
Jane Hathaway

Commodity and Exchange in the Mongol Empire
A Cultural History of Islamic Textiles
Thomas T. Allsen

State and Provincial Society in the Ottoman Empire
Mosul, 1540–1834
Dina Rizk Khoury

The Mamluks in Egyptian Politics and Society
Thomas Philipp and Ulrich Haarmann (eds.)

The Delhi Sultanate
A Political and Military History
Peter Jackson

European and Islamic Trade in the Early Ottoman State
The Merchants of Genoa and Turkey
Kate Fleet

Reinterpreting Islamic Historiography
Harun al-Rashid and the Narrative of the ʿAbbāsid Caliphate
Tayeb El-Hibri

The Ottoman City between East and West
Aleppo, Izmir, and Istanbul
Edhem Eldem, Daniel Goffman and Bruce Masters

A Monetary History of the Ottoman Empire
Sevket Pamuk

The Politics of Trade in Safavid Iran
Silk for Silver, 1600–1730
Rudolph P. Matthee

The Idea of Idolatry and the Emergence of Islam
From Polemic to History
G. R. Hawting

Classical Arabic Biography
The Heirs of the Prophets in the Age of al-Maʾmūn
Michael Cooperson

Empire and Elites after the Muslim Conquest
The Transformation of Northern Mesopotamia
Chase F. Robinson

Poverty and Charity in Medieval Islam
Mamluk Egypt, 1250–1517
Adam Sabra

Christians and Jews in the Ottoman Arab World
The Roots of Sectarianism
Bruce Masters

Culture and Conquest in Mongol Eurasia
Thomas T. Allsen

Revival and Reform in Islam
The Legacy of Muhammad al-Shawkani
Bernard Haykel

Tolerance and Coercion in Islam
Interfaith Relations in the Muslim Tradition
Yohanan Friedmann

Guns for the Sultan
Military Power and the Weapons Industry in the Ottoman Empire
Gábor Ágoston

Marriage, Money and Divorce in Medieval Islamic Society
Yossef Rapoport

The Empire of the Qara Khitai in Eurasian History
Between China and the Islamic World
Michal Biran

Domesticity and Power in the Mughal World
Ruby Lal

Power, Politics and Religion in Timurid Iran
Beatrice Forbes Manz

Postal Systems in the Pre-Modern Islamic World
Adam J. Silverstein

Kingship and Ideology in the Islamic and Mongol Worlds
Anne F. Broadbridge

Lightning Source UK Ltd.
Milton Keynes UK
UKHW011936201019
351986UK00001B/33/P

9 780521 174497